# Join the Recommended Country Inns® Travelers' Club and Save!

The Recommended Country Inns® guides are the preeminent guidebooks to the finest country inns in the United States. Authors personally visit and recommend each establishment described in the guides, and **no fees are solicited or accepted for recommendation in the books.**

Now the Recommended Country Inns® guides offer a special new way for travelers to enjoy extra savings: through the Recommended Country Inns® Travelers' Club. Member benefits include savings such as:

- Discounts on accommodations
- Discounts on food
- Discounts on local attractions

**How to Save:** Read the profile for each inn to see if it offers an incentive to members. For participating establishments, look for information at the end of the inn's profile or in the index at the end of the book. Simply mention that you are a member of the Recommended Country Inns® Travelers' Club when making reservations, and show your membership card when you check in. All offers are subject to availability.

**How to Join:** If you wish to become a member of the Recommended Country Inns® Travelers' Club, simply fill out the attached form and send it by mail to:

Recommended Country Inns® Travelers' Club
c/o The Globe Pequot Press
PO Box 833
Old Saybrook, CT 06475
Or fax to: 860-395-2855

A membership card will be mailed to you upon receipt of the form. Please allow four to six weeks for delivery.

*Sign up today and start saving as a Recommended Country Inns® Travelers' Club member!*

(All offers from participating inns expire May 31, 2001, unless otherwise mentioned.)

D0424193

# *Recommended Country Inns®*
# *Travelers' Club Membership Form*

Name: _____

Address: _____

City _____, State _____ Zip _____

Phone _____ Fax _____ E-mail _____

Age:   18–35 _____;      36–50 _____;      over 50 _____

Sex:   Male _____      Female _____

Marital Status:   Single _____      Married _____

Annual Household Income:

   under $35,000 _____;   $35,000–$75,0000 _____;   over $75,000 _____

Credit cards:

   Mastercard _____;      Visa _____;      Amex _____;

   Discover _____;      Other _____

Book purchased at: Store Name: _____;

City _____, State _____

## Mail completed form to:
Recommended Country Inns® Travelers' Club
c/o The Globe Pequot Press
PO Box 833
Old Saybrook, CT  06475
Or fax to:  860–395–2855

MA

# *Recommended*
# COUNTRY INNS®

## MID-ATLANTIC and CHESAPEAKE REGION

Delaware / Maryland / New Jersey / New York / Pennsylvania
Virginia / Washington, D.C. / West Virginia

### *Eighth Edition*

by Suzi Forbes Chase
illustrated by Olive Metcalf

The Globe Pequot Press

OLD SAYBROOK, CONNECTICUT

# About the Author

SUZI FORBES CHASE has been writing about food and travel—and particularly about country inns—longer than she likes to admit. As the author of *Country Inns and Back Roads* she traveled from east to west and back again researching, inspecting, and writing about inns from British Columbia to Florida. Today, however, she confines most of her country inn research to the states closest to home. She is a resident of New York State. Suzi is also the author of *Recommended Bed and Breakfasts: Mid-Atlantic States* (The Globe Pequot Press) and *The Hamptons Book: A Complete Guide* (Berkshire Press) and the editor of *ZagatSurvey to Long Island Restaurants*.

ISBN 0-7627-0295-8
ISSN 1078-5523

Cover photo: Nicholas DeVore/Tony Stone Images
Cover, text, and map design: Nancy Freeborn/Freeborn Design

Manufactured in the United States of America
Eighth Edition/First Printing

# Contents

Introduction. . . . . . . . . . . . . . . . . . . . . . . . . . . . . . . . . . . . . . . . . . vi
How to Use This Inn Guide . . . . . . . . . . . . . . . . . . . . . . . . . . . x
Delaware and Maryland . . . . . . . . . . . . . . . . . . . . . . . . . . . . . 2
New Jersey. . . . . . . . . . . . . . . . . . . . . . . . . . . . . . . . . . . . . . . 64
New York. . . . . . . . . . . . . . . . . . . . . . . . . . . . . . . . . . . . . . . 102
Pennsylvania. . . . . . . . . . . . . . . . . . . . . . . . . . . . . . . . . . . . 246
Virginia and Washington, D.C.. . . . . . . . . . . . . . . . . . . . . . 333
West Virginia . . . . . . . . . . . . . . . . . . . . . . . . . . . . . . . . . . . 434

**Indexes**
Alphabetical Index to Inns. . . . . . . . . . . . . . . . . . . . . . . . . . 460
The Most Romantic Inns . . . . . . . . . . . . . . . . . . . . . . . . . . . 462
Best Buys in the Mid-Atlantic States . . . . . . . . . . . . . . . . . . 463
Inns Especially Suited to Family Travel. . . . . . . . . . . . . . . . . 464
Inns Especially Suited to Business Travelers. . . . . . . . . . . . . 465
Inns with Wheelchair Accessibility. . . . . . . . . . . . . . . . . . . . 466
Inns That Accept Pets (with prior permission). . . . . . . . . . . 467
Inns Offering Travelers' Club Benefits. . . . . . . . . . . . . . . . . . 468

# Introduction

"Broad, wholesome, charitable views (of distant places) cannot be acquired by vegetating in one's little corner of the earth."

—Mark Twain, *Innocents Abroad*, 1869

*I* would like to take this opportunity to introduce myself. For fourteen years Brenda Boelts Chapin did a wonderful job of writing this book—a book that I used frequently myself. Then, in 1997, when she decided to go on to other challenges, I was asked to become the editor, a task that I eagerly accepted. Now, for the eighth edition of this venerable guide to inns in the Mid-Atlantic region, I have become the author—a position that I hope to retain for many, many years.

When I first started writing about country inns and bed-and-breakfast establishments, there were no more than 500 inns in America. Most were pale shadows of the sophisticated hostelries we know today. Frequently, a B&B then consisted of a room (or several rooms) in a family home. In fact, my mother used to open her home to paying travelers on occasion, and it gave us all a marvelous exposure to people who had ideas and experiences different from our own. I have always been grateful for this education.

Today, however, innkeeping has become a full-time professional occupation. Over the last twenty years, the number of country inns and bed-and-breakfast establishments has increased dramatically and the American Bed and Breakfast Association now estimates there are about 30,000 B&Bs and country inns in America (although when I race across the countryside from one inn to another, it sometimes seems to me as if there were that many just in the Mid-Atlantic region).

## WHAT EXACTLY IS A COUNTRY INN?

Various writers and organizations have their own definitions of a country inn and how it differs from a bed-and-breakfast. We all agree that, in general at least, a country inn will have a restaurant, while a bed-and-breakfast (by definition) will not. Nevertheless, the two often are referred to synonymously and the distinctions do become blurred. For purposes of this book, I have attempted to adhere to a definition of a country inn that includes an establishment with at least ten guest rooms and a restaurant.

Actually, there are not two, but three, categories of "inns" in America. The first is what we term a "home-stay" or a "guesthouse." This is what my mother had—a room in a private home that is either open seasonally or where the owner has another full-time job and opens his or her home to paying guests merely to provide supplemental income. In other words, the guesthouse is not a full-time occupation. Frequently, there is one bath shared by all the guests and there are no guest televisions or telephones. These establishments are generally not included in guidebooks and they are never included in mine.

A bed-and-breakfast, on the other hand, *is* usually a full-time job for the innkeepers—one they have obtained a license to run. They may offer as few as two or three rooms, but they provide more amenities than a guesthouse owner, and they generally are hands-on managers, perhaps fixing and serving breakfast to their guests and interacting directly in many helpful ways. Someone staying in a bed-and-breakfast can expect to receive breakfast in the morning and often snacks or drinks in the afternoon. Furthermore, most B&Bs today offer private in-room baths for their guests (and many now offer in-room televisions and telephones), as well as a common room that may include a fireplace, a library, or a game room. Outside, there may be a swimming pool or a tennis court. The establishment will not have a restaurant, however. In general, a B&B offers a more private and intimate place to stay than a country inn, with the number of rooms ranging from two to ten.

Guests who stay in a country inn will, in general, find a larger establishment, run by a professional staff—and there will frequently be a restaurant on premise. There will usually be more than ten rooms, but not always. A country inn is officially licensed as a business by the innkeepers. Furthermore, a country inn often is more impersonal than a B&B. In larger inns, you may never meet the owners at all.

In this book, I have concentrated on guiding you to the best country inns in the Mid-Atlantic region. Even though the above distinction seems clear-cut, if you take a close look, you'll see that within these pages there are some large bed-and-breakfasts included. Partly, this is because even though you will find *many* new inns in this edition, a number of smaller bed-and-breakfasts have been included in these pages for many years, and even though they don't have a restaurant, they certainly don't deserve to be dropped. Also, I am continuously traveling the countryside inspecting new inns, but I update this book every other year. In some cases I found fabulous new bed-and-breakfasts that I wanted to tell my readers about sooner rather than later. For a more thorough compilation of all the bed-and-breakfasts in our region, read my companion book, *Recommended Bed & Breakfasts: Mid-Atlantic States*.

# HOW DID I SELECT COUNTRY INNS
## FOR THIS BOOK?

My goal is to search out the very best country inns in the Mid-Atlantic region and to describe them to you in such a way that you can make an informed decision about where to stay. I want you to know both the pros and cons of each inn so that you will not be disappointed with your choice. In order to do that, every year I criss-cross the Mid-Atlantic region from Lake Ontario to the Cumberland Gap and from the Atlantic Ocean to the Ohio and Kentucky borders, searching out the finest country inns. I generally visit more than 600 inns and bed-and-breakfasts a year—and put almost 10,000 miles on my car—so that I know my descriptions are on target. My visits include stops at old, reliable inns and at brand new ones.

I assure you that every inn in this book (with two to three exceptions) has been personally inspected by me and, in my opinion, each meets the highest standards of cleanliness, maintenance, decor, and friendliness. Of the inns I inspect each year, only about 20 percent make it into the pages of a book. Naturally, I include those I consider to be the best. My pledge to you is that my decisions are strictly independent. Under no circumstances were inns able to pay to be included. No fees of any kind are accepted.

Although I have an enormous database of inns and bed-and-breakfasts in my computer, I learn about new inns from a variety of sources. I always ask local innkeepers, as well as the chambers of commerce, about new inns when I am traveling. I frequently receive letters from readers and from new innkeepers telling me about inns. In addition, I subscribe to newsletters, magazines, and newspapers. There is seldom a day that goes by that I don't add a new inn to my database or change a note about an old one.

On my first visit to an inn, I arrive unannounced and do a thorough inspection. I take copious notes in hardbound books that I later index, and I add the dates of my inspections, the book where my complete notes will be found, and my overall comments to my computer database. This approach has one major drawback: On occasion, there is no one home at the inn I want to see, and then I must wait to review that inn on another visit. On the other hand, the approach works because I know I am seeing the inn just as it will look to paying guests and not spruced up for a visit by a travel writer. If, after my inspection, I believe the inn warrants inclusion in my books, I usually schedule a return visit to stay there.

It was no easy task to select 210 inns from the vast number that are now open. I believe the ones I have chosen have the highest standards of cleanliness, superb maintenance, and friendly on-site innkeepers or managers. If an inn is lacking in any of those qualities, I did not include it. In addition, if an inn has been in business fewer than two years, or if there are new owners, I will generally give it time to season.

I believe most travelers today prefer rooms with private baths, so most of the inns in this book offer a private in-room bath. I also look for inns with comfortable common areas, including verandas, porches, and gardens, and those offering something extra—perhaps afternoon tea, or evening wine and cheese, or a swimming pool. Yet, I also believe I have a responsibility to offer my readers a selection of inns that provide a variety of styles, prices, and amenities and that cover the entire Mid-Atlantic geographic area.

Country inns reflect the architectural and decorative styles of the buildings they occupy as well as the interests of the innkeepers who own them, and that's what makes them so interesting. So whether you're looking for an intimate, romantic retreat with a whirlpool tub and a truffle on the pillow at turndown, or a gourmet dinner of superlative food and wine, or an adventure-packed weekend of cross-country skiing, you're sure to find what strikes your fancy in these pages.

I take my responsibility very seriously. Changes in inns inevitably take place and your personal experiences add to my knowledge about an inn. I encourage you to write and tell me both your happy and your unfortunate experiences. You may write to me at The Globe Pequot Press, P.O. Box 833, Old Saybrook, CT 06475.

Thank you for using this book. Happy travels!

Suzi Forbes Chase

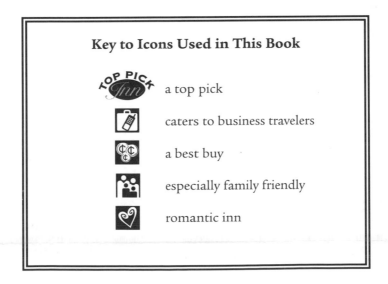

### Key to Icons Used in This Book

a top pick

caters to business travelers

a best buy

especially family friendly

romantic inn

# How to Use This Inn Guide

## INTRODUCING . . . A NEW FORMAT

This guidebook contains 210 full descriptions of inns in the Mid-Atlantic region, which consists of Delaware, Maryland, New Jersey, New York, Pennsylvania, Virginia, Washington, D.C., and West Virginia. If you have used this guide in the past, you will see several significant design changes in this edition:

*Icons:* To give you a quick overview of an inn's special qualities, we have added descriptive icons to this book. You can select an inn quickly by looking for a particular icon. If you are traveling with your family, for example, look for the family icon—an assurance that this inn accepts children. If you are traveling on business, look for the business icon, which indicates those inns that provide space and amenities to make your business trip more productive. The following descriptions will tell you the criteria I used in selecting an icon.

The inns I selected as my "Top Picks" are my personal favorites. They meet the very highest standards of excellence in every way—from decor and ambience to friendliness, cleanliness, maintenance, and cuisine. These are the inns I love to visit most.

The inns I selected as offering a setting conducive to romance generally include such features as whirlpool tubs, in-room fireplaces, and rooms with a certain sense of privacy. They all have private bathrooms. Beyond these basics, however, each of these inns has a certain ambience that lends itself to romance—a quality that is hard to describe, but one in which the innkeepers have conspired to weave a web of fantasy, or whimsy, or *romance* into the fabric of their inn.

To identify an inn as one that offers exceptional value, I chose those in which a couple could spend a night for under $90 including breakfast. When lunch and dinner are also offered by the inn for a fixed price, the price will be stated in a different way.

Inns identified by the family-friendly icon accept children of all ages or accept those eight years or older. They often have additional facilities that will be attractive to children, such as horseback riding, a swimming pool, or cross-country skiing.

📱 For an inn to be considered especially appropriate for business travelers, I identified only those that have a telephone in each guest room (especially if a telephone is equipped with dataport so a traveler can plug in a computer). I looked for those that have a desk or work space in the room, as well as a television (and often a VCR). A fax and copier should be available for use, and sometimes there are also meeting or conference rooms.

*Supplemental list of inns:* At the end of each state chapter is a list of supplemental inns—almost 200 throughout the entire Mid-Atlantic region—bringing the total number of inns identified in this book to more than 400. Although I have offered a thumbnail sketch of each supplemental inn, these come without recommendation and they are not indexed in the back. In some cases the additional inns are B&Bs and were not included because this is a country inns book. In other cases, I may have been unable to inspect them recently or perhaps they did not achieve the standard of excellence necessary for a full description. Regardless, they are placed here to help you find a place to stay if your first choice was fully booked.

## GENERAL DESCRIPTION

Throughout this book, the states are listed alphabetically and the inns within each state are listed alphabetically by town. Preceding each state, you will find a map identifying the location of each inn, as well as a table of contents. At the beginning of each inn description, you will also find a list of important details such as rates, size of inn, restaurant prices, amenities, facilities, and policies.

In the back of the book are the indexes—an overall index of inns and and special indexes. Each of the inns warranting a particular icon, for example, is indexed under that icon in the back. If you are traveling with a wheelchair-bound person, or with pets, you will also find an index in the back that identifies inns that offer the necessary facilities to accommodate you and your companion.

## CAVEATS

*Rates:* The rates in this book are based on double occupancy. Although they were accurate at the time of publication, you may find slight differences. It is always best to ask for the exact rate when you book—and be sure to ask if the rate includes all taxes, gratuities, and service charges. Inns will often require a deposit to hold the room. You should also ask about the inn's refund policy in case you are unable to come when planned.

*Credit cards and personal checks:* American Express, Visa, and MasterCard are generally accepted by all inns. If you plan to use a credit card or to pay with a personal check, however, you should inquire in advance in case specific forms of identification are required.

*Telephones:* I have indicated those inns that have telephones in the guest rooms, as well as those that have dataport connections. If the rooms are not equipped with telephones, I have tried to indicate where a common telephone is located or, in some cases, if the innkeepers have portable telephones that guests can take to their rooms.

*TV:* More and more inns are providing televisions in the rooms. If you are opposed to such an intrusion, you might ask to have it removed. In some cases, it is so well hidden that you may need to ask its location to view it.

*Pets:* I have indicated those inns in which well-behaved pets are permitted to stay and I have also included an index at the end of the book. Please note, however, that innkeepers definitely want to be notified in advance if you plan to bring your pal along. In some cases they have specific rooms that are suitable for pet occupancy.

*Wheelchair access:* If I have stated that an inn has wheelchair accessibility, then at least one room has a door wide enough for a wheelchair to pass through and also meets the approved ADA requirements for use of the bathroom. These inns also have common rooms that allow for maneuverability of a wheelchair. If there's a particular inn that you wish to visit and it is not identified as wheelchair accessible here, however, you should inquire anyway. Perhaps the bathroom does not have *all* the ADA requirements, but you may feel there are enough to accommodate your particular needs.

*Smoking:* Many inns restrict smoking, and the number of nonsmoking inns is now greater than those that permit smoking. I have indicated which inns do and do not allow smoking. If an inn permits smoking, I have also specified if they offer designated nonsmoking rooms.

*Recommended Country Inns® Travelers' Club:* Many of the inns in this book provide discounts to people who buy the book and become members of the Recommended Country Inns® Travelers' Club. To receive your discount, please fill out the form in the front of this book and mail it to The Globe Pequot Press, P.O. Box 833, Old Saybrook, CT 06475. You will receive a membership card by return mail. There is no charge for membership and you will reap substantial discounts.

*Recommended*

# COUNTRY INNS®

## MID-ATLANTIC and CHESAPEAKE REGION

# Delaware & Maryland

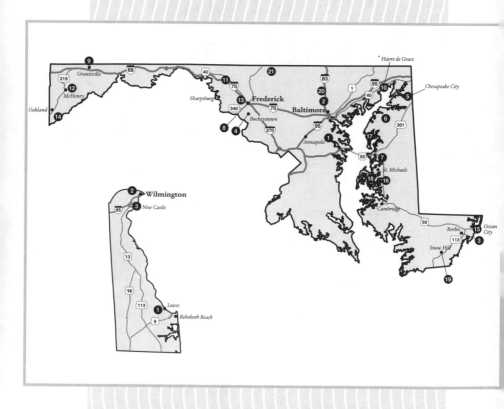

# Delaware and Maryland

*Numbers on map refer to towns numbered below.*

## Delaware

1. Lewes, New Devon Inn .......................................... 4
2. Montchanin, The Inn at Montchanin Village* ................. 5
3. New Castle, Armitage Inn............................................ 8

## Maryland

1. Annapolis, William Page Inn................................ 11
2. Baltimore,
   Celie's Waterfront Bed and Breakfast ....................... 12
   Mr. Mole Bed & Breakfast .................................. 14
3. Berlin,
   Atlantic Hotel............................................. 15
   Merry Sherwood Plantation* .............................. 17
4. Buckeystown, The Catoctin Inn .......................... 19
5. Chesapeake City,
   Inn at the Canal.......................................... 21
   Ship Watch Inn .......................................... 22
6. Chestertown,
   Brampton Bed & Breakfast ................................ 25
   Great Oak Manor* ........................................ 26
7. Easton, Ashby 1663 Bed and Breakfast* ..................... 29
8. Frederick,
   The Turning Point Inn..................................... 31
   Tyler-Spite Inn .......................................... 33
9. Grantsville, Elliott House Victorian Inn .................... 34
10. Havre de Grace, Vandiver Inn ............................ 36
11. Keedysville, Antietam Overlook Farm* ..................... 37
12. McHenry, Lake Pointe Inn*................................ 39
13. Middletown, Stone Manor*................................ 41
14. Oakland, Carmel Cove Inn................................ 43
15. Ocean City, The Lighthouse Club Hotel ... at Fager's Island.... 45
16. Oxford, Combsberry* ..................................... 47
17. Rock Hall, The Inn at Osprey Point....................... 49
18. St. Michaels, The Inn at Perry Cabin* ..................... 51
19. Snow Hill, River House Inn............................... 54
20. Stevenson, Gramercy Mansion B&B ........................ 56
21. Taneytown, Antrim 1844 Country Inn* ..................... 57

*A Top Pick Inn

# New Devon Inn
## Lewes, Delaware 19958

**INNKEEPERS:** Suzanne Steele and Judith Henderson; Dale Jenkins, proprietor

**ADDRESS/TELEPHONE:** 142 Second Street (mailing address: P.O. Box 516); (302) 645-6466 or (800) 824-8754; fax (302) 645-7196

**E-MAIL:** newdevon@dca.net

**WEB SITE:** www.Beach-net.com

**ROOMS:** 26, including 2 suites; all with private bath, air-conditioning, and telephone. Designated nonsmoking rooms. Wheelchair accessible. Children over the age of 16 welcome.

**RATES:** Seasonal: $50 to $170, double occupancy; continental breakfast. Two-night minimum June through September and holiday weekends. Request special packages.

**OPEN:** All year.

**FACILITIES AND ACTIVITIES:** Restaurant (entrees $15 to $27). Nearby: Cape Henlopen State Park, Zwaanendael Museum, Lewes Bay Beach, restaurants, shops, biking.

**BUSINESS TRAVEL:** Desks, meeting rooms, and fax available.

*L*ewes is a charming little historic village located along the edge of the Lewes-Rehoboth Canal—a center for fishermen and boaters. The car ferry to Cape May provides a direct link between New Jersey and the DelMarVa Peninsula and a much more relaxing and pleasant way to travel than driving around. Travelers in the know will stop in Lewes to browse through the antiques and gift shops and the art galleries and to stay at the New Devon Inn, which is located in the heart of town.

Innkeeper Dale Jenkins, who is also a real estate agent, named the former hotel after the mythical island James Michener created for his book *Chesapeake,* a novel rich in the lore of the Chesapeake Bay region. You enter the inn by passing along a wide hallway flanked by an animation art shop and a jewelry store. In the lobby there are lustrous heart-pine floors, two unusual elephant chairs, and an ornate cage elevator that is a reminder of the hotel's 1926 origins. You may decide to peruse the morning paper here or to take it to the pretty Garden Room, an oasis of wicker, green plants, and sunlight. Up a short flight of stairs, the music room contains an antique bellows organ and Victorian-era furnishings.

In the morning you go down to the lower lobby for freshly baked muffins or sticky buns and coffee that is elegantly served in delicate antique cups. The inn's television is located here as well.

The guest rooms are furnished with lovely Victorian antiques—many of Eastlake design. Although the rooms are small, they all have a private bath, and the beds are swathed in elegant designer linens. My favorite is Room 108, a bright corner room that overlooks Second Street. At night a luscious chocolate and a cordial await at bedside.

The Buttery, a charming restaurant located just beyond the lobby of the New Devon Inn but under separate management, serves both lunch and dinner. Among the dinner specialties you might select rainbow trout encrusted in cornmeal and served with wilted radicchio, spinach, and toasted pine nuts or a roast half duckling with fruited bread stuffing and raspberry-Chambord sauce. Elegant, freshly baked cakes and pies are dessert specialties.

HOW TO GET THERE: From points west take Route 9 east (becomes Savannah Road) into Lewes. In town turn left onto Second Street; inn is 1 block on the left at the corner of Second and Market Streets.

# The Inn at Montchanin Village
Montchanin, Delaware 19710

INNKEEPER: Brooke Johnson White; Daniel and Missy Lickle, proprietors

ADDRESS/TELEPHONE: Route 100 and Kirk Road (mailing address: P.O. Box 130); (302) 888–2133 or (800) COWBIRD; fax (302) 888–0389

E-MAIL: montchan@gte.net

WEB SITE: www.montchanin.com

**ROOMS:** 33, including 25 suites; all with private bath, air-conditioning, telephone, television, minirefrigerator, coffeemaker, hair dryer, porch, dataport, robe, iron, ironing board, and wet bar; 9 with fireplace, 2 with whirlpool. No smoking inn. Wheelchair accessible.

**RATES:** $170 to $450, double occupancy; includes full breakfast. Two-night minimum some weekends, holidays, and special events.

**OPEN:** All year.

**FACILITIES AND ACTIVITIES:** Dining room open for dinner daily 5:30 to 10:00 P.M. (entrees $21 to $28). Nearby: museums and gardens.

**BUSINESS TRAVEL:** Dataport, voice mail, and dual-line telephone in all rooms; 7 with desk; fax available; meeting space for twenty-five people.

*M*ontchanin is a tiny hamlet named for Anne Alexandrine de Montchanin. She was the grandmother of Eleuthère Irénée duPont, founder of the DuPont Gunpowder Company. The inn is located in a cluster of buildings built in the early 1800s to house laborers from the nearby DuPont powder mills. The complex includes several houses, a cluster of cottages, a former blacksmith shop, a schoolhouse, and a massive stone and post-and-beam barn.

The restoration is the ambitious undertaking of local preservationists Missy and Daniel Lickle. When they acquired the property, they sought an adaptive use that would preserve the quaint buildings in their original setting. They achieved this goal admirably. The entire six acres are on the National Register of Historic Places. Work continues on the inn, where the next project is to restore the massive fieldstone barn, which will eventually house the inn's guest reception room and a library where a fieldstone fireplace will offer cozy warmth.

The restoration is so true to the village's origins that even the original tiny concrete outhouses remain as garden curiosities. Privy Lane leads guests to the restaurant in the former blacksmith shop, where an elegant full breakfast is served every morning to inn guests—and it's complimentary.

The guest rooms are luxuriously furnished with antique four-poster and canopy beds, armoires, and painted blanket chests. There are chain-stitched rugs on hardwood floors, graceful moldings, and sponged walls. Nine of the units have fireplaces, and almost all have either a private garden, porch, balcony, or terrace. The beds are swathed in pretty fabrics and dressed in Frette sheets, and the marble baths have every possible luxury, including oversized whirlpool tubs in some. Look carefully and you'll see whimsical displays of Dan and Missy's cow and bird collection—in the bathroom tiles, on the bath mats, and peeking out of unexpected places throughout the rooms.

The blacksmith shop now houses Krazy Kat's Restaurant, which is setting records of its own for fine dining. One of the area's top chefs is at its helm; he designed the kitchen as well as the menu. The fanciful paintings of costumed dogs and cats that decorate the walls will delight and amuse you. You'll find such dishes as pan-roasted pork porterhouse crusted with brandy pepper and laced with caramelized pearl onions and rosemary demicream, or grilled Atlantic salmon and shrimp bouillabaisse. The restaurant is open for breakfast, lunch, and dinner.

The inn is in the Brandywine Valley, where the Wyeth family has been painting for years. It's close to Winterthur Museum and Gardens, Longwood Gardens, Brandywine River Museum, and Wilmington. Although there are no sports facilities on the premises, a golf course is located 2 miles away, and this is a terrific area for bicycling.

HOW TO GET THERE: From I–95 take the Concord Pike/Route 202 exit. Travel north on Route 202 to Route 141. Turn left onto Route 141, continuing to the Rockland Road intersection. Turn right onto Rockland Road, passing the DuPont Country Club. Continue on Rockland Road over the Brandywine River and bear left at the fork, just past the river. At the corner of Rockland Road and Route 100, turn right onto Route 100 north. Travel approximately 500 feet and turn into the entrance at Kirk Road and Route 100.

## Brick-a-brack

The Foyer of Krazy Kat's restaurant at The Inn at Montchanin Village is laid with bricks. To give them a deep, rich, and lustrous gloss, the owners have developed their own unique polish. They rub and buff the floors with two coats of brown paste wax (they use Kiwi), which, they say, gives the bricks a warm color and a hard, sealed finish.

# Armitage Inn
## New Castle, Delaware 19720

INNKEEPERS: Stephen and Rina Marks

ADDRESS/TELEPHONE: 2 The Strand; (302) 328–6618;
fax (302) 324–1163

E-MAIL: armitageinn@earthlink.net

ROOMS: 5; all with private bath, air-conditioning, telephone, and television; 2 with fireplace, 3 with whirlpool. No smoking inn. Children over the age of 12 welcome.

RATES: $105 to $150, double occupancy; includes full breakfast. Two-night minimum may apply weekends April through November.

OPEN: All year.

FACILITIES AND ACTIVITIES: Tennis courts and a public park accessible through the garden gate. Nearby: playhouse, concert hall, dinner theater, Winterthur, Longwood Gardens, Brandywine Valley.

BUSINESS TRAVEL: Desks in all rooms; dataports.

*N*ew Castle is one of my favorite towns. It's so authentically Colonial that I have no difficulty imagining myself walking along the narrow brick sidewalks, lighted by flickering street lamps, garbed in a dress with a voluminous skirt, a bonnet securely fastened over my curls, and my gloved hand gently resting on the arm of a handsome gentleman wearing a tall hat and tails. Perhaps we've been to a party at the home of Revolutionary War hero Zachariah Van Leuvenigh, whose handsome brick house still stands on The Strand, a greensward that rolls down to the banks of the Delaware River. Peter Stuyvesant laid out New Castle in 1651, when the area was still under Dutch rule, and it was near here that William Penn first landed in 1681.

Today Van Leuvenigh's gracious house with its fine views is known as the Armitage Inn. Stephen and Rina Marks spent almost a year polishing the wide-plank, red-pine floors of this center-hall Colonial, which has a splendid staircase that reaches to the second floor. To the right, a gracious dining room waits for us to sample a scrumptious gourmet breakfast, but for now the elegant parlor, with its fire glowing in the hearth, beckons us.

We looked through the extensive library, selected a book, and spent a toasty winter afternoon in pure relaxation. Beyond the library the oldest room in the house, which dates to the 1600s, contains its original massive brick cooking fireplace and beehive oven. Beyond that are a screened porch and a walled garden.

The guest rooms have canopy beds so high that they require a step stool. Some are draped in filmy fabric, and some have hand-crocheted canopies. Televisions are tucked into period reproduction furniture. The marble-and-tile baths are spacious; they all have hair dryers, and some have whirlpool tubs. Our favorite room is the White Rose Room, which has a little nook that overlooks The Strand and the Delaware River. During the day the river is alive with traffic, but at night we were lulled to sleep by foghorns. In the morning a flock of geese called overhead.

HOW TO GET THERE: Traveling on I–95 take exit 5A (if coming from the south, take I–295 toward New Jersey and take exit 5A) onto Delaware Route 141 south. At the intersection of Routes 9 and 273, turn north on Route 9 and travel for ½ mile. Bear right to New Castle via Delaware Street. Continue on Delaware Street through the village to The Strand. The inn is on the right.

# Select List of Other Inns
# in Delaware

### The Bay Moon Bed & Breakfast
1128 Kings Highway
Lewes, DE 19958
(302) 644–1802 or (800) 917–2307 (pager)

*6 rooms; 4 with private bath. Features oak decor; in center of town.*

### Blue Water House
407 East Market Street
Lewes, DE 19958
(302) 645–7832 or (800) 493–2080

*6 rooms; all with private bath. In a building that resembles a lighthouse; distant ocean views.*

### The Boulevard Bed and Breakfast
1909 Baynard Boulevard
Wilmington, DE 19802
(302) 656–9700

*6 rooms; 4 with private bath. In 1913 brick house in residential area; simple but comfortable furnishings.*

# Maryland

## William Page Inn
### Annapolis, Maryland 21401

**INNKEEPER:** Robert Zuchelli

**ADDRESS/TELEPHONE:** 8 Martin Street; (410) 626–1506 or
(800) 364–4160; fax (410) 263–4841

**E-MAIL:** WmPageInn@aol.com

**WEB SITE:** www.williampageinn.com

**ROOMS:** 5, including 1 suite; 3 with private bath; all with air-conditioning, 2 with whirlpool, 1 with television. No smoking inn. Children over
the age of 12 welcome.

**RATES:** $95 to $195, double occupancy; includes full breakfast. Two-
night minimum weekends mid-March through November.

**OPEN:** All year.

**FACILITIES AND ACTIVITIES:** Off-street parking. Nearby; restaurants,
U.S. Naval Academy, William Paca Mansion, boating tours, guided tours
of Colonial Annapolis, State House, historic mansions.

**BUSINESS TRAVEL:** Desks in 3 rooms, fax available, computer rentals;
valet service.

One of the things I like best about the William Page Inn is its proximity to the U.S. Naval Academy. It's an easy walk through the
impressive wrought-iron gates, where we never tire of watching the
daily noontime drill of the "plebes" in the quadrangle.

The brown-shingled house, with its broad side porch, appears modest at
first glance, but for more than fifty years it served as the Democratic Club of
Annapolis. The living room, in particular, has the look of a private club. The
guest rooms are named for characters in *Charlotte's Web* by E. B. White. Why?
"Because I liked the whimsy," explained innkeeper Robert Zuchelli. Each of
the rooms has its own distinctive character highlighted by fine antiques.
There are four-poster and rice beds in the rooms, and the Fern Room has a
wonderful Victorian bed and an elaborate Victorian dressing table. Temple-
ton has its own private bath with a whirlpool tub, while Wilbur and Charlotte share a hall bath.

My favorite is The Marilyn Suite (a name not from *Charlotte's Web*), which is located on the third floor. It has a romantic ambience enhanced by a mauve-and-blue decor. The dormered windows have window seats, and a skylight is perfectly placed to shed moonlight across the handsome sleigh bed. This is the only room with a television. A two-room bath includes a whirlpool tub and a shower.

Do you remember Charlotte's children saying, "We take to the breeze; we go as we please?" And so do we. But our breezes are bound to return us frequently to the William Page Inn.

HOW TO GET THERE: From Route 50 exit onto Rowe Boulevard. Follow Rowe past three traffic lights to stop sign. Turn left onto College Avenue. At light turn right onto King George Street. Continue to Gate 1 of Naval Academy and turn right onto East Street. Turn right at stop sign at Martin Street. Pull into driveway of inn.

# Celie's Waterfront Bed and Breakfast
## Baltimore, Maryland 21231

INNKEEPER: Celie Ives

ADDRESS/TELEPHONE: 1714 Thames Street; (410) 522–2323 or (800) 432–0184; fax (410) 522–2324

E-MAIL: Celies@aol.com

WEB SITE: www.bbonline.com/md/celies

ROOMS: 7; all with private bath, air-conditioning, TV, telephone with dataport and answering machine; 2 with balcony and/or fireplace; 4 with whirlpool tub. No smoking inn. Wheelchair accessible. Children over the age of 10 welcome.

RATES: $125 to $225, double occupancy; includes continental breakfast. Two or three nights for whirlpool rooms on weekends and special events; two or three nights all rooms on holiday weekends.

**OPEN:** All year.

**FACILITIES AND ACTIVITIES:** Roof deck, courtyard/garden. In charming historic district with shops and restaurants. Near Harborplace, aquarium, science center, Oriole Park at Camden Yards, Baltimore Museum of Art.

**BUSINESS TRAVEL:** Desk, telephone with dataport and answering machine, cable TV and VCR, minirefrigerator, coffeemaker, hair dryer, iron and ironing board in all rooms; fax and newspapers available; flexible breakfast time.

Just outside the door of Celie's, the cobblestone streets, the melange of waterfront taverns and shops, and the old but still-working wharfs are reminders of early Fells Point, Baltimore's first deepwater port. This is where Baltimore's famous clipper ships were built. Yet just across the street, the picturesque brick police station places the district directly in the present, as this station is the one used in the popular television program *Homicide: Life on the Streets,* and the bar near Celie's is also featured. You may even see the series being filmed.

Celie's is a wonderful oasis of peaceful calm, entered along a long brick passageway. Although it looks as if it began life with the rest of the area in the 1730s, it was actually built in 1990, when the district was undergoing a massive revitalization. The city asked for proposals to fill this vacant lot, and Celie's was chosen. She built a cozy lobby with a fireplace and a breakfast room where a pine sideboard holds the breakfast goodies. Just beyond, a brick-walled courtyard includes a gently splashing fountain and lush plants as well as garden furniture. Nevertheless, the favorite retreat at Celie's is the rooftop deck where a bird's-eye view of the harbor is bound to delight both day and night.

The guest rooms hold every amenity a tourist or a business traveler might want. There are desks, cable televisions, VCRs, refrigerators stocked with soft drinks, telephones with dataports and answering machines, coffeemakers, and hair dryers. The furnishings are crisp and smart, incorporating a combination of antiques and new furniture. Several of the guest rooms have balconies, some have fireplaces, and some have whirlpool tubs.

**HOW TO GET THERE:** From Pratt Street in downtown Baltimore, proceed east and turn right onto President Street. Turn left onto Fleet Street and right onto Ann Street. At Thames Street, turn right again. The B&B is in the middle of the block—a gray building with rose trim.

# Mr. Mole Bed & Breakfast
## Baltimore, Maryland 21217

**INNKEEPERS:** Paul Bragaw and Collin Clarke

**ADDRESS/TELEPHONE:** 1601 Bolton Street; (410) 728–1179;
fax (410) 728–3379

**ROOMS:** 5, including 2 suites; all with private bath, air-conditioning,
and telephone with dataport. No smoking inn. Children over the age of
10 welcome.

**RATES:** $105 to $135, double occupancy; includes full breakfast. Two-
night minimum on weekends.

**OPEN:** All year.

**FACILITIES AND ACTIVITIES:** Enclosed parking. Nearby: Mechanic Theater, Myerhoff Symphony Hall, Lyric Opera House, Antique Row, Wal-
ters Art Gallery, Lexington Market, Oriole Park at Camden Yards, Babe
Ruth Birthplace, Inner Harbor, Science Museum, National Aquarium.

**BUSINESS TRAVEL:** 5 blocks from train. Telephone with dataport and
voice mail plus desk in room; fax available.

*I* love the droll whimsy juxtaposed with the sophisticated elegance
of Mr. Mole. Part fairy tale and part urbane splendor, the B&B
strikes the right note on both counts. As most of you know, the
name was inspired by the character in *Wind in the Willows*.

Located in a nineteenth-century brick townhouse, the B&B has 14-foot ceilings in the
adjoining living, drawing, and breakfast rooms,
all painted a brilliant Kodak yellow and each
with a carved marble fireplace. In the hallway
Collin Clarke painted leaves all over the walls.
Throughout the rooms, Collin's blue-and-white
porcelain collection and Paul Bragaw's ecclesias-
tical antiques and small boxes delight the eye.
Heavy drapes frame the windows.

The guest rooms have an equal measure of
caprice and grace. The enormous London Suite,
for example, has two bedrooms and a sitting
room, which has bottle-green wainscoting and cardinal-red walls. The red-
lacquered four-poster bed is draped with red, green, and white plaid. The

Garden Suite is furnished with antique white wicker, and the bed is swagged in buttery linen. There's a private overhanging porch.

Unlike many B&Bs, guests at Mr. Mole select their breakfast from a buffet of breads, cheeses, and fruits and then are free to sit at a private table of their own choosing, where they can be as solitary or as sociable as they choose.

**HOW TO GET THERE:** From I-95 take exit 53 to I-395. Exit onto Martin Luther King, Jr., Boulevard, bearing right, and continue 2 miles. Turn left on Eutaw Street, go ⁶/₁₀ mile, turn right at fourth stoplight onto McMechen Street. Go 1 block to stop sign at Bolton Street. Inn is diagonally across intersection.

# Atlantic Hotel 🏨 💲
## Berlin, Maryland 21811

**GENERAL MANAGER:** Gary Weber

**ADDRESS/TELEPHONE:** 2 North Main Street; (410) 641-3589 or (800) 814-7672; fax (410) 641-4928

**WEB SITE:** www.atlantichotel.com

**ROOMS:** 17, including 1 suite; all with private bath, air-conditioning, telephone, and TV. Smoking permitted on porches and in lounge only. Wheelchair accessible.

**RATES:** $75 to $160, double occupancy; full breakfast. Two-night minimum weekends late May to early September.

**OPEN:** All year.

**FACILITIES AND ACTIVITIES:** Restaurant (entrees $23 to $30), Drummer's Cafe (entrees $13 to $24). Nearby: Old Globe Theater building—a combination of art gallery, bookstore, gift shop, and cafe, with entertainment ranging from folk performers to puppet shows. Assateague Island National Seashore, which has miles of beaches and marshlands, is popular for hiking, swimming, and fishing.

**BUSINESS TRAVEL:** Desks in 6 rooms.

*I* remember the first time I drove through Berlin, a little inland village on Maryland's Eastern Shore about 10 miles from Ocean City. It was a brilliant, sunny spring day. People were strolling in and out of shops and commenting on the fine weather. The Atlantic Hotel was the most popular magnet. In the center of town, this quaint three-story Victorian brick building dates to 1895 and is on the National Register of Historic Places. Across the front there's a covered brick veranda embellished with pillars and iron-lace trim. A bevy of rockers occupy the space in summer, and planters overflowing with an abundance of colorful flowers create a border.

Drummer's Cafe is a popular spot for lunch and casual dining both summer and winter. We love the old-world ambience that includes a tin ceiling and a cozy sitting area around the fireplace in winter, especially on Fridays and Saturdays, when there's a pianist. In summer the patio in back is a congenial place for lunch or dinner. The formal dining room is noted for its gourmet dishes and exceptional wine list. Do not miss the delectable crab cakes or the house-made desserts.

The guest rooms are perfectly acceptable but not fabulous. There are a smattering of Victorian antiques—the handsome bed and armoire in Number 11 is especially stunning, as is the brass bed in the suite, Number 25. The baths are small, although there are several with claw-foot tubs. Overnight guests have the use of the Ladies Parlor, a second-floor retreat where we enjoyed the old-fashioned pastimes of reading and writing.

HOW TO GET THERE: From Washington, D.C., take Route 50 east across the Chesapeake Bay Bridge and stay on Route 50 for approximately 90 miles to Berlin. Turn south onto Maryland Route 818, which is Main Street. The inn is on the left.

# Merry Sherwood Plantation
## Berlin, Maryland 21811

**INNKEEPER:** W. Kirk Burbage

**ADDRESS/TELEPHONE:** 8909 Worcester Highway; (410) 641–2112 or (800) 660–0358; fax (410) 641–9528

**ROOMS:** 8, including 1 suite; all with air-conditioning, 6 with private bath, 3 with wood-burning fireplace, 1 with Jacuzzi. No smoking inn.

**RATES:** $95 to $175, double occupancy; includes full breakfast. Two-night minimum weekends.

**OPEN:** All year.

**FACILITIES AND ACTIVITIES:** Eighteen acres of gardens. Nearby: Assateague Island National Seashore, 8 miles away; golf, horseback riding, bird-watching, bicycling; historic Berlin.

**RECOMMENDED COUNTRY INNS® TRAVELERS' CLUB BENEFIT:** 25 percent discount, Monday to Thursday; call ahead for availability on weekends.

*A*s we drive under the canopy of sugar maple trees that line the circular driveway, the magnificent seafoam green plantation mansion, trimmed with darker shades of green and sparkling white, looms ahead. A fanciful cupola crowns the confection. We imagine we see Elizabeth Henry Johnson—the young girl for whom the 8,500-square-foot,

twenty-seven-room house was built in 1859—surveying her lands while waiting for her husband.

The restoration of the mansion, which is listed on the National Register of Historic Places, was the dedicated work of local businessman Kirk Burbage, whose family has lived in Berlin for some 200 years. He spent two years reviving the former ruin, and his painstaking attention to detail is apparent throughout.

We arrived in time for iced tea, which was being served in the front parlor. In the ballroom creamy, arched marble fireplaces gleam, heavy damask drapes frame doorways, and lace panels cover windows. Priceless antiques include Victorian settees, a square grand piano, and a massive carved chair with lion's-head arms and bearing a brass portrait of Queen Victoria. It's said to have been made for an anticipated visit to the United States by the queen, which never took place. We sat and sipped, talking to the other guests while we all thoroughly enjoyed a narrative about the house's history and its restoration.

The house contains impressive furnishings and decor throughout. There's a magnificent chandelier in the dining room, the parlor has an organ, and the library has polished paneled walls. There are nine elegant fireplaces. We were especially impressed by several bookcases in the library that open to reveal closets. Some of the books are leather-bound first editions. Beyond the library an inviting side porch contains wicker and rattan furniture, and we sat here imagining how gorgeous the gardens must be during the summer. *Summer Living* magazine has been assisting in the development of the gardens and landscaping on the eighteen-acre property. We wished we had been able to come at a time when the flowers and trees were in bloom.

The guest rooms are equally impressive, furnished with museum-quality antiques and lush fabrics. In the Harrison Room, for example, there's a mas-

## *Whispers from the Past*

The soft rustle of silk, the delicate laugh of a lady, the faint whiff of an unidentifiable perfume: These are only a few of the sensations guests in the Harrison Room of Merry Sherwood Plantation have reported. They may feel a fresh breeze, although the windows are shut, or find that the picture of a beautiful young girl that sits on a dresser has been moved ever so slightly so that she can gaze across the gardens to see the roses in bloom.

Benign and appealing, the girl seems to appreciate the company of her guests. Who is she and why is she still here? No one seems to know. It's not the original mistress, but whoever she is, she seems to have loved this home so much she simply cannot yet leave. No matter. Guests who feel her presence say she imparts a gentle peace that they cherish as a special memento of their visit to Merry Sherwood.

sive Gothic Revival bed and a Victorian fainting couch that can be converted into a double bed. The Chase Room has an unusual bed with 5-foot posts carved into beehive finials. The Johnson Room has a carved canopy bed.

Before going out to dinner, we climbed the mahogany stairs to the cupola, lined with windows, to survey the estate's domain. Later, in the library, we spent a pleasant evening finishing a jigsaw puzzle.

We breakfasted regally the next morning in a formal dining room that boasts a brass chandelier. We were seated at a mahogany Empire-style table with Victorian rosewood chairs. If you're lucky perhaps you, too, will have oatmeal-butterscotch muffins followed by ham-and-broccoli strata, as we did.

**HOW TO GET THERE:** From Baltimore and Washington, D.C., follow Route 50 east to Berlin (it's 6 miles before Ocean City). Take the Route 113 exit and travel south for 2½ miles. Merry Sherwood Plantation is on the right.

# The Catoctin Inn
## Buckeystown, Maryland 21717

**INNKEEPER:** Paula VanHoose; Terry and Sarah MacGillivray, proprietors

**ADDRESS/TELEPHONE:** 3619 Buckeystown Pike (mailing address: P.O. Box 243); (301) 874–5555 or (800) 730–5550; fax (301) 874–2026

**E-MAIL:** Catoctin@Fred.net

**WEB SITE:** www.catoctininn.com

**ROOMS:** 20, including 11 suites and 3 cottages; all with private bath, air-conditioning, telephone (most with dataport), TV, and VCR; 14 with minirefrigerator, coffeemaker, hair dryer, iron, ironing board, whirlpool tub; 16 with fireplaces; 8 with balconies or porches. One room designated smoking. Wheelchair accessible.

**RATES:** $95 to $175, double occupancy; includes continental breakfast; full breakfast available for additional charge $2.80 to $3.95. Two-night minimum some weekends.

**OPEN:** All year except Christmas Day.

**FACILITIES AND ACTIVITIES:** Four-course dinner Saturday nights (prix fixe $69 per couple); parking on premises, four acres of lawns and gardens, bicycles available. Nearby: Civil War Medical Museum, Monocacy National Battlefield, Appalachian Trail.

**BUSINESS TRAVEL:** Desks, telephones with dataports and voice mail, TVs, VCRs, coffeemakers, irons, ironing boards, and minirefrigerators in rooms; conference room, fax, IBM compatible computer, laser printer available; flexible breakfast hour.

**RECOMMENDED COUNTRY INNS® TRAVELERS' CLUB BENEFIT:** 10 percent discount, Monday to Thursday.

*I*f enthusiasm and hard work can guarantee a successful inn, then Terry and Sarah MacGillivray have their success assured. When they opened their inn in 1991, they had five rooms in the 1780s manor house and operated their antiques business out of the huge carriage barn. In 1995 they renovated several cottages on the property to create spacious and charming suites with gas fireplaces and whirlpool tubs. Still not satisfied, in 1996 they converted the brick stable hand's quarters into eight spacious guest rooms, complete with gas fireplaces and marble baths with whirlpools.

By this time they realized that the numerous business travelers who visit the nearby corporate headquarters needed more than merely comfortable accommodations. So they included such amenities as telephones with dataports and voice mail, televisions and VCRs, coffeemakers, irons, ironing boards, and minirefrigerators in the rooms. In addition they converted the carriage house (the antiques business succumbed to the demands of innkeeping) to a conference facility plus even more guest rooms. On my last visit they were upgrading the dining rooms and adding a new kitchen and a new entrance to the inn.

The guest rooms come in a variety of styles. My favorite is the Summer Kitchen, a brick outbuilding with a gas fireplace, a two-poster bed, and a lovely antique dresser. The wonderful marble bath has a two-person whirlpool tub and a shower. The stable hand's building offers spacious rooms with gas fireplaces and painted furniture. Handsome quilts cover the beds.

A four-course dinner is served every Saturday night, beginning with wine and cheese in the ornate 1780s library. It contains two marble fireplaces and such curiosities as a chestnut Federal dresser with a marble top that came from Robert E. Lee's estate. The entree sometimes comprises a roast beef tenderloin with mushrooms as well as a baked crab cake imperial. For dessert you might try the peanut butter chocolate mousse cake. It's pure decadence.

**HOW TO GET THERE:** Traveling west on I-70, take exit 54. Turn right at the light onto Route 85. At the second light, stay to the right and continue on Route 85. The inn is 5 miles farther on the left before you go down the hill into Buckeystown.

# Inn at the Canal 📱 💲

## Chesapeake City, Maryland 21915

**INNKEEPERS:** Mary and Al Ioppolo

**ADDRESS/TELEPHONE:** 104 Bohemia Avenue (mailing address: P.O. Box 187); (410) 885-5995; fax (410) 885-3585

**ROOMS:** 7, including 1 suite; all with private bath, air-conditioning, telephone with dataport, TV, and radio; 4 with deep European soaking tubs. No smoking inn. Children over the age of 10 welcome.

**RATES:** $80 to $130, double occupancy; includes full breakfast, afternoon refreshments. Two-night minimum.

**OPEN:** All year except December 24 and 25.

**FACILITIES AND ACTIVITIES:** Antiques shop, parking; in historic district. Nearby: Canal Museum, waterside seafood restaurants, fishing, boating.

**BUSINESS TRAVEL:** Desks in four rooms; TV, telephone with dataport; fax available.

*E*arly one morning we took a walk through the slumbering historic streets of Chesapeake City. The tranquility we saw was in marked contrast, we knew, to the lusty, brawling, muddy boomtown that sprang up when the Chesapeake and Delaware Canal was under construction. What remains today is a peaceful village of interesting old houses, one of which is now an elegant bed-and-breakfast.

Inn at the Canal is located in the historic Brady-Rees house, a three-story Victorian that dates to 1870. Henry Brady owned the tugboats that plied the canal and it's said that although he and his wife were proud parents of two daughters, he longed for a son. So much so, in fact, that he promised his wife a grand new house if she produced one. She did—and he built this house. There are stained-glass windows and 12-foot ceilings painted with extraordinary scenes that are still awaiting restoration. Mary and Al Ioppolo have filled their inn with lovely antiques. I especially love the carved oak sideboard in the dining room. We could have whiled away the afternoon walking along the village streets and browsing through the art galleries and antiques shops (including one at the inn) or reading one of Mary's interesting historical books on the front porch wicker swing, but we couldn't resist the huge porch on the back of the house that looks across the gardens and adjacent streets to the canal. The parade of ships is mesmerizing.

The guest rooms are filled with lovely antiques. There are four-poster and canopy beds, and sinks are often ensconced in pretty oak dressers. The baths are beautifully restored but often include old fixtures. In Room 4, for example, which has a wonderful view, the tub in the bath is surrounded with elegant walnut paneling.

Mary fixes a full breakfast. One March morning we started with a fruit cobbler, moved on to caramel French toast, and finished with apple coffee cake.

**HOW TO GET THERE:** From I-95, take exit 109 (Elkton, Maryland) onto Route 279 west. Follow this to Route 213 south. Travel 7 miles and cross the Chesapeake City Bridge. At the far end turn right to South Chesapeake City and go under the bridge to the stop sign. Turn left onto George Street and travel 3 blocks. Turn right onto Second Street and go 1 block. Turn left onto Bohemia Avenue. The inn is on the right.

# Ship Watch Inn 🖺 🖾
## Chesapeake City, Maryland 21915

**INNKEEPERS:** Thomas and Linda Vaughan

**ADDRESS/TELEPHONE:** 401 First Street (mailing address: P.O. Box 153), (410) 885-5300; fax (410) 885-5784

**WEB SITE:** www.chesapeakecity.com

**ROOMS:** 8; all with private bath, air-conditioning, telephone with dataport, TV, and radio; 4 with whirlpool tub. Wheelchair accessible. Smoking on outside decks only.

**RATES:** $90 to $135, double occupancy; includes full breakfast. Two-night minimum holiday weekends.

**OPEN:** All year.

**FACILITIES AND ACTIVITIES:** Parking, hot tub on outside deck, waterside setting, in historic district. Nearby: restaurants, boating, tours of nearby horse farms.

**BUSINESS TRAVEL:** Telephones with dataports, corporate rate, early breakfast.

*W*as there ever a more appropriately named inn? Bordering the banks of the Chesapeake and Delaware Canal, this inn may be carved out of a 1920s house, but it was totally renovated in 1996 by Tom and Linda Vaughan, descendants of the original owners, to become a fabulous waterfront inn. Guests are greeted by a wooden statue of a captain, who stands sentry at the door.

There are polished pine floors. A massive oak buffet in the hallway holds local brochures, while a comfortable living room holds a buffet filled with plates of sticky buns, pies, cookies, and drinks. Doors lead from the living room to the deck.

The hallways are sponged with ivory paint, and the guest rooms are spacious, smart, and pretty. Every room has a large porch and a fabulous view of the passing maritime traffic. There are iron beds dressed with pretty designer linens, and four of the new tile baths have whirlpool tubs. Room 2 has an oak double bed and a sink in an oak dresser, but my favorite is Room 4, which has a queen-sized iron bed, an armoire, and a gray tile bath with a double whirlpool tub and a floral pedestal sink.

A full breakfast is served either in the dining room or on the porch. The entree could include such delicacies as French toast strata with apple cider syrup or herbed scrambled eggs in vol-au-vents with mushroom sauce.

Following dinner at the excellent Bayard House, a seafood restaurant with decks overlooking the canal, we came back to the inn and relaxed in the hot tub on the deck, sipping a glass of wine and watching the brilliantly lighted ships pass silently through the canal—some so close we felt we could have reached out to touch them.

HOW TO GET THERE: From I–95, take exit 109 (Elkton, Maryland) to Route 279 west. Follow this to Route 213 south. Travel 7 miles and cross the Chesapeake City Bridge. At the far end turn right to South Chesapeake City and go under the bridge to the stop sign. Turn left onto George Street and go to the end. The inn is the last house on the right.

# The Chesapeake and Delaware Canal

The 363-mile-long Erie Canal was the greatest of America's man-made canals. Its barges, pulled by mules along a towpath, carried goods from Buffalo on Lake Erie to the Hudson River and eventually to New York.

The Erie Canal is long gone. The Chesapeake and Delaware Canal, on the other hand, is very much alive. Completed in 1829, it shortened the water route between Philadelphia and Baltimore by more than 300 miles. It has been widened and dredged numerous times through the years and now carries some 1,500 massive freighters and other commercial vessels through the 14-mile trough that connects Delaware Bay to Chesapeake Bay. Part of the Intracoastal Waterway, it's said to be the third largest carrier of tonnage in the world, following only the Suez and Panama Canals.

When first opened, the C & D Canal had its own towpath on which mules pulled barges laden with goods. Chesapeake City, Maryland, was the hub of canal traffic—the place where, according to *The Ocean Highway,* one of the Federal Writers' Project books, "barge captains saluted each other with musical blasts from horns, while their wives hung out the wash on clotheslines rigged from the deck house. Barge householding included a menagerie of chickens, pigs, and even cows. Showboats from the Chesapeake Bay circuit sometimes tied up at canal towns, and many floating emporiums traveled a leisurely pace from village to village selling tinware, dress goods, steel traps, and other odds and ends."

Today you can review this interesting segment of American history at the Canal Museum in one of the original pumphouses in Chesapeake City. Afterward, lunch or dinner in one of the seafood restaurants on the banks of the canal might reward you with a view of a towering freighter or an elegant yacht passing so close you feel as though you can reach out and touch it.

# Brampton Bed & Breakfast
## Chestertown, Maryland 21620

**INNKEEPERS:** Michael and Danielle Hanscom

**ADDRESS/TELEPHONE:** 25227 Chestertown Road; (410) 778–1860; fax (410) 778–1805

**E-MAIL:** brampton@friend.ly.net

**ROOMS:** 10, including 2 suites and 2 cottages; all with private bath and air-conditioning; 2 with television, 8 with desk, 2 with Jacuzzi, 8 with fireplace. Wheelchair accessible. No smoking inn.

**RATES:** $105 to $195, double occupancy; includes full breakfast and afternoon tea. Two-night minimum most weekends. Corporate rates available.

**OPEN:** All year.

**FACILITIES AND ACTIVITIES:** Thirty-five acres, pond, sunroom. Nearby: restaurants, Chestertown Tea Party Festival (May), hiking, birding, sailing, golf, horseback riding, bicycling.

**RECOMMENDED COUNTRY INNS® TRAVELERS' CLUB BENEFIT:** Stay two nights, get third night free, Monday through Thursday, excluding holidays, subject to availability.

My family roots run deep through Chestertown. My father and his brothers and sisters were reared nearby, and my aunt was on the Board of Regents of Washington University for many years. Among her many accomplishments, she wrote a fascinating history of the town. I still love to poke around the interesting little back roads near Chestertown, imagining the many adventures my father says he had as a boy. But regardless of motive, you, too, can have interesting adventures along Chestertown's back roads when you stay at Brampton.

The magnificent 1860 plantation-style house stands tall against the sky high on a hill overlooking its thirty-five acres. On the National Register of Historic Places, it was built to impress. Its massive windows reach from the polished pine floors to the 12-foot ceilings, flooding the rooms with light. Across the front, a veranda contains wicker furniture where I love to sit in the afternoon with a tall iced tea and some of Danielle's freshly baked cookies.

There are seven guest rooms in the main building—all furnished with period antiques. My favorite is the Fairy Hill Suite in the former kitchen. It has a sitting room with a large wood-burning fireplace; the bedroom, with a cherry four-poster bed, is up a flight of stairs. The Smokehouse, a little cottage in back, has beamed ceilings, a woodstove, and another four-poster bed. For utter privacy, however, the two suites in the Garden Cottage, located in a field a short distance from the main house, would be my choice. They have wood-burning fireplaces, private brick patios, and double whirlpool tubs in the baths. A peaceful quiet pervades your thoughts in this secluded place, where the concerns of a busy executive melt away.

Danielle, who is Swiss, prepares a full gourmet breakfast every morning that may include puffed pancakes with poached pears, or, perhaps, an egg dish. These will be served at individual tables in the formal dining room, along with freshly baked muffins and breads, fruit, and juice.

**HOW TO GET THERE:** From Chestertown proceed 1 mile south on Route 20, following the signs toward Rock Hall, Maryland. The inn, surrounded by great trees, is located on the left side of the road.

# Great Oak Manor 💟
## Chestertown, Maryland 21620

**INNKEEPERS:** Don and Dianne Cantor

**ADDRESS/TELEPHONE:** 10568 Cliff Road; (410) 778–5943 or (800) 504–3098, fax same as phone

**E-MAIL:** innkeeper@greatoak.com

**WEB SITE:** www.greatoak.com/great oak

**ROOMS:** 11, including 1 suite; all with private bath, air-conditioning, telephone, desk, and radio; 5 with fireplace, 2 with TV and VCR. No smoking inn. Not appropriate for children.

**RATES:** $95 to $185, double occupancy; includes full breakfast and afternoon tea. Two night minimum on three-day weekends.

**OPEN:** All year.

**FACILITIES AND ACTIVITIES:** On twelve acres overlooking Chesapeake Bay, gardens, private beach (beach chairs provided). Nearby: golf course, marina, tennis courts, swimming pool, bicycling, fishing.

**BUSINESS TRAVEL:** Desk in all rooms, fax, dataport, copier, printer available.

*D*ianne and Don Cantor were cruising up the Intracoastal Waterway when they "found" Chestertown. Don had just sold his high-tech California company and Dianne, a stained-glass artist, knew she could practice her craft anywhere. Stopping to inquire about houses for sale, a realtor mentioned a derelict manor house on the water. Dianne recalls today, "*Water* was the operative word. We didn't even hear the word *derelict*." That was in 1993, and today all evidence of neglect is far behind.

Great Oak Manor has one of the most interesting histories of any house on the Eastern Shore. The twenty-five-room Federal brick manor house was built in 1938 by Russell D'Oench, a W. R. Grace heir. In 1946 it was purchased by Frank Russell, who turned it into an exclusive executive sportsman's retreat. In addition to hunting, fishing, and golfing on the estate, its renown grew as the place to win (or lose) big time in the high-stakes gaming hall.

Today we enjoy the estate, which now contains twelve acres, for the elegant architecture found in the manor house, for the peaceful ambience of the gardens, and for the mesmerizing views of the Chesapeake Bay from its bluff-top perch. The grand common rooms are richly paneled; there are carved icons over the doors, and the fireplace mantels are exquisitely carved. I love the cozy Gun Room, where a hand-painted map of the original 1,700-acre spread pulls up to reveal a bar, and a fire glows in winter in the brick fireplace.

The massive gaming room, hidden away on the third floor, is now the Russell Room. It has pine paneling, a giant stone fireplace, and a beamed cathedral ceiling. D'Oench is a spacious room, which also has a fireplace and a fabulous view of the bay. One of my favorite rooms, however, is Marmaduke, which has a fireplace mantel with an icon of a mountain and oak leaves that was a symbolic reminder of the D'Oench's honeymoon in Sun Valley.

# The Legend of Great Oak Manor

Was John F. Kennedy a guest at Great Oak Manor? Legend says he was . . .

Frank Russell's 1,100-acre estate on Chesapeake Bay, known in the 1940s and 1950s as Great Oak Farm, was perhaps the first executive retreat in the United States. Discretion about who was in attendance was assured by the private airstrip and hangars, private boat dock and marina, and the policies of Mr. Russell. Catering to "the highly specialized needs of the small top-executive conference," Mr. Russell recognized that "the executive mind never rests, but sometimes functions best away from desks, away from the too-close scene of business, away from interruptions that snap the thread of thought."

That was the stated function of the Farm, but any executive invited to visit knew there was more than met the eye. A day of shooting grouse or Canada geese was followed by round after round of drinks before the brick fireplace in the Gun Room, which itself was followed by a convivial feast in the dining room. After dinner the men would retire to a hideaway oak-paneled, cathedral-ceilinged gambling hall on the top floor, where a stone fireplace would crackle in the winter. Thousands were won and lost in a single night in games of roulette, blackjack, and poker.

Guy Lombardo, Authur Godfrey, and Robert Mitchum were frequent guests and the persistent rumor that John F. Kennedy was also a guest may or may not be based in fact. He might have enjoyed the hospitality of the Farm when he launched his Eastern Shore campaign for president of the United States. The event took place nearby, but there's no written record revealing where he stayed. Regardless of the Farm's rules, could one of the otherwise-discreet staff members have been so awed by Kennedy's presence that he or she told a friend or a relative about the future president's stay? It's certainly possible—and so the rumor persists.

Breakfast is served in the mornings in the dining room. In addition to a buffet of freshly baked muffins, fresh fruit, and cereals, there will be an entree such as blueberry pancakes or cheese eggs.

The estate has its own beach as well as lovely gardens. Benches are strategically placed along the lip of the bluff, where spectacular sunsets can be viewed. A marina, golf course, tennis courts, and swimming pool are just next door. Guests can arrive by boat, and fishing excursions can be arranged with advance notice.

**HOW TO GET THERE:** From Baltimore/Washington, D.C., take Route 50 east across the Chesapeake Bay Bridge to Route 301 north. Follow this to Route 213 north. Follow Route 213 through Centreville and into Chestertown. Pass Washington College and turn left at the traffic light onto Route 291 (Morgnec Road). When it dead ends, turn right onto Route 20. Turn right onto Route 514. After crossing Route 298, continue on Route 514 for another $1^8/_{10}$ miles. Turn left onto Great Oak Landing Road. Pass silos and go through first set of brick pillars; continue past golf course. Continue straight ahead through second set of brick pillars to large brick manor house.

# Ashby 1663 Bed and Breakfast
## Easton, Maryland 21601

**INNKEEPERS:** Cliff Meredith and Jeanine Wagner

**ADDRESS/TELEPHONE:** 27448 Ashby Drive (mailing address: P.O. Box 45); (410) 822-4235 or (800) 458-3622; fax (410) 822-9288

**E-MAIL:** info@ashby1663.com

**WEB SITE:** www.ashby1663.com

**ROOMS:** 12 suites; all with private bath, air-conditioning, telephone, and TV; 9 with whirlpool tub, 7 with fireplace, 6 with patio or deck. No smoking inn. Children over the age of 12 welcome.

**RATES:** $215 to $595, double occupancy; includes full breakfast and complimentary cocktails. Two-night minimum when stay includes Saturday night from April to November.

FACILITIES AND ACTIVITIES: On twenty-three acres; waterfront views, pool, lighted tennis court, exercise room, billiards room, dock for private boats, paddleboat, canoe. Nearby: golf courses, restaurants, antiques shops, boating, fishing, hunting, the Talbot County Historical Society, the Historic Avalon Theatre, annual waterfowl festival.

The gracious Greek Revival mansion on the banks of the Miles River was abandoned and crumbling when it was purchased by Cliff Meredith and Jeanine Wagner in 1985. The team was undaunted, however, and immediately began a restoration that virtually rebuilt the house from top to bottom. Palladian-style windows now open the living room to views of the pool, terrace, and spa with the Miles River beyond, and a graceful stairway sweeps up from the mellow heart-pine floors of the entrance hall to the second and third levels of the house.

Elegant antiques grace all the rooms, and the chairs and sofas are covered with sophisticated English prints and stripes. In the dining room an antique Waterford crystal chandelier illuminates the handsome fireplace and mahogany dining room table.

The library has a marble fireplace and a bay window overlooking the garden. The screened porch has iron and wicker furniture and offers views of the formal gardens.

The guest rooms are gracious and refined. The Robert Goldsborough Suite on the second floor contains a canopy bed that's lushly skirted, flounced, and covered with a rich peach-and-green fabric. There's a fireplace and a wall of windows that overlook the pool and the bay. The marble bath, however, is the pièce de résistance. It has a raised double whirlpool tub with a view of the bay from the floor-to-ceiling windows, as well as a fireplace, which casts a seductive glow across the room. There are five rooms in the manor house and two more in the George Goldsborough House. The inn is located on an undulating point of land that juts into the Miles River and provides a half mile of waterfront. Miles River Cottage, a new building directly on the banks of the Miles River, was completed in 1996. It contains five additional guest rooms with terrific views of the river, fireplaces, canopy beds, and whirlpool tubs. Several of the rooms have private decks.

Service at Ashby 1663 is as gracious as the decor. Every evening guests gather in the library for complimentary cocktails—an opportunity to become acquainted with one another as well as their hosts. On sunny days and warm evenings they enjoy the use of the pool and the lighted tennis court, or they may play a game of billiards, ride one of the inn's bicycles along the quiet country roads, or exorcise all hint of stress by indulging in a stint on the tanning bed, the massage machine, or the sauna machine. On the other hand, they may decide to retain the fitness regime they enjoy at home by using the treadmill, stair master, bicycles, or rowing machine in the inn's exercise room.

Breakfast is served every morning in the formal dining room or on the sunporch. In addition to fresh fruits and juices and freshly baked muffins and breads, guests may enjoy an entree of asparagus in crepes with hollandaise sauce or baked French toast with bananas and walnuts topped with maple syrup.

HOW TO GET THERE: From Washington, D.C., take Route 50 across the Chesapeake Bay Bridge and follow it to Easton. At Airport Road turn right and travel to the stop sign. Turn right again onto Goldsborough Neck Road and bear left at the fork, traveling past the NO OUTLET sign. Turn left again at the sign that reads ASHBY 1663. Continue on the paved road for ¾ mile to the B&B.

# The Turning Point Inn
Frederick, Maryland 21701

INNKEEPER: Charlie Seymour

ADDRESS/TELEPHONE: 3406 Urbana Pike; (301) 831–8232; fax (301) 831–8092

ROOMS: 7, including 2 cottages; all with private bath, air-conditioning, telephone, and television; 2 with Jacuzzi. Cottage wheelchair accessible. Pets allowed with prior permission. Limited smoking inn.

RATES: $75 to $150, double occupancy; includes full breakfast.

OPEN: All year.

FACILITIES AND ACTIVITIES: Dinner nightly except Monday (entrees $17.95 to $35.00), lunch Tuesday to Friday, Sunday brunch, wine cellar; on six acres. Nearby: Antietam Battlefield, Harper's Ferry, New Market (antiques capital), hiking at Sugarloaf Mountain, Gettysburg Battlefield.

*I* parked the car and walked along the pretty garden path to the beautifully painted Georgian Colonial mansion. Inside I was pleased to find an absolutely stunning mauve-colored living room, decorated with antique tables and chairs. The restaurant at the Turning Point Inn, located in four of the house's main-floor rooms, has become one of the biggest attractions, however. Chef William Erlenbach has developed a distinctive award-winning style that is earning accolades. A typical Gourmet Food and Wine Pairing Dinner will include five courses, each paired with personally selected wines. An entree might feature a plank-roasted tenderloin of beef with a crisp onion crust and a cassoulet sauce, while the dessert at one recent dinner consisted of a delicate squash brûlée napoleon with honey hazelnut layers and burnt honey crème anglaise.

It's obvious that Charlie Seymour hasn't slowed down for a minute since he took over management of The Turning Point Inn from his parents in

1991. It had been a "turning point" in their lives when they purchased it in 1985, and it became one in Charlie's life then. Formerly with a brokerage firm in Washington, D.C., Charlie has consistently improved the inn under his management.

The guest rooms are as lovely as the dining rooms. I particularly like the Victorian Room, which has a gray iron bed and a lovely bath with pink tiles. The Blue Room has a four-poster bed. Although the baths are on the small side, they are exquisitely decorated. The Carriage House offers both spaciousness and seclusion. It has a sitting room on the main floor and a bedroom on the second floor.

HOW TO GET THERE: From I–270 take exit 26 toward Urbana, turn east onto Route 80, and proceed to the stop sign; turn right on Route 355, go 2/10 of a mile, and turn right into the inn's lane.

# Tyler-Spite Inn ♥
## Frederick, Maryland 21701

**INNKEEPERS:** Bill and Andrea Myer; Joe Steiner, manager

**ADDRESS/TELEPHONE:** 112 West Church Street; (301) 831–4455;
fax (301) 662–4185

**ROOMS:** 10; 4 with private bath and the rest shared; all with air-
conditioning, hair dryer, robe, iron, and ironing board; five with fireplace. Wheelchair accessible. No smoking inn. Children over the age
of 10 welcome.

**RATES:** $180 to $275, double occupancy; includes full breakfast and
high tea. Two-night minimum holiday weekends.

**OPEN:** All year.

**FACILITIES AND ACTIVITIES:** On one acre; pool, formal gardens, parking, in the heart of the Frederick National Historic District, which
includes 33 blocks of historic and architecturally significant buildings.
Nearby: restaurants, Francis Scott Key Museum, the Barbara Fritchie
House and Museum.

**BUSINESS TRAVEL:** Telephone and TV on premise; fax and photocopier
available.

*D*r. John Tyler was both a feisty individual and an innovative doctor who performed the first cataract operation in America. When
the town decided in 1814 to cut a road through a piece of unde-
veloped property right where he wanted to build his home, he decided to
outsmart them. The night before the road crew was to begin, he brought in
a crew of his own who worked all night, laying the foundation for his grand
house. When the town fathers arrived in the morning, they found the good
doctor rocking peacefully in his favorite rocking chair. He knew that the
town was prohibited from seizing land if there was a significant structure
being built.

The Tyler-Spite House, where not only Dr. Tyler lived but also, later, U.S.
Congressman Jacob Kunkel and Civil War Colonel John Maulsby, would be
considered a significant structure by anyone's definition. It has 13-foot ceilings, eight fireplaces (many with marble mantels) elegant carved moldings,
and spacious rooms. Today it is listed on the National Register of Historic
Places. In addition to this structure, however, the B&B includes elegant
accommodations in the Nelson House, which is next door.

Bill and Andrea Myer, who have lovingly restored the mansions, have done so with careful attention to its original features, and they have furnished it with museum-quality antiques—much as it might have been furnished when it was new. There are priceless oil paintings, Oriental rugs on polished pine floors, and even the mahogany campaign desk on which General Douglas MacArthur signed the peace treaty in Manila. In back there's a lovely walled garden that includes a brick patio, formal flower beds, and a swimming pool.

The guest rooms are equally elegant, with fireplaces, canopy featherbeds, and antique chests and tables. Rather than alter the historic structure, the Myers have opted to offer some guest rooms with shared baths.

Guests enjoy an abundant breakfast that may include a soufflé, Belgian waffles, or fried green tomatoes. On weekends there will be a formal high tea, and at night there's a decanter of sherry in each of the guest rooms.

**HOW TO GET THERE:** From any freeway follow signs for the Frederick National Historic District. Continue to Church Street in the center of town. The B&B is on the right, opposite the old Court House.

# Elliott House Victorian Inn
## Grantsville, Maryland 21536

**INNKEEPERS:** Eleanor and Jack Dueck

**ADDRESS/TELEPHONE:** 146 Casselman Road; (301) 895–4250 or (800) 272–4090

**E-MAIL:** edueck@mail.gcnet.net

**WEB SITE:** www.elliotthouse.com

**ROOMS:** 7; all with private bath, air-conditioning, telephone, TV, VCR, and hair dryer; 3 with fireplace and/or deck. Wheelchair accessible. No smoking inn. Children over the age of 12 welcome.

**RATES:** $95 to $140, double occupancy; includes full breakfast. Two-night minimum holiday weekends.

**OPEN:** All year.

**FACILITIES AND ACTIVITIES:** On seven acres; hot tub, pool table, Ping-Pong table, large deck. Nearby: Spruce Forest Artisan Village, trout fishing, hiking, bird-watching.

On a recent trip to look at inns in Maryland's western panhandle, innkeepers kept telling me not to miss a newcomer in Grantsville. I can never resist a recommendation from other innkeepers, so I made a detour to see what they were so excited about. I wasn't disappointed.

Jack and Eleanor Dueck were both English teachers, lecturers, and consultants in Canada before becoming innkeepers. In 1994 they located an 1870s Victorian on seven acres along the historic National Pike Road (the first U.S. road built by the government). They opened their B&B in 1997. Nearby are the 1798 Stanton Mill, operated for many years by the Elliott family, and the 1813 Stone Arch Bridge, which was featured in a 1998 *National Geographic* article. Curving along the back of the property is the Casselman River, which is noted for its trout fishing.

The parlor of the inn has a gas fireplace and a comprehensive library. In the games room there's another fireplace as well as a pool table, Ping-Pong table, and games table. A hot tub offers a relaxing way to unwind after a day of hiking or driving.

The guest rooms are charmingly decorated with quilts made by a local craftsperson, and the baths are all finished in tile. There are pedestal sinks and stenciling in all. My favorite room is the Drover's Cottage, a two-level former wash house that has a living room with a fireplace and a spacious deck. Upstairs there's a bedroom with a picture window offering views of the countryside and the Casselman River. The cottage has a full bath upstairs and a powder room downstairs.

One of the most unique features of the inn, however, is its setting. It is located adjacent to the Spruce Forest Artisan Village, a collection of small log cabins used by working artists, musicians, and craftsmen. During the summer more than one hundred juried artisans, musicians, and storytellers work either in the cabins or under the shade of the massive spruce trees. Visitors can watch them at work and also purchase art directly from the artists. The Penn Alps restaurant is located in a famous 1818 stagecoach stop—the only remaining log cabin on the National Pike. The restaurant, which is open for breakfast, lunch, and dinner, features reasonably priced dishes served buffet style. Inn guests are given a coupon for a complimentary breakfast at the restaurant.

HOW TO GET THERE: Traveling west on I–68, take exit 22. Stay in the right lane and continue to the stoplight at Alternate Route 40. Turn left on Alternate Route 40 and go 2 miles. The Elliott House is on the right behind the Penn Alps restaurant. Traveling east on I–68, take exit 19 and follow the signs to Grantsville. Turn right at the light onto Route 40 and go 1 mile. Just after the bridge, turn left into the Penn Alps restaurant parking lot. Elliott House is straight ahead through the parking lot.

---

# Vandiver Inn 🎭 🏛
## Havre de Grace, Maryland 21078

**INNKEEPER:** Suzanne Mottek

**ADDRESS/TELEPHONE:** 301 South Union Avenue; (410) 839-5200 or (800) 245-1655; fax (410) 939-5202

**ROOMS:** 9, including 3 suites; all with private bath, air-conditioning, and telephone; 5 with desk, 3 with fireplace and/or deck, 1 with Jacuzzi. Wheelchair accessible. No smoking inn.

**RATES:** $75 to $130, double occupancy; includes full breakfast.

**OPEN:** All year.

**FACILITIES AND ACTIVITIES:** Twig gazebo in backyard. Nearby: Havre de Grace Decoy Museum, Waterfront Promenade, Tudor Hall (home of John Wilkes Booth), fishing, bicycling, boating, golfing.

**BUSINESS TRAVEL:** Desk in five rooms, modem hookup, fax available; 20 percent corporate discount Sunday to Thursday.

*H*avre de Grace is a charming little town that was named by Lafayette during one of the French general's visits. Roughly translated, it means merciful (or graceful) harbor. It is strategically located at the point where the Susquehanna River spills into Chesapeake Bay. Its place in history was assured when it almost became the U.S. capital, missing out to Washington, D.C., by only one vote. Along the streets of its National Historic District, seventeenth- and eighteenth-century homes continue to reflect the elegance of a bygone era.

The Vandiver is among the finest of Havre de Grace's homes. Built in 1886 the spacious seafoam-green Victorian boasts bay and dormer windows, a broad porch across the front containing wicker chairs, and a wealth of fabulous stained and leaded glass. Gingerbread drips from the overhangs.

The inn contains nine guest rooms, all of which are decorated with Victorian antiques. Although the decor is not elegant, the rooms are comfortable and restful. My favorite is the John Rodgers Suite, a second-floor room with an antique Victorian Bed, a fireplace, and a private porch. There's a private bath with a claw-foot tub and a shower. The newest room, completed in April 1998, is the Joseph C. Fair Room. It has a working fireplace as well as a Jacuzzi on the sunporch. All the rooms have private baths, although the bath for the G. Arnold Pfaffenbach Room is accessed from the hall instead of from the room.

A full breakfast is served daily. Themed dinners—such as those featuring a region's wines, a murder mystery dinner, or a romantic Valentine's Day celebration—take place throughout the year. Call for a schedule.

**HOW TO GET THERE:** From I–95, take exit 89 (Route 155 east). Follow the signs to Route 40. Bear right onto Ohio Street. At the traffic light turn left, crossing Route 40, and turn onto Otsego Street. Follow Otsego Street as it bears right onto Union Avenue. The Vandiver Inn is 7 blocks farther on the left.

# Antietam Overlook Farm
## Keedysville, Maryland 21756

**INNKEEPERS:** John and Barbara Dreisch

**ADDRESS/TELEPHONE:** P.O. Box 30; (301) 432–4200 or (800) 878–4241

**ROOMS:** 5; all with private bath, air conditioning, telephone, fireplace, garden tub, hair dryer, desk, iron, and ironing board; four with balcony. No smoking inn. Children over the age of 11 welcome.

**RATES:** $115 to $160, double occupancy; includes full breakfast. Two-night minimum if stay includes Saturday night.

**OPEN:** April to February.

**FACILITIES AND ACTIVITIES:** On ninety-one acres. Nearby: Antietam National Battlefield, restaurants.

*I*f my goal is to retreat from the world for a few days, I always head for Antietam Overlook Farm. This top-of-the-world, ninety-one-acre aerie is so peaceful and so quiet that you may not even hear or see the other guests except at breakfast. What you might see from your private screened porch instead are grazing deer, wild turkeys feeding on grain, or an abundance of birds enjoying the bounty of the numerous feeders. Or you might imagine that scouts may have used this very perch to observe troop movement on the Antietam Battlefield below.

John and Barbara Dreisch, who built their mountaintop sanctuary in 1988, zealously guard the peaceful solitude of their guests. There's an electrically controlled gate at the entrance, all large rooms are thoroughly soundproofed, and each is absolutely private so that if you are immersed in bubbles in your garden tub (a deep soaking tub surrounded by plants found in each room), you can gaze at the deer and watch the flames flickering in the fireplace in utter privacy. As Barbara says, "We provide whatever our guests could possibly need—and then we leave them alone."

The guest rooms contain no cutesy antiques or frilly pillows. Instead there are fantastically comfortable beds, equally comfortable chairs, and spacious baths equipped with every amenity a guest might want.

Of course, should you prefer the company of others, there's a lovely country room with a massive stone fireplace that's lighted by a wagon-wheel chandelier. Quilts, flags, and folk art complement the hand-hewn beams and posts and the yellow-pine walls and ceiling. A service bar is equipped with coffee, tea, wine, soda, and liqueurs, and guests help themselves whenever they want. A full  breakfast is served here every morning. It might include a baked potato, pepper, and onion frittata with cheese; homemade maple and raisin blended country sausage; fried tomatoes; and orange French toast with spicy marmalade sauce, as well as an array of homemade breads with jams, curds, and chutneys and local fruits and juices.

**HOW TO GET THERE:** Call for directions. Near Sharpsburg and Boonsboro, Maryland, as well as Charles Town, Harpers Ferry, and Shepherdstown, West Virginia.

# Lake Pointe Inn 📱 💝
## McHenry, Maryland 21541

INNKEEPER: Carol McNiece; George and Linda Pettie, owners

ADDRESS/TELEPHONE: 174 Lake Point Drive; (301) 387–0111 or (800) 523–5253; fax (301) 387–0190.

ROOMS: 9, not including Sang Run House; all with private bath, air-conditioning, telephone with private line, TV, VCR, radio, and hair dryer; one with desk and whirlpool tub. No smoking inn. Children over the age of 16 welcome.

RATES: $108 to $178, double occupancy; includes full breakfast, snacks, beverage bar, and hors d'oeuvres. Two-night minimum on weekends.

OPEN: All year except Christmas Eve.

FACILITIES AND ACTIVITIES: On lake with dock, canoes, kayak, pontoon boat; mountain bikes, tennis court, volleyball, badminton; hot tub on deck. Nearby: Wisp Mountain Resort, which has downhill ski slopes, golfing, hiking, biking, cross-country skiing, horseback riding.

BUSINESS TRAVEL: Guest rooms have TV and VCR and telephones with private lines. Sang Run House offers two large meeting rooms, sitting room with fireplace, copier, fax, multiple telephone lines, and Internet access.

*L*ake Pointe Inn has evolved over the years, adapting to its setting and to its various uses. Originally the site of the summer home of Dr. James McHenry, staff surgeon to General George Washington, in 1890 Jonas Glotfelty built a substantial farmhouse on a prominent site overlooking his spreading farmlands. He would be amazed today to see that his farmhouse is at the edge of a fifty-six-acre lake, created in 1925 by the local electric company. In 1939 the present great room was created. It has a massive stone fireplace and wormy chestnut beams, columns, and paneling. There's an oak floor and a wall of windows overlooking the lake. In 1996, following an extensive renovation by current owners George and Linda Pettie, the inn opened to guests. The great room continues to be the cozy focal point of the inn. Furnished with Mission-style furniture and decorated with fine Arts and Crafts fabrics, ironwork, pottery, and rugs, the room is inviting and snug.

A broad wraparound deck faces the lake, and guests often begin the morning with a cup of coffee here as they watch the sun rise or relax with a glass of wine in the evening after a day of skiing at nearby Wisp Mountain Resort before going to dinner. In the summer there's a private swimming dock, where canoes and kayaks await and where guests are taken on lake excursions on the inn's pontoon boat.

The guest rooms are lovely. Were I to choose a favorite, it might be the McHenry Room, which has a Mission-style bed and a two-person whirlpool tub in the lovely bathroom. There are views of the ski runs at Wisp Mountain and the lake. The guest rooms on the third floor have private baths, although they are reached from the hallway.

Carol McNiece is the accomplished innkeeper who saw to our every need. Every floor has a complimentary hot and cold beverage bar, so we began the day with a cup of coffee before starting off on a hike. On our return we enjoyed a wonderful breakfast that included an entree of scrambled eggs with leeks on a puff-pastry base with a mushroom tarragon sauce. After a day of bicycling on two of the inn's six mountain bikes, we found a bowl of fresh fruit, freshly popped popcorn, and homemade cookies waiting. But I must admit that the hot tub on the deck offered the most welcome relaxation.

Most recently, the nearby Sang Run House was renovated into four guest rooms with private baths plus two large meeting rooms. This has proven an especially popular place for corporate meetings and conferences.

HOW TO GET THERE: From I-68, take exit 14 onto Route 219 south and continue for 12½ miles to McHenry. Turn right at the Citgo station onto Sang Run Road. In 2 blocks turn left onto Marsh Hill Road. In ¼ mile, turn left onto Lake Pointe Drive and follow the loop road either right or left to the inn.

# Stone Manor 💚
## Middletown, Maryland 21769

**INNKEEPERS:** George and Judith Harne

**ADDRESS/TELEPHONE:** 5820 Carroll Boyer Road; (301) 473–5454; fax (301) 371–5622.

**E-MAIL:** Stonemanor@juno.com

**WEB SITE:** www.ourhome.net./stonemanor

**ROOMS:** 6, including 5 suites; all with private baths and air-conditioning, CD players, whirlpool tubs, robes, and hair dryers; 4 with balconies or patios, 3 with fireplaces. Limited wheelchair access. No smoking inn.

**RATES:** $125 to $250, double occupancy; includes an extensive continental breakfast and a welcoming plate of fruit and cheese.

**OPEN:** All year.

**FACILITIES AND ACTIVITIES:** On 144 acres with hiking and walking trails, restaurant serving lunch and dinner and Sunday brunch (four- or five-course prix fixe dinner $45 to $55; brunch $20). Nearby: golfing, horseback riding, whitewater rafting, tennis, boating.

**BUSINESS TRAVEL:** Telephones, TVs, VCRs available for guest rooms; fax and copier available; meeting rooms.

When you meander down country lanes as I so often do, you are apt to discover many surprises. One of my favorite surprises occurred in the hills of Maryland just west of Frederick and northeast of Harpers Ferry, West Virginia. Traveling up and down the terrain in the foothills of the Catoctin and Blue Ridge Mountains one spring afternoon, I passed miles and miles of rural farmland where fields of wheat and corn create their colorful patchwork and Holstein cows contentedly graze. Turning down first one byway and then the next, had I not had a particular destination, I would have believed myself to be thoroughly lost.

Yet once I reached my ellusive quarry, I couldn't have been happier with my find. Stone Manor, as the name suggests, is an impressive and elegant mansion built entirely of massive local gray stones. Constructed in three stages, from 1760 to the 1970s, the manor was converted to a country inn in 1991 by Judith Harne, an engineer and now general manager of the inn, and her architect husband, George. A heavy oak door opens to a warm and cozy entry, and the living room features hardwood floors, Oriental carpets, and antiques. The dining rooms, where fabulous dinners are served nightly, are intimately located in several of the downstairs rooms. My favorite place to relax, however, is the library on the second-floor landing—an open room filled with interesting books and containing tables piled high with magazines and more books.

The guest rooms are spacious and enchanting—each is named for a flower. My favorite is Thistle, a feminine, cathedral-ceilinged room with skylights and containing a wonderful bed with thistle finials and a two-level bath—a charming and intimate bower. Gardenia, on the other hand, is a two-room suite with a fireplace in both the sitting room and the bedroom and a bath with a whirlpool tub. It's done in deep, rich fabrics of green, burgundy, and gold.

The dining room at Stone Manor is renowned for its cuisine and wine list. For the ultimate in romantic getaways, you can make advance reservations to have dinner served in your guest room, complete with your own private server.

## Scented Slumber

Innkeeper Judith Harne of Stone Manor in Middletown, Maryland, understands the power of aromatherapy. The inn has developed an extensive herb garden, but, in addition to using the herbs in the inn's cuisine, Judith puts them to other uses as well. For example, she ties a bundle of fragrant herbs with a fine silk ribbon and places them on her guests' pillows at turndown along with a note describing the symbolic meaning of each herb. She reminds her guests that rosemary is for remembrance; that lavender is for devotion; thyme is for strength and courage; sage is for domestic happiness. She also combines these scents into the inn's own bath salts and places them in the bathrooms. Guests insist they have only the sweetest of dreams at Stone Manor.

**HOW TO GET THERE:** From Baltimore take I–70 west to U.S. 340 and then follow it west to Charles Town, West Virginia. Take the Lander Road/Jefferson exit and bear right off the exit ramp toward Jefferson. At the stop sign in Jefferson, turn left and proceed 4/10 mile. Turn right onto Old Middletown Road and go 2 1/10 miles to Sumantown Road. Turn left onto Sumantown Road. Proceed for 6/10 mile and turn left onto Carroll Boyer Road. The inn is at the end of the first road on the right.

# Carmel Cove Inn
## Oakland, Maryland 21550

**INNKEEPER:** Ed Spak

**ADDRESS/TELEPHONE:** Glendale Road, Deep Creek Lake (mailing address: P.O. Box 644); (301) 387–0067; fax (301) 387-2394

**WEB SITE:** www.carmelcoveinn.com

**ROOMS:** 10; all with private bath, air-conditioning, telephone, and radio; 4 with decks, 3 with whirlpool tub, 2 with fireplace. No smoking inn. Children over the age of 12 welcome.

**RATES:** $100 to $150, double occupancy; includes full breakfast; afternoon wine, microbrewed beers, and cheese; evening liqueurs and chocolates. Two-night minimum summer weekends; three-night minimum holidays.

**OPEN:** All year.

**FACILITIES AND ACTIVITIES:** On two acres; tennis court, outdoor hot tub, billiards table, dock, fishing equipment, paddleboat, canoes, mountain bike, cross-country ski and/or hiking trails on premises. Nearby: restaurants, Wisp Mountain Resort, whitewater rafting on the Youghiogheny River, Swallow Falls.

**BUSINESS TRAVEL:** Telephones with private lines.

*I* love to find an innkeeper who is bursting with enthusiasm for his job. That's Ed Spak. He couldn't wait to show me around his inn, and he is a fountain of knowledge about the inn's history. He told me that the Discalced Carmelite Fathers, who wore no shoes, chose this isolated spot on Deep Creek Lake in Maryland's panhandle for its luxurious beauty and its utter tranquility. This was their sacred retreat—the place where they could commune with God in an undisturbed and beautiful natural setting. They built their simple retreat house with their own hands and with the help of local masons, who donated a day of their own time to build the stone foundation for the chapel.

Today, the blue-gray shingled structure is the cornerstone of a fifty-three-acre lakeside community. The former chapel, with its tall beamed cathedral ceiling, boasts a cozy woodstove at one end and conversation areas defined by elegant sofas and chairs. Interesting decor includes a coffee table made from a huge bellows.

The guest rooms are a far cry from the simple little cubicles once occupied by the monks. They are spacious and refined—some with fireplaces and some with private decks. My favorite decor is in Room 9, which has a lovely oak bed with a high headboard and footboard, an oak dresser, and an armoire. An old butter churn is used for an end table.

A sumptuous breakfast is enjoyed in the breakfast room, which has a stone fireplace, natural knotty-pine walls, and a beamed ceiling. Guests receive a full gourmet breakfast that might include Southern-style bourbon French toast, homemade pepper-and-onion sausage, bacon-and-mushroom quiche with cheddar cheese, lyonnaise potatoes, banana bread, fresh honeydew and cantaloupe balls, and a homemade pear tart in addition to juices, coffees, and teas.

HOW TO GET THERE: From I-68 traveling west take exit 14A. Take Route 219 south for approximately 20 miles to Deep Creek Lake. Continue over the Route 219 bridge and along the lake for 2 more miles to Glendale Road. Turn left onto Glendale Road and travel 1 mile, cross over the bridge and bear right at the end. Continue 1 more mile to Carmel Cove. Turn left and then bear left to the inn. From I-68 traveling east take Maryland exit 4 (Friendsville). Travel south on Route 42 to Route 219 south and continue as above.

# The Lighthouse Club Hotel . . . at Fager's Island
## Ocean City, Maryland 28142

**INNKEEPER:** Angela Reynolds

**ADDRESS/TELEPHONE:** Fifty-sixth Street In-The-Bay (mailing address: 201 Sixtieth Street); (410) 524–5400 or (888) 371–5400; fax (410) 524–3928

**E-MAIL:** island@damv.com

**WEB SITE:** www.fagers.com

**ROOMS:** 23 suites; all with private bath, air-conditioning, three telephones, TV, VCR, minirefrigerator, coffeemaker, hair dryer, whirlpool tub, balcony or deck, and robe; 8 with fireplace and desk. Smoking permitted. Not appropriate for children.

**RATES:** $79 to $275, double occupancy; includes continental breakfast and sodas in minirefrigerator. Two-night minimum from mid-June through Labor Day and every weekend and holiday.

**OPEN:** All year.

**FACILITIES AND ACTIVITIES:** On three acres; Fager's Island Restaurant is open for lunch (entrees $6 to $9) and dinner (entrees $17 to $29). Passes provided for Ocean City Health and Racquet Club. Nearby: golfing, tennis, fishing, hiking, biking, bird-watching, excursions through Assateague National Park, sunning on the beautiful sandy beaches, walking along the boardwalk, Bay Star Dinner Theater.

**BUSINESS TRAVEL:** Lunch and dinner room service; telephone, TV and VCR, desks in rooms; fax available.

**RECOMMENDED COUNTRY INNS® TRAVELERS' CLUB BENEFIT:** Stay six nights, get seventh night free (valid year-round); 10 percent discount for Lighthouse Suites, December and January, excluding holidays; 10 percent discount on Lighthouse Suites, Monday to Thursday, February to April, excluding holidays. All subject to availability; you must identify yourself as a Travelers' Club member.

*I*f visions of vast sandy beaches spin through your dreams, head for Ocean City, where 10 miles of sparkling white sand offer unlimited space for romantic walks, shell gathering, and sunning. The Lighthouse Club Hotel, on the bay side, is snuggled among natural wetlands that are populated by snowy egrets and cranes. Beyond is peaceful Isle of Wight Bay.

The white clapboard, octagonal Lighthouse Club was fashioned after the Thomas Point Lighthouse. It became a luxurious B&B in 1988—a welcome relief from the beachy motels and high-rise hotels along the strip. On entering the three-story reception area, guests are drawn to the floor-to-ceiling library that offers a selection of books for every taste.

Two levels of guest rooms enjoy private decks with views of the marsh and bay. The fifteen units on the second floor, called the Lighthouse Suites, are slightly smaller than the eight huge Lightkeeper Suites on the top floor. On the second floor the rooms are furnished in quiet tones of beige and white to blend with the marshlands outside. They have queen-sized mattresses on bamboo platforms and Jacuzzis in the white marble baths. On the third floor the suites have four-poster beds, gas fireplaces, spacious desks, and double Jacuzzis. All rooms and suites have minirefrigerators with ice makers and a wet bar. There are televisions and VCRs in armoires, three telephones per suite, and a built-in stereo system.

Unlike most B&Bs, a continental breakfast is brought to the room at night when the beds are turned down and a chocolate is laid on the pillow. The breakfast of fresh fruit, juice, and breakfast breads can be prepared at your leisure, and there's a coffeemaker in the room. What could be finer than waking to a spectacular sunrise and enjoying breakfast on your private deck as you watch the birds in the marsh?

Fager's Island Restaurant and Bar is located along a boardwalk spanning the marshes. It offers elegant dining on local seafood on spacious bayside decks or in cozy indoor surroundings.

HOW TO GET THERE: From Washington, D.C., take Route 50 across the Chesapeake Bay Bridge and continue east for approximately 90 miles, passing Cambridge and Salisbury. Take Route 90 toward North Ocean City. At the junction of Route 90 and Coastal Highway, turn right onto Coastal Highway. Turn right at Fifty-sixth Street Bayside. The Lighthouse Club is directly ahead.

# Combsberry 💚
## Oxford, Maryland 21654

**INNKEEPER:** Catherine Magrogan; Dr. Mahmood and Ann Shariff, proprietors

**ADDRESS/TELEPHONE:** 4837 Evergreen Road; (410) 226–5353; fax (410) 228–1453

**WEB SITE:** www.combsberry.com

**ROOMS:** 7, including 2 suites and 2 cottages; all with private bath, air-conditioning, and hair dryer; 5 with fireplace, 4 with whirlpool tub and/or porch or patio. No smoking inn. Children over the age of 12 welcome.

**RATES:** $250 to $395, double occupancy; includes full breakfast and cocktail/tea hour. Two-night minimum weekends preferred.

**OPEN:** All year except Thanksgiving, Christmas, and Easter.

**FACILITIES AND ACTIVITIES:** On nine acres; formal English garden, private dock, swimming, fishing, crabbing, paddleboat, canoe. Nearby: historic Oxford-Bellevue Ferry across Tred Avon River, Oxford Museum, Oxford Customs House, Tilghman Island Seafood Festival.

*S*ometimes, my most important bed-and-breakfast discoveries are the result of recommendations by other innkeepers. This was certainly the case with Combsberry. I was on a B&B inspection trip on the Del-MarVa Peninsula, and an innkeeper insisted that I *must* see the new inn that had just opened in Oxford. I love to be the first to report a new discovery, so I couldn't resist.

Combsberry is one of those gentle brick plantation homes tucked away off the road where the unsuspecting cannot see them. Construction of the manor house began in 1738, meaning that parts of it are 260 years old. Set among arching weeping willows and towering magnolia trees on the banks of Island Creek, the sense of tranquility is almost palpable.

Combsberry's common rooms are inviting and gracious. The living room, which still has the original wide-plank pine floors, includes elegant antiques, Oriental rugs, and English chintz fabric draped across the windows. A green-paneled library with a fireplace is reached through a wide archway painted with flowers. In front there's a tile-floored sunroom with magnificent views of the water. French doors lead to a formal garden enclosed by a tall brick wall.

The guest rooms, which are spacious, refined, and lovely, are also quite different. Were I to chose a favorite, it might be the Victoria Garden Room, which is entirely decorated in blue and white. There's blue-and-white-checked wallpaper and a blue and white rug. The wrought iron bed has a floral spread, and there are pretty English chintz curtains on the windows. Chairs and tables are in white wicker, and there are glorious views of the water from both the bedroom and the bath. A pretty door leads to the formal garden. But I also love Oxford Cottage, a private two-story cottage that has a brick, ivy-covered terrace. In the first-floor living room, there's a fireplace; in the upstairs bedroom, there's a brass and white iron bed. A Carriage

House was completed in 1997 to house a living room with a fireplace as well as two additional guest rooms. These have hand-painted furniture, whirlpool tubs in the baths, and glorious water views. Both rooms have a fireplace.

For breakfast guests have the option of dining formally in the dining room or informally in the bright country kitchen. Personally, I can't resist one of the kitchen cafe tables, set along the bay window-wall that offers views of the water. I love the omelette that Catherine prepares with crab caught at the B&B's pier. Or perhaps she'll fix her Combsberry casserole that includes hash browns, cheese, ham, and onions baked in an egg and milk sauce. In addition there will be fresh fruit and juice and sweet breads and muffins.

HOW TO GET THERE: From Washington, D.C., and Baltimore take Route 50 across the Chesapeake Bay Bridge. Stay on Route 50 to Route 322 south, the Easton Parkway. Then take Route 333 south toward Oxford and continue for 6 8/10 miles. Turn left onto Evergreen Road. Turn left again at the second driveway through the brick pillars. Drive down a long driveway to the inn.

# The Case
## of the Missing Husband

It was a balmy spring evening and the guests at Combsberry had all returned from their various dinner engagements. But it was too lovely outside to consider bed, so they lingered on the lawn, in the garden, and down by the dock talking together, enjoying the warm bay breezes and the sweet smells of spring. Eventually, however, every guest retired and the house grew quiet. On returning to her room, however, one guest was shocked to find that her husband, who she thought had gone to bed several hours earlier, was nowhere to be found. She woke the innkeeper and a search of the entire inn revealed no trace of him. Soon they began a search of the grounds and there he was—fast asleep and gently swaying in the hammock down at the water's edge, blissfully unaware of the concern for his whereabouts.

# The Inn at Osprey Point
## Rock Hall, Maryland 21661

**INNKEEPER:** Christine Will

**ADDRESS/TELEPHONE:** 20786 Rock Hall Avenue; (410) 639–2194; fax (410) 639–7716

**E-MAIL:** innkeeper@ospreypoint.com

**WEB SITE:** www.ospreypoint.com

**ROOMS:** 7, including 1 suite; all with private bath, air-conditioning, and TV; 1 with fireplace, 1 with whirlpool tub; telephone available. No smoking inn.

**RATES:** $125 to $160, double occupancy May to November, $105 to $140 December to April; includes continental breakfast. Two-night minimum holiday weekends.

**OPEN:** All year.

**FACILITIES AND ACTIVITIES:** Restaurant open for dinner (entrees $13 to $21); thirty acres that include dock, marina, beach, fishing, crabbing, canoeing, nature trails, picnic tables and grills, children's play area, swimming pool, bicycles, horseshoes, volleyball.

**BUSINESS TRAVEL:** Meeting rooms, fax available, desk in 3 rooms.

The Chesapeake Bay and its tributaries are lined with old watermen's villages where fishing and shell fishing were the principal occupations for many years. Rock Hall, on Swan Creek, still has an active fishing fleet, and its seafood restaurants feature the daily catch. Otherwise it's a sleepy, back-roads town. The Inn at Osprey Point, located on thirty acres within the Osprey Point Yacht Club, includes a 160-slip marina, a boon to all the folk who love to cruise the Chesapeake and to come here on private boats.

The setting and demeanor of the inn are reminiscent of one found in a New England fishing village, although the inn is actually a reproduction of the Coke-Garrett House in Colonial Williamsburg. The crisp white clapboard exterior has dormered windows, and the rooms look out on the marina. A sandy beach is an inviting place for children and adults to cool off after a day of sight-seeing.

The guest rooms of the inn are just as those at the beach should be: spacious, refreshing, and smartly furnished. My favorite is Bolero, a second-floor room containing wide-plank pine floors covered with Oriental carpets, a beamed ceiling, a fireplace surrounded by Delft tiles, and a four-poster maple bed topped with a fishnet canopy. From the cushioned window seat there are lovely views of the water. The small marble-floored bath has a shower. The largest room is Escapade, which has both a bedroom and a sitting room as well as a marble bath containing a whirlpool tub. There are terrific water views.

A restaurant is located in two main-floor rooms, which are decorated with prints of sailing ships and watery Monet-like scenes. Both rooms have wonderful big fireplaces and there's a convivial bar as well. The most popular entree is a plate of broiled Maryland jumbo lump crab cakes served with a remoulade sauce; steak, pork chops, seafood stew, and freshly caught fish are also available.

**HOW TO GET THERE:** From Washington, D.C., take Route 50 east across the Chesapeake Bay Bridge and continue on Route 301/50 until it splits. Take Route 301 north for 5 miles to Route 213 north. Follow Route 213 through Centreville and into Chestertown. After passing Washington College, take Route 291 for ¼ mile to Route 20. Turn right onto Route 20, traveling south to Rock Hall, which is approximately 13 miles. At the blinking light in Rock Hall, continue straight ahead for approximately 1 more mile. The inn is on the right in the Osprey Point Yacht Club.

# The Inn at Perry Cabin
## St. Michaels, Maryland 21663

**INNKEEPER:** Stephen Creese; Sir Bernard Ashley, proprietor

**ADDRESS/TELEPHONE:** 308 Watkins Lane; (410) 745–2200 or (800) 722–2949; fax (410) 745–3348

**E-MAIL:** Perrycbn@friend.ly.net

**WEB SITE:** www.keswick.com/keswick.html

**ROOMS:** 41, including 6 suites; all with private bath, air-conditioning, cable television, telephone, radio, hair dryer, desk, robes, iron, and ironing board; 18 with balcony or patio. Smoking permitted; designated non-smoking rooms. Wheelchair accessible. Pets allowed.

**RATES:** $195 to $695, double occupancy; includes full breakfast and afternoon tea.

**OPEN:** All year.

**FACILITIES AND ACTIVITIES:** Lunch ($30), dinner ($65), cocktail service, docking privileges. Library, conservatory, garden room, snooker room with snooker table and fireplace. Swimming pool, sauna, and steam room. Bicycles and boats available. Nearby: St. Michaels Maritime Museum and village.

**BUSINESS TRAVEL:** Telephone, desk, and fax available; conference center with audiovisual equipment.

Purser Samuel Hambleton served as aide-de-camp to Commodore Oliver Hazard Perry during the War of 1812, where he distinguished himself in the Battle of Lake Erie. Following the war Hambleton retired to Maryland's Eastern Shore, where he built a fine manor house with a wing that resembled Perry's cabin on the flagship *Niagra*. And this is how The Inn at Perry Cabin got its name.

The elegant but comfortable inn secured its current status, however, through the foresight and ambition of Sir Bernard Ashley, a cofounder of the Laura Ashley Company. Ashley's vision was to model his inn along the lines of an English country house hotel but infuse it with the warm informality of American hospitality. He created an inn that has all the creature comforts his guests might want but with a relaxed and unpretentious air.

The numerous common rooms include a wicker- and greenery-filled, brick-floored conservatory and an adjoining snooker room with a fireplace. There's a living room, a morning room, and a library (can you find the door disguised as a bookshelf?), all of which have fireplaces. In the sunny, brick-floored side porch, guests can enjoy a variety of board games under the watchful eye of a party of teddy bears assembled in an antique wicker stroller. The inn also includes a state-of-the-art meeting room, a fitness center, and an indoor swimming pool. Located on twenty-five acres bordering the Miles River, there's a dock for those who wish to arrive by water. Bicycles are available for meandering along the country lanes.

The guest rooms are spacious and charming—all are decorated with Laura Ashley fabrics, wallpa-  pers, china, and furniture. I love Suite 22, but all the rooms are lovely. This one has a living room with a private deck and an upstairs bedroom with a wonderful view of the water. The elegantly carved bed is draped in a pretty floral fabric and antique tables serve as nightstands. A bowl of fruit and bottled water awaited our arrival, and I could become addicted to the buttery oatmeal-raisin cookies left on a pretty floral Laura Ashley plate at our bedside when we returned from dinner. If you wish to sleep late, you can "put out the cat," a cute little stuffed one that can be hung from the outside doorknob.

Meals at The Inn at Perry Cabin are superb. In the first place, the dining rooms are positively elegant and there are lovely views across the manicured lawns to the river. You might start your five-course dinner as we did, with a lobster bisque flavored with cognac, and then move on to a light salad. Next I enjoyed a fillet of Atlantic salmon on jumbo lump crab with a caramelized ginger sweet-and-sour sauce, while my husband had the roast breast of squab on artichokes and mushrooms with a red onion tart-tatin. My favorite dessert is a fluffy-light bread pudding with a crème anglaise sauce, but a

# Blue Crabs

I will never forget my first taste of Maryland's famous blue crabs, or the ambience in which they were eaten. I was sitting with friends—all of us casually attired—at a picnic-style table on a pier that jutted out into the Miles River just before it tumbles into the Chesapeake Bay. It was a balmy evening of clear skies and calm seas. The gentle waves slapped against the pilings, and nearby the rigging of sailboats at anchor joined in the chorus.

We shared a pitcher of pale beer as we waited for our feast. Our waitress arrived with placemats and plastic bibs. She handed us each a wooden mallet and a knife. Then came a wooden cutting board and an overflowing platter of dull red-colored crab steamed in hot spices that penetrated the shell and seasoned the sweet, white meat. The rock-hard shells yielded to the mallets. Soon the table was littered with pieces of shell, flecks of butter, and sopping napkins.

Hilde Gabriel Lee, in *Taste of the States: A Food History of America*, says that the blue crab of the Chesapeake Bay (so called because of the color of its underside) may shed its shell as many as twenty-three times in its lifetime of about three years, and each time it does so, its size is increased by one-third. The average blue crab is about five to seven inches across. During the twenty-four-hour period in which the blue crab is molting, its shell is also edible. Then it becomes the delicacy known as soft-shell crab, when it may be cleaned and then fried (perhaps after dipping in a buckwheat batter) and eaten.

The hard-shell blue crab is the basis for Maryland's famous crab cakes, and it is also used in salads and soups. Nevertheless, in my opinion, there is no finer way to eat them than straight from the steamer with mallet and knife in hand, washing them down with pale beer while sitting on a pier in the Chesapeake Bay.

pumpkin mousse in a tuille was wonderful also. The wine list is exceptional; so is the selection of cognacs, liqueurs, ports, and sherries.

The Inn at Perry Cabin is one of my top picks because of its friendly staff who unobtrusively see to the smallest details to make their guests' stay memorable. This is why the inn has received numerous awards and why such celebrities as Diane Sawyer, Mike Nichols, Paul Newman, Joanne Woodward, and others return again and again.

HOW TO GET THERE: From Washington, D.C., take Route 50 across the Chesapeake Bay Bridge. Remain on Route 50 for approximately 30 miles to Easton. One-half mile after the Easton Airport, bear right onto Route 322. Go 2 miles. At the traffic light, turn right onto Route 33 to St. Michaels. Pass through the village; the inn is on the right just beyond.

# River House Inn

## Snow Hill, Maryland 21863

INNKEEPERS: Larry and Susanne Knudsen

ADDRESS/TELEPHONE: 201 East Market Street; (410) 632–2722; fax (410) 632–2866

ROOMS: 8, including 1 suite and 1 cottage; all with private bath and air-conditioning; 6 with fireplace, 2 with Jacuzzi. Suite suitable for families. Dogs permitted with prior permission. Two rooms wheelchair accessible. No smoking inn.

RATES: $100 to $175, double occupancy; includes full breakfast and afternoon wine and snacks. $20 additional person, $10 additional child. Two-night minimum June to September and holidays.

OPEN: All year.

FACILITIES AND ACTIVITIES: Dinner by advance arrangement ($30 per person for four courses, including wine). Located on Pocomoke River. Nearby: river tour aboard The Otter; canoeing, bicycling, golfing, boating; Chincoteague and Chesapeake Bay.

RECOMMENDED COUNTRY INNS® TRAVELERS' CLUB BENEFIT: Stay two nights, get third night free, Monday to Thursday; or free river tour with two-night stay.

*T*f you appreciate the excesses of Victorian architecture, you will love River House. It is a confection of gingerbread icing, multiple gables with keyhole trim, black wrought-iron lace reminiscent of New Orleans, and various-sized porches. In front there's an impressive wraparound veranda, while across the back, double porches offer views of the Pokomoke River just beyond the sloping lawns and gardens on the inn's two acres.

Larry and Susanne Knudsen opened their inn to guests in 1991. Originally there was only The River House, which is still the heart of the inn. The cardinal-red twin parlors, with their duet of fireplaces, draw you in with the warmth of their decor. The breakfast room and dining room are here as well,

where guests feast on Susanne's River House eggs—a combination of eggs shirred in cream and topped with herbs and cheese—or her croissant French toast with dried fruits.

Now, in addition to River House, guest rooms are located in River Cottage, an 1890s carriage house converted to a guest room, and in Riverview Hideaway, a new building the Knudsens built at the river's edge in 1996. Each of the rooms includes antique and reproduction furniture, and four of the rooms have either canopy or four-poster beds. The River Room has a fabulous carved French bedroom suite, and the West Room has an early mahogany Chippendale-style suite with carved phoenixes.

Snow Hill is a charming village with a past. Take a walking tour of the historic old homes, or, perhaps, borrow one of the inn's bicycles for a longer excursion. Or join up with Larry, who is a riverboat captain, for one of his tours along the Pokomoke River on his boat the *Otter*.

**HOW TO GET THERE:** From the intersection of Route 12 and Market Street in Snow Hill, go east a few hundred yards on Market and turn left on Green Street, then right into the parking space.

# Gramercy Mansion B&B
## Stevenson, Maryland 21153

**INNKEEPERS:** Anne Pomykala and Cristin Kline

**ADDRESS/TELEPHONE:** 1400 Greenspring Valley Road (mailing address: P.O. Box 119); (410) 486–2405; fax (410) 486–1765

**WEB SITE:** www.angelfire.com/md/pomykala

**ROOMS:** 10, including 1 suite; 5 with private bath and the rest shared; all with air-conditioning, TV, and robes; 5 with telephone, VCR, desk, radio, coffeemaker, hair dryer, iron, and ironing board; 3 with whirlpool tub and/or fireplace. No smoking inn.

**RATES:** $65 to $90, single occupancy; $165 to $279, double occupancy; includes full breakfast. Additional adult $25 per person, additional child $10.

**OPEN:** All year.

**FACILITIES AND ACTIVITIES:** On forty-five acres that include an organic herb farm, nature trails, tennis court, Olympic-sized swimming pool. Nearby: Baltimore is twenty minutes away.

The elegant 1902 English Tudor house that is now the cornerstone of Gramercy Mansion B&B was built on this hilltop by Alexander Cassatt, a brother of Mary Cassatt, the poignant impressionist painter and printmaker, as a wedding present for his daughter. Through the years it has been a gracious family home to railroad magnates and political dignitaries, but in 1951 it embarked on a fascinating new life. The estate became the home of Koinonia, where Christian ambassadors, in a Point Four Program initiated by President Truman, were trained in literacy methods and organic gardening. When the Peace Corp was established in the 1960s, Koinonia became its training ground, offering seminars on world peace, education, literacy, race relations, hunger, and much more. Most of the outbuildings built during this period now contain apartments. The estate was purchased at auction by the Pomykala family in 1985, and a continuous restoration effort has been under way ever since. In 1986 the mansion was the site of a decorator's show house.

The mansion is impressive to say the least. There are dark boxed beams, multiple fireplaces, a library with oak paneling, and a wide terrace that serves as a breakfast room in summer. In winter breakfast is served in the handsome dining room, which has another fireplace, dark boxed beams, and walls covered in forest-green fabric. Wonderful English and American antiques furnish the rooms.

There are five magnificent guest rooms. My favorite is the blue Garden Suite. It has a bedroom with an antique French bed, a sunporch with lattice walls that overlooks the pool and gardens, and a sitting room with a fireplace and an ornately carved Victorian walnut bed. The bath has deep blue tiles, a fabulous marble sink, and a large whirlpool tub. (There are also five smaller "back hall" rooms that, although beautifully furnished with single beds, share a hall bath.)

A breakfast menu is offered to guests every afternoon, allowing them to make a choice of, perhaps, an omelette of tomatoes, onions, cheese, mushrooms, and freshly picked herbs; banana, raspberry, or blueberry pancakes; or poached, scrambled, or fried eggs; as well as fruit, juice, and breakfast breads.

In addition to the walking trails throughout the property and the swimming pool and tennis court, guests may visit the seven-acre organic farm that continues to use the horticultural principles established by the Koinonia Foundation.

HOW TO GET THERE: From downtown Baltimore follow I-83 (the Jones Falls Expressway) north to I-695. Take the left exit onto I-695 west and Falls Road. Follow Falls Road north toward Brooklandville. At the second light, turn left onto Greenspring Valley Road. Go 1 mile, through the light at Greenspring Avenue, to the first driveway on the right.

# Antrim 1844 Country Inn
Taneytown, Maryland 21787

INNKEEPERS: Richard and Dorothy Mollett

ADDRESS/TELEPHONE: 30 Trevanion Road; (410) 756-6812 or (800) 858-1844; fax (410) 756-2744

E-MAIL: azmz94a@prodigy.com

ROOMS: 23, including 8 suites and 6 cottages; all with private bath, air-conditioning, radio, hair dryer, desk, robes, and CD player; 10 with whirlpool tub and fireplace; 1 with TV and VCR. Children over the age of 12 welcome. Wheelchair accessible. No smoking, except in tavern.

**RATES:** $200 to $350, double occupancy; includes full breakfast, afternoon snacks, and evening hors d'oeuvres. Special packages available on holidays. Two-night minimum if stay includes Saturday night and some holidays.

**OPEN:** All year, except Christmas Eve.

**FACILITIES AND ACTIVITIES:** Tavern, twenty-three acres, swimming pool, 2 Nova grass tennis courts, croquet lawn, bowling green, golf-chipping green, volleyball, badminton, horseshoes, formal gardens. Dinner by reservation Wednesday to Sunday (fixed price $55, higher on holidays). Nearby: 12 miles to Gettysburg. Golf courses: Wakefield Valley, Carroll Valley, Bear Creek.

**BUSINESS TRAVEL:** Desk in all rooms; telephone, fax, and copy machine available; conference rooms; flip charts.

*Y*our day unfolds gently. You might begin with a cup of fresh coffee presented at your door by a wooden butler along with the morning paper. It's one of those lazy days with no particular place to be or time to be there. Perhaps you'll enjoy a game of tennis before breakfast, or a stroll in the gardens.

You may have slumbered in the third-floor Brandon Room with its raspberry walls and green-and-raspberry canopy over the bed. You would have admired the antique dresser and drop-leaf table, and you certainly would have reposed in the raspberry-colored whirlpool tub while admiring the view of the gardens and cottages on the twenty-three-

acre estate grounds below—perhaps you would have turned out the lights and basked in the glow of the fat candles on the rim of the tub.

Other guest room options include the Boucher Suite, which has a canopy bed facing a fireplace and two balconies, the Lamberton Room, with its 1790s canopy bed with turned posts; and the Clabaugh Room, which has a half-tester Empire-style rosewood bed. Additional rooms with whirlpool tubs and fireplaces are found in the Ice House, the Cottage, the Smith House, the Barn, and (opened in 1998) the Carriage House.

Eventually you go down to breakfast, which is served in a room with lacquered green walls and red drapes. You'll have fruit and juice, sweet breads and muffins, and, maybe, Belgian waffles or an omelette. Later you'll browse through the books in the library or spend an hour or two reading in one of the elegant twin parlors with their matching marble fireplace mantels or, perhaps, out on the veranda.

As the day warms you'll decide whether to take a swim in the pool; engage in a game of badminton, horseshoes, croquet, or lawn bowling; or, maybe, practice your putting on the inn's putting green. This, of course, is all merely a prelude to dinner.

Chef Sharon Ashburn has created a distinctive Antrim cuisine that marries the local regional flavors and ingredients with the delicacy of French cuisine. Even if you are unable to stay here, you should come for dinner. The setting is romantic, charming, and elegant. You might be seated in the original brick-floored smokehouse, the summer kitchen, the slave kitchen, or the new room that also has a brick herringbone floor and looks as old as the rest. The silver and crystal will sparkle, and fresh flowers will brighten the crisp white cloths. You will appreciate the oil portraits on the walls that glow in the light of the candlestick lamps.

You will start the event at 6:30 P.M. in the inn's common rooms. You might chat quietly together or with other guests as staff persons pass hors d'oeuvres and glasses of wine. At 7:30 you will be seated. Your dinner may start with an *amusée*—on one recent visit, a squab egg served in phyllo. The next course might be a sweet potato vichyssoise with crispy caramelized pecans in the center, followed by a spinach salad with chicken livers and bacon bits and a pansy on top. Next comes a sherbet intermezzo. You may have chosen a beef filet for your entree. If so, it is tender and juicy and accompanied by a red-wine sauce, roasted potatoes, carrots, zucchini, beans, and okra. Dessert will be positively decadent. A plate of five selections is shared by two people. Among the offerings you may find a cinnamon crème brûlée, a white chocolate cheese cake, a bourbon-pecan pie, a cylinder of spun sugar filled with fresh berries, and chocolate chip ice cream.

HOW TO GET THERE: From Baltimore Beltway I-695 take exit 19 onto I-795 north. Exit onto Route 140 west to Taneytown. In town turn left onto Trevanion Road and go 150 feet to inn on right. From Frederick take I-94 north to Taneytown. Turn right at light on Route 140, proceed ½ mile, turn right at fork onto Trevanion Road. Go 150 feet to inn on right. Signs indicate where to park.

# Select List of Other Inns in Maryland

### Prince George Inn
232 Prince George Street
Annapolis, MD 21401
(410) 263-6418
E-mail: pginn@annap.infi.net
Web site: www.princegeorgeinn.com

*4 rooms (2 with private bath) in brick townhouse.*

### Two-O-One
201 Prince George Street
Annapolis, MD 21401
(410) 268-8053
E-mail: twoOonebb@aol.com

*3 rooms and 1 suite; all with private bath; in elegant townhouse furnished with top-quality antiques.*

### Abacrombie Badger Bed & Breakfast
58 West Biddle Street
Baltimore, MD 21201
(410) 244-7227

*12 rooms; all with private bath; in 1890s brick townhouse across from Meyerhoff Symphony Hall.*

### Ann Street B&B
804 South Ann Street
Baltimore, MD 21231
(410) 342-5883

*2 rooms and 2 suites; all with private bath; in historic twin brick townhouses in Fells Point.*

### The Inn at Buckeystown
3521 Buckeystown Pike
Buckeystown, MD 21717
(800) 272-1190 or (301) 874-5755

*3 rooms, 2 suites, 2 cottages; all with private bath; in Victorian mansion; restaurant.*

## The Imperial Hotel

208 High Street
Chestertown, MD 21620
(410) 778-5000

*11 rooms and 2 suites; all with private bath; in restored 1904 hotel in the heart of town; restaurant.*

## The White Swan Tavern

231 High Street
Chestertown, MD 21620
(410) 778-6500

*4 rooms and 2 suites; all with private bath; in restored historic 1733 tavern.*

## Currier House B&B

800 South Market Street
Havre de Grace, MD 21078
(800) 827-2889 or (410) 939-7886
E-mail: janec@currier.bb.com

*4 rooms; all with private bath; in 1800s house filled with family antiques and mementos.*

## Spencer Silver Mansion

200 South Union Avenue
Havre de Grace, MD 21078
(410) 939-1485

*3 rooms and a two-story stone cottage; all with private bath; in fabulously ornate restored Victorian.*

## Middle Plantation Inn

9549 Liberty Road
Mount Pleasant, MD 21701
(301) 898-7128

*3 rooms; all with private bath; in rebuilt log cabin on twenty-six acres in tiny village.*

## National Pike Inn

9 West Main Street
New Market, MD 21774
(301) 865-5055
Web site: www.newmarketmd.com/natpike.htm

*4 rooms and 1 suite; 3 with private bath; in village known as antiques capital of Maryland.*

## The Oak and Apple Bed & Breakfast

208 North Second Street
Oakland, MD 21550
(301) 334-9265

*5 rooms; 3 with private bath; in Colonial Revival house in Maryland's western panhandle.*

## Robert Morris Inn

Morris Street
Oxford, MD 21654
(410) 226-5111

*34 rooms; all with private bath; in riverside inn dating to 1710; restaurant.*

## Moonlight Bay Inn

6002 Lawton Avenue
Rock Hall, MD 21661
(410) 639-2660

*5 rooms; all with private bath; in waterfront B&B with adjacent marina.*

## Dr. Dobson's B&B

200 Cherry Street
St. Michaels, MD 21663
(410) 745-3691

*2 rooms; both with private bath; with decor featuring historic quilt collection.*

## Tarr House B&B

Green Street
St. Michaels, MD 21663
(410) 745-2175

*2 rooms; both with private bath; in charming 1667 brick village house.*

## Victoriana Inn

205 Cherry Street
St. Michaels, MD 21663
(410) 745-3368

*5 rooms; 2 with private bath; in white waterfront Victorian.*

## The Inn at Antietam

220 East Main Street
Sharpsburg, MD 21782
(301) 432-6601

*4 suites; all with private bath; in white 1908 Victorian adjacent to Antietam Cemetery.*

## Back Creek Inn

Calvert and A Streets
Solomons, MD 20688
(410) 326–2022

*4 rooms, 2 suites, and 1 cottage; all with private bath; in Tidewater country.*

## Chesapeake Wood Duck Inn

Gibsontown Road
Tilghman Island, MD 21671
(800) 956–2070 or (410) 886–2070

*6 rooms and 1 suite; all with private bath; on an island that still supports a skipjack fleet.*

## The Lazyjack Inn

5907 Tilghman Island Road
Tilghman Island, MD 21671
(800) 690–5080 or (410) 886–2215
E-mail: mrichards@skipjack.bluecrab.org

*3 rooms and 1 suite; all with private bath; on island famous for its seafood.*

## Inn of Silent Music

Smith Island
Tylertown, MD 21866
(410) 425–3541

*4 rooms; all with private bath; in eighty-year-old charmingly decorated water-front home on island reached by 9-mile ferry ride.*

## The Inn at Christmas Farm

8873 Tilghman Island Road
Wittman, MD 21676
(800) 987–8436 or (410) 745–5312

*1 room and 4 suites; all with private bath; on thirty-acre waterfront farm near St. Michaels and Tilghman Island.*

# New Jersey

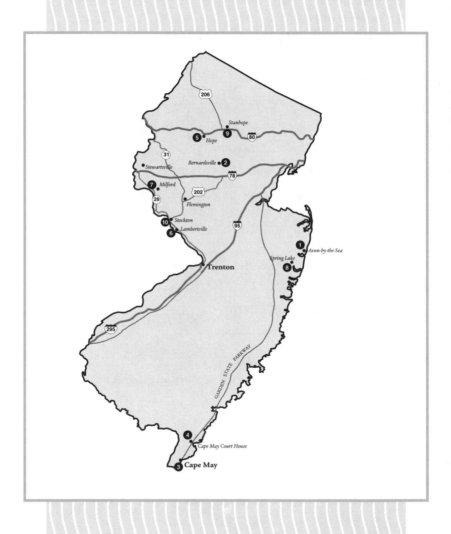

206

Stanhope
9
5  Hope
80

31
Bernardsville  2
78
7  Milford
29
202
Flemington

10  Stockton
6  Lambertville
95

1  Avon-by-the-Sea
Spring Lake
8

Trenton

295

GARDEN STATE PARKWAY

4
Cape May Court House
3  Cape May

Stewartsville

# New Jersey

*Numbers on map refer to towns numbered below.*

1. Avon-by-the-Sea, Cashelmara Inn . . . . . . . . . . . . . . . . . . . . . . . . . . . . 66
2. Bernardsville, The Bernards Inn . . . . . . . . . . . . . . . . . . . . . . . . . . . . 67
3. Cape May,
     The Mainstay Inn* . . . . . . . . . . . . . . . . . . . . . . . . . . . . . . . . . . . . 69
     Manor House Inn . . . . . . . . . . . . . . . . . . . . . . . . . . . . . . . . . . . . 71
     The Queen Victoria* . . . . . . . . . . . . . . . . . . . . . . . . . . . . . . . . . . . 73
     The Southern Mansion* . . . . . . . . . . . . . . . . . . . . . . . . . . . . . . . 75
     The Virginia Hotel . . . . . . . . . . . . . . . . . . . . . . . . . . . . . . . . . . . . 77
4. Cape May Courthouse, The Doctors Inn at Kings Grant . . . . . . . . 79
5. Hope, The Inn at Millrace Pond . . . . . . . . . . . . . . . . . . . . . . . . . . . . 80
6. Lambertville,
     The Inn at Lambertville Station . . . . . . . . . . . . . . . . . . . . . . . . . . . 83
     Lambertville House* . . . . . . . . . . . . . . . . . . . . . . . . . . . . . . . . . . . 84
7. Milford, Chestnut Hill on the Delaware . . . . . . . . . . . . . . . . . . . . . 86
8. Spring Lake,
     La Maison—A B&B and Gallery* . . . . . . . . . . . . . . . . . . . . . . . . . . 88
     Normandy Inn . . . . . . . . . . . . . . . . . . . . . . . . . . . . . . . . . . . . . . . 90
     Sea Crest by the Sea . . . . . . . . . . . . . . . . . . . . . . . . . . . . . . . . . . . 91
9. Stanhope, The Whistling Swan Inn . . . . . . . . . . . . . . . . . . . . . . . . . 93
10. Stockton,
     The Stockton Inn . . . . . . . . . . . . . . . . . . . . . . . . . . . . . . . . . . . . . 94
     The Woolverton Inn* . . . . . . . . . . . . . . . . . . . . . . . . . . . . . . . . . . 96

*A Top Pick Inn

# Cashelmara Inn

**INNKEEPER:** Mary F. Wiernasz

**ADDRESS/TELEPHONE:** 22 Lakeside Avenue; (732) 776–8727 or (800) 821–2976; fax (732) 988–5819

**E-MAIL:** cashelmara@monmouth.com

**WEB SITE:** www.avon-by-the-sea.com/cashelmara

**ROOMS:** 14, including 2 suites; all with private bath, air-conditioning, television, and radio; 7 with fireplace, 4 with minirefrigerator, 2 with whirlpool tub, 1 with private porch. No smoking inn.

**RATES:** $75 to $250, double occupancy; includes full breakfast and afternoon snacks; extra persons $10 if under 11 years of age; $20 if 11 or over. Two-night minimum weekends off-season; three-night minimum Memorial Day weekend and during July and August; four-night mini-mum Fourth of July and Labor Day weekends.

**OPEN:** All year.

**FACILITIES AND ACTIVITIES:** On Swan Lake; badges provided for ocean beach and for municipal swimming pool. Nearby: restaurants, antiques shops, bicycling, golfing, horse racing.

**BUSINESS TRAVEL:** Small conference room; fax and telephone available.

After a top-to-bottom renovation completed in 1997, Cashelmara barely shows her age. Built in 1907 by the U.S. Postmaster General for his summer cottage, the inn had been a seasonal rooming house for many years. Mary Wiernasz purchased it in 1984, but it wasn't until she undertook this wonderful renovation that the inn came into its own.

You'll love the care she took in making her grand house hospitable and elegant. There's a broad veranda across the front of the creamy stucco house, which has multiple dormers. Wooden rockers invite lazy afternoons watching the ducks and swans on Swan Lake just across the lawn. In the lobby and parlors there are elaborate Victorian tables, chairs, and chests, as well as gas fireplaces. In the evening, especially if there's rain and you choose not to close your day with a walk along the boardwalk, you will certainly opt to watch a movie in Mulligan's Grand Victorian Theater, where you will sit on antique velvet theater chairs amid rich velvet wall drapes to watch a movie on the 80-inch television screen. There's even stereo surround-sound, special theatrical lighting, and, yes . . . popcorn.

Each of the guest rooms has been refurbished also. My favorite is the first-floor suite. It has a burgundy sofa, a gas fireplace, a fabulous antique mirrored armoire, and an elaborately carved canopy bed with elegant green-and-yellow-striped drapes and bedskirt. French doors lead to a private porch. The bath has a plum-colored Jacuzzi and a plum and white floor. There are more rooms on the second and third floors. Those on the second have wide windows that offer the best views; those on the third floor have dormer windows.

We love the bright breakfast room with its wall of windows. You might start the day with an omelette or eggs fixed as you like them, or, perhaps, you'll ask for the Cashel McMara, a slice of ham topped with a fried egg, sliced tomato, and melted cheese on an English muffin.

**HOW TO GET THERE:** From the Garden State Parkway, take exit 98 and follow Route 138 east to Route 35. Take Route 35 north to the first light. Turn right onto Sixteenth Avenue and follow this to Ocean Avenue. Turn left and proceed for approximately 1 mile. Cross over the inlet bridge into Avon. Go 7 blocks to Lakeside Avenue. Turn left to the inn, which is on the left.

# The Bernards Inn
Bernardsville, New Jersey 07924

**INNKEEPERS:** Alice and George Rochat, Edward Stone; Steve Malone and Diane Carr, managers

**ADDRESS/TELEPHONE:** 27 Mine Brook Road; (908) 766–0002 or (888) 766–0002; fax (908) 766–4604

**E-MAIL:** info@bernardsinn.com

**WEB SITE:** www.bernardsinn.com

**ROOMS:** 20, including 4 suites; all with private bath, air-conditioning, telephone with dataport, TV, radio, minibar, hair dryer, robes, iron, and ironing board. Smoking permitted; designated nonsmoking rooms.

**RATES:** $115 to $215; includes continental breakfast.

**OPEN:** All year.

**FACILITIES AND ACTIVITIES:** Restaurant open lunch (entrees $11 to $14) and dinner (entrees $23 to $28), parking, membership in local YMCA health club. Nearby: U.S. Equestrian Center, U.S. Golf Museum, Jockey Hollow National Park.

Desks, television, and telephones with dataports in every room; express check out, same-day laundry, complimentary shoe shine, room service.

Although The Bernards Inn, a 1907 Mission-style stone and stucco structure, has been welcoming visitors for more than ninety years, its recent metamorphosis from dowdy dowager to pretty princess has given it the same cachet it had when it first opened. Owner Alice Rochat is an interior designer and renovator, and although she and her husband, George, have owned the inn since 1980, their renovation was not completed until the mid-1990s. Now the inn has a vintage ambience as well as thoroughly modern creature comforts.

A fire was crackling in the lobby hearth when we arrived, and we admired the handsome carved mahogany mantel. We were staying in Room 2, a spacious area decorated in shades of green. There was a handsome antique armoire containing a minibar and television and a large antique carved mahogany bed with a matelassé spread. The lovely tiled bath had a pedestal sink.

Dinner is an elegant event. Executive Chef Edward Stone has developed a distinctive regional cuisine. I started with a salad of corn and mâché that was topped with crispy sweetbreads. It was terrific. For an entree I had roasted Muscovy duck served with a saga blue cheese polenta and a spring vegetable ragout. My husband had sautéed black sea bass and cockles, which came with a plum tomato Provençal. An excellent wine list presents a broad selection of offerings. We shared a wonderful warm Belgian chocolate cake for dessert.

HOW TO GET THERE: From I–287 traveling north take exit 26B (Mt. Airy Road/Bernardsville). Bear right at the first light. Go 2 miles to the traffic light and make a left onto Route 202 south. Go 1 block to inn, which is on the corner on the right. From I–287 traveling south take exit 30B (Bernardsville/Route 202) and go to the light. Make a left onto Route 202 south and follow Route 202 south through two traffic lights. Go straight for 1 block to the inn, which is on the right.

# The Mainstay Inn

## Cape May, New Jersey 08204

**INNKEEPERS:** Tom and Sue Carroll; Kathy Moore, manager

**ADDRESS/TELEPHONE:** 635 Columbia Avenue; (609) 884–8690

**WEB SITE:** www.mainstayinn.com

**ROOMS:** 16, including 7 suites; all with private bath; 4 suites with fireplace, whirlpool, television, telephone, snack kitchen, and VCR. One room wheelchair accessible. No smoking inn. Children 6 and older welcome in Officers' Quarters; children 12 and older welcome in main inn and cottage.

**RATES:** $110 to $295, double occupancy; $10 less for single; includes full breakfast, afternoon tea, and beach passes. Additional person, $20. Three-night minimum in season; two-night minimum spring and fall weekends.

**OPEN:** All year; reduced number of rooms mid-December to mid-March.

**FACILITIES AND ACTIVITIES:** Nearby: restaurants, beach, historic Cape May mansions, bicycling, bird-watching, sailing, trolley rides, state park, lighthouse museum, carriage rides.

**RECOMMENDED COUNTRY INNS® TRAVELERS' CLUB BENEFIT:** Stay one night, get second night free, Sunday to Thursday, late October to late April, excluding Thanksgiving, Christmas, and Presidents Day week, subject to availability.

*I* never return to The Mainstay Inn without remembering my first visit in the 1970s. The entire B&B movement was in its infancy, but Tom and Sue Carroll had the foresight to recognize that the grand Victorian mansions of Cape May would make lovely B&Bs. They opened their first in the late 1960s, and then sold that to buy their dream "cottage" in 1971. In the almost thirty years they have owned The Mainstay, they have continuously expanded and improved the property. Along the way they added a neighboring house that they call The Cottage and a building across the street that they converted into four elegant suites called The Officers' Quarters. Their fledgling business was eventually copied by others, and there are now more than one hundred B&Bs in Cape May.

Tom and Sue are the kind of hands-on innkeepers that innkeeping used to be all about, and their B&B is a reflection of their love of history and architecture. The original inn was built as a gambling club in 1872, and much of the paneling, stained glass, and woodwork remains. Tom and Sue have added elaborate Bradbury and Bradbury wallpapers and borders to enhance the vintage feeling. I have spent many lazy afternoons in a rocking chair on the porch listening to the clip-clop of the horses hooves as they pull tourists through town. I have spent an equal amount of time up in the belvedere, where the salty sea breezes whisper through the sycamore trees.

The guest rooms are as refined and elegant as the common rooms—Bradbury and Bradbury wallpapers and borders are used, and all rooms are furnished with magnificent antiques that are true to the period. You will sleep in a magnificent Victorian walnut bed in Henry Clay, for example, and in a brass bed in the Grant Suite. In the newer Officers' Quarters, the suites are decorated with country Victorian or country pine furnishings. The living rooms contain gas fireplaces, there are private decks, and each suite has its own snack kitchen. The large,  modern baths have whirlpool tubs, separate steam showers, and back-lighted stained-glass windows that cast a romantic glow throughout the room.

Except in summer, Sue prepares a sumptuous full breakfast for her guests. Generally it's served in the dining room, but we have sometimes taken our coffee out to the veranda. In summer a hearty continental breakfast is served on the veranda. Guests in the Officers' Quarters are given a continental breakfast that they can prepare themselves in their kitchen.

Don't miss afternoon tea at The Mainstay. If you are staying there, it's included in the price of your room, but if you weren't fortunate enough to book a room, you can pay a nominal fee and be taken on a tour of the inn and then enjoy tea on the veranda. You'll savor such delicacies as tea sandwiches, cheese daisies, and almond cake squares or lemon bars. Undoubtedly you'll want to leave with a copy of Sue's new cookbook, *Breakfast at Nine, Tea at Four.*

HOW TO GET THERE: From the Garden State Parkway merge onto Lafayette Street. Turn left onto Madison, right onto Columbia, to 635 on the right.

# Honeymoon Redux

Two couples, unknown to each other, were celebrating their twenty-fifth anniversaries at The Mainstay Inn in Cape May. Sitting in rocking chairs on the broad veranda, they began talking. They were surprised to learn that both couples had spent their honeymoons in Bermuda, but they were even more surprised and delighted to discover that they had actually met each other on their honeymoons. They recalled the fun they had had together and their disappointment over the years that they had lost touch. They now plan to return to The Mainstay to celebrate their anniversaries together.

# Manor House Inn

## Cape May, New Jersey 08204

**INNKEEPERS:** Nancy and Tom McDonald

**ADDRESS/TELEPHONE:** 612 Hughes Street; (609) 884–4710; fax (609) 898–0471

**WEB SITE:** www.manorhouse.net

**ROOMS:** 10, including 1 suite; all with private bath and air-conditioning; 1 with television, 1 with Jacuzzi. No smoking inn. Children over the age of 12 welcome.

**RATES:** $85 to $217, double occupancy; includes full breakfast, beach tags, and beach chairs. Two-night minimum weekends; three-night minimum throughout July and August.

**OPEN:** All year except January.

**FACILITIES AND ACTIVITIES:** Nearby: ocean beach 2 blocks away, Cape May house tours, Christmas festivities, walking street of shops and restaurants.

**RECOMMENDED COUNTRY INNS® TRAVELERS' CLUB BENEFIT:** 10 percent discount, Sunday to Thursday, excludes July and August.

*N*ancy McDonald had been coming to Cape May since she was a child. When she and Tom married, they began visiting Cape May together, and their favorite place to stay was the Manor House. Eventually they decided to purchase their own inn and create one with all the ambience they loved so much at the Manor House. Just as their quest was beginning, they booked a room at the Manor House to participate in a cooking class. To their surprise, longtime owners Tom and Mary Snyder, who by this time knew the McDonalds well, said that they were ready to sell. The happy result is that the McDonalds purchased their dream inn, the Snyders sold it to a couple they knew would love and appreciate it, and we have the joy of being able to continue to stay in one of Cape May's finest inns.

On a quiet side street but in the heart of the historic village, the Manor House offers peace and tranquility. We entered a foyer rich with burnished chestnut and oak. On the stair landing a polished oak window seat was sur-

veyed by an ornate stained-glass window. Nancy invited us to the parlor, where, since it was winter, a fire crackled in the hearth. A selection of sweet and savory treats, as well as port and sherry, were waiting. With the soft strains of classical music playing in the background, we soon relaxed from our drive and allowed ourselves to be pampered. In the

warm weather guests sit in the beautiful and secluded English garden, which is alive in the spring with more than 150 different varieties of tulips.

Nancy and Tom have owned the Manor House since early 1995. Just as it did before, food plays an important role at the inn. Nancy is a gourmet cook and a connoisseur who knows the best places for lunch and dinner, and she fixes a superlative breakfast for her guests. The menu is prepared every afternoon so that guests can anticipate the morning meal. The hot entree might include a tomato tart, with tomatoes fresh from the garden in season, a lemon-ricotta pancake, or, perhaps, orange-custard French toast. Fresh fruit, hot-from-the-oven muffins or bread, and freshly squeezed juice accompany the meal. Rather than a buffet-style breakfast, Tom serves the courses. Guests are served in two seatings.

The guest rooms are tasteful and refined instead of fussy and Victorian. Number 9 has a turn-of-the-century French bed and green wallpaper, while Number 8 has red walls and a fantastic antique Victorian walnut dresser.

Room 6 stretches across the front of the house and has a sleeping and a sitting area as well as a bath with a whirlpool tub. Some of the bathrooms are small, however, and two of the rooms share a bath.

**HOW TO GET THERE:** From the Garden State Parkway or the Lewes Ferry, take Route 109 south into Cape May. After crossing the bridge and passing the marina, you will be on Lafayette Street. Continue about 8 blocks to Franklin Street. Turn left onto Franklin, go 2 blocks, and turn right onto Hughes Street. The inn is in the second block on the left.

# The Queen Victoria
## Cape May, New Jersey 08204

**INNKEEPERS:** Dane, Joan, and daughter Elizabeth Wells

**ADDRESS/TELEPHONE:** 102 Ocean Street; (609) 884–8702

**E-MAIL:** Quinn@bellatlantic.net

**WEB SITE:** www.queenvictoria.com

**ROOMS:** 21, including 6 cottages; all with private bath, air-conditioning, radio, and minirefrigerator; 8 with whirlpool tub, 6 with television, 3 with gas fireplace, 2 with telephone; VCR available for rent. Wheelchair accessible. No smoking inn.

**RATES:** $85 to $280, double occupancy; includes full breakfast, afternoon tea, parking, beach towels, and passes. Additional adult or child, $20. Three and four-night minimums during busy seasons and holidays. Two-night minimum weekends. Request special quiet-season packages and midweek and second-night rates, which begin at $75, from November to March. Payment by check preferred.

**OPEN:** All year.

**FACILITIES AND ACTIVITIES:** Complimentary bicycles, use of butler's pantry. Nearby: beach 1 block, restaurants, historic tours of Cape May, bird-watching, fishing, Christmas tours, and Dickens Extravaganza.

**RECOMMENDED COUNTRY INNS® TRAVELERS' CLUB BENEFIT:** Stay one night, get second night free, Monday to Thursday, November to March.

*J*oan and Dane Wells were historic preservation advocates long before they arrived in Cape May. Joan had been executive director of the Victorian Society of America, and Dane was Main Street Manager for Philadelphia. Both were dedicated to achieving a meticulous restoration of their inn and to furthering the unique Victorian character of Cape May. Much of the town's attractiveness today is the result of their efforts.

With its picturesque turrets, bay windows, and gingerbread trim, The Queen Victoria is a superb example of Cape May's Victorian architecture. Dane and Joan began restoring it in 1980. Since then five buildings have been added to the property. They range in style from Regents Park, a charming little cottage, to The Queen's Hotel, which has rooms well suited to business travelers and where breakfast is not included in the room rate. Other buildings include Prince Albert Hall, a former Victorian home that now contains rooms with whirlpool tubs, the Carriage House, and The Queen's Cottage, which has a pretty garden in the rear.

Each building (except for the Carriage House and Regent's Park) has its own parlor or common sitting area; some have two. Each also has a parlor  stocked with coffee, tea, sodas, popcorn, and much more for guests' use. Hand-painted wallpaper embellishes the walls. When seated around the expansive tables in one of the dining rooms for breakfast or afternoon tea, guests often discuss Joan's collection of Van Briggle pottery, the silver displayed in the cabinets, or the impressive furniture.

Each guest room has antique Arts and Crafts or Mission-style furniture. There are walnut and oak headboards, brass beds, and marble-topped dressers. Handmade quilts lend a country touch.

Breakfast might include such temptations as the inn's renowned granola, fresh-baked muffins and breads, fresh fruit and juice, and an entree such as Aunt Ruth's baked eggs and cheese with savory sausage patties.

The ocean is only a block away, and guests often borrow the inn's bicycles to ride along the boardwalk. There are myriad activities at the inn throughout the year. During the first week of December, guests are invited to help decorate a variety of Christmas trees in typical Victorian styles. The Dickens Extravaganza open house and a series of musical events are also held at Christmastime.

**HOW TO GET THERE:** From the southern end of the Garden State Parkway, continue straight into town (more than 1 mile) to merge with Lafayette Street. At second stoplight, turn left onto Ocean Street. Go 3 blocks; inn is on the right.

# The Southern Mansion 🖤 📱
## (Home of the George Allen Estate)
Cape May, New Jersey 08204

**INNKEEPERS:** Shawn Kirkpatrick and Fiona McGrath; managers, Joseph Bray and Denise Cortina

**ADDRESS/TELEPHONE:** 720 Washington Street; (609) 884–7171 or (800) 381–3888; fax (609) 898–0492

**E-MAIL:** mansion@jerseycape.com

**WEB SITE:** www.southernmansion.com

**ROOMS:** 23; all with private bath, air-conditioning, telephone with dataport, radio, television, minirefrigerator, hair dryer, desk; 12 with private porch or balcony. Children over the age of 12 welcome. No smoking inn.

**RATES:** $195 to $350, Memorial Day to October; $100 to $250, October to Memorial Day, double occupancy; includes full breakfast and afternoon tea (exception: $100 rate does not include breakfast). Three-night minimum Memorial Day to October; two-night minimum October to Memorial Day.

**OPEN:** All year except Christmas Day.

**FACILITIES AND ACTIVITIES:** On two acres that include parking, gardens, concierge; beach towels, chairs, and tags provided. Nearby: excellent restaurants, historic district, ocean beaches, boardwalk.

**BUSINESS TRAVEL:** Desks, telephones with dataports, televisions in rooms; fax and copier available; meeting rooms with full audiovisual capabilities.

For more years than we like to remember, the George Allen Estate sat forlornly behind its high privet hedge becoming ever more decrepit. The magnificent 14,000-square-foot 1863 Italianate villa had been inhabited for many years by humans, dogs, cats, and assorted wild animals. A family with contracting experience came to its rescue in 1994 and spent millions restoring it to its former grandeur. It's now the showplace of Cape May.

Today the incredible inlaid floors in the dual parlors are polished to reveal the walnut, mahogany, and red tulip border, and the lustrous bird's-eye maple star in the middle of the floor gleams. Twin marble fireplaces are enhanced by massive mirrors that reach to the 14-foot ceilings, and twin crystal chandeliers hang from ceiling medallions. Along one side a marble-topped Victorian buffet holds afternoon snacks of fresh lemonade, home-made cookies, and tea. My favorite retreat, however, is on the very top of the building. From the wide central hallway, you can climb to the screened-in belvedere to drink in the fabulous view of the village with the ocean beyond.

The guest rooms are spacious and ornate; the ceilings are 13 feet high, and the smallest room is 300 square feet. Because of the rooms' size, it was possible to decorate fearlessly and with drama. One room has sapphire-blue walls; another, butterscotch. One of my favorites is Room 3, which has vermilion walls. It's furnished with an ornately carved bed and a beautiful armoire containing a sink. The bath has a shower with hand-painted tiles.

Not only has the elaborate mansion been restored, but a new wing was added to the house in a style that is so sympathetic to the original that it's hard to tell the two apart. The rooms in the new wing are as spacious as those in the original mansion, and it also contains a massive ballroom for events or meetings.

A full breakfast is served every morning. Fruit, juice, muffins, croissants, and breads are set up on the buffet in the dining room, and guests may help themselves to as much as they want. The entree is served at the table. One of our favorites is Texas French toast, a thickly sliced French bread that is dipped in a cinnamon batter before being sautéed. It is served with a fresh fruit compote—fruits that have been macerated in sugar.

**HOW TO GET THERE:** From the end of the Garden State Parkway or the Lewes Ferry, take Route 109 south into Cape May. After crossing the bridge and passing the marina, you will be on Lafayette Street. Continue on Lafayette Street through the first traffic light. Turn left at the second street, which is Jefferson. Go 2 blocks. The B&B is straight ahead on the corner of Washington Street.

# The Virginia Hotel 🖼 💲 📱
## Cape May, New Jersey 08204

**MANAGER:** Joanne Galloway; Curtis Bashaw, proprietor

**ADDRESS/TELEPHONE:** 25 Jackson Street (mailing address P.O. Box 557); (609) 884–5700 or (800) 732–4236; fax (609) 884–1236

**WEB SITE:** www.virginiahotel.com

**ROOMS:** 24; all with private bath, air-conditioning, telephone with dataport and voice mail, television, VCR, radio, desk, and robes; 3 with private porch, 2 with whirlpool tub. Smoking permitted.

**RATES:** $120 to $295 Memorial Day weekend to mid-October, $80 to $275 mid-October to Memorial Day weekend, all double occupancy; includes continental breakfast. Three-night minimum high season; two-night minimum rest of year except three-night minimum holiday weekends.

**OPEN:** All year.

**FACILITIES AND ACTIVITIES:** Restaurant: The Ebbitt Room, dinner (entrees $22 to $28), bar, lobby with piano entertainment throughout July and August and weekends the rest of the year; valet parking; room service; garden; book, periodical, and video library; beach towels, chairs, and tags provided; in historic district. Nearby: ½ block from ocean beach and boardwalk.

**BUSINESS TRAVEL:** Desk, telephone with dataport and voice mail, TV, VCR in all rooms; copy and fax service available; room service, conference room with full audiovisual capabilities.

When Curtis Bashaw purchased The Virginia Hotel in 1989, it was sheathed in asbestos siding and had been condemned. Alfred and Ellen Ebbitt, who built Cape May's first hotel in 1879, would not have recognized it. Today it's hard to believe that it had ever fallen to such a state. The set of double porches across the front incorporate elaborate gingerbread that drips with Victorian excess, and the entire hotel is wonderfully bright and appealing.

Located in the heart of Cape May's shopping district and ½ block from the beach, the Virginia Hotel is now one of the finest places to stay in Cape May. The lobby is situated up a flight of stairs from the street. It is smartly furnished and includes a fireplace and a baby grand piano where a pianist can be heard every night in July and August and on weekends the rest of the year. Shelves of books line the walls, and there's a magnificent stained-glass window in the landing. We love to sit in the wicker chairs on the veranda in summer, or on one of the enclosed garden porches any time of year, with a tall, cool glass of lemonade to read or to watch the crowds meandering by on the street below. In summer breakfast may be eaten on the veranda as well. A walled garden in back contains benches and pathways beside the lush beds of flowers.

The Ebbitt Room has earned a reputation as one of the finest restaurants in Cape May. It has charming decor in muted tones of gray-green, with huge bouquets of flowers that create secluded niches for the romantic and intimate tables. A small bar has light and contemporary furnishings enhanced by Bradbury and Bradbury wallpaper in a William Morris pattern. Chef Christopher Hubert has created a distinctive award-winning cuisine. Typical entrees include grilled Atlantic salmon with lobster mashed potatoes and sautéed Chilean sea bass in a fine herbed crust. Don't miss the warm chocolate torte with crème anglaise.

The guest rooms come in various sizes, but all are decorated in the same sophisticated style, using shades of gray-green and peach and custom-designed furniture supplemented with a smattering of antiques. The best rooms are on the second floor. The Jackson and the Virginia Rooms, as well as Room 204 have private verandas with views of the ocean. Planter boxes overflow with flowers. The tiled baths are modern and bright.

HOW TO GET THERE: From the end of the Garden State Parkway or the Lewes Ferry, take Route 109 south into Cape May. After crossing the bridge and passing the marina, you will be on Lafayette Street. Continue on Lafayette Street to the stop sign at its end. Turn left onto Jackson Street. The inn is 1½ blocks further on the left.

# The Doctors Inn at Kings Grant
## Cape May Courthouse, New Jersey 08210

INNKEEPER: Dana Suchanoff

ADDRESS/TELEPHONE: 2 North Main Street; (609) 463–9330;
fax (609) 463–9194

ROOMS: 6, including 2 suites; all with private bath, air-conditioning,
fireplace, telephone with dataport, television, radio, minirefrigerator,
coffeemaker, hair dryer; 5 with whirlpool tubs, 2 with VCR, 1 with a
steam shower, 1 with a balcony. Wheelchair accessible. No smoking inn.
Children over the age of 6 welcome.

RATES: $125 to $170, double occupancy; includes full breakfast and
afternoon refreshments. Two-night minimum May to September.

OPEN: All year.

FACILITIES AND ACTIVITIES: Bradbury's Restaurant serving lunch
(entrees $7.00 to $13.00) and dinner (entrees $20.00 to $27.00). On one
acre with parking, lovely gardens, gazebo; exercise room with bicycle, stair
stepper, Nordic Track, electronic massage table, and sauna.

BUSINESS TRAVEL: 20 percent discount, Monday to Thursday; business card
required to receive discount. Desk and telephone with dataport in room.

RECOMMENDED COUNTRY INNS® TRAVELERS' CLUB BENEFIT: Stay
two nights, get third night free, Monday to Thursday.

*T*his grand pink-stucco Italianate Victorian mansion, located in a
village 13 miles north of Cape May, was built in 1854 and restored
as an inn in 1994. It is so named because British rulers William
and Mary granted 1,000 acres (the inn continues to sit on one of these acres)
to a Doctor Cox in 1690 to thank him for his loyalty to the crown. Is it a
coincidence or destiny that from that time since, the inn has always
belonged to a doctor?

The common rooms of the inn contain elaborate Victorian decor. There
are damask drapes at the windows, crystal chandeliers hanging from ceiling
medallions, and fancy moldings. In the parlor there's a fireplace, a grand
piano, and a variety of board games. The lovely gardens include a fountain
and a gazebo.

Each of the guest rooms has a gas fireplace and ornate Victorian antique
furnishings. The Albert Elmer Wood Room, for example, has a bed with a tall
Victorian headboard and a matching marble topped Victorian dresser. The

bath has a marble floor and countertop and is fancifully painted and papered in green.

Innkeeper Dana Suchanoff is a culinary school graduate, and she makes sure the breakfasts she serves are healthful and delicious. Guests eat in the dining room, where the meal always includes freshly baked muffins and breads, cereals, juice, and fruit salad. The entree may consist of a frittata with green peppers, onions, and roasted red peppers, accompanied by home fries and English muffins. Or perhaps there will be a blueberry strata served with maple syrup and sausage.

HOW TO GET THERE: From the Garden State Parkway traveling south, take the East Mechanic exit (just past exit 10) and turn right onto East Mechanic Street. The inn is ¼ mile on the right, on the corner of East Mechanic and Main Streets.

# The Inn at Millrace Pond
Hope, New Jersey 07844

INNKEEPERS: Charlie and Cordie Puttkammer; Jeff Foster, manager

ADDRESS/TELEPHONE: Johnsonburg Road (mailing address: P.O. Box 359); (908) 459–4884 or (800) 7INNHOPE; fax (908) 459–5276

ROOMS: 17, in 3 historic buildings; all with private bath, air-conditioning, desk, and telephone with dataport; 10 with television, 5 with whirlpool tub. Three rooms wheelchair accessible. Designated no smoking rooms.

RATES: $95 to $165, double occupancy; includes continental breakfast. Two-night minimum weekends, although single Saturday nights may be booked if rooms are still available on Monday of the requested week.

OPEN: All year except Christmas Day.

FACILITIES AND ACTIVITIES: Dinner daily (entrees $19 to $25), tavern, twenty-three acres, ten-acre pond, hiking, tennis court. Nearby: shops, factory outlets, Waterloo Village (twenty minutes), Poconos (thirty minutes), golf, antiquing, canoeing, and fishing.

BUSINESS TRAVEL: Telephone and desk in room; fax and computer available; conference space, corporate rates; complete conference center.

*T*he mellowed creamy limestone walls of the old mill complex have weathered gently with time. The setting of The Inn at Millrace Pond is so peaceful, I often think how pleased the Moravians who built these buildings in 1769 would be to see how beautifully their handiwork has weathered the ages. On one fall visit we had enjoyed a game of tennis on the inn's court and then sat quietly beside the pond to relax. When we looked up, three deer were silently grazing nearby. We returned to the inn along the trail that parallels the millrace.

The mill complex is owned by Charlie and Cordie Puttkammer, who have continuously improved the property since they purchased it in 1994. They had previously lived in Washington, D.C., and in India. The original mill is now a restaurant. It includes a stream that courses down the hill from the pond, right through the lowest level of the mill. You can walk down the massive hand-hewn plank stairs in the mill and cross a bridge that spans the race. Stone walls keep the temperature crisp and cool, and the inn puts this chamber to good use as storage for its excellent wines. The giant waterwheel stands to one side. Beyond the waterwheel there's a brick-floored tavern with a massive stone walk-in fireplace. This is where the kitchen was originally located.

The formal dining room is located on the main floor of the mill. Its hand-hewn posts and beams are illuminated by Colonial-style chandeliers and candles in hurricane shades. It's a sophisticated but casual room enhanced by checked curtains and oak floors—an alluring room that complements the distinctive cuisine. We once had an entree of boneless breast of duck with cranberry mascarpone that was served with cheese polenta and a dried fruit confit. For dessert, the restaurant specializes in American comfort food such as carrot cake and an apple tart with a warm caramel sauce.

Guest rooms are located in the old mill as well as in the Millrace House (which has a wonderful enclosed stone veranda for guests to use), the restored miller's home, and Stone Cottage. The decor of the rooms in the inn includes period reproduction four-poster and canopy beds, wide-plank pine floors, and beautiful examples of stenciling. My favorite rooms, however, are the secluded and romantic ones in Stone Cottage. These have also appealed to Barbra Streisand, who stayed here while filming portions of *The Prince of Tides*. Nick Nolte and Dustin Hoffman have also been guests.

In 1997 an 1883 clapboard building was moved to the property. It has been converted into a conference center. There are computer hookups and audiovisual capabilities as well as meeting rooms.

**HOW TO GET THERE:** From I–80, take exit 12 (Blairestown/Hope). Follow Route 521 south for 1¼ miles to the blinking red light in the center of Hope. Turn left onto Route 519 and drive ²⁄₁₀ mile over the old Moravian bridge to the inn, which is on the left. There's a large parking lot behind the inn.

## *Moravian Mill*

In 1769 several families who had immigrated to America from Moravia, a country that is now part of the Czech Republic, built a series of stone buildings in western New Jersey. Recognizing that they could capture the water that flowed down the hillside from a ten-acre pond to turn a waterwheel, they crafted a mill from the distinctive local stone, placing the waterwheel and the millrace on the lowest level. Neighboring farmers would bring their grain to the mill to be ground, and while they were there, they would tether their horses in the stone barn, have them shod at the blacksmith shop, or have a wagon wheel repaired at the wheelwrights' house. It's said that when George Washington and his starving troops were wintering at Jockey Hollow near Morristown during the Revolutionary War, grain was ground here and transported to his encampment to feed his men.

Although the Moravians operated the mill for some forty years, by the 1950s its future seemed uncertain. The mill was deserted and unused, and the remaining buildings were serving as rental houses.

The quaint village of Hope, where the mill was located, is built from the same stone and in the same style as the mill. Its buildings include a general store, a church, and other buildings that supported the mill complex. Today the village and the mill complex are all listed on the National Register of Historic Places.

# The Inn at Lambertville Station
Lambertville, New Jersey 08530

**INNKEEPER:** Lisa Leventhal

**ADDRESS/TELEPHONE:** 11 Bridge Street; (609) 397–4400 or
(800) 524–1091; fax (609) 397–9744

**ROOMS:** 45, including 8 suites; all with private bath, air-conditioning,
telephone with dataport, television, and radio; suites have fireplaces and
whirlpool tubs. Wheelchair accessible. Smoking permitted but some
rooms designated nonsmoking.

**RATES:** $95 to $235, double occupancy; includes continental breakfast.
Two-night minimum holiday weekends.

**OPEN:** All year.

**FACILITIES AND ACTIVITIES:** Lambertville Station restaurant in
restored train station serving lunch (entrees $7.00 to $9.00) and dinner
(entrees $11 to $22); lobby honor bar, parking. Nearby: New Hope,
Pennsylvania, Bucks County Playhouse; hiking and bicycling trail paral-
leling Delaware River.

**BUSINESS TRAVEL:** Desk and telephone with dataport in all rooms; corporate rate; fax, copier, and typing service available. Conference room
with slide projector, television, and VCR.

The Inn at Lambertville Station was built in 1983, and, since it parallels the Delaware River, several of the rooms have lovely river
views. Adapting a clever decorating theme, each of the guest rooms
is named for an exotic or foreign destination. A hybrid of sorts, it's too big to
be classified as a typical country inn. It's the friendly staff, the interesting
lobby, and the use of authentic antiques that made it a candidate for the
pages of this book.

The three-story lobby is small but spectacular. Raised above the entrance,
it has a gas fireplace, an impressive honor bar, and a television—all comple-
mented by lovely antique tables and chairs. Excellent oil portraits climb the
walls to the cathedral ceiling. Through French doors there's a deck overlooking Swan Creek.

The inn is adjacent to a canal with a walking trail. One morning we rose
early to take a walk along the creek, where we stood mesmerized as we
watched the water tumble over a waterfall.

The guest rooms are disappointing. Although they are spacious and offer
promise, they are currently exhibiting weary signs that include stained car-

pets and damaged furniture. The baths, however, are clean and bright, although they have a chain hotel appeal. A recent change of management, however, leads us to hope improvements are coming soon.

Lambertville Station restaurant, on the other hand, is absolutely top-notch. The charming old building has been beautifully restored, and there are tables on multiple levels from which to choose. The gray stone walls and stained-oak wainscoting provide a lovely backdrop. We started our meal with a basket of bread that included an unusual but excellent coconut bread, which was followed by crispy crab cakes in a remoulade sauce served with garlic-flavored red bliss mashed potatoes. The meal ended with a cold zabiglione with fresh strawberries.

**HOW TO GET THERE:** From I–95 take New Jersey exit 1; travel north on Route 29 for 10 miles to Lambertville. Turn left onto Route 179 toward New Hope. The inn is on the left in 4 blocks. Enter the parking lot by driving past Lambertville Station restaurant.

# Lambertville House
## Lambertville, New Jersey 08530

**INNKEEPERS:** George and Jan Michael; Brad Michael, manager

**ADDRESS/TELEPHONE:** 32 Bridge Street; (609) 397–0200 or (888) 867–8859; fax (609) 397–0511

**E-MAIL:** innkeeper@lambertvillehouse.com

**WEB SITE:** www.lambertvillehouse.com

**ROOMS:** 26, including 8 suites; all with private bath, air-conditioning, telephone with dataport, television, desk, radio, hair dryer, robes, and whirlpool tub; 22 with gas fireplace, iron, and ironing board; 9 with patio or balcony. Wheelchair accessible. Not recommended for children under 12. No smoking inn.

**RATES:** $180 to $399, double occupancy; includes continental breakfast. Two-night minimum some holiday and special-event weekends.

**OPEN:** All year.

**FACILITIES AND ACTIVITIES:** Courtyard with fountain, garden, parking; discounted rate at local health club. Nearby: on Main Street of Lambertville near excellent restaurants, antiques and gift shops, art galleries.

**BUSINESS TRAVEL:** Desk, telephone with dataport, and TV in each room; four corporate meeting rooms with audiovisual capabilities.

**RECOMMENDED COUNTRY INNS® TRAVELERS' CLUB BENEFIT:** 10 percent discount, Monday to Thursday.

For years we used to watch in dismay as the forsaken but historic old Lambertville House sank deeper and deeper into its depression. Built in 1812 it served originally as a stagecoach stop and, over the years, hosted President Andrew Johnson and General Ulysses S. Grant. Purchased in 1996 by a local custom home builder and his wife, George and Jan Michael, the stone and stucco building has finally been lovingly and elegantly restored. Although it took two years to complete the restoration, it's now listed on the National Register of Historic Places. Were you to enter from Bridge Street, you would pass along a corridor of stone walls and elegant antiques shops. In a display case are several artifacts found during the restoration of the building.

In the lobby the original stone walls have a rustic texture that contrasts with the mustard-colored sponged walls. A masculine and intimate common room has a wine-colored rug, a leather sofa, and tapestry wing chairs before

a gas fireplace. In back there's a covered slate porch furnished with iron furniture. We would later sip a glass of complimentary wine here, while a spring shower washed the brick courtyard.

Although the guest rooms are new, they have an old-world ambience created through the use of antique and reproduction furnishings and fabrics. You can't go wrong. Every room has an armoire holding a television and walls decorated with artwork by local artists; most have gas fireplaces. All the baths have granite counters and marble or tile floors, and each has a whirlpool tub; the suites all have two-person whirlpools. My favorite room is the Spire Suite, which has a two-person whirlpool on a private screened porch that also serves as a sitting room. There's a fabulous bath with a two-person glass shower and a pedestal sink. In the bedroom a bed with a high headboard and footboard enjoys the warmth of a fire in an original stone hearth, and built-in bookshelves hold a variety of tomes.

On the lower level a charming breakfast room has a tile floor and another working gas fireplace. A continental breakfast of cereal, fresh-baked muffins, croissants, fruit, and juice is served during the week. On weekends this is supplemented by a hot dish such as a quiche.

**HOW TO GET THERE:** From I–95 take New Jersey exit 1 and travel north on Route 29 for 10 miles to Lambertville. Turn left onto Route 179 toward New Hope. The inn is on the right in 2½ blocks.

# Chestnut Hill on the Delaware
## Milford, New Jersey 08848

**INNKEEPERS:** Linda and Rob Castagna

**ADDRESS/TELEPHONE:** 63 Church Street (mailing address: P.O. Box N); (908) 995–4200 or (908) 995–9761; fax (908) 995–0608

**E-MAIL:** chhillinn@aol.com

**ROOMS:** 6, including 1 suite and 1 cottage; 4 with private bath; all with air-conditioning; 5 with telephone, 4 with television, 1 with Jacuzzi; cottage with fireplace. Wheelchair accessible. No smoking inn. Children over the age of 12 welcome.

**RATES:** $95 to $150, double occupancy; includes full breakfast. Two-night minimum weekends. No credit cards.

**OPEN:** All year.

**FACILITIES AND ACTIVITIES:** 40-foot deck on banks of Delaware River, a river walk, picnic area, cushions, umbrellas, benches, dock, gardens, parking. Nearby: restaurants, Hunterdon Hills Playhouse, Bucks County Playhouse, tennis, rafting and tubing on the Delaware River.

*T*he inn is a Victorian gem. Rob and Linda painted it in shades of green ranging from seafoam to forest. I'll never forget the time I arrived to find Ron precariously hanging from a ladder as he painted the elaborate grapevine wrought iron that marches across the porch and down the columns. It creates a pretty frame for those of us who love to spend the afternoon rocking on the porch and watching the lazy river roll by.

You'll be greeted in the entrance hall by a mannequin dressed in nineteenth-century splendor graciously welcoming guests to her home. "May I show you to my parlor?" she seems to say. The tiny parlor to the right of the hall is intimate and charming with wonderful examples of antique Victorian furniture and silver.

In the Eastlake Parlor, on the opposite side of the hall, shelves of an old apothecary cabinet are filled with Linda's unique gift items (don't miss this!), and there's also an organ, a piano, a fancifully carved fireplace mantel, and another gentlelady mannequin. This one is dressed in the clothes worn by the actual lady of the house around the turn of the century.

The guest rooms are charmingly decorated. Teddy's Place, on the third floor, includes more than 150 teddy bears who gladly share their room with their visitors. There's a brass bed and a bath with a sink in a Victorian dresser. The utterly romantic Country Cottage, an adorable cottage next door to the main house, has a private deck and a fireplace.

Rob and Linda's hands-on attention to their guests' comfort is evident throughout the inn. At night when guests return from dinner, they find a personalized good-night note waiting for them on the stair newel, as well as chocolates and warm cookies in their room. For guests who want to learn to make the beautiful notecards that Linda uses, she gladly offers before-departure lessons.

Breakfasts are served in formal style with fine china, silver, and linen in the ornately Victorian dining room. They include fresh seasonal fruit, delicious sausage and baked German apple pancake, and a variety of omelettes and pastries. It's a chance to sit back and savor.

HOW TO GET THERE: From I-78 take exit 11 (Pattenburg). Follow Route 614 for 8 miles south to Spring Hill. Turn left onto Route 519 and travel 3 miles south to Milford. In Milford turn right onto Bridge Street and then right onto Church Street. At the end of Church Street, turn left; the inn's parking lot is straight ahead.

# La Maison—A B&B and Gallery
## Spring Lake, New Jersey 07762

**INNKEEPERS:** Barbara Furdyna and Peter Oliver; Paula Jordan, manager

**ADDRESS/TELEPHONE:** 404 Jersey Avenue; (732) 449–0969 or
(800) 276–2088; fax (732) 449–4860

**WEB SITE:** www.bbianj.com/lamaison

**ROOMS:** 8, including 2 suites and 1 cottage; all with private bath, air-conditioning, telephone, and television; 1 with Jacuzzi. Cottage with fireplace and private garden. Pets and children allowed in cottage only. Wheelchair accessible. No smoking inn.

**RATES:** $150 to $350, double occupancy; includes full breakfast, wine and hors d'oeuvres in afternoon, and beach and tennis passes. Two-night minimum weekends; three -night minimum weekends July and August.

**OPEN:** All year except January.

**FACILITIES AND ACTIVITIES:** Bicycles available. Nearby: ocean beach 4 blocks, jogging, walking, croquet, health club membership.

*A*s we drove along Ocean Avenue, the tangy smell of salt air reminded us of childhood afternoons spent romping in the surf. Beaches are still my favorite destinations, and this white-sand beach stretches for 2 miles. Spring Lake's boardwalk was alive on this sunny day with bicyclists, joggers, in-line skaters, and walkers.

Spring Lake is a peaceful and charming seaside Victorian village unaffected by the fast-food emporiums and honky-tonk dives that characterize some other sections of the New Jersey shore. Stately mansions with broad lawns line the well-kept streets, and the village has an impressive collection of antiques shops, decorator showrooms, and cafes.

La Maison, on a quiet side street, is perfectly suited to this fine-arts community. On entering the unassuming building, we found ourselves in a captivating French country home and art gallery. Colorful watercolors and oils fill the walls and climb the stairs, and all are for sale. Barbara described many of the local scenes in the paintings, and she knows the artists (one is Peter, her husband and partner). It's worth coming here to purchase the art even if you can't spend the night.

Barbara Furdyna is a gracious and engaging innkeeper who adores France, so wherever you look you can imagine yourself in a little tucked-away corner of France. Barbara was a French major in college and studied at the Sorbonne. The inn is romantic and seductive. We relaxed in the parlor with its gorgeous Persian rug and cozy fireplace, sipping sherry and munching hors d'oeuvres that had been laid out on the antique desk.

You'll find light and airy guest rooms with sleigh beds, carved armoires, iron beds, and ornate French iron chairs. The baths are spacious. I especially like the King Juan Carlos Room, with its sexy bath that contains a two-person whirlpool and a skylight in the cathedral ceiling, through which we could view a full moon. A wonderful little cottage in back has a gas fireplace and its own private garden. Children and small pets are welcome to accompany their parents here.

Breakfast is served *en famille* in the formal dining room or on the covered porch in summer. We started with mimosas, and then Barbara brought a tray of freshly baked muffins and breads, followed by Belgian waffles with whipped cream.

Barbara offers complimentary beach, pool, and tennis passes to her guests (chairs and umbrellas, too) as well as membership in the Atlantic Club, a full-service health club. She also has bicycles for her guests to use.

HOW TO GET THERE: From the Garden State Parkway, take exit 98 onto Route 34 south. Follow Route 34 to the traffic circle and then take Route 524 east to Spring Lake. After crossing the railroad tracks, take the second right onto Fourth Avenue. Proceed for 5 blocks and turn right onto Jersey Avenue. La Maison is the second house on the right.

# Normandy Inn ▪

## Spring Lake, New Jersey 07762

**INNKEEPERS:** Michael and Susan Ingino; Jeri Robertson, manager

**ADDRESS/TELEPHONE:** 21 Tuttle Avenue; (908) 449–7172 or (800) 449–1888; fax (908) 449–1070

**E-MAIL:** normandy@bellatlantic.net

**WEB SITE:** www.normandyinn.com

**ROOMS:** 19, including 2 suites; all with private bath, air-conditioning, telephone, television, and radio; 6 with fireplace, 2 with Jacuzzi. No smoking inn.

**RATES:** $136 to $329; children under 10, $10, over 10, $20; includes full breakfast. Three-night minimum July and August if stay includes Saturday, two nights weekends most other months. Twenty percent less off-season.

**OPEN:** All year.

**FACILITIES AND ACTIVITIES:** Bicycles. Nearby: restaurants, ocean beach 1 block away, shopping, Garden State Art Center.

**RECOMMENDED COUNTRY INNS® TRAVELERS' CLUB BENEFIT:** 20 percent discount, midweek, October to April, two-night minimum, subject to availability. Advance reservations required.

*S*pring Lake is one of those discoveries you can't wait to share with best friends. Its uncluttered boardwalk, beautiful beach, and lovely residential tree-lined streets are welcome and inviting.

Along one of the quiet side streets, the Normandy Inn stands out. This is a true Victorian "painted lady," with its gables and turrets, arched windows, and multiple porches painted in shades of olive, gold, jade, terra cotta, and burgundy. The wide front veranda is filled with white wicker tables and chairs. Inside, innkeepers Michael and Susan Ingino refer to the fabulous furniture as Rococo Revival or Renaissance Revival style—suffice it to say, it's very ornate and lovely.

The guest rooms are furnished with antiques as well. You will find a full tester empire-style bed in Room 101, and in other rooms there are brass beds, iron beds, and carved walnut beds with high headboards. Work has been under way for several years to upgrade the baths; two now have whirlpool tubs, and six have marble floors and new fixtures. Gas fireplaces were recently added to four more rooms.

Breakfast is served in a room so large that it often seems more like a camp dining room than an inn breakfast room. Guests are seated at individual tables, where they can order a full breakfast from a menu. It will include eggs prepared any way you like them, pancakes, or French toast; meat, fruit, juice, cereal, and coffee, tea, or chocolate.

**HOW TO GET THERE:** From Garden State Parkway take exit 98 and follow Route 34 to first circle. Go ¾ of way around the circle to Route 524 east; follow this to ocean. Turn right onto Ocean Avenue, go right onto Tuttle, and ½ block to the inn.

# Sea Crest by the Sea
## Spring Lake, New Jersey 07762

**INNKEEPERS:** John and Carol Kirby

**ADDRESS/TELEPHONE:** 19 Tuttle Avenue; (732) 449–9031 or (800) 803–9031; fax (732) 974–0403

**E-MAIL:** jk@seacrestbythesea.com

**WEB SITE:** www.seacrestbythesea.com

**ROOMS:** 12, including 2 suites; all with private bath, air-conditioning, telephone with dataport, television, and VCR; 8 with fireplace, 3 with whirlpool tub. No smoking inn. Not appropriate for children.

**RATES:** $155 to $255, double occupancy; includes full breakfast and afternoon tea. Two-night minimum weekends October to May; three-night minimum June to September and all holidays.

**OPEN:** All year.

**FACILITIES AND ACTIVITIES:** Nearby: ocean beach 1 block, bicycling, walking along boardwalk, band concerts on lawn by lake in summer, plays at Community House.

*L*et there be no doubt. This is an inn designed for adults who wish to escape to a romantic fantasy world for a few days. The lovely Victorian seaside town itself offers an authentic backdrop for a weekend of make-believe. It has remained virtually the same since it became a fashionable resort in the late 1800s.

Sea Crest by the Sea is a typical example. Its broad front veranda offers a bevy of wicker chairs in which to sit to smell the tangy salt breezes. Once you enter the ornate front door, however, you are totally immersed in a Victorian spell. If you arrive at the proper hour, Carol and John may be offering afternoon tea—a sampling of freshly baked cookies and cakes, washed down with tea in antique china teacups. You will sit either in the front parlor, which has a fireplace, or in one of the dining rooms.

You might choose the guest room with a Casablanca theme. If so, you will enter the room through a bead curtain and perhaps try on the trench coat hanging on the back of the door. You will certainly snuggle into the rattan bed sometime during your stay to watch "the" video on your room's VCR. Or maybe you've opted for Papillion, the butterfly room, located in a garret on the top floor and offering a fireplace and two dormer windows with views of the ocean. You might drift off to sleep in the iron bed, while visualizing yourself effortlessly floating through space with the bright butterflies that are stenciled on the walls.

A plentiful breakfast will be shared at two common tables with the other guests. In addition to the usual array of cereals, fruit, and juices, Carol might fix her feather-light buttermilk scones and a sesame seed frittata with watercress.

HOW TO GET THERE: From the Garden State Parkway, take exit 98 onto Route 34 south. Follow Route 34 to the traffic circle and then take Route 524 east to Ocean Avenue. Turn right. Go 1 block, and turn right onto Tuttle Avenue. The inn is on the left in 1 block.

# The Whistling Swan Inn
## Stanhope, New Jersey 07874

**INNKEEPERS:** Paula Williams and Joe Mulay

**ADDRESS/TELEPHONE:** 110 Main Street; (973) 347–6369; fax (973) 347–3391

**E-MAIL:** wswan@worldnet.att.net

**WEB SITE:** bbianj.com/whistlingswan

**ROOMS:** 10, including 1 suite; all with private bath, telephone with dataport, radio, television, and air-conditioning. No smoking inn. Children over the age of 12 welcome.

**RATES:** $95 to $170, double occupancy; includes full breakfast. Two-night minimum stay on holidays, special event weekends, and all fall weekends.

**OPEN:** All year.

**FACILITIES AND ACTIVITIES:** Nearby: Waterloo Village (open Tuesday through Sunday from mid-April through December, except for holidays), golf courses, USGA Golf House Museum, Mining Museum. Horseback riding, hiking, bicycling, cross-country skiing. Lake Hopatcong, Musconetcong River, Delaware Water Gap. Flea markets and antiquing.

**BUSINESS TRAVEL:** Phone, photocopier, television, fax, and secretarial services available; desk in 8 rooms; dataport in all rooms; corporate rates.

When the Morris Canal was in operation, offering a water route for barges journeying between the Delaware and the Hudson Rivers, Stanhope was a bustling boomtown. During this period, grand homes were built for the prosperous townsfolk. The gracious Queen Anne Victorian that Joe and Paula Muloy purchased in 1985 for their inn was built in 1905. The rich tiger-oak columns, floors, fretwork, and fireplace mantels are fabulous, as is the beautiful stained glass. Many of the lovely antiques in the common rooms came from the home of Paula's grandmother.

The guest rooms reflect the same elegant Victorian ambience as the common rooms. Distinguishing features in each room are the antique working radios that Joe collects and the beautiful afghans that Joe's mother made. The rooms are named for nearby attractions. Walnut Valley has an iron bed and a rosebud motif, Harmony has an iron canopy bed and a wicker chaise lounge. Although each of the rooms has a private bath, most have showers. But for those who like to take a leisurely bath, perhaps *à deux,* the home's original bath has been turned into a Victorian-style spa. Twin claw-foot tubs sit side by side, providing a romantic and memorable way to bathe.

A full breakfast is served every morning in the dining room. Paula may start the meal with a baked French toast or a garden-pie egg dish, as well as warm muffins or fruit bread, and it might end with fresh local strawberries served with crème brûlée or a cold peach fruit soup.

**HOW TO GET THERE:** From I–80 take exit 25 (eastbound) or 27B (westbound), follow Route 206 until it becomes Route 183. At traffic circle go ⅔ way around toward Netcong. At Hess Gas Station (located on right) turn left onto Main Street. Follow Main Street to Number 110.

# The Stockton Inn

Stockton, New Jersey 08559

**INNKEEPER:** Kathryn Vogt; Robin Hannan and Jack Boehlert, managers

**ADDRESS/TELEPHONE:** 1 Main Street (mailing address: P.O. Box C); (609) 397–1250; fax (609) 397–8948

**ROOMS:** 11, including 8 suites; all with private bath, air-conditioning, telephone, radio, coffeemaker, television, 8 with fireplace, 5 with mini-refrigerator. Smoking permitted.

**RATES:** $95 to $170, double occupancy; includes continental breakfast. Two-night minimum if stay includes a Saturday night.

**OPEN:** All year.

**FACILITIES AND ACTIVITIES:** Dining room open for lunch (entrees $6.50 to $13.95), dinner (entrees $16.95 to $23.95), and Sunday brunch. Nearby: Delaware Canal towpath ¼ mile, Mercer Museum, James Michener Art Center, art galleries, antiques shops.

The impulse is always there. I feel like bursting into a verse of "There's a Small Hotel with a Wishing Well" whenever I visit The Stockton Inn and see the little stone wishing well in the meandering courtyard garden. But then, this is the inn that the song was written about. Lorenz Hart often visited the inn and he wrote the song in 1936 for *On Your Toes*. It was later reprised for *Pal Joey*.

It was in the 1930s also that artist Kurt Wiese (who had illustrated the original *Bambi* book) began painting the colonial murals of Bucks and Hunterdon County sites that line the walls of three of the dining rooms. R. A. D. Miller later added more wall paintings in exchange for food and lodging. Our favorite has always been Toby's room, the original brick-floored tavern with its fireplace and romantic ambience.

The inn, built in 1710 from locally quarried stone, was originally a private residence. Through the years it has witnessed numerous historical events. George Washington used the nearby ferry to help move supplies and troops across the Delaware during the Revolution, and a tavern opened in the building in 1832, when the D & R Canal became a popular waterway. In the 1940s, 1950s, and 1960s, band leader Paul Whiteman closed his radio and television shows by announcing he was on his way to "Ma

Colligan's" for dinner, and for many years it was a retreat for famous writers and artists. (For some sixty years the inn was known as Colligan's Inn.)

Now the inn has regained its former luster. It includes guest rooms in the original stone structure as well as in three other historic buildings. The spacious guest rooms are especially well suited to business travelers. They feature period reproduction furniture, modern baths, stereos, coffeemakers, telephones, and televisions. Most have fireplaces, separate sitting areas, draped beds, and refrigerators.

Guests dining at the inn can opt for one of six romantic rooms, but the favorites are the mural rooms, especially on cold winter days, when a fire glows in the stone fireplaces and candles softly illuminate the paintings.

During the summer, when the outside terraces are open, we love to sit beside one of the waterfalls or near the pond. The Garden Bar has a dance floor; a combo or pianist plays on weekend nights.

**HOW TO GET THERE:** From New York take the New Jersey Turnpike south to exit 14 and follow I–78 west to exit 29. Follow I–287 south to Route 202 south and take the second Lambertville exit onto Route 29, traveling north to Stockton. The inn is in the center of the village.

# The Woolverton Inn
## Stockton, New Jersey 08559

**INNKEEPERS:** Elizabeth and Michael Palmer

**ADDRESS/TELEPHONE:** 6 Woolverton Road; (609) 397–0802 or (888) AN–INN–4U; fax (609) 397–4936

**E-MAIL:** woolbandb@aol.com

**WEB SITE:** woolvertonbnb.com

**ROOMS:** 10, including 2 suites; all with private bath and air-conditioning; 3 with fireplace, 2 with Jacuzzi. No smoking inn. Wheelchair accessible. Children over the age of 12 welcome.

**RATES:** $90 to $210, double occupancy, includes full breakfast and afternoon refreshments. Two-night minimum weekends; three-night minimum holiday weekends.

**OPEN:** All year.

**FACILITIES AND ACTIVITIES:** Located on ten acres with croquet lawn, hiking trails, and horseshoes pit on property. Nearby: Delaware River towpath and park ½ mile, canoeing, rafting, historical sites, boutiques, antiques shops.

**BUSINESS TRAVEL:** Fax and telephone available, early breakfast and late check-in, meeting room and services.

**RECOMMENDED COUNTRY INNS® TRAVELERS' CLUB BENEFIT:** Stay two nights, get third night free, Monday to Thursday.

*T*n the 1980s The Woolverton Inn was my special secret retreat. I would come on summer afternoons, to sit either on the upstairs porch or on the flagstone veranda, and write. In the evening after dinner, I would play the piano or complete a jigsaw puzzle into the wee hours of the morning. But then the innkeeper moved away and it just wasn't the same.

Therefore, it was with a keen sense of hope that I visited The Woolverton Inn again in late 1994, when I learned that it had been purchased by Elizabeth and Michael Palmer, an enthusiastic couple who had great plans for the majestic, 1792 stone manor house. By early 1996 the renovations were complete, and I found that this magnificent manor house once again met—and exceeded—my expectations. Private baths have been added to every guest room, and two rooms even have two-person Jacuzzis. There are canopy beds, lush fabrics, fireplaces in two rooms, and walls charmingly handpainted with flowers or pastoral scenes. The guest rooms are named for people who have had a connection to the house. My favorite is Amelia's Garden, which has a

olive Metcalf

four-poster cherry bed with a fishnet canopy, a pretty sitting room, and an elegant bath with pink walls and a lovely walnut dresser outfitted with a sink.

Downstairs, in the living room, the piano remains in the corner, and the game table by the window is just waiting for a couple to put a jigsaw puzzle together. The antique furniture is elegantly upholstered, oil paintings embellish the walls, and a fire glows in the hearth in cool weather. On the wicker-filled side porch, guests relax with a book and enjoy the gardens, perhaps while enjoying tea, coffee, or lemonade with cookies, cheese, and fruit, which are offered every afternoon.

A full gourmet breakfast is served in the formal dining room. Elizabeth might prepare a baked apple or poached pear for the fruit course and perhaps an entree of blueberry johnnycakes or creamy scrambled eggs with asparagus and chives.

The inn is located on ten acres. Sheep graze in a meadow. There are a stone spring house, a picturesque barn that may one day be restored, and a carriage house with two guest rooms. Hiking trails meander about, and there's a croquet lawn and a horseshoes pit. For those of us who love country inns with a deep-felt passion, we can add another to our collection of favorites.

**HOW TO GET THERE:** From New York take the New Jersey Turnpike south to exit 14 and follow I–78 west to exit 29. Follow I–287 south to Route 202 south and take the second Lambertville exit onto Route 20, traveling north to Stockton. Travel through the village to the fork. Veer right onto Route 523 and go for ²/₁₀ mile. Turn left onto Woolverton Road. The inn is reached along the second driveway on the right.

# Select List of Other Inns in New Jersey

## Bay Head Gables Bed & Breakfast

200 Main Avenue
Bay Head, NJ 08742
(800) 984–9536 or (732) 899–9844

*11 rooms; all with private bath; in 1914 shingle-style house.*

## Conover's Bay Head Inn

646 Main Avenue
Bay Head, NJ 08742
(800) 956–9099 or (732) 892–4664

*12 rooms; all with private bath; in well-known B&B.*

## Fairthorne Bed & Breakfast

111 Ocean Street
Cape May, NJ 08204
(800) 438–8742 or (609) 884–8791

*6 rooms; all with private bath; in 1892 whaling captain's Colonial Revival–style house.*

## Hotel Macomber

727 Beach Avenue
Cape May, NJ 08204
(609) 884–3020

*33 rooms; some with private bath; in 1911 oceanfront hotel that is undergoing restoration.*

## The Humphrey Hughes House

29 Ocean Street
Cape May, NJ 08204
(800) 582–3634 or (609) 884–4428

*11 rooms; all with private bath; in home that once belonged to a Cape May founder.*

## Inn at 22 Jackson

22 Jackson Street
Cape May, NJ 08204
(800) 452–8177 or (609) 884–2226

*5 rooms; all with private bath; in whimsical and romantic small B&B.*

## Henry Ludlam Inn

1336 Route 47
Dennisville, NJ 08270
(609) 861–5847

*5 rooms; all with private bath; in early nineteenth-century farmhouse.*

## Chimney Hill Farm

207 Goat Hill Road
Lambertville, NJ 08530
(609) 397–1516

*8 rooms; all with private bath; in elegant stone manor house.*

## Inn at Sugar Hill

5704 Mays Landing-Somers Point Road
Mays Landing, NJ 08330
(609) 625–2226

*6 rooms; most with private bath and some with view of Great Egg Harbor; restaurant.*

## The Wooden Duck

140 Goodale Road
Newton, NJ 07860
(973) 300–0395

*5 rooms; all with private bath; in charming B&B in rural setting in northern New Jersey.*

## Northwood Inn

401 Wesley Avenue
Ocean City, NJ 08226
(609) 399–6071

*8 rooms; all with private bath; in 1894 Queen Anne Victorian.*

## Castle by the Sea

701 Ocean Avenue
Ocean City, NJ 08226
(800) 622–4894

*9 rooms; all with private bath; in elaborate gingerbread Victorian.*

## Ocean Plaza

18 Ocean Pathway
Ocean Grove, NJ 07756
(888) 891–9442 or (732) 774–6552

*18 rooms; all with private bath; in recently restored former boarding house; close to ocean.*

## Hollycroft Inn

506 North Boulevard
South Belmer, NJ 07762
(800) 679–2254 or (732) 681–2254

*8 rooms; all with private bath; in unusual stone-and-log Adirondack-style lodge at the beach.*

## Holly Thorn House

141 Readington Road
Whitehouse Station, NJ 08889
(908) 534-1616

*5 rooms; all with private bath; in former barn converted to elegant B&B.*

# New York

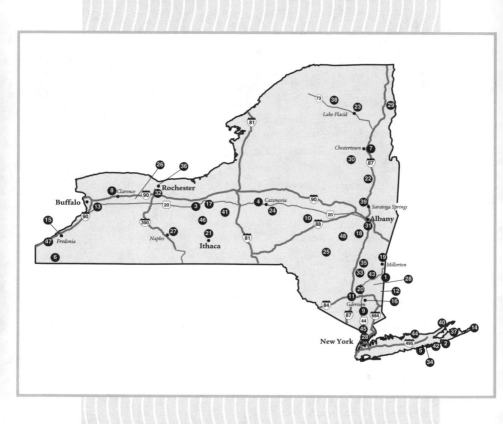

# New York

*Numbers on map refer to towns numbered below.*

1. Amenia, Troutbeck . . . . . . . . . . . . . . . . . . . . . . . . . . . . . . . . . . . . . . . 105
2. Bridgehampton, Bridgehampton Inn* . . . . . . . . . . . . . . . . . . . . . 108
3. Canandaigua,
   Acorn Inn . . . . . . . . . . . . . . . . . . . . . . . . . . . . . . . . . . . . . . . . . . . . . 109
   Morgan-Samuels B&B Inn. . . . . . . . . . . . . . . . . . . . . . . . . . . . . . . 111
4. Cazenovia,
   The Brewster Inn . . . . . . . . . . . . . . . . . . . . . . . . . . . . . . . . . . . . . . 113
   Lincklaen House . . . . . . . . . . . . . . . . . . . . . . . . . . . . . . . . . . . . . . . 115
5. Center Moriches, The Lindenmere Estate B&B* . . . . . . . . . . . . . . 116
6. Chautauqua, The Maple Inn . . . . . . . . . . . . . . . . . . . . . . . . . . . . . 119
7. Chestertown, The Friends Lake Inn . . . . . . . . . . . . . . . . . . . . . . . 121
8. Clarence, Asa Ransom House* . . . . . . . . . . . . . . . . . . . . . . . . . . . . 123
9. Cold Spring, Plumbush Inn. . . . . . . . . . . . . . . . . . . . . . . . . . . . . . . 125
10. Cooperstown, The Cooper Inn* . . . . . . . . . . . . . . . . . . . . . . . . . . 126
11. Cornwall, Cromwell Manor Inn* . . . . . . . . . . . . . . . . . . . . . . . . . 128
12. Dover Plains, Old Drovers Inn* . . . . . . . . . . . . . . . . . . . . . . . . . . 130
13. East Aurora, The Roycroft Inn* . . . . . . . . . . . . . . . . . . . . . . . . . . 133
14. East Hampton,
    East Hampton Point Cottages . . . . . . . . . . . . . . . . . . . . . . . . . . 136
    The Hedges Inn . . . . . . . . . . . . . . . . . . . . . . . . . . . . . . . . . . . . . . . 138
    The Huntting Inn . . . . . . . . . . . . . . . . . . . . . . . . . . . . . . . . . . . . . 139
    J. Harper Poor Cottage* . . . . . . . . . . . . . . . . . . . . . . . . . . . . . . . . 141
    The Maidstone Arms* . . . . . . . . . . . . . . . . . . . . . . . . . . . . . . . . . 143
    1770 House. . . . . . . . . . . . . . . . . . . . . . . . . . . . . . . . . . . . . . . . . . . 145
15. Fredonia, The White Inn . . . . . . . . . . . . . . . . . . . . . . . . . . . . . . . . 146
16. Garrison, The Bird & Bottle Inn . . . . . . . . . . . . . . . . . . . . . . . . . . 149
17. Geneva,
    Belhurst Castle & White Springs Manor. . . . . . . . . . . . . . . . . . . 151
    Geneva on the Lake Resort . . . . . . . . . . . . . . . . . . . . . . . . . . . . . 153
18. Greenville, Greenville Arms 1889 Inn . . . . . . . . . . . . . . . . . . . . . 155
19. Hillsdale, Aubergine . . . . . . . . . . . . . . . . . . . . . . . . . . . . . . . . . . . . 157
20. Hopewell Junction, Le Chambord . . . . . . . . . . . . . . . . . . . . . . . . . 158
21. Ithaca,
    Buttermilk Falls Bed & Breakfast. . . . . . . . . . . . . . . . . . . . . . . . . 159
    Hanshaw House Bed & Breakfast. . . . . . . . . . . . . . . . . . . . . . . . . 161
    Rose Inn" . . . . . . . . . . . . . . . . . . . . . . . . . . . . . . . . . . . . . . . . . . . . . 163
22. Lake Luzerne, The Lamplight Inn Bed and Breakfast. . . . . . . . . 166
23. Lake Placid, Lake Placid Lodge* . . . . . . . . . . . . . . . . . . . . . . . . . . 168

*A Top Pick Inn*

24. Leonardsville, The Horned Dorset Inn . . . . . . . . . . . . . . . . . . . . . 171

25. Lew Beach, Beaverkill Valley Inn. . . . . . . . . . . . . . . . . . . . . . . . . 172

26. Mumford, Genesee Country Inn. . . . . . . . . . . . . . . . . . . . . . . . . . 174

27. Naples, The Vagabond Inn. . . . . . . . . . . . . . . . . . . . . . . . . . . . . . 176

28. New York City,
    Bed and Breakfast on the Park . . . . . . . . . . . . . . . . . . . . . . 178
    The Inn at Irving Place* . . . . . . . . . . . . . . . . . . . . . . . . . . . . 179
    Inn New York City. . . . . . . . . . . . . . . . . . . . . . . . . . . . . . . . 181
    Le Refuge . . . . . . . . . . . . . . . . . . . . . . . . . . . . . . . . . . . . . . 183

29. North Hudson, Elk Lake Lodge . . . . . . . . . . . . . . . . . . . . . . . . . 185

30. North River, Highwinds Inn . . . . . . . . . . . . . . . . . . . . . . . . . . . 187

31. Old Chatham, Old Chatham Sheepherding Company Inn* . . . . 189

32. Pittsford, Oliver Loud's Inn* . . . . . . . . . . . . . . . . . . . . . . . . . . . 193

33. Poughkeepsie, Inn at the Falls. . . . . . . . . . . . . . . . . . . . . . . . . . 195

34. Quogue, The Inn at Quogue . . . . . . . . . . . . . . . . . . . . . . . . . . . 196

35. Rhinebeck,
    Beekman Arms. . . . . . . . . . . . . . . . . . . . . . . . . . . . . . . . . . . 198
    Belvedere Mansion* . . . . . . . . . . . . . . . . . . . . . . . . . . . . . . 200

36. Rochester, 428 Mt. Vernon—A B&B Inn . . . . . . . . . . . . . . . . 202

37. Sag Harbor, American Hotel . . . . . . . . . . . . . . . . . . . . . . . . . . . 204

38. Saranac Lake, The Point* . . . . . . . . . . . . . . . . . . . . . . . . . . . . . 205

39. Saratoga Springs,
    Adelphi Hotel. . . . . . . . . . . . . . . . . . . . . . . . . . . . . . . . . . . 207
    Batcheller Mansion Inn* . . . . . . . . . . . . . . . . . . . . . . . . . . . 209
    Union Gables Bed & Breakfast . . . . . . . . . . . . . . . . . . . . . . 211

40. Shelter Island,
    Chequit Inn . . . . . . . . . . . . . . . . . . . . . . . . . . . . . . . . . . . . 213
    Olde Country Inn . . . . . . . . . . . . . . . . . . . . . . . . . . . . . . . . 215
    The Ram's Head Inn. . . . . . . . . . . . . . . . . . . . . . . . . . . . . . 216

41. Skaneateles,
    Hobbit Hollow Farm* . . . . . . . . . . . . . . . . . . . . . . . . . . . . 218
    Sherwood Inn. . . . . . . . . . . . . . . . . . . . . . . . . . . . . . . . . . . 220

42. Southampton, The 1708 House* . . . . . . . . . . . . . . . . . . . . . . . 221

43. Stanfordville, Lakehouse Inn . . . On Golden Pond* . . . . . . . . . . 224

44. Stony Brook, Three Village Inn. . . . . . . . . . . . . . . . . . . . . . . . . 227

45. Tarrytown, The Castle at Tarrytown* . . . . . . . . . . . . . . . . . . . . 229

46. Trumansburg, Taughannock Farms Inn. . . . . . . . . . . . . . . . . . . 231

47. Westfield, The William Seward Inn . . . . . . . . . . . . . . . . . . . . . . 233

48. Windham, Albergo Allegria Bed & Breakfast . . . . . . . . . . . . . . . 235

* A Top Pick Inn

# Troutbeck 📱
## Amenia, New York 12501

**INNKEEPER:** James Flaherty; Garret Corcoran, manager

**ADDRESS/TELEPHONE:** Leedsville Road; (914) 373-9681 or (800) 978-7688; fax (914) 373-7080

**E-MAIL:** jbflaherty@worldnet.att.net

**ROOMS:** 42, including 8 suites; 37 with private bath; all with air-conditioning, telephone with dataport, desk, and radio; 8 with fireplace and balcony; 6 with whirlpool tub. Smoking permitted. Children over the age of 12 welcome.

**RATES:** $700 to $1,000. Friday 5:00 P.M. to Sunday 2:00 P.M.; $400 to $600 for one weekend night, per couple; includes breakfast, lunch, and dinner every day and all drinks and facilities. Taxes and 15 percent gratuities additional. Two-night minimum holiday weekends.

**OPEN:** Midweek reserved for executive groups. Weekends open as a country inn.

**FACILITIES AND ACTIVITIES:** Friday and Saturday dinner for outside diners (entrees $20 to $28); Sunday brunch $26; Saturday lunch served. Tennis courts, walled gardens, outdoor and indoor swimming pools, fitness center, pool table; on 422 acres, hiking, cross-country skiing, brook and creek. Nearby: Vanderbilt Mansion, Roosevelt Home, antiquing. Jim Flaherty maps out individualized tours.

**BUSINESS TRAVEL:** Desk and telephone with dataport in all rooms, fax, photocopy service, audiovisual equipment, computers with Internet access; extensive meeting and conference space available.

*T*he red, yellow, orange, and rust leaves of fall covered the ground, crunching under our feet as we walked along the pathways. We had been hiking on Troutbeck's trails, and as we approached the stone bridge across the stream, we stopped at the gazebo to rest and admire the sprawling English stone country house. Built by Colonel Joel Springarn and his wife, Amy, in the 1920s, it has a slate roof, leaded windows, and a fascinating history. Springarn was a professor, literary critic, and horticulturist and the couple attracted the leading liberals of the day. The NAACP was formed within these walls; Lewis Mumford memorialized the estate in his book *Sketches from Life;* Sinclair Lewis, John Burroughs, and President Theodore Roosevelt all stayed here.

By the time James Flaherty and Robert Skibsted purchased the property in 1978, however, it had been abandoned for some thirty-five years. There was no glass in the windows, no water, no electricity, and no heat. The beauty of the inn and its grounds today is a testament to what hard work and perseverance can do.

During the week Troutbeck is an executive retreat, specializing in high-level conferences; on weekends, however, it becomes a romantic getaway for country inn travelers, as well as a popular spot for weddings.

The public rooms include oak floors, stone walls, leaded casement windows, and beamed ceilings. There's a Victorian bar in the Red Room, where guests gather for drinks and hors d'oeuvres before dinner, a cozy living room with a beamed ceiling, a paneled library with another fireplace, and a poker room.

The guest rooms are located in the main house, in the new ballroom wing, and in the Century Farmhouse. They are decorated with antiques and period reproductions. Some rooms have canopy beds, and most have private baths.

Gourmet meals are the norm at Troutbeck, and they are served in delightful dining rooms—several with stone walls, beamed ceilings, and fireplaces—to the accompaniment of soft candlelight and fresh flowers, an utterly romantic and seductive setting. One night we had a fabulous rack of lamb for two that was served with a bread pudding of chanterelles and porcini and an organic field-green salad with pears. For dessert, we devoured a warm chocolate cake with a soft center on a pool of crème anglaise.

**HOW TO GET THERE:** From New York take I-684 north from Brewster and then Route 22 north to Amenia. From Amenia take Route 343 toward Connecticut; go 2$^4$/$_{10}$ miles, turn right onto Route 2, cross bridge, and turn right into Troutbeck.

# Notable Quotables

Troutbeck, which straddles the Connecticut and New York borders, has seen more than its share of well-known visitors. Its first owners were the Benton family from the Lake District of England, who in 1765 named their estate Troutbeck after their ancestral home in Great Britain. While they owned Troutbeck they were friendly with both Emerson and Thoreau. Its second owners, Colonel Joel Elias Springarn and his wife, Amy, were well known to the liberals and literati of the 1910s and 1920s. Among their famous guests were Lewis Mumford, Ernest Hemingway, President Theodore Roosevelt, Sinclair Lewis, and W. E. B. Du Bois. It was Mr. Springarn who said, "I have a dream . . . of a unified Negro population," and it was at Troutbeck that the NAACP was conceptualized.

Sinclair Lewis was so taken by its setting that he said of Troutbeck (supposedly to Mr. Springarn), "You live in a cathedral of trees." Those magnificent sycamore trees that were planted when the Bentons first purchased the property in 1765 still overlook the elegant stone manor house.

Lewis Mumford, another frequent visitor, said of Troutbeck, "Nestled under a hill, secure against visual intrusion, this house cultivates its innerness; though numerous doors open onto lawn and terrace, Troutbeck itself gives a sense of being snug, protected, inviolate."

# Bridgehampton Inn

Bridgehampton, New York 11932

**INNKEEPERS:** Anna and Detlef Pump; Maureen Brown, manager

**ADDRESS/TELEPHONE:** 2266 Main Street; (mailing address P.O. Box 1432); (516) 537–3660; fax (516) 537–3589

**ROOMS:** 8, including 2 suites; all with private bath, air-conditioning, telephone, and television. No smoking inn.

**RATES:** $140 to $360, double occupancy, continental breakfast. Two-night minimum weekends; three-night minimum holiday weekends.

**OPEN:** March to December.

**FACILITIES AND ACTIVITIES:** Gardens. Nearby: ocean beaches, Corwith Museum, Friday talks by celebrity authors at library in summer, restaurants, antiques shops, boutiques.

What a joy it is to see a formerly derelict house refurbished and gleaming. The 1795 mansion that houses the Bridgehampton Inn sat forlornly on the edge of fashionable Bridgehampton for years until local caterer Anna Pump and her husband, Detlef, transformed it into their classy inn.

I remember what it looked like in 1993 when Anna and Detlef purchased

it, and I remember the painstaking restoration that took place until the inn opened a year later. Today it is both a reflection of its historic past and of the Scandinavian heritage of its owners. Detlef is a builder, and Anna enjoys a terrific decorating sense. The inn is infused with their style.

When we arrived one dark evening, a welcoming fire glowed in the living-room fireplace, and wine and cheese were waiting in the bright breakfast room. The polished oak floors were covered with Oriental carpets, and a Victorian sofa was upholstered in a lovely forest-green velvet. A glass bowl of oranges sat on an antique table, while a pitcher of daffodils graced the mantel.

The guest rooms are unique, each furnished with a hand-carved four-poster bed and elegant antiques. Room Number 6 is furnished with a spectacular, eight-piece antique Biedermeier suite. All the rooms have wall-to-wall carpeting, burnished antique chests and tables, and a serene and restful atmosphere. This is an inn to relax and wind down in; its proximity to New York City means that many guests come for that very reason. The gray marble baths have deep European sinks, wide countertops, and spacious showers with a center head, similar to those in Denmark.

Anna is known as the premier caterer in the Hamptons, and her breakfasts reflect her expertise. A continental breakfast featuring homemade blueberry muffins, scones and croissants, fresh juice and fruit can be supplemented, for an additional charge, with an egg dish accompanied by smoked salmon and ham.

On sunny summer days guests relax in the spacious gardens or on the covered porch or patio. The inn is merely five minutes from premier golf courses and three minutes from the glorious Hamptons beaches. Antiques shops, superior restaurants, and historic museums are all within walking distance of the inn. An old-fashioned soda fountain, cafe, and ice cream parlor, the Candy Kitchen, is just down the street. They still make their own ice cream and sell grilled-cheese sandwiches.

HOW TO GET THERE: From New York City take I–495 (Long Island Expressway) to exit 70 (Manorville) and follow Route 111 to Highway 27 (Sunrise Highway). Take Highway 27 (which becomes Montauk Highway) for 25 miles to Bridgehampton. Traveling east on Montauk Highway, the road becomes Main Street as it reaches Bridgehampton. The inn is on the left ¼ mile beyond the traffic light at the entrance to Bridgehampton Common shopping center.

# Acorn Inn
## Canandaigua, New York 14424

INNKEEPERS: Joan and Louis Clark

ADDRESS/TELEPHONE: 4508 Route 64 South, Bristol Center;
(716) 229–2834; fax (716) 229–5046

WEB SITE: www.dreamscape.com/acorninn

ROOMS: 4; all with private bath, air-conditioning, television, VCR, radio, hair dryer, and robes; 2 with fireplace; telephone jack in all rooms, telephone available on request. No smoking inn. Children over the age of 12 welcome. Some dogs permitted with prior permission.

**RATES:** $105 to $200, double occupancy; includes full breakfast; 25 percent discount on two or more nights Monday through Thursday from November through April, subject to availability. Two-night minimum weekends in July, August, October, and holidays.

**OPEN:** All year, except closed for two weeks in April and in September.

**FACILITIES AND ACTIVITIES:** On one acre; gardens with fountain and pools, hot tub in garden. Nearby: Bristol Mountain (skiing), Finger Lakes Performing Arts Center, Bristol Valley Theatre, Sonnenberg Gardens and Mansion, golfing.

*S*ometimes the nicest things come in the smallest packages. That's certainly true of the Acorn Inn. Although it has only four rooms and baths, every single detail is so scrupulously thought out that guests are assured of a memorable stay—and they keep coming back again and again. Before Joan and Louis Clark purchased their 1795 former stagecoach stop and turned it into an inn, they had been antiques dealers. You will find beautiful examples of fine Oriental rugs as well as American and English antiques.

The inn is located adjacent to Route 64; you enter and immediately gravitate toward the Gathering Room with its large Rumford fireplace. There are mellow pine floors, oil paintings and antique mirrors on the walls. Baskets and dried flowers hang from the beams. A wall of bookshelves is filled with interesting books, and the sofas and chairs are covered with pretty toile and checked fabrics.

The guest rooms are spacious and beautifully furnished. There are canopy beds, designer linens, and comfortable seating areas. The baths are lovely, with modern fixtures and stenciling decorating the walls. I especially like The Bristol, a spacious room in the former ballroom that has a gas woodstove, a canopy bed, a fainting couch, and numerous books in cases. A window seat in a bay window overlooks the gardens. Should you wish to watch a video on the VCR, the television has a 26-inch screen. The bath, with a soaking tub and a separate shower, is decorated with acorn stenciling.

Breakfast is served in a country dining room that looks out onto a lovely garden. Joan serves the meal on antique china with heirloom silver. You will always have freshly squeezed orange juice, and you might also be treated to one of Joan's stratas. There may be a fresh summer-vegetable-medley or blueberry strata or, perhaps, a vegetable and spinach dish.

**HOW TO GET THERE:** From I–90 (New York State Thruway) traveling west, take exit 43 (Manchester/Canandaigua) and follow Route 21 south past Canandaigua. At the junction with County Road 32, follow that for 7½ miles to Route 64. Turn left (south) onto Route 64; the inn is the fourth house on the right. From I–90 traveling east take exit 45 (Victor) onto Route 96 east to Victor. In Victor take Route 444 south to Routes 5/20. Turn left (east) and continue 1 mile to Route 64. Turn right (south) and continue on Route 64 for 5½ miles to the inn, which is on the left.

# Morgan-Samuels B&B Inn
## Canandaigua, New York 14424

**INNKEEPERS:** John and Julie Sullivan

**ADDRESS/TELEPHONE:** 2920 Smith Road; (716) 394–9232; fax (716) 394–8044

**ROOMS:** 6; all with private bath, air-conditioning, fireplace, radio, hair dryer, robes, and CD player. 2 with Jacuzzi. No smoking inn. Children over the age of 7 welcome.

**RATES:** $129 to $255, double occupancy; includes full breakfast and afternoon tea. Two-night minimum weekends May through mid-November.

**OPEN:** All year.

**FACILITIES AND ACTIVITIES:** Dinner for eight or more by reservation (approximately $50 each); BYOB. Forty-six acres, tennis court. Nearby: horse-drawn sleigh rides during winter, Canandaigua Lake, Sonnenberg Gardens and Mansion, Rose Hill Mansion, Bristol Playhouse, wineries.

**RECOMMENDED COUNTRY INNS® TRAVELERS' CLUB BENEFIT:** 10 percent discount, Monday to Thursday, November 15 to July 1, except holidays.

*B*uilt in 1810 the Morgan-Samuels English-style mansion is composed of stone, brick, hand-hewn beams, and multiple fireplaces. It is named for Judson Morgan, an actor and farmer who built the original mansion in 1810 and for a subsequent owner, Howard Samuels, who invented the plastic bag. John and Julie Sullivan purchased the forty-six-acre estate in 1989 and converted it to a wonderful inn. Every year they make new improvements—most recently, in 1997, they added two more fireplaces so that every guest room has its very own, and they completely reworked the gardens.

Located on a rise at the end of a maple-lined driveway, the mansion is truly impressive in its sylvan setting. John is both the inn's chef and a Holstein breeder. The inn is still a working farm, and, in addition to numerous cows (and often heifers from May to October), you are likely to see chickens, ducks, and turkeys roaming the grounds.

The common rooms are abundant and striking. There's a garden room with a slate floor, a living room with a huge stone fireplace; and a cozy library with another fireplace and a game table as well as a television, VCR, and video library. A tearoom and four beautiful and very different patios—one with a pond, another reached through an antique steel gate through an archway, and still another with a well and a statue—complete the picture. Elegant oil paintings, museum-quality antique furniture, and classical music in the background make this a very special inn.

Were I to choose my favorite room, it would be the Victorian Room, which has a canopy bed, a fireplace, French doors leading to a private balcony, and a bathroom with stone walls that includes a Jacuzzi surrounded by marble, stone, and wood. It has a romantic medieval feeling.

John, sometimes accompanied by his ten-year-old son, Jonathan, makes an early morning jaunt to the farmers' market to select the freshest ingredients, and they obtain their bread from a nearby Trappist monastery. John prepares the kind of breakfasts that you write home about. If the morning is balmy, you may eat on a patio or in the garden room; otherwise you'll probably eat in the beamed dining room. You'll start with a fabulous fresh fruit platter, fresh muffins and rolls, and juice. Then he may have fixed one of his special omelettes or, perhaps, French toast.

A wonderful afternoon repast that includes stuffed mushrooms and imported cheeses is offered every afternoon. The Sullivans will provide fresh local apple cider, or guests may bring their own wine. Candlelight dinners will be arranged if enough guests express an interest.

HOW TO GET THERE: From I–90 (New York State Thruway) traveling west, take exit 43 (Manchester/Canandaigua) and turn right onto Route 21. Proceed to Route 488 and turn left. Turn right at the first intersection onto East Avenue and go to the first stop sign. Continue straight for ¾ mile to the inn, which is on the right.

# The Brewster Inn
## Cazenovia, New York 13035

INNKEEPER: Richard Hubbard

ADDRESS/TELEPHONE: 6 Ledyard Avenue (mailing address: P.O. Box 507); (315) 655–9232; fax (315) 655–2130

ROOMS: 17, including 1 suite; all with private bath, air-conditioning, telephone, television, radio, iron, and ironing board; 4 with fireplace and whirlpool tub, 1 with private porch or balcony. Wheelchair accessible. No smoking inn.

RATES: $90 to $225, double occupancy; includes continental breakfast. Two-night minimum on weekends.

OPEN: All year.

FACILITIES AND ACTIVITIES: Restaurant open for dinner daily (entrees $18 to $20) and brunch on Sunday; bar. On three acres; parking, lakefront, exercise room, private dock. Nearby: golfing, cross-country skiing, fishing, tour Lorenzo (mansion of John Lincklaen, the founder of Cazenovia), picnic at Chittenango Falls State Park.

*B*enjamin Brewster helped John D. Rockefeller establish Standard Oil and then decided he needed a summer resting place. Consequently, in 1893 he began constructing the magnificent estate we now know as The Brewster Inn on the southern tip of Cazenovia Lake. It's an imposing three-story structure of shingles and brick with fabulous woodwork in the lobby and stairwell. The ceilings and walls are entirely paneled in rich mahogany and oak, and the spindles on the stairs are gracefully twisted.

They are painted a creamy ivory, which makes the area light and bright, although it does hide the luster of the natural woods.

Eight guest rooms in the Carriage House were completed in 1993, and there are nine more rooms in the mansion. Those in the mansion vary in size, but all have private baths and six have lake views. I was fortunate enough to stay in Room 2, which is furnished with one of the most fabulous antique bedroom suites I have ever seen. It includes an Eastlake half-tester bed with a heavily carved headboard and footboard, a matching high dresser with a mirror, and a chest. A gas fireplace faces the bed. Oak floors are covered with Oriental rugs, and there are views of the lake. The bath is equally impressive. The original platform tub sits on a black-and-white tile floor, and there's a fabulous old porcelain sink on porcelain legs. A glass towel bar holds the towels. A door in the bath leads to an enclosed sitting porch with a television. Not only is this *my* favorite room, but I am told that it is also the favorite room of Alec Baldwin and Kim Bassinger.

Under no circumstances should you miss dinner at The Brewster Inn. Owner Dick Hubbard is an expert on wines, and his wine list reflects a wide but very knowledgeable selection that offers variety in type, style, and price. The food is equally impressive. I started my evening with a lovely Caesar salad topped with house-made croutons, and then I followed it with a wonderful duck that was crispy on the outside and moist and tender inside. It was served with a tangy cherry sauce; a wedge of a baked potato pie made with thin slices of Yukon gold, russet, and sweet potatoes; and fresh vegetables. For dessert I had a Sambuca soufflé with a side of crème anglaise. It was a fabulous meal.

HOW TO GET THERE: From I–90 (New York State Thruway), take exit 34 (Canastota) to Route 5 west. Go 7 miles; turn south onto Route 13 and travel 9 miles to Cazenovia. In the village turn west onto Route 20 and continue through town. The inn is on the right in about ½ mile. From Syracuse take I–81 south to exit 15 (Lafayette) and proceed east on Route 20 for 17 miles to Cazenovia. The inn is on the left before you reach the town.

# Lincklaen House

## Cazenovia, New York 13035

**INNKEEPER/CHEF:** Dan Kuper, Mary Margaret Budlow

**ADDRESS/TELEPHONE:** 79 Albany Street; (315) 655-3461; fax (315) 655-5443

**E-MAIL:** linkhouse@aol.com

**WEB SITE:** www.cazenovia.com/lincklaen

**ROOMS:** 18, including 1 suite; all with private bath, air-conditioning, telephone, television. Pets allowed. No smoking inn. Wheelchair accessible.

**RATES:** $100 to $150, double occupancy; includes continental breakfast and happy hour Wednesday to Saturday.

**OPEN:** All year.

**FACILITIES AND ACTIVITIES:** Dinner Wednesday to Sunday (entrees $17 to $24); lunch Wednesday to Saturday; Sunday brunch (entrees $15 to $18). Call in winter. Tavern. Nearby: Labrador ski area in Truxton, horseback riding and cross-country skiing in Highland Forest, Turning Stone Gambling Casino. Seasonal: Winter Festival, Lorenzo Carriage Driving Competition, antiques fair in Madison.

**BUSINESS TRAVEL:** Telephone in room; desk in 5 rooms; fax machine available; conference room.

**RECOMMENDED COUNTRY INNS® TRAVELERS' CLUB BENEFIT:** 10 percent discount, subject to availability.

The charming town of Cazenovia has streets lined with handsome brick buildings that house fashionable dress and gift shops, antiques stores, and art galleries, and in its midst stands a hotel with a pedigree. Built along a popular early stagecoach route, this was the first hotel designed to accommodate a prosperous and wealthy clientele who were looking for more refined lodging than had previously been available.

Under new ownership since 1997, changes are taking place in this old-time hostelry. We hope to soon see a marked improvement in the guest rooms, which on our last visit were spare and practical, but characterless. Nevertheless, they were spotlessly clean and furnished with period reproduction furniture interspersed with Hitchcock beds. Stenciling decorated the rooms and baths.

One enters a black-and-white tile foyer to a lobby with lace curtains on the tall windows and a massive fireplace. In the East Room there are elegant period sofas and chairs. The formal dining room is located down a hallway where another fireplace graces a wall. My favorite restaurant, however, is the charming Seven Stone Steps, downstairs. It has low beamed ceilings and a bumpy original floor with wide pine boards; oil murals of Cazenovia that were painted in 1940 circle the walls. There's often a guitarist or a jazz combo here at night.

Innkeeper and chef Dan Kuper was formerly the chef at the Brewster Inn. For dinner you might start with a baked escargot that was steeped in a champagne-hazelnut sauce and then have an entree of tenderloin en croûte, a filet of beef with lobster meat and asparagus wrapped in a puff pastry and finished with a wild mushroom demiglace.

**HOW TO GET THERE:** From I–90 (New York State Thruway), take exit 34 (Canastota) to Route 5 west. Go 7 miles on Route 5, then turn south onto Route 13 and travel 9 miles to Cazenovia. The inn is in the center of town. From Syracuse take I–81 south to exit 15 (Lafayette) and proceed east on Route 20 for 17 miles to Cazenovia.

# The Lindenmere Estate B&B
## Center Moriches, New York 11934

**INNKEEPER:** Jennie Magaro

**ADDRESS/TELEPHONE:** 16 Sedgemere Road (mailing address: P.O. Box 1252); (516) 874–2273; fax (516) 878–5445

**WEB SITE:** www.lindenmere.com

**ROOMS:** 12, including 4 cottages; all with private bath, air-conditioning, television, VCR, desk, and robes; 6 with water views, 4 with whirlpool tub. Wheelchair access. No smoking inn. Children over the age of 12 welcome.

**RATES:** $125 to $275, double occupancy; includes full breakfast; lower rates midweek for two small rooms with single beds and large private baths, including full breakfast. Two-night minimum May to October.

**OPEN:** Valentine's Day to Columbus Day weekend.

**FACILITIES AND ACTIVITIES:** On thirteen acres bordering Moriches Bay; private beach, 50-foot swimming pool and pool pavilion, lighted Har-tru tennis court, two private docks, volleyball, horseshoes, croquet, nature path, flower gardens, fishing. Nearby: restaurants, golfing.

**BUSINESS TRAVEL:** Desk in some rooms, computer jack in all rooms; fax and copier available. Meeting room.

**RECOMMENDED COUNTRY INNS® TRAVELERS' CLUB BENEFIT:** Stay two nights, get third night free, Monday to Thursday; 10 percent discount for three-night stay on weekends.

As you enter the wrought-iron gates and drive along the driveway lined with majestic hundred-year-old linden trees, you catch sight of the beautiful house with its panoramic waterfront views. Then you understand why Imelda Marcos loved this place so much. It is one of the most spectacular settings of any inn in this book. The shingle-style house extends along Moriches Bay, with only a broad colonnaded, covered veranda and an expanse of green lawn separating it from the water. There's a bench down by the water, as well as a boardwalk and a dock. At night, after a swim in the pool, which is right at water's edge, guests often sit on the dock trying to count the multitude of stars while whispering romantically to one another.

The sixteen-bedroom and seventeen-bathroom house was built as a private residence in 1905. The classic, shingle-style mansion is rumored to have been designed by Stanford White, who left a legacy of other similar houses on Long Island. The hurricane of 1938 destroyed much of the mansion, and for a number of years it was abandoned. After World War II it was rebuilt and opened as the Lindenmere Hotel, but eventually that closed, too. Local residents remember when Philippine President Ferdinand Marcos and his wife, Imelda, purchased the estate in the early 1980s. Imelda lavished attention and wealth on the mansion, installing grand staircases and remodeling the baths to include marble floors and 24-karat gold and onyx fixtures. When the president was deposed in 1987, the government seized the house and attempted to sell it for $4.5 million. In 1996 Dr. Peter Magaro and his wife, Jennie, purchased the thirteen-acre estate. They opened it as a bed-and-breakfast in 1997.

Today the graciousness of the past remains. Guests enter a foyer with a piano and shelves of books and videos. A grand living room contains a fireplace, a cardinal-red velvet sofa and puffy chairs upholstered in a Ralph Lauren fabric of yellow and rose. The oak floors are covered with Oriental rugs. Beyond, a dining room has an elegant Victorian walnut marble-topped sideboard and a fabulously carved oak buffet. But as lovely as the rooms are, what you can't resist is the pull of that fabulous water view. You're drawn like a magnet through the French doors to the veranda to gaze at the water.

The guest rooms are spacious, classic, and simple. About half have views of the water, but those on the second floor are spectacular. My two favorite rooms are the lodge-like Room 6, which has slanted wood ceilings, a panoramic view, and a whirlpool tub in the bath, and Room 7, which has a handsome oak Craftsman-style bed, a wonderful view, and another whirlpool tub in the bath.

The grounds include a large, pagoda-like pool house with a marble floor and a giant barbecue. It has a wooden cathedral ceiling that rises steeply to a skylight and walls of glass encircled by columns that match the house. The views are breathtaking, as they are from the pool that lies beside it. Classy chaise lounges sit on a flagstone terrace. The property also includes a spectacular perennial garden and a nature walk that parallels the shoreline but travels through the woods.

Breakfast is served in the formal dining room, where a typical menu will include fresh fruit and/or berries and juices, home-baked breads, cereals, and an entree such as quiche Lorraine with home fries and fried apples or corn cakes with maple syrup and bacon, ham, or sausage.

HOW TO GET THERE: From I-495 (Long Island Expressway) take exit 69 (Wading River). At the stop sign at the top of the ramp, turn right onto Wading River Road. Travel approximately 3 to 4 miles and turn right at the second stop sign onto Chichester Street. Go 1 mile to its end and turn left onto Main Street in Center Moriches. At the first traffic light turn right onto Union Street. Follow Union Street for 1 mile to Sedgemere Road. Turn left onto Sedgemere Road and cross a small bridge over the creek. The inn is the first right turn after the bridge. Ring the bell at the wrought-iron gates and announce yourself, then proceed ¼ mile to the main house.

# The Maple Inn  ¢¢¢
## Chautauqua, New York 14722

**INNKEEPERS:** Tom and Linda Krueger

**ADDRESS/TELEPHONE:** 8 Bowman Avenue (mailing address P.O. Box
46); (716) 357–4583

**ROOMS:** 11, including 5 suites; all with private bath, air-conditioning,
small kitchen, and private porch. Wheelchair access. No smoking inn.
Not appropriate for children.

**RATES:** $75 to $125 per night, double occupancy, from Labor Day to
Memorial Day; $850 to $1,200 per week, double occupancy, from
Memorial Day to Labor Day.

**OPEN:** All year.

**FACILITIES AND ACTIVITIES:** On the grounds of Chautauqua Institution, with access to all the cultural and recreational activities of the
institution, including twelve tennis courts, three beaches, boat dock,
thirty-six-hole golf course; and an incredible array of classes, lectures,
and concerts.

**RECOMMENDED COUNTRY INNS® TRAVELERS' CLUB BENEFIT:** Stay
two nights, get third night free.

e have talked for years about spending a week at Chautauqua
Institution. We would attend lectures and concerts, have picnics
down by the lake, ride our bicycles along the lakeside roads, play
tennis every day, and immerse ourselves in the activities of this renowned
adult summer camp. We have not yet escaped for a week, but we did come for
a day in late March.

Founded in 1874 as a summer training conference for Sunday school
teachers, the Chautauqua Institution soon developed into the nation's premier intellectual retreat. Then and now the primary purpose of a week or a
summer at Chautauqua is to attend classes, lectures, and concerts (often
taught by leading authorities) to broaden the intellect, while also following
a variety of leisure pursuits that include programs of music, opera, dance,
theater, and religious services. All these are combined with recreational activities such as golf, tennis, boating, and swimming.

When the camp was first founded, charming Victorian cottages were
built side by side along the narrow, tree-studded streets to create a Victorian
village where the focus is on the activities on sparkling Chautauqua Lake as

well as around the Amphitheater, Norton Hall, and the Hall of Philosophy. The cottages remain and have regularly been passed along from generation to generation. A hotel on the grounds, the Athenaeum, has 160 rooms and a huge veranda across the front with fabulous views of the water. The entire village is on the National Register of Historic Places.

The Maple Inn was built in 1894, and it became an inn in 1909. It has been owned by Tom and Linda Krueger since 1983. It's a pristine white-clapboard structure that's more colonial in appearance than Victorian, with a double deck across the front where wicker furniture resides in summer.

We entered a smartly decorated reception room with neat and comfortable overstuffed chairs on a navy-blue carpet. Unlike most bed-and-breakfasts, The Maple Inn offers individual kitchens for its guests, so there is as much or as little interaction among guests as they choose. There are two room sizes. The two-room suites have a combination living/dining room and kitchen with a separate bedroom and bath, while the studios have a bedroom with an efficiency kitchen occupying one wall. White is the predominant color, with accents of blue and green. The furniture includes pretty antique dressers, tables, and chests painted in white.

What could be finer than sipping that first cup of coffee on your private deck while contemplating which of the many activities you'll take in today? You'd be sharing the experience with such notables as Paul Newman and Robert Redford, who visited in 1988, and President Bill Clinton, who came in 1996.

HOW TO GET THERE: From I–90 (New York State Thruway), take exit 60 onto Route 394 (Westfield) south for 10 miles to the main gate of the Chautauqua Institution. Enter the property and turn right. Go 2 blocks and turn left onto Bowman Avenue. The inn is 2 more blocks on the left.

# The Friends Lake Inn
## Chestertown, New York 12817

**INNKEEPER:** Sharon Taylor

**ADDRESS/TELEPHONE:** 963 Friends Lake Road; (518) 494-4751;
fax (518) 494-4616

**E-MAIL:** friends@netheaven.com

**WEB SITE:** www.friendslake.com

**ROOMS:** 16, including 10 suites; all with private bath, air-conditioning,
radio, robes, iron, and ironing board; 8 with whirlpool tub, 6 with private deck or patio, 2 with fireplace; pay telephone in coat room. No
smoking inn. Children over the age of 12 welcome.

**RATES:** $225 to $350, double occupancy; includes breakfast and dinner;
$135 to $285, double occupancy; includes full breakfast. Promotional
and midweek packages available. 18 percent meal gratuity added. Two-
night minimum weekends.

**OPEN:** All year except closed Tuesday and Wednesday mid-March to
mid-May.

**FACILITIES AND ACTIVITIES:** Restaurant serving dinner (entrees $18 to
$29); Bistro has bar menu (entrees $7.00 to $11.00), breakfast ($3.25 to
$5.95), lake-view bar. Nordic ski center on premise with 32 kilometers of
groomed cross-country ski and snowshoeing trails (hiking in summer),
as well as ski and snowshoe rentals and lessons. Gazebo and hot tub by
backyard pond, private beach, two canoes, swimming. Nearby: Gore
Mountain downhill skiing, ice skating, sledding, snowmobiling, whitewater rafting on the Hudson River, horseback riding.

**BUSINESS TRAVEL:** Conference room; fax, copier available.

**RECOMMENDED COUNTRY INNS® TRAVELERS' CLUB BENEFIT:** Stay
two nights, get third night free, excluding holiday weeks and weekends.

*t* was October when we first visited, and a huge bowl of bright red
apples sat on the reception desk inviting all who entered to sample
the local provender. The air was crisp and the sun shone brightly
against the tan clapboard exterior. Sharon explained to me that the original
part of the inn was built as a farmhouse in the 1860s, but by the end of the
century it was being used as a boardinghouse for tanners, which was then the
primary trade in Chestertown.

Sharon and Greg Taylor have owned the inn since 1904, and they are continuously adding to it and making improvements. Now, in addition to the main dining room, which has its original tin ceiling and huge brick fireplace, there's an informal bistro, which has an oak floor and another fireplace. The Mission-style furniture is comfortable and stylish.

Although the inn is noted for its outdoor activities and the Nordic Ski Center it operates in the winter, guests also come for the award-winning fine dining. Greg is an exceptional wine aficionado. His cellar of more than 20,000 bottles has earned the inn a "Best of Excellence" Award from the *Wine Spectator,* and there are twenty wines by the glass, an extensive list of micro-brews, and an impressive array of aged ports, cordials, single-malt scotches, and liqueurs.

Needless to say, the food is also outstanding. One night we had the duo of farm-raised venison, a delicious combination of noisettes and a chop brushed with orange oil and served with caramelized sweet onions and cranberry relish. It was absolutely delicious.

The guest rooms are spacious and stunning. Several have whirlpool tubs and fireplaces. Room 3 has a four-poster bed, two balconies, and a Jacuzzi in the room; Room 17 has a two-person whirlpool tub with a view and a pine canopy bed. Waverly fabrics are used lavishly on the beds, windows, and canopy drapes.

HOW TO GET THERE: From the south take I–87 (Adirondack Northway) to exit 23 (Warrensburg) and then follow Route 9 through Warrensburg to Route 28. Follow Route 28 for approximately 5 miles to Friends Lake Road. Turn right. The inn is on the left in 4.3 miles. From the north take I–87 (Northway) south to exit 25 (Chestertown). Turn right onto Route 8 west. Travel 3½ miles to Friends Lake Road. Turn left and then bear right at the first fork in the road. Turn right at the next intersection and continue for about 3 miles to the inn.

# Asa Ransom House ▦ ▨

## Clarence, New York 14031

**INNKEEPERS:** Judy Lenz and Robert Lenz

**ADDRESS/TELEPHONE:** 10529 Main Street; (716) 759–2315;
fax (716) 759–2791

**E-MAIL:** innfo@asaransom.com

**WEB SITE:** www.asaransom.com

**ROOMS:** 9, including 3 suites; all with private bath, air-conditioning,
telephone with dataport, television, radio, desk, fax, hair dryer, iron, and
ironing board; 7 with fireplace, 5 with balcony or porch, 3 with CD
player. Wheelchair access. No smoking inn.

**RATES:** $155 to $225, Sunday to Thursday, includes breakfast and dinner; $95 to $155 Sunday to Thursday, includes full breakfast; $205 to
$285 Saturday, includes breakfast and dinner; all double occupancy; less
for single occupancy.

**OPEN:** Closed January, Christmas, occasional holy days, and every Friday. Saturday dinner served to houseguests only.

**FACILITIES AND ACTIVITIES:** Dinner Sunday through Thursday
(entrees $12 to $25); lunch on Wednesday; tea on Thursday afternoon;
reservations appreciated. Taproom, gift shop. Nearby: Niagara Falls (28
miles), Artpark in Lewiston, opera in Lancaster, antiquing, golf, sports,
winery tours.

**BUSINESS TRAVEL:** Desk, telephone with dataport, fax machine, television, all in room. Meeting rooms.

*W*hen I think of the perfect country inn, the Asa Ransom House
often comes to mind. Prim and proper, clad in its ivory clapboard
and brick, it sits on three acres behind a neat fence, with a broad
front lawn shielded from the street by trees and gardens. In 1799 Asa Ransom, a young silversmith, saw an ad offering land in a wilderness area now
known as Clarence to "any proper man who would build and operate a tavern upon it." Not one to let opportunity pass him by, Ransom bought the
land and soon constructed a log home and a tavern. In 1801 he added a
sawmill and, two years later, a gristmill—the first in Erie County. These buildings did not survive, but the library, Sunshine Square Gift Shop, and snug

(the cozy bar) of the present building date to 1853, and remnants of the grist-mill are visible in back.

Innkeepers Judy Lenz and Robert Lenz purchased the inn in 1975 and have decorated it with lovely antiques and period reproduction pieces. Judy is such an expert interior decorator that she has even decorated period rooms in museums. Nevertheless, this inn is her masterpiece. She personally made

all the window treatments in the inn (and they are fabulous), and she stenciled a number of the guest rooms and the public rooms herself. When you see the stenciling in Room 3, you will understand that she is as much an artist as an innkeeper.

The guest rooms are large and lovely, with clever touches that you are sure to appreciate. Guests who wish to watch a favorite television program will be advised where to find the television in their room, but if you've come to escape the "tube," it is so well hidden you won't even know it's there. In Room 3, for example, it's hidden in the ornate fireplace mantle; in Room 6, it's behind a lovely painting. Every room has an antique radio, and there's a selection of old radio programs on cassettes to listen to. Were I to name a favorite room (and it's hard), I would select Room 7, which has blue toile walls in the bedroom, a blue carpet, a navy-blue sofa, a bed with a fishnet canopy, a gas fireplace, and a private porch that overlooks the pond and gardens in back. In the lovely bath the walls are finished in a blue-and-white stripe.

Guests can choose from two dining rooms, each with a fireplace. The Ransom Room is formal, and a jacket is required for men, while the Clarence Hollow room is more informal. The same selection of seafood (the salmon Kiev is particularly tasty), meat, chicken, and vegetarian selections are available.

Be sure to take time to wander through the herb garden, which has more than seventy varieties along its neat rows. A brochure carefully maps out the garden layout and offers a complete description of each herb.

HOW TO GET THERE: From I–90 (New York State Thruway) traveling west, take exit 48A (Pembroke) and turn south onto Route 77. At the junction with Route 5, go west. You will reach the inn in 11 miles on the left. Route 5 is Main Street in Clarence. From I–90 traveling east, take exit 49 and go north on Route 78. At the junction with Route 5, go east for 5¼ miles to Clarence.

# Plumbush Inn
## Cold Spring, New York 10516

**INNKEEPERS:** Gieri Albin and Ans Benderer

**ADDRESS/TELEPHONE:** 1656 Route 9D, (914) 265–3904;
fax (914) 265–3997

**ROOMS:** 3; all with private bath and air-conditioning; 1 with telephone,
television, coffeemaker, and hair dryer. Smoking permitted. Not appropriate for children.

**RATES:** $125 to $150, double occupancy; includes continental breakfast.

**OPEN:** All year; closed every Monday and Tuesday.

**FACILITIES AND ACTIVITIES:** Restaurant open Wednesday to Sunday
for lunch (entrees $7.00 to $14.00) and dinner (entrees a la carte $27 to
$29; prix fixe $32 to $36). On five acres; gardens, parking. Nearby: U.S.
Military Academy at West Point; Appalachian Trail; Boscobel, an exquisitely restored Hudson River mansion.

*S*wiss-trained Gieri Albin has been the host and Ans Benderer the chef
of Plumbush Inn in the Hudson River Valley for more than twenty
years, and although the romantic restaurant takes precedence over the
guest rooms, all three rooms are furnished with nice antiques and have private baths. In my opinion, the best room is the Marquesa Suite, a spacious
affair with slanted ceilings, an iron-and-brass bed, a lovely antique Victorian
settee, and antique tables and dresser. The other two rooms share a sitting
room, which has a television. The rooms were created in 1986 and although
decorated with nice antiques seem gaunt and undernourished compared
with the elaborate decor in the dining rooms.

The plum-colored (yes, it really is) building is a sprawling plantation-
style home whose construction was begun in the early nineteenth century.
It was then the country home of the Marquise Agnes Rizzo dei Ritti, a lady
of American lineage who married a nobleman of Italian extraction. In the
late 1860s Victorian elements were added to the house to give it its present
appearance. It has a wraparound porch, Victorian detailing, dormers, and
multiple fireplaces.

The main floor of the mansion is composed of a series of dining rooms.
Each is individually decorated with beautiful oil paintings and has a fireplace. One is dark and intimate with oak-paneled walls. Another has pretty,
splashy rose wallpaper on the walls; a third is on a bright porch with views of

the gardens. There are tall candles, fresh flowers, and elegant china, silver, and crystal stemware.

One evening I had a sautéed breast of duck with brandied plum sauce. It was outstanding. On another night, when my husband was able to accompany me, he had a brook trout (they have a tank in the kitchen) that he pronounced the best he'd ever had, and I had an ambrosial filet of beef Wellington. The house dessert specialty is Swiss apple fritters, which come with vanilla sauce.

**HOW TO GET THERE:** From Manhattan take the Henry Hudson Parkway north to the Saw Mill River Parkway; follow this north to the Taconic Parkway and then follow the Taconic Parkway north to the exit onto Route 301 west (Cold Spring). Follow this to Route 9D. Follow Route 9D south 3¼ miles to the inn, which is on the left.

# The Cooper Inn
## Cooperstown, New York 13326

**MANAGER:** Steven C. Walker

**ADDRESS/TELEPHONE:** Corner of Main and Chestnut Streets (mailing address: P.O. Box 311); (607) 547–2567; reservation line (800) 348–6222; fax (607) 547–1271

**WEB SITE:** www.cooperinn.com

**ROOMS:** 15, including 5 suites; all with private bath, air-conditioning, telephone with dataport, television, radio, desk, hair dryer, iron, and ironing board. No smoking inn.

**RATES:** $80 to $235, double occupancy; includes continental breakfast; additional person in room, $15. Two-night minimum holiday weekends.

**OPEN:** All year.

**FACILITIES AND ACTIVITIES:** On three acres; guests have the use of all the recreational facilities of the Otesaga Resort Hotel including The Leatherstocking Golf Course, tennis, pool or lake swimming, canoes, powerboats, and fishing on Lake Otsego. Discounted tickets available to Clark Sports Center, a full exercise and fitness center, including basketball court, indoor running track, racquetball and squash courts, bowl-ing center, swimming pool, diving pool, aerobics studios, and rock-climbing walls. Nearby: National Baseball Hall of Fame and Museum, Fenimore House Museum and The American Indian Wing, The Farm-ers' Museum, Glimmerglass Opera.

**BUSINESS TRAVEL:** Telephone with dataport, desk, television in room; fax, copier, and conference room available.

*J*ames Fenimore Cooper's father founded Cooperstown in 1786, a few years before James was born. The boy undoubtedly played in the streets where The Cooper Inn now stands—well before baseball was invented here by Abner Doubleday in 1839. The handsome Federal brick building was built in 1812 by publisher Henry Phinney, and it was expanded in 1936, when it first became an inn. There's a columned portico, white shut-ters, and elegant corbels that support wide overhanging eves. In 1998 a top-to-bottom renovation reduced the room count and created fifteen rooms that are spacious and elegant.

The inn is located on three acres of grounds that include formal gardens and a circular driveway. We entered a wide front-to-back hallway fur-nished with antique tables and chairs. The twin parlors are elegant and refined, with oil paintings hanging on peach-colored walls and unusual stepped woodwork

over the doors and windows. Wing chairs and sofas are covered in lovely tapestry fabrics. A roof deck for summer relaxation was being designed on my last visit.

There's a smart game and television room with a rose carpet and coordi-nated drapes and a breakfast room filled with bookshelves, where the conti-nental breakfast of hot and cold cereals, fresh fruit and juices, fresh-baked muffins, and toast is served along with coffee, tea, and hot chocolate.

The guest rooms are furnished with period reproductions. The rooms I visited all had peach-colored walls and beautiful floral fabrics. The new baths are sparkling and modern with tile floors and walls. It can now be said that The Cooper Inn is one of the nicest places to stay in Cooperstown.

When staying at The Cooper Inn you have the best of both worlds. It is located in the heart of Cooperstown, within walking distance of the National

Baseball Hall of Fame and Museum as well as all the shops and summertime activity. It's owned by the proprietors of the huge Otesaga Resort Hotel, which offers all its facilities to guests of The Cooper Inn. Yet the inn is so secluded behind its fence and gardens that it seems to be in a quiet and insulated world of its own.

**HOW TO GET THERE:** From I–90 or I–87 (both New York State Thruway) take exit 25A to I–88 south toward Oneonta. Travel about 60 miles to exit 17 and take Route 28 north for 20 miles to Cooperstown. Route 28 becomes Chestnut Street. The inn is on the corner of Chestnut and Main Streets.

# Cromwell Manor Inn
## Cornwall, New York 12518

**INNKEEPERS:** Dale and Barbara O'Hara

**ADDRESS/TELEPHONE:** Angola Road; (914) 534–7136

**WEB SITE:** www.virtualcities.com/ny/cromwell.htm

**ROOMS:** 13, including 3 suites; all with private bath, air-conditioning, and radio; 7 with fireplace, 1 with whirlpool tub. Wheelchair accessible. No smoking inn. Children over the age of 7 welcome.

**RATES:** $145 to $275, double occupancy; includes full breakfast. Two-night minimum on weekends.

**OPEN:** All year.

**FACILITIES AND ACTIVITIES:** On seven acres with gardens. Nearby: across the street from the 4,000-acre Black Rock Forest and adjacent to the Museum of the Hudson Highland. A short pathway from the inn grounds leads to the Jones Farm Country Store, where you can buy local jams, preserves, maple syrup, baskets, and craft items.

*D*ale O'Hara had traveled the world, but one day in 1984, while driving along a back road near West Point, he spotted a run-down brick mansion with a FOR SALE sign that seemed to call to him. The next day he owned the mansion—and his wandering days were over. He had a mission. For six years he scraped, painted, scraped more, repaired, replaced, and fixed; and along the way he met and married Barbara. When they decided to turn the mansion into a country inn, it took two more years to obtain the proper permits and to install thirteen new bathrooms—one for each of the guest rooms. Finally, in 1993, they were ready.

The curious name intrigued me. Dale said that David Cromwell, a descendant of that British fellow, Oliver, built the Greek Revival manor house with its six stately white, two-story columns across the front in 1820. A cottage closer to the road actually dates to 1764.

In the manor house the elegant formal parlor has an ornate marble fireplace mantel, which is a lovely contrast to the chrysanthemum-yellow walls. There are Empire sofas and chairs upholstered in a white-on-white fabric, an antique secretary with a roll-top desk and glass doors above, and an antique coffee table with a lyre base.

The guest rooms are uniquely decorated with lovely antiques also. The Oliver Cromwell Suite is the most elegant. There's a fireplace with a wooden mantel and brick hearth, a canopy bed with English floral draperies that match those on the windows, a spinning wheel, and comfortable wing chairs.

The bath is located in the mansion's former kitchen. It has a green tile floor with a whirlpool tub and a separate shower. A fabulous arched stained-glass window in shades of red and pink lends a romantic tone to the room. Another of my favorite rooms in the main house is the Saffron Room, which has a fabulous yellow damask fabric on the bed and drapes and a bath with sparkling white tile.

For those seeking privacy or for families, The Chimneys is the answer. This cottage, which was built in 1764, has wide mellow-pine floors and a living room with an antique hand-carved Flemish sideboard. One bedroom has a massive stone fireplace and a cannonball bed. There's a private tiled bath with stenciled walls. A second bedroom also has a fireplace, and the bath has a claw-foot tub on a red tile floor. There are hand-hewn posts and green walls. Upstairs a small room has a pretty quilt on a bed piled high with stuffed animals and brightened by a skylight. A bath here has a quilt for a shower curtain and stenciled cupboards.

Breakfast is served at individual tables in a room that once held a kitchen. Dale's collection of delicate models of square-rigged galleons sits above the pine cabinets. In summer you may also take breakfast on a pretty painted porch, where guests can view the natural woodland, gardens, and little fish pond. The most popular breakfast entree is a decadent but yummy caramelized French toast.

**HOW TO GET THERE:** The inn is 5 miles north of West Point. From New York City cross the George Washington Bridge and follow the Palisades Parkway north. Stay on the Palisades Parkway to its end at Bear Mountain. At the traffic circle, take 9W north for 11¼ miles to the Angola Road (Cornwall) exit. At the end of the exit ramp, turn left onto Angola Road and continue for ³/₁₀ mile. The B&B is on the right.

# Old Drovers Inn ♥
## Dover Plains, New York 12522

**INNKEEPERS:** Alice Pitcher and Kemper Peacock

**ADDRESS/TELEPHONE:** Old Route 22 (mailing address: P.O. Box 100); (914) 832–9311; fax (914) 832–6356

**E-MAIL:** Old_Drovers_Inn@juno.com

**WEB SITE:** www.olddroversinn.com

**ROOMS:** 4; all with private bath and air-conditioning; 3 with fireplace. Pets by prior approval. Children over the age of 12 welcome. Smoking permitted.

**RATES:** $350 to $450, weekends per couple, includes full breakfast and dinner; $175 to $250, double occupancy, midweek; continental breakfast. Two-night minimum if Saturday stay included.

**OPEN:** All year, except two weeks in January.

**FACILITIES AND ACTIVITIES:** On twelve acres. Dinner Thursday through Tuesday; Saturday, Sunday, and holidays served from noon (entrees: $17 to $35). Nearby: Hyde Park, golf courses, horseback riding, antiquing, country drives, fairs and festivals.

*E*lizabeth Taylor and Richard Burton reserved the entire inn and its discreet staff for some secluded and romantic private time when they finished filming *Cleopatra*. After opening night of *Phantom of the Opera*, Andrew Lloyd Weber and Sarah Brightman didn't reserve the entire inn, but they did retreat to the Meeting Room, with its vaulted ceiling and fireplace, probably with a bottle of champagne and a privately served dinner to celebrate. Recently Barbra Streisand received some much-needed rest and relaxation when she stayed in the Cherry Room. Another guest, the Marquis de Lafayette, was likely content with more humble accommodations at the inn.

Today as you enter the low-slung doorway from the street of this inn that's steeped with history and pass under the ancient beamed ceiling, dark with age and smoke, you might pull up a stool to the old oak bar and savor the warmth from the mammoth stone fireplace. Listen carefully. History is preserved so thoroughly at the Old Drovers Inn that you can almost hear the banter of the eighteenth-century drovers and their rough-tongued sidekicks. The more gentlemanly drovers, or cattle owners, were accustomed to driving their cattle to market in New York along this road, timing  their journey to stop here for drink, refreshment, gambling, and sleep. The anklebeaters, the dust-covered cowboys who urged the cattle onward, were lucky to receive a bed of straw in the stables.

Alice Pitcher and Kemper Peacock have so perfectly preserved the inn and its unique atmosphere that few places on the East Coast offer such elegant accommodations in such a thoroughly historic setting. Dinner guests enter the inn just as their rowdy predecessors did, on the ground floor, proceeding into the intimate dining room by passing the bar, where Charlie Wilbur will greet them by name and deliver their favorite drink to the table almost before they have time to sit down. Beware! Mixed drinks are served in double portions here. A waiter will bring a large blackboard menu to the table and hang it from a hook on a beam. You may wish to start with the hearty cheddar cheese soup, a specialty of the house. I must say that I love everything on the menu, but the browned turkey hash with mustard sauce is a specialty, as is the double cut rack of lamb chops with Charlie's tomato chutney.

There are only four guest rooms, but they are all special—all but one has a working fireplace—and they are decorated with English chintz fabrics, canopy beds, and antique dressers, tables, and chests. They sometimes have quirky elements as well. The tiny bath in one requires that you peek around the corner to shave. The largest is the Meeting Room. It was originally the inn's ballroom and later became the village meeting hall.

Overnight guests park behind the inn and enter on the second floor, where the wide entry hall includes a sitting area before a fireplace. You will probably be greeted by one or all of Alice's adorable Yorkshire terriers: Gordon Bennett, Goodness Gracious, or Jeepers Creepers. A remarkable feature of this incredible inn is that those of us who love to travel with our pets are welcome to bring them here with us.

Other common rooms include a paneled parlor furnished with antique sofas and chairs and a cozy library decorated with bright English chintz and including a fireplace and a multitude of books. There's a lovely shell corner

## Please Pass the Ps

One of the more curious tales of a country inn involves the Old Drovers Inn in Dover Plains, New York. The romantic and elderly inn was built in 1750, and, as unusual as it seems, every single owner from that time to this has had a last name beginning with a *P*.

First there was farmer Ebenezer Preston, who operated an extensive farm on the acreage that included his farmhouse. He or his descendants eventually opened the house to travelers for food, libation, and rest and called the place the Clearwater Tavern. The Preston family owned the building for almost 200 years.

In 1937 the tavern was sold to Olin Chester Potter, who operated it until his death in 1952, at which time his son, James Potter, assumed control. It was Mr. Potter who sold the inn to Alice Pitcher and Kemper Peacock in 1988.

There's another odd twist to this tale, however. The beautiful murals in the Federal Room are frequently admired by guests of the inn. They were painted by Edward Paine, another man who made a significant contribution to the history of the inn—and another person with a last name beginning with a *P*.

cabinet whose twin is now featured in the American Wing of the Metropolitan Museum of Art. Breakfast is served in the Federal Room, a room lined with historical murals of the area, painted in the style of the Hudson River School of painters by Edward Paine in 1942.

**HOW TO GET THERE:** From New York City take I-684 to Brewster, then take Route 22 north. On Route 22 a sign for the inn is 3 miles south of Dover Plains. Turn east and drive ½ mile. Inn is on the right. Dinner guests enter on the ground floor; overnight guests park in back and enter on the second floor.

# The Roycroft Inn  📱 👥
## East Aurora, New York 14052

**INNKEEPER:** Martha B. Augat

**ADDRESS/TELEPHONE:** 40 South Grove Street; (716) 652-5552; fax (716) 655-5345

**E-MAIL:** mbaugat@roycroftinn.com

**WEB SITE:** www.someplacesdifferent.com

**ROOMS:** 22; all with private bath, air-conditioning, telephone with dataport, television, VCR, desk, radio, robes, whirlpool tub. Wheelchair accessible. No smoking inn.

**RATES:** $120 to $250, double occupancy; includes continental breakfast.

**OPEN:** All year.

**FACILITIES AND ACTIVITIES:** Restaurant open for lunch Monday to Friday (entrees $5.50 to $9.95), dinner (entrees $13 to $23), and Sunday brunch ($15), sometimes including a jazz combo. On Roycroft campus, which includes the 1899 chapel; the 1902 blacksmith/copper shop, where art galleries now reside; the furniture, leather, and bookbindery, where you can buy pottery, collectibles, books, and art. There's also a courtyard garden, and you may receive a complimentary pass to a local health club. Nearby: Elbert Hubbard Roycroft Museum, numerous crafts and antiques shops.

**BUSINESS TRAVEL:** Desk, telephone with dataport, television, and VCR in all guest rooms; meeting rooms, fax, and copier available; audiovisual equipment.

*E*lbert Hubbard was a visionary, there's no dispute about that. Primarily an author and lecturer, he first gained fame in 1899 with an essay that urged readers to accept responsibility. As his popularity grew and his publications increased in number and stature, he built a print shop that specialized in expert printing and fine bookbinding. Soon he added other crafts to his enterprise, including copperware, leather goods, and the manufacturing of solid Mission-style furniture. The influence of William Morris, who Hubbard had met at his Kelmscott Press and crafts complex in 1894 in Hammersmith, England, was evident.

Hubbard's village of artisans were knows as "the Roycrofters." To accommodate the increasing visitors to East Aurora, who were attracted to Hubbard's lectures and ideas, he built The Roycroft Inn.

Simple and straightforward, the guest rooms held no illusions of grandeur. They were small boxes; some shared a common sitting room, and all shared hall bathrooms. Sleeping porches offered additional sleeping accommodations, and Hubbard carved a name into the door of each room, naming them either after a friend who had visited here or for a prominent figure of the day whom he admired. But the purpose for coming to The Roycroft  Inn wasn't to repose in a room; the purpose was to learn by listening to lectures, watch the crafts being created, or engage in stimulating conversation.

Hubbard and his wife died in the sinking of the *Lusitania* in 1915, and although his son carried on the enterprise for an additional twenty-three years, the complex eventually deteriorated and was closed. In 1993 the Margaret L. Wendt Foundation of Buffalo provided the funding to perform a historically accurate restoration of the inn and it reopened to the public in 1995. The inn and the surrounding buildings making up the Roycroft Campus are on the National Register of Historic Places.

Today the guest rooms are more spacious and luxurious than in Hubbard's day, with twenty-two rooms, each containing a private bath with a whirlpool tub. Nevertheless, the ambience and character of the former Roycrofters are flawlessly preserved. There are original and lovingly reproduced Roycroft beds, tables, chairs, and chests. The maple floors are polished, on the beds a woven throw in a leafy pattern has fringed edges, the ceilings have wide bead boards, and the walls are covered with a Roycroft-designed leafy wallpaper. The baths also have maple floors (they were once rooms) and beautiful Roycroft-designed tiles with acorns in relief.

# Elbert Hubbard Lives On

Elbert Hubbard, the founder of the Roycroft Arts and Crafts community, was a Renaissance man of his day, a period that began in 1883 and ended (much too soon) with his drowning when the SS *Lusitania* was sunk by a German submarine in 1915. Enthusiastic, energetic, intelligent, and loquacious, he left us with his philosophy in these quotations:

- "Produce great people; the rest follows."
- "Men are homesick amid this sad mad rush for wealth and place and power. The calm of the country invites and we would fain do with less things and go back to simplicity."

Every room at The Roycroft Inn contained a journal where guests were invited to record their thoughts. Among them were the following:

*October 31, 1922*
I've gazed, from the harbor, on Naples
And tramped o'er the Appian Way,
Climbed the Palatine Height
While the soft morning light
On the dome of St. Peter's made play.
I've been bathed in the joy of old London
Have strolled through the Bois of "Paree"
But, wherever I've been
The Old Roycroft Inn
Went with me in sweet memory.

*March 20, 1922*
Elbert, old Boy, I thought you were Bunk;
I came here tired and thoroughly funked.
After a sleep full of rest, I woke up with zest . . .
I'm sorry, Elbert, I thinked the wrong thunk.

The huge lobby of the inn was originally Hubbard's grand salon, where most lectures were held. The reception area was the music room. The fabulous murals that line the walls were painted in 1905 by Alexis Jean Fournier. They have now been restored and rehung. On the opposite side of the building, the Roycroft print shop is now another massive lobby that leads the way to the series of dining rooms.

This is an inn to explore and appreciate. Few places are restored in such a historically accurate fashion. Yet the friendliness of the staff, who obviously take as much pride in their work as the former Roycrofters did, and the excellent facilities, including the wonderful dining rooms and the food they serve, make it the kind of place I want to return to again and again.

**HOW TO GET THERE:** East Aurora is located 50 miles southeast of Buffalo. From I–90 east of Buffalo, take exit 54 onto Route 400, the Aurora Expressway. Follow this for 14 miles to East Aurora. Take the Maple Street exit and turn right onto Maple Street. Follow this for 2 miles to its end. Turn left onto Main Street and go 2 blocks. Turn right onto Grove Street. The inn is on the left.

# East Hampton Point Cottages
East Hampton, New York 11937

**INNKEEPER:** Dominique Cummings

**ADDRESS/TELEPHONE:** 295 Three Mile Harbor Road/Hog Creek; (516) 324–9191; fax (516) 324–3751

**E-MAIL:** cottages@easthamptonpoint

**WEB SITE:** www.easthamptonpoint.com

**ROOMS:** 13, consisting of 12 cottages and 1 suite; all with private bath, air-conditioning, telephone, television, radio, minirefrigerator, hair dryer, deck or patio, and robes; 12 (all cottages) with full kitchens, coffeemakers, and whirlpool tubs. Smoking permitted. Pets allowed in some units with prior permission.

**RATES:** $100 to $400, double occupancy. Additional person, $20. Weekly rentals only in July and August; two-night minimum stay weekends in May, June, September, October, and New Years' weekend; three- or four-night minimum some holiday weekends.

**OPEN:** All year.

**FACILITIES AND ACTIVITIES:** Waterfront restaurant serving lunch (entrees $6.00 to $17.00) and dinner (entrees $20 to $35); outdoor pool, tennis court, dock, marina (mechanic on duty), ship's store, exercise room with stairmaster, bicycle, treadmill, etc.; van service to town and beach. Nearby: golfing, sailing, horseback riding, ocean beaches, wineries.

"ummertime, and the living is easy." This old Gershwin tune always lingers in the back of my mind when I think about East Hampton Point. How can you resist the fabulous deck of the restaurant overlooking the harbor, where you can relax with a tall, cool drink after a day at the beach and watch the sun sink beyond the horizon as it serves up the most spectacular sunsets imaginable? Your friends may have arrived by boat and docked at the pier, and as the day turns quieter, the sounds of rigging slapping against masts sings a seafarer's lullaby.

The cottages were built in stages during the 1980s—little beachy places tucked away among the trees. Then the spectacular restaurant was built down by the water, and eventually the complex was purchased by a local team who transformed everything into a premier retreat.

The cottages are still located amidst the trees, but they now are connected by brick pathways bordered by abundant flower beds. A former chapel at one end of a path houses exercise equipment and a television to make the time pass more quickly. The cottages range in size and amenities, but each has a full kitchen. Cottage 5 has a kitchen with a Mexican tile floor and counters, as well as bleached pine cabinets. There's a private deck with a view of the marina and a powder room with wainscoted walls. Upstairs the bedroom has a cathedral ceiling and pine furniture. There's a terrific view of the marina. The bath is spectacular, with a tile floor and a skylight over the whirlpool tub, as well as pine cabinets, wainscoting, and a separate shower.

The pool is secluded amidst its own trees, and beside the tennis court there's a trellis that shelters tables and chairs. A continental breakfast is available at the ship's store by the marina for a charge in the summer. It will include fresh fruits, juice, bagels, muffins, croissants, and scones.

The restaurant offers a combination of dining options. You may want to sit in the formal dining room, or, perhaps, if it's a warm night you may want to sit on the outside deck. Part of the deck is reserved for informal dining, and there's a separate deck menu. The handsome bar is distinguished by the presence of a polished mahogany 5.5-liter sloop that is suspended from the ceiling.

**HOW TO GET THERE:** From New York City take I–495 (Long Island Expressway) east to exit 70 (Manorville). At the stop sign turn right (south) and follow this to its end at Route 27 (Sunrise Highway). Follow Route 27 east about 30 miles to East Hampton. At the traffic light by the pond in East Hampton, turn left and drive through town. Bear left just before the windmill and follow Three Mile Harbor Road for 4³⁄₁₀ miles to the turnoff for the inn and restaurant.

# The Hedges Inn
## East Hampton, New York 11937

**INNKEEPER:** Linda Calder

**ADDRESS/TELEPHONE:** 74 James Lane; (516) 324–7100; fax (516) 324–5816

**ROOMS:** 11; all with private bath, air-conditioning, telephone, radio, hair dryer, robes, iron, and ironing board; 4 with desks. No smoking inn.

**RATES:** $225 to $350, double occupancy; includes continental breakfast. Two-night minimum weekends November to June; three-night minimum weekends July to October; five-night minimum Fourth of July and Labor Day weekends.

**OPEN:** All year.

**FACILITIES AND ACTIVITIES:** Restaurant (James Lane Cafe) open May to Labor Day weekend serving dinner (entrees $18 to $30). Parking, courtyard, beach passes provided. Nearby: ocean beaches, golfing, tennis, Guild Hall Theatre, historic museums.

This historic house has a story to tell. Located as it is at the very entrance to the village, it enjoys a location that places it on the edge of Town Pond and midway between the village and the beach. The Hedges family, one of the founders of East Hampton, owned the property from 1652 to 1923, and it is believed that part of this current house may actually be as old as 1774. After the Hedges family sold the house, it went through several metamorphoses, including a very fancy summer boarding house in the 1930s. From 1954 to 1964, however, the little house was one of the most talked-about places in the Hamptons, for this was the site of Henri Soulé's famous Hampton outpost—a branch of his renowned Manhattan eatery, Le Pavillion.

The Hedges Inn, painted a crisp white and sitting behind a decorative picket fence, is one of the prettiest inns in the Hamptons. There are shutters at the windows, and colorful flowers spill from planter boxes. A broad front porch seems to be made for relaxation on gentle summer afternoons. Crisp and bright, the public rooms of the inn have polished bleached-pine floors and white walls. The main dining room has a fireplace, and French doors lead to an enclosed and tented garden room, which is surrounded by planter boxes filled with flowers and has a flagstone floor. This is an utterly romantic place to eat in the summer. A small flagstone terrace is a lovely place to have a before- or after-dinner drink.

The guest rooms are cheerful and light. In 1998 they received a complete Crate and Barrel makeover. They now have pine and wrought-iron beds, the wainscoting is painted a soft creamy color, and there's pretty new art on the walls. Forest-green carpeting covers the floors.

**HOW TO GET THERE:** From New York City take I–495 (Long Island Expressway) east to exit 70 (Manorville). At the stop sign turn right (south) and follow County Road 111 to its end at Route 27 (Sunrise Highway). Follow Route 27 east about 30 miles to East Hampton. At the traffic light by the pond, you will see the inn straight ahead.

# The Huntting Inn 🛎️ 📱
East Hampton, New York 11937

**INNKEEPER:** Linda Calder

**ADDRESS/TELEPHONE:** 94 Main Street; (516) 324–0410; fax (516) 324–6122

**ROOMS:** 18, including 1 suite; all with private bath, air-conditioning, telephone, television, radio, hair dryer, iron, and ironing board; 12 with desk, 1 with whirlpool tub. No smoking inn.

**RATES:** $225 to $475, double occupancy; includes continental breakfast. Two-night minimum weekends November to June; three-night minimum weekends July to October; five-night minimum Fourth of July and Labor Day weekends.

**OPEN:** All year.

**FACILITIES AND ACTIVITIES:** Dinner nightly (The Palm Restaurant) April to October; Thursday to Sunday from November to March, but please confirm (entrees $20 to $35). Tavern, parking, garden, on two and a half acres. Nearby: beach, tennis privileges, golf, charter fishing, boating, swimming, sailboarding, bicycling, horseback riding, shopping, Guild Hall Theater, museums.

BUSINESS TRAVEL: Desk in 12 rooms; fax available; meeting room.

Built originally as the home of the Reverend Nathaniel Huntting, the second pastor to minister to the spiritual needs of the souls of East Hampton, the core of the building dates to 1699. Over the years it was added to and expanded as more space was needed. Today the quirky narrow hallways that twist and turn are the residue of these additions. The house was opened to travelers during the Revolutionary War and became a full-time boardinghouse in the 1870s. It has never looked back.

The sparkling white clapboard building has black shutters and sits behind a white picket fence. Located in the heart of the village, it's possible to walk from here to all the shops and galleries. A lovely side garden has benches, and we have often composed ourselves in this quiet spot before or after a day at the beach.

The well-known Palm Restaurant, the original of which opened on Second Avenue in Manhattan in 1920, is located on the main floor. The decor of dark wooden booths, dark wainscoted walls, tin ceilings, oak mirrors, and Victorian light fixtures remains in the original restaurant, and this theme has been adapted to The Palm here, too. The restaurant is noted for its enormous (and fabulous) steaks, lobster, and side dishes such as an overflowing platter of cottage fries and deep-fried shoestring onions (we usually order a combination platter of a half portion of each). In addition to the  restaurant, there's a cozy bar with an old-world oak bar and more wooden booths on the opposite side of the lobby. In back, there's a quiet room for reading or just relaxing.

The guest rooms vary in size and decor—all have period reproduction furniture, floral chintz fabrics, and a private bath.

HOW TO GET THERE: From New York City take I–495 east to exit 70. Take County Road 110 to Route 27. Follow Route 27 east about 30 miles into East

Hampton to where it merges with Main Street. The inn is at 94 Main, on the right side past the Presbyterian Church and Guild Hall Theater. Watch for the white picket fence.

# J. Harper Poor Cottage
East Hampton, New York 11937

**INNKEEPERS:** Gary and Rita Reiswig

**ADDRESS/TELEPHONE:** 181 Main Street; (516) 324–4081; fax (516) 329–5931

**E-MAIL:** info@jharperpoor.com

**WEB SITE:** www.jharperpoor.com

**ROOMS:** 5; all with private bath, telephone, television, VCR, desk, and robes; 4 with fireplace, 3 with whirlpool tub, 1 with balcony. Radio, minirefrigerator, hair dryer, fax, CD player, iron, and ironing board available. No smoking inn.

**RATES:** $195 to $450, double occupancy; includes full breakfast. Three-night minimum in July and August, four-night minimum holiday weekends, two-night minimum weekends rest of year.

**OPEN:** All year.

**FACILITIES AND ACTIVITIES:** On one acre with beautiful sunken gardens; parking, beach passes, and towels provided; wine and a fully stocked bar. Nearby: Guild Hall and John Drew Theater, ocean beaches, tennis, golfing, fishing.

**BUSINESS TRAVEL:** Desk, telephone, television, and VCR in room; dataport and computer line available; fax, conference room available.

The J. Harper Poor Cottage is one of the most unique buildings in East Hampton, although that fact is not readily apparent from the street, as it's hidden away behind a buff-colored stucco wall. The original section, a saltbox, dates to the early eighteenth century. You can still see its hand-hewn oak beams and cooking fireplace in the breakfast room. It began to take on its distinctive English manor house appearance in 1885 when it was enlarged and the mullioned windows and the carved lintel angels were added to the entrance. In 1900 the house was purchased by James Harper Poor, who hired English architect Joseph Greenleaf Thorp to give it an Arts and Crafts appearance. Current owners Gary and Rita Reiswig have impeccably restored the house to this period.

Comfortable, inviting, restful, and gracious, this inn has developed through its various incarnations from the time the Reiswigs first purchased it, and it is with tremendous pride that I highly recommend it now. You enter the spacious entry hall and feel as though you have been transported into an elegant early twentieth-century home. A library to the left holds an oak library table and chairs, and along the wall are several thousand volumes neatly arranged in oak bookcases. To the right is the breakfast room, which has French doors opening to a wisteria-covered loggia, raised-panel pine walls, and a woodstove. Beyond the library the massive living room has a

plaster-relief ceiling, oak-paneled walls, an oak window seat in the bay window, and a huge fireplace with a floor-to-ceiling tile surround. William Morris–design linen covers the chairs and is mirrored by a hand-blocked paper border.

The guest rooms are decorated with as much flair as the common rooms, and all are romantic—all but one have a working fireplace. I believe my favorite is Number 13, which has a little balcony overlooking the village green. It has hand-hewn oak beams and paneled walls. There's an iron bed with a matelassé spread, an antique oak secretary with books filling the shelves, and a fabulous bath. The largest room is Number 11, which has both a bedroom (with a wonderful Arts and Crafts bed) and a sitting area—decorated in a William Morris–inspired green floral pattern that seems to bring the lovely garden right inside the room. There's a window seat by the mullioned windows for viewing the gardens. The bathroom is positively romantic. It has a whirlpool tub-for-two, a separate shower, and pedestal sinks.

You may relax with a glass of wine in the living room or out on the courtyard while you admire the gardens after you arrive, allowing the pressures of the drive to melt away. You will certainly go to one of the fine local restaurants for dinner. If it's a balmy summer day, you will have breakfast the next morning on the courtyard. You will start with coffee, juices, and breakfast breads. For an entree, you might be served a frittata, an omelette, or, perhaps, pancakes.

HOW TO GET THERE: From New York City take I–495 (Long Island Expressway) east to exit 70 (Manorville). At the stop sign turn right (south) and follow County Road 111 to its end at Route 27 (Sunrise Highway). Follow Route 27 east about 30 miles to East Hampton. At the traffic light by the pond, turn left. You are now on Main Street. The inn is on the left.

# The Maidstone Arms

East Hampton, New York 11937

INNKEEPER: Coke Anne Saunders; William S. Valentine, manager

ADDRESS/TELEPHONE: 207 Main Street; (516) 324–5006; fax (516) 324–5037

E-MAIL: maidarms@aol.com

WEB SITE: www.maidstonearms.com

ROOMS: 19, including 6 suites and 3 cottages; all with private bath, air-conditioning, television, and telephone; 3 with fireplace and/or patio. No smoking except in Water Room.

RATES: $175 to $350, double occupancy; includes continental breakfast. Two- to four-night minimum most weekends and holidays.

OPEN: All year.

FACILITIES AND ACTIVITIES: Restaurant serving breakfast, lunch (entrees $8.50 to $15.50), and dinner (entrees $19 to $29). Water Room Lounge with woodstove for drinks or a cigar. Nearby: Atlantic Ocean (walking distance), village shops, museums, movie theater, bicycling, water sports, and boating.

BUSINESS TRAVEL: Desk in 7 rooms; fax and copy machines available; small conference room.

*I*t is at the Maidstone Arms that East Hampton marks the changing of seasons. In springtime the lawn becomes a carpet of golden daffodils under the huge elm tree in front. Throughout the summer the front porch and stairs are filled with planters that overflow with bright flowers. In fall, as pumpkins cover the fields, the porch of the Maidstone Arms is piled with pumpkins, cornstalks, and huge gourds in an array of red, orange, yellow, and green. In winter, hopefully as snow is falling, the giant evergreen tree in front is covered with thousands of twinkling lights, and the entire village turns out for its holiday lighting and to sing carols and drink hot cider.

This gracious and refined country inn epitomizes all that a country inn should be. In crisp white clapboard with blue and white awnings, it regally surveys Town Pond. The Water Room, a common room that stretches along the front of the inn and overlooks Town Pond, has an appropriate sporting theme of duck decoys, fishing pictures, and antique fishing gear. You might enjoy a game of backgammon or chess, read a book, or have a lively conversation with friends while sipping a cognac and enjoying a cigar here. In winter a fire may be burning in the handsome woodstove, but in summer the French doors may be thrown open to the pretty back garden, where you will certainly want to sit.

The guest rooms are charmingly decorated—some have canopy beds, some four-posters, and some iron or brass beds—all use pretty floral or checked fabrics, quilts, and matelassé spreads. One of my favorites is Number 14, which has a verdigris iron bed and a pretty sitting porch with wicker

furniture that looks out toward Town Pond. The baths are lovely with hexagonal-tile floors and tiled walls.

William Valentine has been setting a standard for dining in the Hamptons ever since he accepted the position of chef here in 1993 (he is now general manager as well). At least one meal in the Hamptons should be eaten here. In the first place, the two dining rooms are delightful. The Boat Room has a more informal feeling, with its wide pine floors, ship prints on the walls, and its huge fireplace. The continental breakfast for inn guests is served here every morning. The China Room, which also has a fireplace, has a cheerful ambience with a plaid carpet and blue and white plates decorating the butter-yellow walls. Chef Valentine's signature entree is a roast rack of lamb with roasted garlic herb orzo, while his signature dessert is a mille-feuille of espresso, mascarpone, and chocolate.

**HOW TO GET THERE:** From New York City take I–495 (Long Island Expressway) east to exit 70 (Manorville). At the stop sign turn right (south) and follow County Road 111 to its end at Route 27 (Sunrise Highway). Follow

Route 27 east about 30 miles to East Hampton. At the traffic light by the pond, turn left. You are on Main Street. The inn is on the left across from Town Pond.

# 1770 House
## East Hampton, New York 11937

INNKEEPERS: Wendy and Burt Van Deusen; Adam and Joi Perle

ADDRESS/TELEPHONE: 143 Main Street; (516) 324–1770; fax (516) 324–3504

ROOMS: 8, including 1 cottage; all with private bath, telephone, and air-conditioning; 2 with fireplace, 1 with television. No smoking inn. Children over the age of 12 welcome.

RATES: $120 to $280, double occupancy; includes full breakfast. Lower rates in winter. Three-night minimum July and August and holiday weekends, two-night minimum other weekends.

OPEN: All year.

FACILITIES AND ACTIVITIES: Gardens, parking. Nearby: beach, bicycling, boating, swimming, ice skating, museums, Guild Hall Theater and Art Gallery, antiques shops, boutiques, restaurants of East Hampton.

Wendy (Perle) Van Deusen, her husband, Burt, and her brother and sister-in-law, Adam and Joi Perle, are carrying on the grand tradition started by their parents, Mim and Sid Perle, in the late 1970s. This picture-perfect, white-clapboard inn along a tree-shaded street in a lovely village is filled with the traditions, family mementos, and antiques that are cherished by their guests.

This is "a timely inn." Everywhere you look are visuals. Clocks—ornate French grandfathers', beautifully carved American timepieces, mantel clocks, and decorative clocks—merge into a soft tick-tocking in the dining room.

The original post office of East Hampton forms one part of the small inn office. There are lovely stained-glass windows that flash red and gold jewels across dining-room tables and a coat of arms over the dining-room fireplace mantel. The cozy library is paneled in fruitwood. Its fireplace casts a warm glow across the tiny bar and the shell corner cabinet filled with fine porcelain.

Each of the guest rooms is uniquely decorated with antiques; most have canopy beds. Number 2 is as spacious and as snug as a country hideaway can be. Pretty chairs are pulled up in front of a fireplace in a paneled wall—just the spot to sip a glass of port after dinner and strategize about the following day's activities, at least until the inviting canopy bed beckons. Number 3 has an antique highboy and canopy bed. The upstairs rooms are reached along a circuitous hallway that leads past a hall fireplace and a divided bench. The cottage in back offers privacy and seclusion.

Wendy is a fabulous trained chef, so you know that breakfast, which is served in the formal dining rooms, will be special. She may have picked herbs from the garden in back for a light frittata, and it is certain that the rich bounty of the Hamptons' fruits and berries will be featured.

**HOW TO GET THERE:** From New York City take I–495 (Long Island Expressway) east to exit 70 (Manorville). At the stop sign turn right (south) and follow County Road 111 to its end at Route 27 (Sunrise Highway). Follow Route 27 east about 30 miles to East Hampton. At the traffic light by the pond, turn left. You are on Main Street. The inn is on the left.

# The White Inn
Fredonia, New York 14063

**INNKEEPERS:** Robert Contiguglia and Kathleen Dennison

**ADDRESS/TELEPHONE:** 52 East Main Street; (716) 672–2103 or (888) FREDONIA (for reservations only); fax (716) 672–2107

**E-MAIL:** inn@whiteinn.com

**WEB SITE:** www.whiteinn.com

**ROOMS:** 24, including 11 suites and 1 cottage; all with private bath, air-conditioning, telephone, television, and radio; 23 with hair dryer, iron, and ironing board; 18 with desk; 2 with fireplace; 2 with whirlpool tub. Wheelchair accessible. Smoking permitted; designated nonsmoking rooms.

**RATES:** $69 to $189, double occupancy; includes full breakfast. Roll-away, $10. Two-night minimum college weekends.

**OPEN:** All year.

**FACILITIES AND ACTIVITIES:** Breakfast, lunch, dinner (entrees $13 to $22 with salad), tavern, gift shop. Nearby: Lake Erie, winery tours, antiquing, skiing, Chautauqua Institution, 1891 Fredonia Opera House, Amish country, music and cultural events of university.

**BUSINESS TRAVEL:** Telephone and television in rooms; desk in 18 rooms; copy machine and fax available; conference space.

**RECOMMENDED COUNTRY INNS® TRAVELERS' CLUB BENEFIT:** 10 percent discount, Sunday to Thursday, except holidays and holiday weekends.

*C*hautauqua County's Fredonia was the mythical town in the Marx brothers movie *Duck Soup,* and the Marx brothers played here during their touring days. It's an all-American village, site of the first Woman's Christian Temperance Union, the first Grange, and the first natural gas well in the country. Keeping within the classic American tradition, Duncan Hines visited here and gave The White Inn his seal of approval.

The White Inn once belonged to Dr. Squire White, who built his first house here in 1811. After it was consumed by fire, his son built a substantial brick dwelling in 1868. The architecture of several rooms in the current inn date to this period. The home remained in the White family until 1918, when it was turned into a hotel.

Robert Contiguglia and Kathleen Dennison met while in hotel school at Cornell. They graduated in 1991, and they married the day after graduation.

They purchased The White Inn in 1993 and have been renovating and redecorating ever since.

The guest rooms have some lovely antique furniture, and above all the doors, where the transom used to be, local artist Peggy Kurtz has painted local scenes. I was especially impressed by the Victorian oak bed with its high headboard and footboard in the Devillo White Room, as well as the matching dresser and the oak table with its ornately carved legs. In the Isabelle White Room, there's a beautiful Eastlake bed and a matching marble-topped dresser and chest. A cautionary note: Several of the baths are tiny, and those that I inspected on my last visit in 1998 still needed attention. You'll see antiques in the wide hallways with sales tags on them. Should you like it, you may take a table home with you.

The dining room at The White Inn is sizable, offering several options in which to dine. In the main dining room you will enjoy a fine gourmet meal accompanied by either local wines (there are several wineries nearby) or other fine wines, or you can eat in the more informal lounge. In the dining room you might have Lamb Wyoming, a boneless saddle of lamb with a lamb stuffing flavored with almonds, spinach, shallots, and garlic. While eating in the lounge perhaps you'll have the Lamplighter Chicken, a grilled chicken breast topped with bacon and melted Swiss cheese and served with a peppercorn sauce and french fries.

HOW TO GET THERE: From I–90 take exit 59 (Dunkirk/Fredonia). At the first light, turn left onto Route 60 south. At the second light, turn right onto Route 20 west. Travel 1³/₁₀ miles to Fredonia, where Route 20 becomes Main Street. The inn is on the right in the center of town.

# The Ghost of Isabelle White

In 1918 when Isabelle White sold the house that had been occupied by the White family since 1811, she did so with remorse. How could she ever find a happiness and a peace to equal the hours she had spent in her delightful bedroom? Little did she know that the house would soon become a commercial hotel!

Since Robert Contiguglia and Kathleen Dennison have owned the inn, guests have told them about some strange goings-on in Isabelle's former room, now the Isabelle White Room. Apparently she sometimes wanders the halls at night, and twice guests have reported seeing an image of a woman in the room. One night, as a couple were peacefully sleeping, the woman had a vivid dream of a woman coming to tell her that she would soon have a child. One year later the couple brought their newborn son to stay in Isabelle's room with them to show him off to their benevolent friend.

# The Bird & Bottle Inn
## Garrison, New York 10524

INNKEEPER: Ira Boyer

ADDRESS/TELEPHONE: Old Albany Post Road, Route 9
(mailing address: R2, Box 129); (914) 424–3000 or (800) 782–6837;
fax (914) 424–3283

E-MAIL: birdbottle@aol.com

ROOMS: 4, including 1 suite and 1 cottage; all with private bath, working fireplace, and air-conditioning, 2 with desk and porch or patio. Wheelchair accessible. Children over the age of 12 welcome. No smoking inn.

RATES: $225 to $260, double occupancy; includes full breakfast and a dinner credit of $75 per couple; plus 12 percent service charge and 7.25 percent tax. Two night minimum if Saturday night included.

OPEN: All year.

FACILITIES AND ACTIVITIES: On eight acres with stream; historic inn with restaurant serving dinner Wednesday through Sunday (prix fixe price for six courses ranging from $35 to $55, exclusive of wine, gratuity, and tax) and lunch Thursday through Saturday (entrees $7.00 to $10.00); Sunday champagne brunch (entrees $17 to $24); atmospheric Drinking Room. Nearby: village of Cold Spring, Boscobel Mansion, historic Hudson River Museum, Kykuit (Rockefeller estate), wineries, nature center, sailing, biking, hiking, antiquing.

RECOMMENDED COUNTRY INNS® TRAVELERS' CLUB BENEFIT: Stay two nights, get third night free, subject to availability.

*I*love the history and romance that surround The Bird and Bottle Inn. The inn opened in 1761 and soon became a popular watering hole along the New York-to-Albany post road. Historians believe it may have been the site of the September 1780 meeting at which treacherous West Point commander Benedict Arnold agreed to reveal the secrets of West Point's fortifications to British spy Major John André for a handsome sum. It's certain that General George Washington was waiting for Arnold at the nearby home of Beverly Robinson when Arnold slipped away to join the British aboard the sloop *HMS Vulture*.

The atmosphere of those early days remains in the white clapboard building with its double porches and steeply pitched roof. The main floor has an utterly romantic air with low, beamed ceilings and dark paneling in the dining rooms, which are arranged in a series of cozy rooms, each with a fireplace. Firelight mingles with candlelight to play on the walls. There are slanted wide-plank pine floors and wavy panes in the mullioned windows. The Drinking Room, the inn's cozy and seductive bar, is reached along a narrow hallway and has another fireplace.

The guest rooms are charming and romantic, with fireplaces in each one where you can burn real wood—a rarity in inns today. The Beverly Robinson Suite is decorated in a peach-and-beige damask that drapes across the canopy bed. Oriental rugs cover the pine floors and there's a little balcony overlooking the entrance. For the ultimate in privacy, the Nelson Cottage is tucked away amid the gardens. Its carved canopy bed is festooned in shades of pink and cream, and it also has a fireplace. Beware, the bath is difficult to access. In fact, the baths in all the rooms are rather cramped. But you have really come here to soak up the history and to dine.

This is one of my favorite restaurants in the New York area. It's infused with such a sense of romance that I can't imagine a reluctant damsel refusing a proposal here, and there's enough space between tables to ensure privacy. But it isn't just the setting; it's also the food that makes this such a special place. I have enjoyed many Thanksgiving and Christmas dinners here, as well as those  merely intended as a short refuge from the city. It's a leisurely and dress-up experience. You might start with an appetizer of herbed chèvre baked in a puff pastry and served hot with a chilled puree of pear sauce. This will be followed by a soup and then a salad of the day. For an entree your choice may be the salmon, sautéed with a topping of thinly sliced potatoes in a tomato and basil beurre blanc, or the roast pheasant, served with a Madeira, pâté, and truffle sauce. Naturally there's a wonderful wine list from which to choose an appropriate accompaniment. For dessert you might have the chocolate ganache tarte, a sinful confection with a crushed macadamia nut crust and a chocolate ganache center that's served in a pool of caramel sauce with chocolate drizzled over.

There are eight acres in which to walk, but those of us with a romantic streak will head for the little bridge that crosses tumbling Indian Brook or strike out to explore the remnants of the old stone gristmill.

HOW TO GET THERE: From New York City, cross the George Washington Bridge and travel north on the Palisades Parkway. Cross the Hudson River again on the Bear Mountain Bridge, making the first left after crossing the bridge onto Route 9D. Follow Route 9D north for 4½ miles. Turn right onto Route 403 and travel 1½ miles to Route 9. Turn left onto Route 9 north and go 4½ miles to the BIRD AND BOTTLE INN sign. Turn right and go ¼ mile to the inn, which is on the left.

# Belhurst Castle & White Springs Manor
Geneva, New York 14456

INNKEEPERS: Duane R. Reeder; Kevin Reeder, manager

ADDRESS/TELEPHONE: Route 14 South (mailing address: P.O. Box 609); (315) 781–0201, fax same

ROOMS: 26, including 4 suites and 3 cottages; all with private bath, air-conditioning, telephone, television, radio, coffeemaker, and hair dryer; 17 with fireplace, 16 with VCR and CD player, 10 with whirlpool tub. Wheelchair accessible. Smoking permitted.

RATES: $105 to $315, May through October; $65 to $245, November through April; double occupancy; continental breakfast. Cot $30, crib $10 extra.

OPEN: All year.

FACILITIES AND ACTIVITIES: Belhurst Castle on twenty-five acres; White Springs Manor on eighteen acres. Restaurant at Belhurst Castle serving lunch Monday to Saturday (entrees $6.00 to $8.00), dinner nightly (entrees $16 to $30), and Sunday brunch ($15); lounge; parking. Dock on Seneca Lake in front of inn. Nearby: Home of Hobart and William Smith colleges, boating, fishing, waterskiing, sailing, hiking, public golf course, winery tours.

BUSINESS TRAVEL: Desk, telephone, television, VCR in room; meeting rooms.

*A*rich history, a checkered past, and a promising future are all associated with Belhurst Castle. The fantastic and romantic stone castle with its turrets, bays, and gables was constructed between 1885 and 1889 by a New York millionairess Carrie M. Young Harron Collins (she was a descendant of Henry Clay), and it's now on the National Register of Historic Places. In 1932 it was purchased by one of its most colorful owners, Cornelius J. "Red" Dwyer, who turned the property into a speakeasy and gambling casino. He continued to operate the casino until 1952, when the Kefauver Commission convinced him to cease, but the successful restaurant remained under his control until 1975.

Duane Reeder has owned the restaurant and inn (the second and third floors were converted to guest rooms in the 1980s) since 1992. Two guest cottages and the ranch home built in the 1950s by Red Dwyer also contain guest rooms.

It's impossible not to be impressed when catching first sight of Belhurst Castle as you drive along the tree-line drive toward the lake. It was built to impress. I entered the building through the *porte cochere,* which leads to massive paneled oak doors and then to a lobby/entrance hall that is fantastically carved from its 14-foot ceilings to its parquet floor. There's a mag-

nificent carved fireplace here that incorporates a design in turquoise and gold and includes arched niches where carved jesters reside. The tavern has an equally impressive, carved floor-to-ceiling fireplace with a central mirror. A selection of crackers and cheese was set out on a table, and there's a nice selection of local microbrews, as well as wines. Alas, there are also dirty and worn carpets and a general impression that maintenance has not been attended to.

The dining room, on the other hand, shines. With elegant table settings, oil paintings on the paneled walls, and fabulous views of the lake, one soon forgets the problems—and that's especially true when the food arrives. One evening I had a lovely appetizer of tender scallops served in a puff pastry with a sprig of thyme and an entree that included a wonderful almond-coated quail that had been basted with a white-peach and Amaretto sauce and was served on a bed of rice. These may be paired with fine wines, including a good selection of local New York State wines.

The Dwyer Suite in Belhurst Castle includes delicate traceries of iron and pale gold stained-glass windows in the bedroom, which also has a high carved tobacco plantation bed but, unfortunately, no nightstand or bedside lamps. In the living room there are velvet and tapestry-covered chairs and a gas fireplace. A table sits in the turret, where pink-and-yellow stained glass tops the curved windows. There are fabulous views of the lake.

In 1998 Mr. Reeder also purchased White Springs Manor, a fabulous Georgian revival mansion dating to 1806 that sits on eighteen acres on a hill overlooking Seneca Lake about 1½ miles from town. It is anticipated that there will be twelve rooms in the manor house, with eight opening in 1998 and the other four in 1999. The Playhouse, a separate cottage, will also be renovated for guests in 1999.

HOW TO GET THERE: From I-90 (New York State Thruway) take exit 42 onto Route 14 south and go about 5 miles to Geneva. Continue south on Route 14 through the village. The inn is located on the shores of Seneca Lake on the outskirts of Geneva.

# Geneva on the Lake Resort
Geneva, New York 14456

INNKEEPER: William J. Schickel; Alfred and Aminy Audi, owners

ADDRESS/TELEPHONE: 1001 Lockland Road (mailing address: P.O. Box 929); (315) 789-7190 or (800) 343-6382; fax (315) 789-0322

E-MAIL: www.gotlreso@epix.net

WEB SITE: genevaonthelake.com

ROOMS: 30 suites; all with private bath, air-conditioning, telephone with dataport, television, radio, full kitchen, coffeemaker, hair dryer, desk, iron, and ironing board; 6 with balcony, 3 with fireplace and VCR, 1 with whirlpool tub. Wheelchair accessible. Most rooms designated nonsmoking. Pets sometimes permitted with prior permission.

RATES: $105 to $525, double occupancy; includes continental breakfast. Two-night minimum when stay includes Saturday.

OPEN: All year.

FACILITIES AND ACTIVITIES: Restaurant, Lancellotti Dining Room, serving breakfast and dinner nightly (entrees $20 to $40). On ten acres overlooking lake and gardens, 70-foot outdoor pool, boathouse, dock, sailing, croquet, bocci, lawn swing, parking on grounds; complimentary passes to nearby YMCA. Nearby: wineries, Hobart and William Smith colleges, Sonnenberg Gardens and Mansion, Rose Hill Mansion.

**BUSINESS TRAVEL:** Desk, television, telephone with dataport in room; complimentary room service breakfast at any hour; fax and computer with Microsoft Word and Word Perfect software available. Three conference rooms, including full audiovisual capabilities, message and copying services, meal and beverage services.

*U*nder the ownership since 1997 of Alfred and Aminy Audi, the owners of L. and J. G. Stickley, Inc., the furniture manufacturers, Geneva on the Lake has received a top-to-bottom renovation. The imposing 1914 white stucco Italian Renaissance mansion with its red tile roof overlooks Seneca Lake. It was modeled after Villa Lancellotti in Frascati, just outside Rome, and was designed by students of the firm of McKim, Mead, and White. The villa and gardens served as a Capuchin monastery from 1949 to 1974.

In 1979 William Schickel, a noted designer (his nephew is now the manager), undertook a major renovation to bring the villa back to its original elegance. From the colonnade pavilion the eye travels down rows of formal boxwood gardens to huge pillars topped by massive terra-cotta urns that create a frame for the lovely pool and then beyond to the lake—a stunning view. Classic sculptures are scattered throughout the grounds.

The spacious guest rooms are furnished with elegant Stickley furniture in velvet and tapestry fabrics. There are marble fireplaces, balconies, lake views, and four-poster and canopy beds. Modern tile kitchens and baths blend comfortably with the old-world beauty. My favorite is the Library Suite, which has a marble floor with an Oriental rug, a coffered ceiling, a lovely sandstone fireplace, cherry bookshelves, and Stickley furniture in solid cherry. The Classic Suite has a tile entry and a fireplace in both the living room and one of the bedrooms. There's a canopy bed and beautiful Chippendale-style furniture from Stickley.

The Lancellotti Dining Room is as elegant and refined as the rest of the inn. A marble floor and lovely linens, china, silver, and stemware add to the room's grace. One night we started our meal with fresh fruit that had been drizzled with a Finger Lakes seyval blanc and then had a delicious entree of Chicken Jacqueline, a sautéed chicken breast topped with a creamy port wine sauce and served with sliced apples and toasted almonds. The dessert menu features grand-restaurant classics, including bananas Foster, strawberries Romanoff, and baked Alaska.

HOW TO GET THERE: From I–90 (New York State Thruway) take exit 42. At the end of the ramp turn right onto Route 14 south and drive approximately 6 miles to Geneva. Continue south on Route 14 through the village. The inn is located on the outskirts of Geneva on the shores of Seneca Lake.

# Greenville Arms 1889 Inn
## Greenville, New York 12083

**INNKEEPERS:** Eliot and Tish Dalton

**ADDRESS/TELEPHONE:** Route 32, South Street (mailing address: P.O. Box 659); (518) 966–5219; fax (518) 966-8754

**E-MAIL:** ny1889inn@aol.com

**WEB SITE:** www.artworkshops.com

**ROOMS:** 13, including 1 suite; all with private bath and air-conditioning. Wheelchair accessible. No smoking inn. Children over the age of 12 welcome.

**RATES:** $115 to $150, double occupancy; $95, single occupancy; includes full breakfast and afternoon tea. Additional person, $35. Two-night minimum holiday weekends.

**OPEN:** All year except December.

**FACILITIES AND ACTIVITIES:** Set dinners are offered Sunday through Thursday nights (prix fixe $25, plus tax and 13 percent gratuity); on Saturday nights and holiday weekends, a choice of appetizers, entrees, and desserts is offered (prix fixe $36 plus tax and a 13 percent gratuity); wine and beer available but extra. The Hudson River Art Workshops are held in the inn's carriage house from May to October. Swimming pool, conference room, games and play area. Nearby: Catskill State Park, Albany, Hudson River touring, biking, hiking, fishing, golf, nature preserve, Catskill Game Farm.

**BUSINESS TRAVEL:** Conference center and audiovisual equipment available.

**RECOMMENDED COUNTRY INNS® TRAVELERS' CLUB BENEFIT:** 10 percent discount.

If you're a painter or an artist, you already know about the Greenville Arms 1889 Inn and the wonderful Hudson River Valley Art Workshops. Started in 1982 the summer programs have grown over the years to attract teachers and students from all over the world. Eliot and Tish Dalton have created a relaxed yet spirited, creative atmosphere, where students and teachers discuss the day's program at breakfast, set up their easels either in the studio, which occupies the ground floor of the carriage house, or *en plein air* and then reflect on their progress at the dinner table and often well into the evening, sharing thoughts about favorite artists and how they achieved their results.

The inn itself is warm and old-fashioned. Built by William Vanderbilt in 1889, it has beautiful fretwork over the doors on the main floor and a wooden fireplace mantel in the dining room. Upstairs, one guest room has a canopy bed with lace curtains; Room 1, which contains the turret, has another canopy bed, a balcony with wicker furniture, and rose carpeting. More guest rooms are located on the second floor of the carriage house. The nicest of these, which has a private balcony, is the Haymow Room.

The beautiful pool is surrounded by lawns and flower beds, and there's a fountain at one end. An English croquet course and all the necessary equipment for an enjoyable, old-fashioned game are also located on the inn's seven acres.

Tish is the inn's chef. For breakfast she specializes in either buttermilk pancakes or French toast that will feature locally made maple syrup, and the Daltons have included an interesting history about the process of making maple syrup on the breakfast menu. Dinner focuses on American comfort foods such as honey roast chicken, roast pork loin, apple pie a la mode, and peach cobbler.

**HOW TO GET THERE:** Exit I–87 at 21B (Coxsackie–New Baltimore). Turn left on 9W south and go 2 miles to the traffic light. Turn right on Route 81 west, go 13 miles to Greenville, then turn left at light on Route 32S. Inn is on the right. Beware: There are three towns named Greenville in New York. This one is in Green County.

# Aubergine 🏨 💲
## Hillsdale, New York 12529

**INNKEEPERS:** David and Stacy Lawson

**ADDRESS/TELEPHONE:** Intersection Routes 22 and 23 (mailing address: P.O. Box 387); (518) 325-3412; fax (518) 325-7089

**WEB SITE:** www.aubergine.com

**ROOMS:** 4; all with private bath (although two are in the hall), air-conditioning, and desks. No smoking inn. Pets permitted with prior permission.

**RATES:** $85 to $110, double occupancy. Two-night minimum weekends in July and August.

**OPEN:** All year except December.

**FACILITIES AND ACTIVITIES:** Restaurant serving dinner Wednesday to Sunday (entrees $19 to $24); on two acres; parking. Nearby: Catamount Ski area (downhill), hiking, fishing, antiquing, golfing.

**RECOMMENDED COUNTRY INNS® TRAVELERS' CLUB BENEFIT:** 10 percent discount, subject to availability.

*B*uilt in 1783 this brick house, located at the junction of two former stagecoach routes, has been a notable French restaurant for forty years. Formerly the domain of Chef Jean Morel, Aubergine was purchased by Chef David Lawson and his wife Stacy in 1995. David, who was trained in France and who was formerly the executive chef at Blantyre, a Relais & Chateaux castle nearby, is an amazing talent. He can describe in intricate detail how to make bread by using macerated currents instead of yeast and how to prepare silky chocolate from cocoa beans.

The restaurant is the primary raison d'être for this family enterprise, and rightly so, as David's culinary accomplishments deserve a showcase. Each of the four dining rooms has a fireplace topped by a handsome mantel. They are gracious and refined, as are the table settings, which include the finest silver, china, linens, and stemware. Fresh flowers grace the tables. You might start the evening with a napoleon of crispy sweetbreads and roasted sweet-potato puree with rhubarb coulis, then move on to a grilled tournedo of Atlantic salmon on creamy polenta with roasted artichokes and served with a tomato-and-garlic broth. For dessert you might try my favorite, a hazelnut soufflé. Reluctant to end such an evening, you might retire to the tiny and charming tavern, which has a copper-topped bar, for an after-dinner port or aperitif.

The guest rooms are located on the second floor, where there's also a nice common room. They are definitely afterthoughts, however, decorated in a straightforward manner. The Coral Room and the Lavender Room have private in-room baths, while the French and Green Rooms have private baths in the hall. There are shag carpets, crewel spreads on the beds, and shutters on the windows.

HOW TO GET THERE: From New York City take the Henry Hudson Parkway north to the Sawmill River Parkway. At the junction with the Taconic Parkway, take this north to the Hillsdale/Claverack exit. Go east on Route 23 for about 9 miles to the traffic light in Hillsdale. The inn is on the left.

# Le Chambord 🖼 📱
## Hopewell Junction, New York 12533

INNKEEPER: Roy Benich; Kevin McGannon, manager

ADDRESS/TELEPHONE: 2075 Route 52; (914) 221–1941; fax (914) 221–1941

WEB SITE: www.pojonews.com

ROOMS: 25, including 16 minisuites; all with private bath, air conditioning, telephone with dataport, television, desk, radio, hair dryer, iron, and ironing board. Wheelchair accessible. Smoking permitted; designated nonsmoking rooms.

RATES: $125 to $135, double occupancy; includes continental breakfast.

OPEN: All year.

FACILITIES AND ACTIVITIES: Restaurant serving lunch (entrees $14 to $17) and dinner (entrees $20 to $29); on ten acres with parking, gardens; Rajko's, an extensive gift and gourmet shop; exercise room with treadmill, climber, rowers, and Solarflex. Nearby: Mills, Boscobel, and Vanderbilt mansions, West Point Military Academy.

BUSINESS TRAVEL: Desk, telephone with dataport, television in all rooms; conference facility, fax, and copier available.

Longtime innkeeper Roy Benich is a jovial, affable man who loves to cruise the dining room greeting and talking to his guests. But when he isn't, the diners are either admiring the European paintings that cover the walls (they are for sale) or sampling the wonderful cuisine. This has been Roy's domain since 1984. As his guests know the minute they enter the inn, he is also a collector of fine art and antiques and an inveterate traveler who returns home with one-of-a-kind items for his gift shop.

The main inn, a white 1863 Georgian Colonial with a two-story colonnade across the front, is impressive to say the least. As we walked up the driveway one summer afternoon, all the tables on the pretty terrace were filled with ladies at lunch who were thoroughly enjoying themselves. The cuisine of the inn is so French in nature that the menu is in both French and English. For dinner you may have *Carré d'Agneau Rotis à l'Ancienne—pour deux* (pistachio-encrusted rack of lamb for two with baked tomatoes Provençale), as we did, and end the meal with that most French of all desserts, crêpe Suzette, for two. The wine list is the pride of the house, and there's a nice selection of cigars (for use in the downstairs lounge or outside only).

Nine of the guest rooms are on the upper floors of the main building. These are furnished with antiques. The remaining rooms are in a 1990s structure that Roy calls Tara Hall, which is located behind the historic building. The rooms here are similarly styled with period reproduction furniture. The building has a nice lounge area with a fireplace as well as several meeting/conference rooms. A ballroom still further back on the property has proven popular for weddings.

**HOW TO GET THERE:** From New York City take the Henry Hudson Parkway north to the Saw Mill River Parkway. Follow the Saw Mill River Parkway north to the Taconic Parkway. Traveling north on the Taconic, go to the Route 52 exit (Fishkill/Carmel exit) and travel east on Route 52. The inn is ¼ mile on the left.

# Buttermilk Falls Bed & Breakfast
## Ithaca, New York 14850

**INNKEEPERS:** Margie Rumsey; Kristen Rumsey, manager

**ADDRESS/TELEPHONE:** 110 East Buttermilk Falls Road; (607) 272–6767; fax (607) 273–3947

**ROOMS:** 5, including 1 suite and 1 cottage; all with private bath and air-conditioning; 2 with television; 1 suite with double Jacuzzi, fireplace, and VCR. One room wheelchair accessible. No smoking inn.

**RATES:** $95 to $295, double occupancy; includes full breakfast. Two-night minimum special event weekends. No credit cards.

OPEN: All year.

FACILITIES AND ACTIVITIES: On two acres with gardens; walking sticks provided for traversing the forest trails; yoga mats, meditation pillows. Nearby: Buttermilk Falls State Park across lawn, swimming, cross-country skiing. Ithaca restaurants (short drive), Finger Lakes wineries, sailing, hiking gorges, museums, antiquing; Cornell University and Ithaca College.

In 1998 Margie Rumsey celebrated fifty years of ownership of the property that was once part of her grandfather's dairy farm. She moved here as a bride in 1948. Actually, she is the sixth generation of her family to live in this 1825 white-brick house and her granddaughter, Kristen, is the seventh. It was Margie's idea to turn the charming farmhouse into a bed-and-breakfast. She has infused it not only with her warmth and enthusiasm, but also with her uncanny decorating sense.

The rooms are decorated in a crisp Amish/Shaker style and include straight-lined furniture made of beautiful woods. Somehow Margie created guest rooms that retain all the appeal an older house conveys (old pine floors covered by Oriental rugs, wainscoted walls, and fireplaces), and yet she has tucked in such modern conveniences as whirlpool tubs and kitchens. You'll see interesting folk art peeking out of an old cupboard and lovely quilts covering beds. My favorite is the Jacuzzi Suite on the former sunporch. This has

a Jacuzzi in the room, where the flames of the fireplace create a play across the walls; in the spring the roar of Buttermilk Falls creates an utterly romantic mood.

Breakfast is served in a dining room that has a buckboard seat at both ends. Perhaps you'll have whole grain cereal or a sundae of plumped dried fruits, nuts, berries, and seeds. There will be a hot casserole or, perhaps, French toast, as well as bacon or sausage, bread or popovers, and, perhaps, a pie. Afternoon tea includes hot or cold spiced cider and a snack of the season.

Outside there are gardens and lawns to roam, and Buttermilk Falls is just across the road. In the spring the water falls in a tumultuous rush from two terraces into the pool below, and in the summer you can swim here. Be sure to ask Margie for help in deciding what to do while in Ithaca. With roots as deep as hers, she knows all the shortcuts and all the hidden treasures of the area.

**HOW TO GET THERE:** From I–90 (New York State Thruway) take exit 40 to Route 34 south and continue for approximately 49 miles to Ithaca. Continue south through Ithaca to the junction with Route 13. Follow Route 13 to East Buttermilk Falls Road. Turn into Buttermilk Falls State Park. The inn is the second house on the left.

# Hanshaw House Bed & Breakfast
## Ithaca, New York 14850

**INNKEEPER:** Helen Scoones

**ADDRESS/TELEPHONE:** 15 Sapsucker Woods Road; (607) 257–1437 or (800) 257–1437

**WEB SITE:** www.wordpro.com/hanshawhouse

**ROOMS:** 4, all with private bath and air-conditioning. No smoking inn. Well-behaved children welcome.

**RATES:** $72 to $135, double occupancy; includes full breakfast. Packages available; some weekends slightly higher. Two night minimum from May to November when stay includes a Saturday night.

**OPEN:** All year.

**FACILITIES AND ACTIVITIES:** On one and two-thirds acres of gorgeous gardens; a pond, woods, picnic table, barbecue, and parking. Nearby: Ithaca restaurants (5 miles), Sapsucker Woods, Cornell University, shopping, gardens, cultural events, winery touring, hiking, sailing, downhill and cross-country skiing.

*H*elen Scoones's decorating eye and sense of drama have turned a charming and historic 1830s Colonial house into an enchanting English cottage. The minute I drove into the parking area and saw the colorful flower gardens surrounding the front and sides of the white clapboard building with its gray shutters, all framed by a white picket fence, I was sure this would become one of my favorite inns. I was right.

Greeted at the front door by Helen (who was an interior designer in her former life and whose husband, Bill, is a dean at Ithaca College), I was drawn across the beautiful parlor with its lovely sofas covered with imported English chintz fabrics to the wall of windows that frame the fabulous back gardens. Here I saw a pretty pond, terraces, abundant flowers that are coordinated to bloom from early spring through late fall, and numerous bird feeders that attract a happy population of woodpeckers, cardinals, and their friends.

There are four spacious guest rooms, all with their own private bath, and each is delightful and charming. Room 1, on the first floor, includes a front-row view of the gardens and a four-poster bed with a crisp matelassé spread. Another of my favorites is Room 2, which has a marbleized and painted armoire.

One of the things I appreciate about Helen is her interest in encouraging local artists and craftspeople. Anyone who recognizes the name MacKenzie-Childs (they are headquartered nearby in Aurora, New York) knows about their highly original hand-painted china and furniture. Helen sets her breakfast table with MacKenzie-Childs whimsical and captivating china, goblets, and tall candles topped with shades, and throughout the inn you will see traces of these talented designers' wares. Other designers are represented as well. Don't miss the painted pieces by Nancy Ternasky! It takes a talented designer to mix and match the work of artists, and Helen is that. In the guest television room for example, she has combined wicker with colorful green

cushions and a pretty French high-backed bench with pink-striped fabric.

Breakfasts are as creative as the decor. One morning we started with orange juice in those beautiful stemmed glasses and then were served a fresh fruit plate garnished with flowers and mint from the garden. As an entree Helen prepared baked eggs on a crouton with sautéed spinach and scallions and topped with hollandaise sauce. This was accompanied by fresh scallion scones and lemon bread. In the afternoon you can sip fresh-brewed tea and nibble homemade biscotti and cookies on the terrace while you watch the birds at their teatime as well.

Helen has lived in the Ithaca area for many years. She can direct you along the back pathway to Cornell University's Sapsucker Woods Laboratory of

Ornithology, or she may suggest a local winery tour or a visit to the Herbert F. Johnson Museum of Art, the wonderful museum designed by I. M. Pei and located on the Cornell University campus.

**HOW TO GET THERE:** From I-90 (New York State Thruway) take exit 40 to Route 34 south and continue for approximately 47 miles. At the junction with Route 13 (north of Ithaca) turn east onto Route 13 and go to Warren Road. Turn south (right) onto Warren Road away from the airport. Go to the stop sign at Hanshaw Road and turn left. Go approximately 7/10 mile to Sapsucker Woods Road and turn left. The inn is the second house on the right.

# Rose Inn
## Ithaca, New York 14851

**INNKEEPERS:** Charles and Sherry Rosemann

**ADDRESS/TELEPHONE:** Route 34N (mailing address: P.O. Box 6576); (607) 533-7905; fax (607) 533-7908

**E-MAIL:** roseinn@clarityconnect.com

**ROOMS:** 15, including 5 suites; all with private bath, air-conditioning, telephone, radio, robes, and hair dryer; 10 with iron and ironing board, 6 with desk, 4 with whirlpool tub, 2 with fireplace. No smoking inn. Children over the age of 10 welcome.

**RATES:** $110 to $185 rooms, $185 to $275 suites, plus 15 percent gratuity and 11 percent tax, double occupancy; includes full breakfast. Extra person in room, $25. Two-night minimum April to November if stay includes Saturday.

**OPEN:** All year.

**FACILITIES AND ACTIVITIES:** Dinner Tuesday to Saturday (prix fixe $55, 4-course). Wine, gratuity and tax extra. Carriage House restaurant serving dinner Friday and Saturday nights (entrees $17 to $23) with live jazz entertainment. Seventeen acres with fishing pond, apple orchard, rose garden. Nearby: winery tours, ski Greek Peak, lake mailboat tours, bicycling, cultural events, Cornell University.

**BUSINESS TRAVEL:** Desk in 6 rooms, conference center, secretarial services; fax; e-mail.

When I think of romantic inns, the Rose Inn often comes to mind first. For one thing Charles and Sherry Rosemann are friendly and solicitous about their guests needs, but they are also absolutely serious and professional about their inn. Charles has managed hotels in Europe and the United States, and Sherry is a professional interior designer. Together they're an unbeatable team who know just what to do to make every guest's stay memorable.

I love to wake in the Honeymoon Suite (you can stay here even if you're re-creating the mood) to watch the sun rise across the fields—there were two deer one morning—and to hear the birds trilling as I gaze through the Palladian windows. It's a stunning room—all decorated by Sherry in beige; bold chocolate brown; rich, warm caramel; and gray. The bed has an ivory tapestry padded headboard, and the linens are positively luxurious in beige and brown with black-and-white tattersall sheets. You can sit in the two-person whirlpool tub in front of the Palladian windows late at night, with candles burning while you watch the flames from the fireplace. In the morning you can take a shower in the bath that is done all in gray marble. Each of the rooms is distinctive. There isn't a single one that you won't be happy with.

Don't even think of eating elsewhere. Dress in your finest, and plan for a leisurely and fabulous dinner, hopefully in the company of a loved one. The dining rooms occupy a series of parlors that are exquisitely restored to the elegance they knew when the mansion was first built. Pause to take it all in  and you will be rewarded with views of wonderful antiques, such as a corner cabinet hand-painted with flowers and scrolls and filled with antique silver and china. Needlepoint carpets accent the polished parquet pine floors.

Dinner is served on gold-rimmed china, often with a rose motif. You place your order for the appetizer and entree when you make your reservation. Ken Atlas is a fabulous chef. One meal started with a "Bounty of Mushrooms," an artful mélange of mushrooms and herbs in a puff pastry topped with melted brie. The salad was as artistic as the appetizer—various vegetables were presented in cups of radicchio. I had ordered the honey almond duck for my entree, and it was moist and lovely.

You should definitely spend time meandering about the seventeen-acre property. Sit awhile in the 8,000-square-foot formal garden with its wedding chapel; pluck an apple from one of the trees in the orchard if the season is right, or pick berries from the raspberry patch. Sit in the rose garden to admire the varieties. Charles creates terrific jams and jellies from his bountiful gardens that can be purchased in the gift shop.

An 1850s carriage house across the drive serves as a conference room during the week. On weekends it becomes the Carriage House restaurant, where casual dining is accompanied by live jazz.

HOW TO GET THERE: From I–90 (New York State Thruway) take exit 40 to Route 34 south and continue for approximately 36 miles. The inn is on the left, about 10 miles north of Ithaca. From Ithaca head north on Route 34 and travel 6 miles to the intersection with a flashing red light. Turn right and continue for ½ mile. At the fork in the road go left (onto Route 34, *not* Route 34B). The inn is 3½ miles farther on the right.

## Stairway to the Stars

When Abram Osmun built his fabulous mansion between 1848 and 1851, he incorporated the finest materials he could purchase. There were hand-carved doors of chestnut and butternut and parquet floors of quarter-sawn oak. An abundance of rich Honduran mahogany was purchased for the grand stairway that was to sweep from the entrance foyer up three stories to a cupola on the roof. Unfortunately, no one with sufficient skill to execute the intricate design could be found. The wood was stored in the henhouse, and the mansion remained unfinished for some seventy years.

One day, however, a traveling carpenter came to Ithaca looking for work. Hearing of the unfinished staircase, he drove up to the house in his battered truck—and went to work. Over the next two years he erected a magnificent spiral staircase. The rail, constructed in a flowing triple curve, is so exquisitely fashioned that it seems to be made of one solid piece of wood. When the job was done, the man left as mysteriously as he had arrived, leaving behind a legend and a legacy.

Today we continue to marvel at the artistry of the Rose Inn's graceful stairway and the story of how it was built.

# The Lamplight Inn
# Bed and Breakfast 📱
## Lake Luzerne, New York 12846

**INNKEEPERS:** Gene and Linda Merlino

**ADDRESS/TELEPHONE:** 231 Lake Avenue (mailing address: P.O. Box 70);
(518) 696–5294 or (800) 262–4668

**WEB SITE:** www.adirondack.net/tour/lampinn

**ROOMS:** 17, including 5 suites; all with private bath, air-conditioning,
telephone, and radio; 12 with fireplace, 4 with whirlpool tub and/or
deck. Wheelchair accessible. No smoking inn. Children over the age of
12 welcome.

**RATES:** $98 to $189, double occupancy; includes full breakfast. Two-
night minimum weekends most of the year; three-night minimum holiday and special-event weekends. Promotional packages available.

**OPEN:** All year.

**FACILITIES AND ACTIVITIES:** Ten acres with trails, brook, garden.
Restaurant serving dinner Friday and Saturday nights from November
to April and Wednesday to Sunday nights from May to October (entrees
$18 to $21); wine and beer available; service bar in great hall where
glasses of wine, beer, and bottled water may be purchased; extensive gift
shop. Nearby: restaurants, Lake Luzerne, whitewater rafting, cycling,
horseback riding, cross-country skiing, snowmobiling, professional
rodeo summer Friday nights, Lake George (10 miles), Saratoga Springs
(18 miles).

**BUSINESS TRAVEL:** Telephones all rooms; desks in 5 rooms; fax and
copy machine available; conference room.

*W*hen Linda and Gene Merlino enthusiastically tell you about
their inn adventures and the constant improvements they have
made, you understand why their inn is so successful. They just
never slow down. It all began in 1985 when they saw a dilapidated building
sitting forlornly on a hillside outside of town. They did what they knew they
had to do. They bought it and immediately started renovating it into a bed-
and-breakfast. Once that was finished Gene headed down to the Brookside
Guest House, where he created the two-level Morning Glory and Sunflower

Suites. After that was finished he built a new carriage house to match the other buildings; the carriage house contains five rooms, each with a gas fireplace and all but one with a private deck.

The main building was built in 1890 by a wealthy lumberman in a Victorian Gothic style meant to showcase his woods. The clapboard is now painted a cheerful yellow with white trim and deep blue shutters, and there's a wonderful wraparound porch. The sitting area on the main floor is in the vast former great room, and Linda has literally stuffed it with Victorian furniture and plants. There are 12-foot beamed ceilings, chestnut wainscoting and moldings, and two fireplaces. You will spend hours looking at her Mme. Alexander doll collection, and something in the extensive gift shop is sure to

please you. There's a little service bar where you can buy a glass of wine or beer or bottled water.

The guest rooms are comfortable and down home rather than elegant. You'll find white iron, oak, and canopy beds; some quilts; and oak dressers. The baths are clean and adequate. Although all baths are private, several are in the hallway rather than in the room.

Dinner is served at the inn, and it's a relief to know that after a day of skiing or hiking you need go no farther than down the stairs to dine. You might have a roasted duckling breast with Lingonberry-gin sauce for dinner, or maybe you'll choose the salmon pinwheels—rolls of fresh salmon and spinach encased in puff pastry, baked, and served with a buerre blanc sauce.

A wonderful full breakfast is served in the dining room every morning. The recipes for Gene's famous home-fried potatoes, Linda's granola, and the couple's apple crisp are often requested.

HOW TO GET THERE: From I-87 (New York State Thruway) traveling north, take exit 24 in Albany. After the toll booths take entrance 1N to I-87 (Adirondack Northway) toward Montreal. Follow this to exit 21 (Lake Luzerne/Lake George). At the end of the ramp, turn left onto 9N south. Follow 9N south for 11 miles. The inn is on the right.

# Lake Placid Lodge ♥ 📱 👥

Lake Placid, New York 12940

**INNKEEPERS:** Christie and David Garrett; Kathryn Kincannon, managing director

**ADDRESS/TELEPHONE:** Whiteface Inn Road (mailing address P.O. Box 550); (518) 523–2700; fax (518) 523–1124

**E-MAIL:** info@lakeplacidlodge.com

**WEB SITE:** www.lakeplacidlodge.com

**ROOMS:** 37, including 5 suites and 15 cabins; all with private bath, air-conditioning, and telephone with dataport; 35 with private deck or patio, 17 with fireplace. Children welcome. Pets permitted in 2 rooms at $50 per day. Wheelchair access. No smoking inn.

**RATES:** $225 to $650, double occupancy; meals extra. Two-night minimum weekends; three-night minimum holidays.

**OPEN:** Year-round.

**FACILITIES AND ACTIVITIES:** Restaurant serving breakfast, lunch (entrees $14 to $19) and dinner (entrees $24 to $31); pub with lighter menu; room service. Championship 18-hole golf course, four tennis courts, hiking trails, sandy lakeside beach, marina, canoes, fishing boats, paddleboats, Sunfish, open-deck sightseeing barge, mountain bikes, cross-country ski touring center in winter. Nearby: downhill skiing, ice skating, hunting.

**BUSINESS TRAVEL:** Desk in room; dataport; fax and secretarial services available; meeting rooms; audiovisual equipment; photocopy services.

*I*t was a sunny October afternoon when we arrived. We immediately fetched a glass of wine from the cozy bar and retired to Hawkeye, our generous two-level retreat, to watch the sunset from our upper deck. As the sun slid behind Whiteface Mountain, it cast its dark reflection in the waters as we watched the streaking sky change from orange and fuschia to the palest pink. It was then that I realized I could happily stay right here and write for the rest of my life.

This former 1882 Adirondack camp was renovated and opened to guests in 1994. True to its origins, it has a log exterior, and its decks are framed by arching unpeeled birch branches. The guest rooms have beds made of twisted birch trees and walls made of logs, bark, and bead-board panels. There are twig furniture and sofas and chairs dressed in bright patterns. Most rooms have stone fireplaces with log mantels, and several, including Hawkeye, have two fireplaces. Six buildings are scattered about the grounds, each containing several rooms or suites.

Even the smallest rooms on the ground floor of the main lodge seem spacious, and they have their own private patios, with terrific views of the lake.

After we watched the evening spectacle, Managing Director Kathryn Kincannon, full of energy and enthusiasm, escorted me through the inn's common rooms, where some guests were playing billiards and others were completing a jigsaw puzzle, and then down to the marina to see the fleet of restored boats. She pointed out a nature trail that leads past trees labeled with identifying tags. We walked to the boat dock, where several couples were just returning from the sunset cocktail cruise on the inn's open-deck sightseeing barge.

It was warm enough at night to eat on the restaurant deck, romantically lighted by flickering candles. Following a dinner of confit of duck leg with sautéed potatoes and foie gras, and deliciously ending with a summer pudding with raspberries, we returned to our room to contemplate the difficult decision before us: Should we take a relaxing soak in the two-person tub; wrap ourselves against the evening chill and sit on the deck awhile longer, listening to the night sounds; or light the fire in one of the massive stone fireplaces? Reluctant to spoil the mood of this amorous place, we chose the latter and lingered with a port before snuggling into the luxurious featherbed, knowing we would be warm enough to leave the windows open all night as we listened to the loons call across the water.

Bright and early in the morning, as the sun was rising, and with the heavy scent of pine permeating the room, I arose to join Kathryn on the boat deck for tai chi, and my companion did his morning jog around the golf course. We left feeling relaxed, rested, and renewed.

HOW TO GET THERE: From I–87 take exit 30. Travel northwest on Route 73 for 30 miles to Lake Placid. In the village take Route 86 for 1½ miles toward Saranac Lake. At the top of the hill, turn right onto Whiteface Inn Road. Follow it for 1½ miles and turn right at the LAKE PLACID LODGE sign. Travel through the golf course to the lodge.

# Silent Star Speaks

When the inn we now know as Lake Placid Lodge was first built, it was privately owned and attracted a glamorous movie-star set that included Norma Talmadge, a silent screen starlet. She would come here for weeks on end with her main squeeze and by all accounts loved the place as if it were her own. But that was long, long ago. Or was it?

For many years a benign female presence, dressed in a long, black, high-necked dress and with dark hair severely fastened atop her head, has been seen drifting with a fluid grace through the original rooms of the inn. It's usually late at night when few people are around. Sometimes she will turn lights off or on, as if to make her presence known. One of her favorite rooms is the Moose sitting room, where Norma's name was serendipitously recently found carved into the massive stone fireplace.

Although the tales of her presence have been whispered for many years, recent guests of the Lodge may have had a first-hand experience. The couple were sleeping in one of the original rooms located above the dining room. While they were sleeping, a book fell off the fireplace mantel with a thud. The gentleman awoke, rose, and replaced it. Soon, however, it happened again. This time, he placed the book under a stack of six books, and in a horizontal position that would prevent its falling. After a sound night's sleep, the couple awoke to find the *same book* was on the floor again.

Did Norma want them to read it? Or perhaps it held a particular significance for her? We will never know, but it is certainly interesting to speculate.

# The Horned Dorset Inn
Leonardsville, New York 13364

**INNKEEPER:** Bruce Wratten; Daniel Welch, manager

**ADDRESS/TELEPHONE:** Route 8 (mailing address: P.O. Box 142); (315) 855-7898; fax (315) 855-7820

**ROOMS:** 4, including 2 suites; all with private bath and air-conditioning; 2 with fireplace. Smoking permitted. Children over the age of 12 welcome. Pets allowed with prior permission.

**RATES:** $105 to $125, double occupancy; includes continental breakfast.

**OPEN:** All year except Mondays and Christmas Day.

**FACILITIES AND ACTIVITIES:** Dinner Tuesday to Sunday (entrees $21 to $27), gardens. Hiking or cross-country skiing through hundred-acre apple orchard at hilltop. Nearby: Cooperstown, with Baseball Hall of Fame; James Fenimore Cooper House; Farmers' Museum (thirty minutes).

*T*he town is an unlikely setting for a fine restaurant. It's in a rural farming community that long ago saw better days. There are boarded up buildings, a grain elevator, and a tavern. In addition the huge 1860 building, painted gold with white trim, seems graceless when viewed from the street. It originally served as a stagecoach stop, then it became a general store, and finally a supermarket before being gentrified into a restaurant. Ah, but don't let all that deter you, for this is a classic example of finding a beautiful lady hiding behind an ugly veil.

Enter the restaurant and you're transported into a world of elegance, sophistication, and grandeur. The partners have salvaged architectural elements from local grand mansions that were being demolished and incorporated them into their building. A heavily carved railing separates a portion of one dining room from a library complete with elegant paneling and bookcases filled with books. Stained-glass windows cast jewels of light. A garden dining room has a wall of Palladian windows rescued from an old school and woodwork from a private residence in Syracuse. Upstairs there's

a matchbox bar with columns from a local estate and a photograph of the horned Dorset sheep that the partners used to raise and for which this inn is named, as well as a bookcase-lined cigar room that was created in 1998. Dinner is an elegant event with preparations that could compete with New York's finest restaurants—all served on gold-rimmed china and with heavy silver.

The inn? Four guest rooms are located in the white Victorian house with the mansard roof just across the garden next door. Antique tables furnish the common rooms, Oriental rugs cover oak floors, and rich ruby-damask covers antique chairs. You'll want to inspect the display of ornate curling medals displayed in a glass-topped coffee table in the parlor.

The very elegant guest rooms are also furnished with antiques, and two of them have fireplaces. The baths are striking, having marble floors and marble-topped dressers or washstands with sinks ensconced in them.

The Horned Dorset Inn has a sister property, the Horned Dorset Primavera Hotel in Puerto Rico, that is a member of the prestigious Relais & Chateaux organization.

**HOW TO GET THERE:** From I–90 take exit 31 (Utica). Go south on Route 8 for 22 miles to Leonardsville. The inn is on the east side of the road.

# Beaverkill Valley Inn 🎏 📱
Lew Beach, New York 12753

**PROPRIETOR:** Laurance Rockefeller; Christina Jurgens, manager and chef

**ADDRESS/TELEPHONE:** 136 Beaverkill Road; (914) 439–4844; fax (914) 439–3884

**ROOMS:** 20; all with private bath; window fan on request. Wheelchair access in 1 guest room and public areas. No smoking in rooms.

**RATES:** $260 to $395, double occupancy; includes breakfast, lunch, and dinner. $160 to $195, single. Children under 2 free; special rates for children 3 to 12. Bed-and-breakfast plan available, Sunday to Thursday, $170 to $240, double occupancy; includes full breakfast. Two-night minimum weekends; three-night minimum holiday weekends.

**OPEN:** All year.

**FACILITIES AND ACTIVITIES:** Air-conditioned dining room open to public by reservation. Victorian bar, enclosed swimming pool, billiards, Ping-Pong, card room, children's play room, ice-cream parlor, hiking and cross-country ski trails, two tennis courts, pond, sixty acres, 1 mile of Beaverkill Stream.

**BUSINESS TRAVEL:** Desks in 6 rooms; telephone, fax, copier, typewriter, and audiovisual equipment available; conference room.

We moseyed along the little country backroads, skirting puddles from a recent rain. We could smell the heady scents of pine and fir, unadulterated by the fumes of industry. This pristine natural environment is not an accident but a careful plan orchestrated by Laurance Rockefeller, who lives on a farm nearby and whose father has done so much to preserve the natural landscape of Wyoming and St. John's in the Virgin Islands. Larry's goal has been to retain the beauty and century-old landscape of the Beaverkill Valley, and he's done so.

As any fly fisherman knows, the Beaverkill is one of the great trout rivers of America, and the inn's property borders over a mile along its banks. This is where dry-fly fishing originated, and although I don't know exactly what that means, it impresses those who do. The inn was built as a boarding house in 1803 to provide accommodations for pilgrims to this fishing mecca, but by the time Larry Rockefeller bought it in 1981, it had fallen on hard times.

Today, however, the white clapboard building shines again. The broad wraparound porch is filled with pretty white wicker; the living room has comfortable overstuffed chairs and sofas and a fireplace for those chilly afternoons when guests return from an afternoon of cross-country skiing. There's nothing pretentious or snobbish here, though. The entire inn is as comfortable as an old pair of shoes.

The guest rooms are decorated with pine and oak furniture, quilts, and brass or iron beds. A buckboard seat sits in a hallway, and there are stained-

glass windows. The baths are excellent, and a 1997 improvement turned one guest room into two baths so that every room now has a private bath, although five are located in the hall rather than in the room. There are no telephones, televisions, or even radios in the guest rooms, but there is a television and VCR downstairs, as well as telephones in old-fashioned oak telephone booths.

This family-friendly inn offers a variety of activities for everyone. There's an indoor pool and a greenhouse playroom for children. In the old-fashioned ice cream parlor, you can scoop your favorite ice cream and cover it with a variety of sauces and toppings—perfect for the child in all of us. There are tennis courts, hiking and cross-country trails, board games, Ping-Pong, and croquet.

Breakfast, lunch, and dinner are included in the nightly package here (although it is possible to stay as a B&B guest on occasion); an extensive afternoon tea is also served. The inn makes it clear that gratuities are discouraged.

HOW TO GET THERE: From New York City cross the George Washington Bridge to New Jersey, staying in the right lane. Exit immediately to the right onto the Palisades Parkway. Travel north for 19 miles to exit 9 west toward Albany. Take I–87 (New York State Thruway) north to exit 16 (Harriman), and follow Route 17 west for 64 miles to exit 96 (Livingston Manor/Lew Beach). Bear to the right and go under Route 17. Continue for ³/₁₀ mile and turn right at the T intersection. Travel 1 mile and turn right onto Beaverkill Road (Route 151), which turns into Route 152 along the way. Proceed for 7 miles to the hamlet of Lew Beach. Continue straight for 2²/₁₀ miles to a small bridge. The entrance to the inn is just across the bridge.

# Genesee Country Inn
## Mumford, New York 14511

INNKEEPER: Kim Rasmussen; Glenda Barcklow, proprietor

ADDRESS/TELEPHONE: 948 George Street (mailing address P.O. Box 340); (716) 538–2500 or (800) 697–8297; fax (716) 538–4565

E-MAIL: gbarklow@aol.com

WEB SITE: www.geneseecountryinn.com

ROOMS: 9; all with private bath, air-conditioning, television, telephone; 3 with fireplace, 2 with patio or porch. No smoking inn. Children over the age of 12 welcome.

**RATES:** $85 to $135, double occupancy; includes full breakfast and afternoon tea. Two-night minimum some weekends May to October.

**OPEN:** All year.

**FACILITIES AND ACTIVITIES:** On eight acres along stream; gift shop. Nearby: seven restaurants within 5-mile radius, Genesee Country Village and Museum, Eastman Philharmonic, biking and walking tours of historical landmarks, trout fishing.

**BUSINESS TRAVEL:** Telephone in room, desk and fax available; conference room.

**RECOMMENDED COUNTRY INNS® TRAVELERS' CLUB BENEFIT:** 50 percent off second night in Old Mill rooms, Sunday to Thursday, November to March.

The mellow brick walls of this 1833 plaster mill are 2 feet thick, and the streams that converge nearby once turned a waterwheel as they raced beneath the structure to form Spring Creek. Today this creek is the playground of ducks, an occasional egret or crane, and numerous birds, as it's on a migratory flyway. There are also deer, muskrat, and fox, and the creek is noted as one of the premier trout-fishing streams in the area. Lawns and flower beds dip away from the inn down to the water's edge, and a pathway leads to a waterfall, which is my preference for a lovely afternoon picnic.

Glenda Barcklow began her transformation of this old building into her unique bed-and-breakfast in 1982, and, although it seemed perfect long ago, she has never stopped adding new rooms and improving the originals. The maple floors of the common rooms are enhanced by beautifully stenciled walls with lovely old moldings. The Old Mill Shop is filled with needlework

supplies and gifts. Breakfast (perhaps she'll fix strawberry waffles with ham or a cheese omelette) is served in a dining room that overlooks the stream.

Each of the guest rooms has its own distinctive flavor. My favorites are those that overlook the creek where I can throw the windows open at night, smell the crisp perfume of country air, and hear the lush sound of the falls. There are beds with fishnet canopies; pine-paneled walls; and smart, tiled baths. My favorite is The Skivington, which includes a gas fireplace, a fishnet-canopied bed, a beautifully executed quilt, and a private deck where it's possible to spend an entire afternoon reading and writing with only the sounds of the birds as background. In my opinion the Seneca Indians were masters of understatement when they named this place Genesee, meaning "pleasant valley."

Be sure to visit the Genesee Country Village Museum, which is about a mile down the road. It's a fully restored nineteenth-century village of fifty-seven buildings that include churches, schools, and even the house where George Eastman was born. Flower and herb gardens are tucked behind and beside many of the buildings.

**HOW TO GET THERE:** From I-90 (New York State Thruway) take exit 47 and follow Route 19 south to Le Roy. In Le Roy take Route 5 east to Caledonia. Then take Route 36 north to Mumford, turning left onto George Street. The inn is 1½ blocks on the right.

# The Vagabond Inn 🖤
## Naples, New York 14512

**INNKEEPERS:** Celeste Stanhope-Wiley and Mica Pierce

**ADDRESS/TELEPHONE:** 3300 Sliter Road; (716) 554–6271

**ROOMS:** 5, including 3 suites; all with private bath, television, VCR, minirefrigerator, and coffeemaker; 4 with fireplace and whirlpool tub, 3 with patio or deck. No smoking inn. Children over the age of 12 welcome.

**RATES:** $115 to $200, double occupancy; includes full breakfast.

**OPEN:** All year.

**FACILITIES AND ACTIVITIES:** On sixty-five acres with hiking and cross-country ski trails, a 9-hole golf course, swimming pool, and gardens. Nearby: numerous wineries, Bristol Valley Playhouse, fishing, and boating on Canandaigua Lake.

We wound up and up and up into the Bristol Mountains above Canandaigua Lake until we felt we could touch the sun. It was a hot, clear day, and as we climbed above the vineyards, the views got better and better. Lured by one of the most beautiful brochures I've seen and one that promised "serenity" on a mountaintop where "peace, elegance, and romance (will) stir the soul," I was on a mission.

I was not disappointed by all the grand statements, for this truly is a unique inn. The setting is spectacular, and when you walk into the gray contemporary board-and-batten house, the panoramic view from the 60-foot Great Room is of more mountains beyond the gardens, a nine-hole golf course, and a swimming pool. The Great Room is anchored at both ends by massive fieldstone fireplaces, and there are numerous selections of books to curl up with in the leather sofa. You will find the fabulous gift items that cover tables, counters, and windowsills irresistible. There's a vast array of blown glass dishes filled with potpourri, wind chimes, candles, hand-cast steel trays from Mexico, and a huge selection of fine-art jewelry. Celeste Stanhope-Wiley is a world traveler, and she brings back treasures for her shop wherever she goes.

There are five guest rooms, and each is beautifully designed with its occupant's ultimate comfort in mind. The Bristol includes a gas stove and a bed with a fishnet canopy. The fabulous bath has a raised redwood whirlpool tub with wonderful views of the mountains, a separate dining porch, and a sundeck. My favorite, however, is the grotto-like room named The Lodge. It has a stone floor, fieldstone walls, and a massive river-rock fireplace. The huge pine bed is stenciled with a tulip design, there are huge boxed beams, and the "bathing chamber" includes a private hot tub. (Guests can also reserve an outside hot tub.)

Celeste prepares a full and delicious breakfast for her guests, and she arranges a flexible time. She has also thoughtfully provided a full kitchen. She has learned that once her guests return in the evening, they are so mesmerized by the setting that they often prefer to eat in. She suggests that they bring selections from the gourmet shops and wineries nearby; she provides everything else. She has more than 400 videos, and she finds that her guests often snuggle in before their VCR to watch a movie.

HOW TO GET THERE: From I–90 (New York State Thruway) take exit 42. Turn right and then right again onto Route 96 north. Watch for the Log Cabin Tavern on the right. Just beyond take County Road 6 (on the left) to Routes 5 and 20. Turn right (east) onto Routes 5 and 20 and then turn left (south) onto Route 14A. Stay on Route 14A until you reach Route 245. Bear right onto Route 245 and stay on this for about 20 miles to Middlesex. Turn left in Middlesex onto Route 364 and go uphill for ½ mile to Shay Road. Turn right onto Shay Road and continue for 4²⁄10 miles to Sliter Road, which will be on the left. Take Sliter Road to The Vagabond Inn (the last ³⁄10 mile will be on gravel).

# Bed and Breakfast on the Park
New York (Brooklyn), New York 11215

**INNKEEPERS:** Liana and Jonna Paolella

**ADDRESS/TELEPHONE:** 113 Prospect Park West; (718) 499–6115

**ROOMS:** 7; 5 with private bath; all with air-conditioning and television, 2 with garden. No smoking inn. Children welcome in 2 rooms.

**RATES:** $110 to $250, double occupancy; includes full breakfast. Two-night minimum weekends; three-night holiday weekends.

**OPEN:** Year-round.

**FACILITIES AND ACTIVITIES:** Nearby: Brooklyn Museum, Brooklyn Botanic Garden, Brooklyn Library, Brooklyn Academy of Music, Prospect Park, bicycling, antiques shops.

"*You can* see the Statue of Liberty!" I exclaimed happily to my companion as he climbed the stairs to join me. We had just been escorted to the Lady Liberty Room by Liana Paolella, and we walked through the double French doors to our private deck and then up another level to the roof, where the Empire State Building, the World Trade Center, and Lady Liberty herself spread before us.

The Lady Liberty Room, where we would be spending the night, was a Victorian gem. An elaborately swagged canopy bed was fluffed with plush pillows, several Victorian dressers with marble tops held fanciful Victorian lamps, and a plate of freshly baked cookies waited on the nightstand. Liana also proudly showed us the Park Suite, which overlooks Prospect Park. It has a lacy crown-canopy bed, a stunning stained-glass window, and a dressing room that's fully paneled with bird's-eye maple, including the mirrored closet doors and a built-in vanity.

Liana was an antiques dealer when she purchased this grand old house in 1985. It needed a tremendous amount of work, but she knew what to do. Stripping the paneled walls, doors, stair railings, detailed fretwork, and window frames, she converted this Victorian derelict into a rare ruby. She then filled it with antiques that might have been used when it was first built. There are fringed sofas and chairs in one parlor, along with a floor lamp with beaded fringe. Ask to see the powder room hidden behind carved paneling in the vestibule. A marvelous collection of oil paintings intrigued us. Liana said that several were painted by her stepfather.

This is a lovely section of Brooklyn, known as Park Slope. Elegant townhouses and brownstones face tree-lined streets. This wide, gray mansion, built in 1892, still has its original stoop and outside trim. Directly across the street is Brooklyn's crown jewel, the 526-acre Prospect Park, created by Frederick Law Olmsted and Calvert Vaux, designers of Manhattan's Central Park. We walked through the park later in the day to take a ride on the restored carousel and to visit the magnificent Brooklyn Museum, one of New York's secret treasures. We were fascinated by the re-created rooms from New York houses.

It was a warm, balmy night, and Liana had suggested a charming restaurant nearby, which we walked to. The streets were filled with neighbors who were walking and greeting one another. Had we decided to go into Manhattan, it would have been just a fifteen-minute subway ride away.

**HOW TO GET THERE:** From Manhattan take the Brooklyn Bridge to Brooklyn. After crossing the bridge continue to Atlantic Avenue. At the intersection with Fourth Avenue, turn right. Continue on Fourth Avenue for 1 mile to Fifth Street. Turn left onto Fifth and continue to the end. Turn right onto Prospect Park West. The inn is 2 blocks farther on the right.

---

# The Inn at Irving Place
New York (Manhattan), New York 10003

**PROPRIETOR:** Naomi Blumenthal

**ADDRESS/TELEPHONE:** 54–56 Irving Place; (212) 533–4600 or (800) 685–1447; fax (212) 533–4611

**E-MAIL:** irving56@aol.com

**WEB SITE:** www.slh.com

**ROOMS:** 12, including 6 suites; all with private bath, air-conditioning, telephone with dataport, fax, television, VCR, CD player, radio, minirefrigerator, hair dryer, decorative fireplace, robes, iron, and ironing board. Smoking permitted; designated nonsmoking rooms. Children over the age of 12 welcome.

**RATES:** $295 to $925, double occupancy; includes continental breakfast.

**OPEN:** All year.

**FACILITIES AND ACTIVITIES:** Lady Mendl's Tea Room, where high tea is served every afternoon; Cibar, an upscale lounge serving drinks, cigars, and light meals; Verbena, an acclaimed restaurant with a garden, leased to its chef. Room service. Nearby: access to Equinox Health Club; Greenwich Village, Soho, restaurants.

**BUSINESS TRAVEL:** Desk, telephone with dataport, fax, television, VCR in room; pager, cellular telephone, laptop computer with Internet access available; room service; limousines.

As I sat in my room overlooking Gramercy Park's Irving Place late one night, I felt myself transported in time to an earlier New York. Like a page from *Time and Again,* I could imagine Washington Irving emerging from his home across the street to walk briskly to a friend's home for dinner or O. Henry scurrying along in the chilly air to reach the warm, convivial atmosphere of Pete's Tavern to finish writing *Gift of the Magi.* The street has changed little over the years, and these two townhouses, recently converted to a sumptuous bed-and-breakfast inn, retain their original stoops, wrought-iron balustrades, and elegant entrances. The inn is so discreet that there's not even a sign announcing it.

The innkeeper warmly greeted me in the gracious parlor, as cozy as a friend's home with its fire burning in the hearth. I was just in time for afternoon tea in Lady Mendl's Tearoom, and he joined me as he told me about the restoration. "The buildings were in need of tremendous work," he explained, and the owner wasn't sure what to do with them. "She loved the tall ceilings and grand windows and decided  that an elegant, turn-of-the-century-style inn would be a nice addition to the city and a perfect use for the buildings." And it is. The side-by-side townhouses contain elegant moldings, polished floors, burnished banisters (one newel has a bronze Fleur de Mai statue), and elegant furnishings. Every room contains fine antiques, but it's all done with a restrained dignity that would have been foreign in most fussy Victorian homes.

My room, quiet and urbane, is named for Stanford White, who certainly trod this street. It has a carved bed, elaborate ceiling moldings, a magnificent armoire, and an inlaid floor. The sophisticated bath has a tile floor. Another of my favorites is the one named for Washington Irving. It has a matching bed and armoire inlaid with a musical-instrument motif. The room named for O. Henry has a brass bed, a carved armoire, and a huge bath with a pedestal sink.

Rather than leave this rarefied and genteel ambience, I met a friend in the charming restaurant on the ground floor. Verbena is leased to an outstanding chef, and we were fortunate to have chosen a night warm enough to allow us to sit in the pretty outdoor garden, although two fireplaces create a cozy inside atmosphere in winter. I had a sturgeon steak with semolina gnocchi, melted sorrel greens, and roasted carrots. For dessert I had a bittersweet-chocolate soufflé baked in a rum-soaked savarin cake and served with chocolate-chip ice cream, truly an outstanding and unusual dish.

Had I opted to attend the theater, I might have had a light snack downstairs at Cibar, the smart lounge that opened at the inn in 1998. Cozy seating in little nooks and around a fireplace and a handsome bar have made this a popular spot. A wide selection of wines, liqueurs, cognacs, single-malt scotches, and cigars is also available.

The next morning a gentle knock announced my breakfast tray of freshly baked pastries, fruit, and coffee. Although I had opted for breakfast in my room, some guests prefer to eat in the tearoom or the parlor. I wonder which option Edith Wharton would have chosen? Since she generally spent her mornings writing in bed, I imagine she would have done just as I did.

**HOW TO GET THERE:** Irving Place is an extension of Lexington Avenue, separated from it by Gramercy Park. The inn is between East 17th and East 18th streets.

# Inn New York City ♥ 📱
## New York (Manhattan), New York 10023

**INNKEEPERS:** Ruth and Elyn Mensch

**ADDRESS/TELEPHONE:** 266 West Seventy-first Street; (212) 580–1900; fax (212) 580–4437

**ROOMS:** 4 suites; all with private bath, air-conditioning, kitchen, telephone with dataport, television, VCR, CD player, and radio; 2 with fireplace and/or whirlpool tub, 1 with a balcony. No smoking inn. Children over the age of 12 welcome.

**RATES:** $250 to $350, double occupancy; includes continental breakfast. Two-night minimum.

**OPEN:** All year.

**FACILITIES AND ACTIVITIES:** Nearby: Lincoln Center, Riverside Park, Central Park, Museum of Natural History, New York Historical Society.

**BUSINESS TRAVEL:** Telephone with dataport, television, VCR, kitchen in all rooms.

*I* should explain that I absolutely love New York. I never tire of it. Therefore, it was a marvelous pleasure to have found this charming "country" inn tucked away on a side street near Lincoln Center and Riverside Park. Inn New York City has long been my own secret treasure (although I admit I share the secret with several others). When Ruth Mensch and her daughter Elyn converted this townhouse to a four-suite bed-and-breakfast in 1989, they had no idea how popular their inn would become.

I remember my enchantment as they showed me around that first time. In the front parlor the elaborate moldings, inlaid hardwood floors, and crystal chandeliers evoked a nineteenth-century nostalgia. "This is where guests often meet friends before walking to one of the nearby restaurants," Ruth told me.

Although all the guest rooms are decorated with unusual flair, I was especially charmed by my own. Ruth has a knack for taking architectural ornaments and turning them into furniture, or room dividers, or interior decor. My room, The Spa Suite, is on the top floor. It has a king-sized bed with a headboard set into an antique chestnut armoire. The sybaritic bath, however, is the pièce de résistance. It has a double Jacuzzi on a platform, a fireplace with a carved mantel, an old barber chair, a cast-iron foot bath, a Victorian dresser with a sink set into its marble top, a sauna for two, and a glassed-in shower.

I also love The Parlor Suite, which has an 18-foot living room with 12-foot-high ceilings. The vestibule has a stained-glass ceiling, and there's a Baldwin grand piano in the living room. The bedroom has a balcony, a fireplace, and a queen-sized bed with a headboard containing cabinets with stained-glass doors. Every room has personal touches such as private libraries, fresh flowers, and fluffy robes.

It was a warm, balmy afternoon the day we arrived, so we walked over to Central Park and rented a canoe for a ride on the lake. Afterward we sipped a glass of wine on the deck of the Boathouse restaurant while we watched the ducks bob for bread tossed into the water. Later we had dinner at a nearby restaurant.

On returning to the inn, we used several of the bath's pleasures and then snuggled into our room for a peaceful and quiet night's sleep. There's a little kitchen in each suite, and Ruth or Elyn fill the refrigerator with fresh goodies at night before retiring. When we rose in the morning, we popped several delicate fresh muffins into the microwave and read the *New York Times* while nibbling on fresh fruit and sipping freshly brewed coffee.

Shhhhh. Don't tell anyone about our secret.

**HOW TO GET THERE:** The inn is located on the south side of West Seventy-first Street, between Broadway and West End Avenue.

---

# Le Refuge 📖 📷
New York (City Island, Bronx), New York 10464

**INNKEEPER:** Pierre Saint-Denis

**ADDRESS/TELEPHONE:** 620 City Island Avenue; (718) 885–2478 or (212) 737–9279; fax (718) 885–1519

**WEB SITE:** www.cityisland.com/lerefuge

**ROOMS:** 8, including 2 suites; suites with private bath, and all with air-conditioning and television. Pay phone in kitchen. No smoking inn.

**RATES:** $75, double occupancy; $65, single; $140, suites; includes continental breakfast. American Express only card accepted.

**OPEN:** All year.

**FACILITIES AND ACTIVITIES:** Dinner with advance reservation ($40 fixed price for four courses), Sunday brunch ($17.50), and classical concert ($10 to $20). Nearby: seafood restaurants. Pelham Bay Park: horseback riding, hiking, tennis courts, Colgate Sailing School, bicycling, Pelham Bay Golf Course, Split Rock Golf Course, Bartow-Pell Mansion and Museum.

*P*ierre Saint-Denis's romantic French Manhattan restaurant by the same name as his City Island inn has long been one of my favorites. I have spent some of my most enjoyable lunches and dinners in the charming rooms decorated in their bright French Provincial fabrics, and I love the delectable light French food that Pierre creates.

Therefore, it was with great anticipation that I first visited his little inn in 1993. A word about City Island might be in order first. Although merely feet from the mainland, this truly is an island, plopped into Pelham Bay and reached across a drawbridge from Pelham Bay Park. It's such an anomaly that few New Yorkers even know it's here. For most of its life it's served as a fishing community, and a good-sized fleet is still harbored here. Not a tourist haven, what you see is what you get—excellent, down-home seafood restaurants, shops selling tackle and boating supplies, and not much else.

Le Refuge is the exception. Once the home of Saint-Denis and his wife, Emmanuelle, they have created an eight-room inn with a restaurant on the main floor. In keeping with the City Island lifestyle, there are no pretensions of elegance here, either. The rooms are crisply decorated with ginghams and toiles and older painted furni-ture. Only the two suites have private baths; all the rest share. My favorite rooms are on the third floor, where there is French toile paper on the walls and dormer windows, although two rooms on the second floor do have access to the balcony across the front. All the rooms have tele-visions and interesting old-fash-

ioned radios. The suites have telephones in the rooms, but the rest of the guests must use the pay telephone in the kitchen.

A continental breakfast of freshly made croissants and café au lait might be eaten on the back deck if the weather is nice. Dinner is served Wednesday through Sunday, and it's open to visitors as well as inn guests. But one of the most popular weekly events is the Sunday brunch. Diners arrive at noon and enjoy a classical concert before partaking of brunch, which is served at 1:00 P.M.

**HOW TO GET THERE:** From I–95 take exit 8B toward City Island. Cross bridge and turn right before first light. Continue to City Island (around traffic cir-cle), cross two-lane City Island bridge, and turn right on City Island Road. Inn is 200 yards on left.

# Elk Lake Lodge 📷
## North Hudson, New York 12855

**INNKEEPERS:** Percy and Janet Fleming, managers

**ADDRESS/TELEPHONE:** Blue Ridge Road (mailing address: P.O. Box 59); summer (518) 532–7616; fax (518) 532–9262; winter (518) 942–0028; fax (518) 942–7070

**ROOMS:** 14, including 8 cottages; all with private bath; 9 with minirefrigerator, 8 with porch, 5 with fireplace, 2 with kitchen. Smoking permitted.

**RATES:** $95 to $120, May to June; $110 to $140, July to October; per person; includes breakfast, lunch, and dinner; plus 15 percent gratuity. Two-night minimum. Children ages 2 to 6, 50 percent discount; 7 to 12, 25 percent discount. No credit cards.

**OPEN:** May through October.

**FACILITIES AND ACTIVITIES:** Breakfast, lunch, dinner for guests only, BYOB; 12,000-acre private forest preserve located directly on Elk Lake and Clear Pond; canoes, rowboats, swimming, fishing, hiking, mountain climbing, bird and animal watching.

Once you've been to Elk Lake Lodge, you'll probably return again and again, for the experience is unlike any other you may encounter. The trip to the private 12,000 acre forest preserve within the 6,000,000-acre Adirondack Park heightens the anticipation, as your drive leads past gigantic spruce, hemlock, maple, and birch trees. A rabbit may dart across the road, but you will probably see no other cars.

When you reach the lodge the setting is so spectacular and so peaceful that you may be amazed that such a pristine location still exists. Elk Lake is spread before you, a 600-acre clear mountain lake with towering mountains as a backdrop. Just before the main lodge, you'll see Branch River plunging across the rocks beside a picturesque waterwheel.

The lodge itself, although built in 1904, is a neat and trim, impeccably maintained, natural shingled Adirondack-style lodge (although not as grand as several of the others) with a wraparound porch occupied by a herd of Adirondack chairs. The lobby is dominated by a huge stone fireplace and Mission-style tables and chairs with leather cushions. The walls are hung with stuffed animal heads and pelts. Braided rugs are on the polished floors. When you arrive in the afternoon, tea will be waiting on a marble topped table.

There are six small rooms upstairs in the main lodge, with knotty-pine walls, dormer windows, and carpeted floors. Each has a pair of twin beds covered with fabric that imitates a quilt. The baths are tiny. The cabins are definitely the preferable places to stay. These are lovely gray log-and-shingle cottages—each in a secluded and very private setting that offers spectacular lake vistas. Were I to choose a favorite, it might be Windfall because of its secluded spot overlooking the lake. It has a wraparound porch with Adirondack chairs, knotty-pine walls, a huge stone fireplace, and two bedrooms. A new cabin, Cornelia, was completed for the 1998 summer season.

Meals are served communally at specified times, and that may be the only time you see other lodge guests. Dinner is a sit-down affair, and the entree is often fixed on the grill. You may have a New York strip steak or, perhaps, swordfish. One of the most popular desserts is the Yum-Yum Pie, a chocolate pudding pie in a walnut/crumb crust with whipped cream.

The array of activities is virtually endless. You may want to fish for trout or landlocked salmon or canoe across the 200-acre glacial Clear Pond. You might hunt for fabulous photos among the wildflower fields or pick fiddlehead ferns, wild strawberries, or blueberries, raspberries, or blackberries. You might bring your binoculars to spy on the loons who live here or to search for hawks, osprey, or pileated woodpeckers.

HOW TO GET THERE: From I–87 (Adirondack Northway) take exit 29 onto the Blue Ridge Road. Travel west for 4 miles toward Newcomb. Turn right at the sign for Elk Lake Lodge and go 5 miles to the inn, which is at the end of a private road.

# Highwinds Inn
## North River, New York 12856

**INNKEEPER:** Holly Currier

**ADDRESS/TELEPHONE:** Barton Mines Road (mailing address P.O. Box 370); (518) 251–3760 or (800) 241–1923; fax (518) 251–5701.

**WEB SITE:** www.adirondack.net/tour/highwindsinn

**ROOMS:** 4, plus two log cabins; all with private bath. No smoking inn.

**RATES:** $135 to $170, double occupancy; includes full breakfast and dinner.

**OPEN:** All year.

**FACILITIES AND ACTIVITIES:** Restaurant serving dinner (entrees $13 to $23) nightly to house guests and the public; wine available. Tennis court, stocked fishing ponds. Eighteen miles of cross-country trails, hiking trails; on 1,600 private acres contiguous with 108,000-acre Siamese Ponds Wilderness area. Nearby: downhill skiing at Gore Mountain, spring whitewater rafting and canoeing on the Hudson River, horseback riding.

The road winds up the mountain and through the forest to an elevation of 2,700 feet, at which point you pass a garnet mine. The Barton family began mining here in the 1880s, and in the summer you can tour the original mine and visit a small museum to learn how garnets, which are almost as hard as diamonds, are mined for use in industry and for jewelry.

The Barton family are the sovereigns of garnets. They eventually expanded their operation throughout the world, and today they mine fully 90 percent of the world's industrial garnets. Although the hill where their family home was located no longer produces garnets, the family still operates mines on a nearby mountain.

Highwinds Inn was the Barton family home for many summers when the mines were in full operation. The house was built in 1933 by C. R. Barton, whose ancestor began mining here in the 1880s, and was occupied by the family until the 1970s. The handsome stone fireplace in the living room always generates interest. It is studded with garnets. Two antique andirons look like iron elves and have hollow eyes so that the flames can be viewed through them.

Each of the four guest rooms has a panoramic view of the mountains. They are furnished with family pieces that include nice old dressers, beds, and chests.

Dinner is served nightly on a glass-enclosed porch that has stunning views of the mountains. The tables are decorated with African violets when the bounty of the flower garden has waned. You might have an entree of sea bass that's been seared in herbs or a hunter's mixed grill, an interesting combination of grilled antelope, venison sausage, and a smoked wild boar rib. The signature dessert is the Garnet Mine, a fabulous combination of chocolate mousse with cherries and walnuts.

The grounds include beautiful perennial beds, hiking trails, a tennis court, and fishing ponds.

HOW TO GET THERE: From I–87 (Adirondack Northway) take exit 23 (Warrensburg) onto Route 9. Go north on Route 9 for about 5 miles through Warrensburg. At the junction with Route 28, turn left onto Route 28. Continue on Route 28 for about 15 miles. Turn left at Barton Mines Road and go uphill 5 miles on paved road to the mine entrance. Follow the signs and continue another 5 miles to the inn, which is at the top of the hill.

# Old Chatham Sheepherding Company Inn

Old Chatham, New York 12136

**INNKEEPERS:** George Shattuck III and Melissa Kelly; Nancy and Tom Clark, proprietors

**ADDRESS/TELEPHONE:** 99 Shaker Museum Road; (518) 794–9774; fax (518) 794–9779

**E-MAIL:** oldsheepinn@worldnet.att.net

**WEB SITE:** www.oldsheepinn.com

**ROOMS:** 8 (11 by 1999), including 3 suites; all with private bath, air-conditioning, telephone, hair dryer, and robes; 5 with private porch, 3 with fireplace, 2 with whirlpool tub. Children under 12 welcome with prior arrangements. No smoking inn.

**RATES:** $185 to $525, double occupancy; includes full breakfast every day except Sunday, when a continental breakfast is served. Two-night minimum weekends May to November; three-night minimum holiday weekends.

**OPEN:** All year except January.

**FACILITIES AND ACTIVITIES:** Restaurant serving dinner Wednesday to Monday (entrees $18 to $25) and Sunday brunch; patio dining in summer. Walking and hiking on 500 acres; seminars and events throughout the year, ranging from sheep-shearing demonstrations to cooking classes and wine dinners; tennis court, bicycles and cross-country skis available, fishing in Kinderhook Creek on property. Do not miss the Shaker Museum across the street from the inn. Nearby: Mac-Haydn Theater in Chatham features Broadway musicals in summer.

**BUSINESS TRAVEL:** Telephone in all rooms; desk in four rooms; meeting room equipped with telephone, fax, and copier.

olive Metcalf

*I*s this heaven or am I merely dreaming? We are sitting in a wicker rocker on our private porch in the Suffolk Room looking beyond the sunken garden with its fountain to the lush green pastures brimming with sheep. The quiet is punctuated occasionally by a lamb bleating for its mother, but otherwise the air is still. This will always be my favorite memory of the Old Chatham Sheepherding Company Inn—this and the extraordinary cuisine, that is.

"I'm just a farmer at heart," owner Tom Clark laughed one night in the relaxed but sophisticated living room of the inn, as he tried to describe how he and his wife, Nancy, created their unique inn and its unusual by-products. "From the time I raised and exhibited three sheep at the local Dutchess County Fair," he went on to say, "I've had an interest in sheep."

This interest in sheep has led the couple to create an entirely new American business. Not only does the inn offer overnight lodging and a fine-dining restaurant, but on their 500-acre farm, the Clarks also raise sheep that are producing milk used for cheese, yogurt, ice cream, and other products. One morning my companion and I rose early to walk down to the Shaker-style sheep barn to watch the 6:30 A.M. milking and to pet the lambs. The operation is as modern and as interesting as a large-scale dairy operation.

The inn is gracious and charming—but that's not surprising, since Nancy is an interior designer and also an artist. Her luminous watercolors decorate several guest rooms. Fine antiques are liberally combined with unusual new furnishings, and elegant fabrics cover chairs, love seats, and beds. There are carved four-poster beds padded with fluffy lamb's-wool cushions. A nearby cottage contains two suites that are perfect in every detail. The masculine Cotswold Suite has a high four-poster bed, a brick fireplace, and a private deck; the Hampshire Suite is charmingly done in shades of pink and yellow. There are two more suites in a new barn and one suite in the carriage house. The inn is a member of the prestigious Relais & Chateaux.

As elegant as the inn appears, however, innkeeper George Shattuck best described the casual atmosphere when he said, "We want guests to feel comfortable. We know we've achieved our goal when they come to breakfast in their terry robes," and he swears it's actually happened.

The dining room is presided over by Executive Chef Melissa Kelly, a graduate of the Culinary Institute of America and the protégée of such acclaimed chefs as Larry Forgione and Alice Waters. Her rack of lamb was exquisite, as was the grilled ahi tuna. There's a kitchen garden and greenhouse from which she collects her herbs and vegetables every day, but she is noted for her distinctive new cuisine using sheep's milk instead of cow's or goat's. She serves a sheep's-milk yogurt with breakfast every morning and often has a

# Here's to Ewe

When little Tommy Clark won a blue ribbon for his Hampshire lamb at the Dutchess County Fair, he was quoted in the local newspaper as saying that one day he would raise a whole flock. Although he has pursued another line for forty years (he is a venture capitalist), in 1993 he and his wife, Nancy, embarked on a grand new adventure when they purchased a 500-acre farm nestled between the Hudson River and the Berkshire Hills.

Starting with a flock of 150 sheep, they built a huge Shaker-style barn with a milking parlor (a creamery was added in 1998) and began the trial-and-error process of developing a distinctive new line of dairy products. They eventually specialized in Friesia crossbreed sheep from New Zealand because they produce the highest volume of milk, and the flock has now increased to 1,000 head of this unique breed.

At first the milk was sold to nearby Hollow Road Farms, where it was made into cheese and sold under their label. In 1996, however, the Clarks purchased Hollow Road Farms, and their dairy products now are made on the farm and sold under the label of Old Chatham Sheepherding Company Inn.

The farm's products of yogurts and cheeses include a Hudson Valley Camembert, fresh herbed sheep's cheese, and a peppered pyramid. They can be purchased at the inn's gift shop or by mail order by calling (888) SHEEP-60.

Chef Melissa Kelly, an honors graduate of the Culinary Institute of America in nearby Hyde Park, has what she considers to be a dream job. She has been able to develop a wholly new cuisine using dishes created from sheep's milk rather than cow's or goat's. Her enthusiasm for the product and her expertise have won her numerous awards. Her appetizer recipe for Hudson Valley Camembert Crisp, one of her signature dishes, follows:

> 2 5-ounce squares of Old Chatham Sheepherding Company
>     Inn Hudson Valley Camembert
>
> 3 sheets of phyllo dough
>
> 2 tablespoons melted unsalted butter
>
> 1 tablespoon butter for sautéeing
>
> 1 egg, beaten with 1 tablespoon water to form a wash

Cut the square piece of Camembert from corner to corner to form four triangles. Lay a sheet of phyllo on the work counter and lightly brush with butter. Lay the second sheet on top of the first and brush it with butter; do the same with the third. From top to bottom, cut the phyllo into four strips. Place a piece of Camembert at the bottom of each piece and gently fold the phyllo over the Camembert, rolling it to the top of the phyllo strip, being sure all the Camembert is enclosed. Brush the fold with egg wash and refrigerate.

Just before you are ready to serve, heat a skillet over a medium flame and add 1 tablespoon butter. Sauté the cheese triangles just until they are golden and the cheese has melted. Serve with a fruit chutney.

lovely ice cream on the dinner dessert menu. There's also a separate bakery and an impressive gift shop in the carriage house.

The manor house was originally the home of John S. Williams, Sr., whose interest in Shaker life was piqued by his home's proximity to several major Shaker communities. He began collecting examples of Shaker artifacts and eventually opened a museum across the street from his home. The museum contains one of the finest collections of Shaker-made articles in the world.

HOW TO GET THERE: From New York City take the Taconic Parkway north to the exit for Route 295 (the last exit before the end of the parkway). Turn left at the end of the exit ramp and, at the following intersection, turn right onto Route 295 east. Follow Route 295 for 2½ miles into East Chatham. Turn left onto the Albany Turnpike at the sign for Old Chatham and follow this for 3 miles into the center of Old Chatham. After passing the general store turn left onto Route 13 and follow this for 1 mile. Bear right onto Shaker Museum Road and follow this for ½ mile to the inn, which is on the left.

# Oliver Loud's Inn

## Pittsford, New York 14534

**INNKEEPER:** Vivienne Tellier

**ADDRESS/TELEPHONE:** 1474 Marsh Road; (716) 248–5200, bed & breakfast; (716) 248–5000, restaurant; fax (716) 248–9970

**ROOMS:** 8; all with private bath, air-conditioning, television, telephone with dataport, desk, radio, and hair dryer; 1 with a balcony; iron and ironing board available. Wheelchair accessible. No smoking inn. Children over the age of 12 welcome.

**RATES:** $125 to $145, double or single occupancy, continental breakfast.

**OPEN:** All year.

**FACILITIES AND ACTIVITIES:** Dinner Monday to Saturday (fixed price $35 for three courses), lighter menu Monday to Friday in pub; located on Erie Canal. Nearby: International Museum of Photography, Strong Museum, Rochester Museum and Science Center, Susan B. Anthony House, Genesee Country Village and Museum, Ellwanger Garden.

**BUSINESS TRAVEL:** Corporate rate, desk, telephone with dataport, and television in room; fax available.

The pretty buttercup-yellow wood house with white trim and black shutters was as welcome as a lighthouse to a ship on a storm-tossed sea on the cold and rainy night I first arrived. Lights shone from the windows, and one of the innkeepers threw open the door as I ran from the car. A cup of hot tea and a brief spell by the fire in the well-appointed living room soon set me right.

The inn was built in 1812 along the well-traveled stagecoach route between Rochester and Syracuse. Known as a lusty, bawdy drinking-tavern, it nevertheless fell off the wagon when the Erie Canal bypassed the little town of Egypt where it was located. The inn was scheduled for the wrecker's ball when Vivienne Tellier purchased it in 1986 and moved it some 4 miles to its present site. What a coincidence that the inn now sits near the Erie Canal, the origin of its demise all those years ago!

My room for the night was St. Cloud III, a lovely room coordinated in shades of green and pink using Waverly fabrics and wallpapers with splashy geraniums and roses that create a gardenlike setting. The rooms are furnished in high-quality reproduction pieces, and the baths are modern and bright with black-and-white tile floors. A basket containing cheese, crackers, mineral water, and homemade cookies was just what I needed to tide me over until dinner. In the morning a breakfast basket containing a thermos of coffee, fresh muffins and croissants, and juice is left at the door. Guests often eat on the wraparound porch or in the Adirondack chairs beside the canal.

But one of the special treats of staying at Oliver Loud's is to eat at Richardson's Canal House, the inn's historic sister property. Anyone who loves history will revel in the atmosphere of the Canal House. It was built along the banks of the Erie Canal in 1818 and has survived the years virtually unchanged, making it the oldest Erie Canal tavern still in use. In 1979 Vivienne Tellier restored it to reflect its earliest heritage and then filled it with museum-quality antiques, paintings, and artifacts.

I had a marvelous dinner in the Green Room one night—a thoroughly refined and dignified, historically accurate room. Oil portraits (George is included) hang on the walls, and interior shutters frame the windows. I enjoyed an outstanding macadamia nut–crusted chicken and lobster roulade served with an orange chili plum sauce, rice cakes, and asparagus wrapped

with pimento. Salad with a poppy-seed dressing and lightly spiced biscuits preceded the entree. A light tiramisu was sandwiched between rich layers of cake and served on a lattice of chocolate.

A tour of Richardson's revealed other fabulous rooms. The Ochre Room has hand-stenciled walls by Ruth Flowers; the Fireplace Room is heavily stenciled; the Cobblestone Room, where a lighter menu is served, has walls of stone (don't miss the quilt made by Vivienne's staff to celebrate the fifth anniversary of the restaurant) and a stone fireplace; the Rufus Porter Room has mural walls painted in the style of that famed muralist. The upstairs rooms of Richardson's are the most romantic. Each is more heavily stenciled than the last and the tiny Sin Bin Rooms, several only large enough for two, are heavily decorated private little cocoons—the perfect spot to accept a proposal. For summer dining, however, the terrace will beckon as yachts glide by on the glassy waters of the canal only steps away. The entire complex is on the National Register of Historic Places.

**HOW TO GET THERE:** From I–90 (New York State Thruway) take exit 45 onto I–490 west. Proceed on I–490 to exit 27 (Bushnell's Basin). At the end of the ramp turn right onto Route 96 north and drive 400 yards to Richardson's Canal House Village, which is on the right. Turn right onto Marsh Road, and drive through the parking lot of Richardson's Canal House to Oliver Loud's.

# Inn at the Falls

## Poughkeepsie, New York 12603

**INNKEEPERS:** Arnold and Barbara Sheer; Amy Hampson and Donna Fairbairn, managers

**ADDRESS/TELEPHONE:** 50 Red Oaks Mill Road; (914) 462–5770 or (800) 344–1466; fax (914) 462–5943

**E-MAIL:** innatfalls@aol.com

**WEB SITE:** www.innatthefalls.com

**ROOMS:** 36, including 14 suites; all with private bath, air-conditioning, telephone with dataport, television, desk, radio, hair dryer, refrigerator, robes, iron, ironing board, and safe; 15 with VCR, 5 with whirlpool tub. Smoking permitted; designated nonsmoking rooms. Wheelchair accessible.

**RATES:** $135 to $170, double occupancy; includes continental breakfast and glass of port in evening.

**OPEN:** All year.

**FACILITIES AND ACTIVITIES:** On four acres; parking, turndown with chocolates. Nearby: tennis, golfing, pool, Vassar College, Bardavon Opera House, Vanderbilt Mansion, Franklin Delano Roosevelt Museum and Library.

**BUSINESS TRAVEL:** Desks, telephones with dataports, televisions in all rooms; VCR in some rooms. Fax and copy service available. Breakfast room service.

*T*he Inn at the Falls is a bit of an anomaly. It's a new building that looks, in some respects, like a small hotel, but it acts very much like a country inn. Built in 1985, the shingle-style inn is located on Wappingers Creek at a point where it rushes over a small collection of rocks to form a waterfall. The inn's two-story common room has floor-to-ceiling windows that look out on the falls and French doors that lead to a spacious patio. A pink marble fireplace warms toes in winter, and plump sofas and chairs are arranged in small conversation groups. Board games, books, and puzzles are at the ready. Drinks are served from the private for-guests-only bar. The whole atmosphere is a comfortable cross between a country inn and a boutique hotel.

The rooms are spacious and charming. Using high-quality new furniture, they are decorated in either English or Country French or Contemporary style, but no two rooms are alike. There are canopy and brass beds. Half of the rooms have views of the creek, and the other half have views of the parking lot, so if this makes a difference, you should specify. Turndown service includes a chocolate on the pillow.

A continental breakfast consisting of fresh muffins, juices, fruit, and coffee is served in the common room every morning. If you prefer, you can call the desk and have someone bring your selection to your room.

Vassar College and the headquarters of IBM are nearby, making the Inn at the Falls a great alternative to hotels and motels for business travelers. One time as I arrived in the late afternoon, a van of businesspeople were hurrying out with their golf clubs to a nearby course after a day of meetings.

**HOW TO GET THERE:** From New York City travel north on the Henry Hudson Parkway to the Saw Mill River Parkway and continue north to the Taconic Parkway. Still traveling north, continue to Route 55 (Poughkeepsie). Go west on Route 55 for 2½ miles and turn left onto County Road 49. Proceed on County Road 49 to the second traffic light and turn left onto Red Oaks Mill Road. Go ½ mile to the inn, which is on the right.

# The Inn at Quogue
Quogue, New York 11959

INNKEEPER: Theresa Fontana

ADDRESS/TELEPHONE: 47-52 Quogue Street (mailing address: P.O. Box 521); inn (516) 653-6560, restaurant (516) 653-6800; fax (516) 653-8026

ROOMS: 65; 62 with private bath; all with air-conditioning, telephone, television, and radio; 7 with full kitchen, 1 with fireplace. Wheelchair accessible. Smoking permitted. Pets allowed with prior permission (one-time charge of $25 per pet).

**RATES:** $175 to $400, double occupancy; includes continental breakfast; extra person in room, $50. Two-night minimum weekends from Labor Day to Memorial Day; three-night minimum weekends from Memorial Day to Labor Day.

**OPEN:** All year.

**FACILITIES AND ACTIVITIES:** Restaurant serving dinner (entrees $17 to $32), taproom, pool, volleyball; beach parking passes provided, beach chairs and towels available. Nearby: ocean beaches, Quogue Wildlife Refuge, Hampton Theatre Company in Quogue.

*Q*uogue is like a gift from the past. The little hamlet has wide, tree-lined streets that pass huge homes that have been in the same family for generations. Known to Hampton devotees as the quiet Hampton—it's the place where local folk meet and greet at the library or the Quogue Country Market, but where not much else takes place. There's none of the frenetic pace associated with its more glamorous neighbors, and that's just the way old-time Quogue residents want it.

The Inn at Quogue, however, a pretty white-clapboard Colonial built in 1783, has been welcoming outsiders to the village for 215 years. There's a smartly appointed, bright and airy restaurant on the main floor with wide-plank pine floors, bookcases lining the walls, and vases of fresh flowers on the tables. On the opposite side of the center hall, a tap room is equally inviting, with a huge fireplace in a corner and comfortable sofas, tables, and chairs. A pianist is often tickling the ivories at night.

The inn is composed of a wide variety of accommodations. The fifteen rooms in the main inn have the flavor and decor of the historic country inn that it is. Little nooks and crannies invite inspection. Bright chintz fabrics cover windows, and beds and some of the furnishings are antique. Room 14 is the nicest, with wide-plank pine floors, a fireplace, and a bath with a blue-and-white tartan tile floor. Two cottages located behind the inn offer similar decor.

Less desirable are the rooms in the building across the street called the East Building. These are decorated with reproduction furniture. The rooms that are euphemistically referred to as "cottages" are, in fact, former motel rooms built by the previous owner of the inn. I definitely recommend staying in the main inn, if a room is available.

**HOW TO GET THERE:** From New York City take I–495 (Long Island Expressway) east to exit 70 (Manorville). At the stop sign turn right (south) and follow this to its end at Route 27 (Sunrise Highway). Follow Route 27 east about 8 miles to exit 64. At exit 64 turn south onto County Road 104 and take this to route 27A (Montauk Highway). Turn west onto 27A to the intersection with Quogue Street. Follow Quogue Street to the inn. The reservation desk is in the East Building, which is on the right.

# Beekman Arms

Rhinebeck, New York 12572

INNKEEPER: Charles LaForge; Eve Diaz, manager

ADDRESS/TELEPHONE: 4 Mill Street; (914) 876–7077 (fax same) or (800) 361–6517

ROOMS: 59, including 2 suites in 10 buildings; all with private bath, air-conditioning, telephone with dataport, and television; 23 with fireplace. Wheelchair accessible. Pets allowed in some rooms. Designated non-smoking rooms.

RATES: $90 to $140, double occupancy. Children under 12 free. Two-night minimum weekends from May to October.

OPEN: All year.

FACILITIES AND ACTIVITIES: Breakfast, lunch, dinner (entrees $10 to $24), Sunday brunch; tavern; 3½ acres, garden, courtyard. Nearby: Rhinebeck Aerodrome, county fair, Antique Auto Show in May, Antiques Fair in October, Roosevelt and Vanderbilt estates in Hyde Park, golfing, boating, horseback riding.

BUSINESS TRAVEL: Desk and telephone with dataport in all rooms; fax available; complete conference center with all facilities; midweek corporate rates.

*F*or almost 250 years life in Rhinebeck and its neighboring towns has ebbed and flowed around and through the Beekman Arms. And since so much American history took place along the Hudson River, it's natural that much of it took place within these walls. It's true that George Washington, Alexander Hamilton, and Benedict Arnold slept here, and it's possible that the terrible argument that led to the duel ending Hamilton's life at the hands of Aaron Burr began here. In 1888 Benjamin Harrison came to the "Beek" after he was nominated for president, and in the 1930s and 1940s Franklin Delano Roosevelt always came to the Beekman

Arms to address a crowd after his elections as governor of New York State and President of the United States.

In more recent years, especially since New York restaurant owner and chef Larry Forgione became proprietor of the restaurant, it has achieved a revered stature. He has created a regional American cuisine that uses the bounty of the local farmland and the nearby river to create such dishes as cedar-

planked salmon with a soft corn pudding and toasted pumpkin seed vinaigrette, and he adheres to the traditional dishes with his glazed country-style meat loaf served with caramelized onions, country smashed potatoes, and roasted ketchup gravy. There are numerous small rooms to dine in, but my favorite is the atmospheric tavern room with its low beamed ceilings, paneled walls, and wood-burning fireplace.

The guest rooms vary widely in size and style. Happily the historic rooms in the main inn were renovated in 1996, as they had become quite tired. They have slanted floors and reproduction furniture. The rooms in the Delamater 1844 House are preferred, as these are furnished with lovely antiques and decorated with fine fabrics and linens. This beautiful Carpenter Gothic mansion, just a few doors down the street, drips with exotic Victorian gingerbread. A pretty patio in back is a popular place to enjoy the continental breakfast that is served to guests in this building only. Other rooms are located in the conference center and in other buildings scattered about the grounds nearby.

HOW TO GET THERE: From I–87 (New York State Thruway) take exit 19 (Kingston) onto Route 209 east and follow signs for the Kingston-Rhinecliffe Bridge. Cross the Hudson River on the bridge and follow Route 199 to Route 9G. Follow Route 9G south for 1 mile to Route 9 and then go south on Route 9 to Rhinebeck. The inn is on Route 9 in the center of town at the traffic light.

# Belvedere Mansion
## Rhinebeck, New York 12580

**INNKEEPERS:** Nikola and Patricia Rebraca

**ADDRESS/TELEPHONE:** 10 Old Route 9 (mailing address: P.O. Box 785); (914) 889–8000; fax (914) 889–8811

**WEB SITE:** www.enjoyhv.com/belvedere

**ROOMS:** 16, including 1 suite; all with private bath and air-conditioning; 11 with patio or balcony, 3 with fireplace. Smoking in bar only. Children over the age of 8 welcome. Small dogs permitted in some rooms with prior permission.

**RATES:** $85 to $250, double occupancy; includes full breakfast. Two-night minimum weekends May to October; three-night minimum holiday weekends.

**OPEN:** All year.

**FACILITIES AND ACTIVITIES:** Restaurant serving dinner (entrees $18 to $26); swimming pool, pond, walking trails, exercise room. Nearby: the Southlands Foundation, an equestrian center and internationally recognized riding school, which offers horse shows, hunter trials, and lessons; Franklin Roosevelt's Hyde Park home and library; Wilderstein; the Vanderbilt Mansion; the Mills Mansion.

One day, on a visit to the Culinary Institute of America in Hyde Park, as I was driving along Route 9, I discovered an elegant mansion, obviously in the throes of a major renovation. My curiosity was piqued. It seemed too large for a private home, and I was right. This majestic Greek Revival–style house, with its fluted Corinthian columns, was destined to become a stylish new inn. For several years I watched its transformation until it was ready to receive guests.

Innkeeper Patricia Rebraca and her husband, Nick, welcomed us warmly as we walked into the charming foyer of the mansion. On one previous visit I had watched a local artist as he painted a colorful mural on an upstairs wall, and now his artistry was also evident on lustrous panels beside the fireplaces in the first-floor dining rooms.

The guest rooms, located on the second floor and reached by a magnificent carved-cherry staircase, are French jewel boxes, filled with exquisite antique French beds, tables, and armoires and embellished with lush damasks and brocades. (The Rebracas also own an antiques store, Cartouche, in Rhinebeck, which specializes in French antiques.) We stayed in Astor, a large room with garnet walls and a garnet-colored damask duvet on the bed.

Belvedere means "beautiful view," and the view down sloping lawns to Route 9 and then beyond to the Hudson River were, in fact, beautiful. We enjoyed a glass of sherry from the decanter in our room as we watched the sun set. Lafayette, just across the hall, has a similar view and is done in sunny yellows. The baths have smart black-and-white marble tiles, pedestal sinks, and, in some cases, claw-footed tubs.

In addition to the five guest rooms in the mansion, there are ten rooms in an adjacent carriage house. These all have private baths and range in size from The River Queen, which has a sitting area and a king-sized canopy bed, to tiny little rooms (Patricia calls these "cozies") with an alcove just big enough for a double bed.

The dining area is located in three main floor rooms with wood-burning fireplaces, and tables are also placed in the foyer and in the tiny bar. A covered side deck has tables for summer dining. For dinner my pan-seared Atlantic salmon was accompanied by a parsnip pancake and wilted red Swiss chard in a balsamic reduction. My companion sampled the spinach-stuffed roulade of chicken with tarragon au jus and garlic mashed potatoes. We finished by sharing a crepe filled with chestnut mousse and sauced with passion-fruit puree.

In the morning we enjoyed a full breakfast that started with juice and delectable fresh muffins and scones. This was followed by a fruit plate of pineapple, kiwi, blood orange, and banana. We had a choice of eggs Benedict, an omelette, or crepes filled with apples.

The inn is located on ten acres that include a pond overseen by a gazebo—the perfect place to finish the latest romance novel.

HOW TO GET THERE: From New York City take Henry Hudson Parkway north to the Saw Mill River Parkway, following that north to the Taconic Parkway. Continue north to Route 55 and travel west to Poughkeepsie. In Poughkeepsie take Route 9 north. The inn is 5 miles north of Hyde Park and 3½ miles south of Rhinebeck.

# 428 Mt. Vernon—A B&B Inn
## Rochester, New York 14620

**INNKEEPERS:** Claire and Phil Lanzatella

**ADDRESS/TELEPHONE:** 428 Mt. Vernon Avenue; (716) 271–0792 or (800) 836–3159; fax (716) 271–0946

**ROOMS:** 7; all with private bath, air-conditioning, telephone with dataport, desk, and television; 3 with fireplace. Wheelchair accessible. Smoking permitted; designated nonsmoking rooms. Children over the age of 12 welcome.

**RATES:** $110 double, $90 single occupancy; includes full breakfast. Two-night minimum some summer weekends.

**OPEN:** All year.

**FACILITIES AND ACTIVITIES:** On two and one-half acres bordering historic Highland Park. Nearby: restaurants (within five-minute drive), Ellwanger Garden, Museum of Photography, Strong Museum, Rochester Museum of Science and Planetarium. University of Rochester and Medical School.

**BUSINESS TRAVEL:** Desk, telephone with dataport, and television in all rooms; small conference room; corporate rates.

*B*e forewarned. This is such an unexpected and secluded treasure in the busy city of Rochester that you may never want to leave. The Sisters of Mercy, who occupied this handsome 1917 brick hilltop mansion for thirty-six years, must have been most reluctant to come down off their hill—and so were we.

We had spent a most enjoyable afternoon exploring the adjacent 150-acre Highland Park, which was designed in the 1880s by Frederick Law Olmsted, who also was responsible for New York's Central Park. It contains a marvelous collection of rare trees, beautiful flowers, and interesting shrubs all connected by meandering pathways and punctuated by whimsical turn-of-the-century buildings.

The mansion, which was restored by Philip and Claire Lanzatella in 1986, has commodious first-floor common rooms. There are lovely narrow-width oak floors in the foyer and living room. Oriental rugs under a pretty Victorian sofa complement the blue-shadow-striped Victorian fainting couch and the ivory tapestry love seat. There's a square grand piano against a wall, a lovely wood-burning fireplace, and oak window seats. The adjacent solarium has rose-colored walls lined with bird-motif plates and Mission-style furniture.

As we mounted the stairs we stopped to admire the fabulous leaded and stained-glass windows. The guest rooms are on the second and third floors. Room 1 has an antique walnut bed and huge walnut doors to the closet; Room 3 has an oak bed and an ornate oak table with glass ball feet. The walls are decorated with Maxfield Parrish prints. Each of the baths has hexagonal-tile floors and pedestal sinks, although several could use some sprucing up.

Guests can choose their breakfast selections from a printed menu the night before. You might have an omelette, French toast, or pancakes. The meal is served in the ornate dining room that has a carved walnut mantel surrounding the fireplace and a massive oak table. An ornate oak buffet holds antique silver and china and a marvelous collection of Maxfield Parrish prints covers the walls.

HOW TO GET THERE: From I–90 (New York State Thruway) take exit 46 onto I–390 north. Proceed to exit 16 onto Route 15A. Stay to the right after turning right and follow the right lane to South Avenue (about ½ mile). Stay on

South Avenue through two traffic lights. After passing Highland turn right in two more streets onto Alpine Street, which bears to the left and becomes Mt. Vernon. Go 1 block to Doctors Road and turn right. Then turn immediately to the left and go up the hill through the inn's gates, which are on the left.

# American Hotel 🏨
## Sag Harbor, New York 11963

INNKEEPER: Ted Conklin; Noel Love, manager

ADDRESS/TELEPHONE: Main Street (mailing address: P.O. Box 1349); (516) 725–3535; fax (516) 725–3573

ROOMS: 8; all with private bath, air conditioning, telephone, and whirlpool tub. Smoking permitted.

RATES: $175 to $250, double occupancy; includes continental breakfast. Two-night minimum weeknights; three-night minimum weekends; four-night minimum in July and August and on holidays.

OPEN: All year.

FACILITIES AND ACTIVITIES: Restaurant serving lunch Saturday and Sunday and dinner nightly (entrees $20 to $36). Nearby: Bay Street Theatre, boating, fishing, ocean and bay beaches.

*I*n 1877, when the American Hotel received its first guests, it was touted as the most elegant and modern place to stay on Long Island. Formerly an office and apartment building, the property was equipped with all the latest amenities, including indoor baths, steam heat, and electric lights. Purchased in 1972 by Ted Conklin, it remains a sophisticated jewel.

The well-known restaurant is located within four classic rooms that are permeated with old-world elegance—the perfect setting for the wonderful French cuisine and the wines that are contained on the forty-five-page wine list that has won the Grand Excellence Award from the *Wine Spectator* year after year. A fireplace is located in the darkly convivial dining room that also serves as the bar and where cigar smoking is allowed. On Friday and Saturday nights Hunky Page plays the baby grand just as he's done for years.

With a colonnaded entrance, a small porch, and a balcony, the inn has the atmosphere of an exclusive gentlemen's club. The eight guest rooms boast plenty of modern luxuries while retaining a distinctive Victorian ambience. The spacious rooms, all with 10-foot ceilings and 9-foot windows, are furnished with pieces that look as if they might indeed have come from a posh turn-of-the-century men's club: oak tables, alabaster lamps, overstuffed chairs, massive dressers with ornate mirrors, carved walnut armoires, antique typewriters and radios, and antique Oriental rugs worn to faded gentility.

Some of the rooms have mahogany sleigh beds; others feature either carved-walnut or brass beds. The baths are positively luxurious, offering tile floors, double Jacuzzis, luxury toiletries, and fully stocked bars that include cordials, wines, liquors, liqueurs, beers, juices, bottled waters, snacks, and crystal glasses.

HOW TO GET THERE: From New York City take I–495 (Long Island Expressway) east to exit 70 (Manorville) and follow Route 111 south to Highway 27 (Sunrise Highway). Take Highway 27 (which becomes Montauk Highway) for 25 miles to Bridgehampton. At the monument in Bridgehampton, turn north onto the Sag Harbor Turnpike. After about 5 miles, this road becomes Main Street in Sag Harbor. The inn is on the right in the center of town.

# The Point 💚
## Saranac Lake, New York 12983

INNKEEPERS: David and Christie Garrett; Tim and Tina Thuell, managers

ADDRESS/TELEPHONE: HCR #1 Box 65; (518) 891–5674 or (800) 255–3530; fax (518) 891–1152

E-MAIL: thepoint@northnet.org

WEB SITE: www.pointny.com

ROOMS: 11; all with private bath, fireplace, porch or patio, coffeemaker, hair dryer, robes, iron, and ironing board. Very limited smoking. Pets permitted with prior permission.

RATES: $850 to $1,600, double occupancy; includes all meals and recreational facilities. Two-night minimum weekends; three-night minimum holiday weekends.

OPEN: All year except three weeks in early spring.

FACILITIES AND ACTIVITIES: Rowboats, waterskiing, hiking, tennis, sunset cruises, swimming, volleyball, badminton, bicycling, croquet, horseshoes, fishing, cross-country skiing, ice fishing, snowshoeing, and ice skating. Nearby: downhill skiing, golf.

*O*ur biggest decision one cool fall afternoon was whether to take a canoe out on the lake or to play a round of tennis. The canoe won out this day because we decided we wanted to see if we could spot some of the other Adirondack camps that line the shores of Saranac Lake.

It's always seemed to me as if the barons of industry who built these rustic log retreats in the early 1900s must have craved the casual ambience they provided as a total antithesis to their luxurious abodes in the cities. Here they could wear old clothes and tramp through the woods, hundreds of miles in distance and spirit from their fast-paced city lives. The Point was the retreat of William Avery Rockefeller, a great-nephew of John D., and its stone fireplaces, spacious porches, and adjacent cottages are considered among the finest of this type of architecture.

When David and Christie Garrett purchased The Point in 1986, it had already been converted to an inn to accommodate travelers to the 1980 Olympics at nearby Lake Placid. They retained its rustic simplicity but added a wealth of antique furnishings, moose and deer heads on the walls, and Oriental rugs on the hardwood floors. They upholstered the furniture in spritely checked wool fabrics. Today it offers the ultimate in sophisticated but casual accommodations and has earned just about every award bestowed on inns.

The inn is secluded on ten acres that occupy a point of land thrusting into the lake. From the main inn as well as most of the cottages, there are romantic, misty views of the lake in the morning and of the sun glistening over the mountains in the afternoon. There's a beach by the lake for swimming, and the inn also offers

hiking trails, sunset cruises, volleyball, badminton, bicycling, cross-country skiing, and ice skating.

Meals are a highlight of a stay at The Point. One night I had a bouillabaisse that was thick with lobster, scallops, shrimp, clams, mussels, and fish, while my companion had a roasted poussin served with sweet corn fritters, wild mushrooms, and roasted potatoes. For dessert the individual soufflés are luscious, but so is the tarte bordalou (a pear tart with almond cream) and the roule marquis (a dark-chocolate sponge cake rolled with sweet cream and served with fresh raspberries and strawberries).

There are some things that you can never have enough of. Among them are love, chocolate, and The Point.

**HOW TO GET THERE:** From New York City take I–87 (the Northway) to exit 30. Follow Route 73 north for 34 miles to Upper Saranac Lake. Detailed directions to the inn are given when reservations are confirmed.

# Adelphi Hotel 🖼 📱
## Saratoga Springs, New York 12866

**INNKEEPERS:** Gregg Siefker and Sheila Parkert

**ADDRESS/TELEPHONE:** 365 Broadway; (518) 587–4688;
fax (518) 587–0851; Maestro's restaurant (518) 580–0312

**WEB SITE:** www.adelphihotel.com

**ROOMS:** 39, including 17 suites; all with private bath, air-conditioning, telephone, television, and desk; 2 with balcony. Smoking permitted. Pets permitted with prior permission.

**RATES:** $95 to $350, double occupancy; includes continental breakfast. Two-night minimum most weekends; three-night minimum racing weekends.

**OPEN:** May to October.

**FACILITIES AND ACTIVITIES:** Restaurant (Maestro's) serving lunch and dinner (entrees $16 to $19). Garden courtyard, 1920s-style colonnaded pool. Nearby: Saratoga Performing Arts Center, where the Philadelphia Orchestra, the New York City Ballet, and popular artists perform during the summer; Saratoga Raceway; Casino Museum.

**BUSINESS TRAVEL:** Desk, telephone, and television in all rooms. Small meeting room.

*I*magine, if you will, that the year is 1877 and you've come to Saratoga Springs to partake of the waters, to place a few bets on the horses, and to spend some lively evenings in the casino. You will dress in your best finery to promenade down Broadway, nodding and smiling as you pass your friends, and admiring the row of enormous but handsome Victorian hotels that line both sides of the street. It was a swell time, and Saratoga Springs was in her heyday as "Queen of the Spas."

Fire consumed several of these grand hotels, and the vicissitudes of time took their toll on the rest (the Grand Union was the largest and most opulent with 824 guest rooms). Nevertheless, thanks to innkeepers Gregg Siefker and Sheila Parkert, who purchased their hotel in 1979 just as it was about to suffer the same fate as all the rest, the Adelphi survived. It is the only remaining hotel from that opulent age, and what a treat it is to gaze at this magnificent remnant of high Victorian architecture today. It has a facade of Lombard brickwork, wood columns that span three stories, and wide overhanging eaves that drip with masses of gingerbread. Spanning the streetside on the second floor, there's a grand piazza where gentlemen and ladies still sit in wicker chairs or Tennessee rockers behind pots of greenery to observe the plebeians on the street below.

The opulent lobby is a testament to the Gilded Age: Gilt peeks out from pediments, mirror frames, and molded ceilings, and it accents painted swags and columns. Dark woods and hunter-green walls set off the rich, damask-covered Victorian chairs and sofas. There are period prints and engravings—some of stern-looking Victorian personages, others by Maxfield Parrish—lining the walls. Cafe Adelphi, a charming little bar, is located off the lobby. Drinks and desserts are available in the afternoon and evening. Maestro's, a restaurant under separate management and reached through a separate entrance, serves lunch and dinner.

Upstairs the wide hallways are literally covered from floor to high ceilings with paintings, illustrations, prints, engravings and other art that would have been at home here in the late nineteenth century. Gregg and Sheila spent years restoring their gem, rescuing and furnishing one room at a time. Most rooms are strictly Victorian in decor, but no two are alike. They are whimsical, playful, and eclectic. The Riviera Suite has a sitting room with an awning that projects over a mural of stone battlements, and the bedroom has pink walls and a pink painted armoire. Other rooms have high walnut or oak Victorian beds, brass beds, and canopy beds.

In back of the hotel there's a tile-floored loggia and a brick garden courtyard surrounded by flower beds. A brick stairway leads to the flagstone-terraced pool that has a covered colonnade backed by trellises and ferns.

HOW TO GET THERE: From I–87 (Adirondack Northway) take exit 13N (Saratoga Springs) to Route 9N. Follow this into Saratoga Springs, where it becomes Broadway. The hotel is on the left.

# Batcheller Mansion Inn
## Saratoga Springs, New York 12866

**INNKEEPERS:** Sue McCabe; Janet Coon and Eva Gonroff, managers

**ADDRESS/TELEPHONE:** 20 Circular Street; (518) 584–7012 or
(800) 616–7012; fax (518) 581–7746

**ROOMS:** 9, including 4 suites; all with private bath, air-conditioning,
telephone, television, desk, radio, minirefrigerator, hair dryer, robes,
iron, and ironing board; 3 with Jacuzzi, 1 with a balcony. Smoking on
porches only. Children over the age of 14 welcome.

**RATES:** $120 to $280, double occupancy; includes full breakfast Saturday and Sunday and continental breakfast Monday to Friday. Two-night
minimum weekends.

**OPEN:** All year.

**FACILITIES AND ACTIVITIES:** Gardens. Nearby: Congress Park just
across the street, where Saratoga's famed Casino is now open as a
museum; Saratoga Spa State Park includes the original bath houses
where you can still "take the waters."

*S*hortly after George Sherman Batcheller, who had been a Brigadier General in the Union Army, built his opulent twenty-eight-room mansion
on Circular Street, President Ulysses S. Grant paid him a visit. Soon he
was named a judge, then an American representative to Egypt, and, eventually, Ambassador to Portugal. But this was home to Sherman and his family.

The mansion is a fantastic extravagance of turrets, gables, domes, and
towers, and no money was spared on the construction of the house known
as his summer "house of pleasure." In the foyer tiger maple and walnut inlaid
floors sweep beyond a grand stairway. An 1800s Czechoslovakian-crystal
chandelier with milky-blue glass arms hangs from the living room's 12-foot
ceiling. Jeffersonian double-hung windows rise to create a doorway to the
covered porch. The library has a parquet floor and intricately carved bookshelves. Hanging on the walls of several rooms are well-known paintings created by Stuart Williams, a copy artist and a former owner of the inn.

There are nine guest rooms on the second and third floors; all are furnished with museum-quality antiques. One of my favorites is the Katrina

Trask, a feminine suite with a private oval porch reached through a tall window and a king-size bed draped with a lacy canopy. A carved white-marble fireplace mantel is lovely, although it is merely decorative. The large bath has both a tub and a shower. This is the room generally selected as the bridal suite. The largest room in the mansion is the masculine Diamond Jim Brady, which measures 18 feet by 28 feet. In keeping with the character of its namesake, there's a pool table, a king-size canopied bed, a sitting area, and a desk in a work space. The bath has a double Jacuzzi and a two-person shower.

Breakfast is served in the dining room, which has 12-foot ceilings, fabulous carved wood moldings over the doors and windows, and a beautiful fireplace. During the week a continental breakfast is served, but on weekends guests may also choose either an egg dish or pancakes.

Gardens surround the house, which is located across the street from Congress Park, where the famed Casino attracted the aristocrats of the day. It is said that solitaire originated here, as well as the club sandwich. The building is now a museum, gift shop, and art gallery.

**HOW TO GET THERE**: From I–87 (Adirondack Northway) take exit 14. At the end of the ramp turn right onto Union Avenue (Route 9P). Traveling west for 2 miles, follow Union Avenue to its end. Turn left onto Circular Street. The inn is located straight ahead after 1 long block.

# Union Gables
# Bed & Breakfast
## Saratoga Springs, New York 12866

**INNKEEPERS:** Jody and Tom Roohan; Colleen Braim, manager

**ADDRESS/TELEPHONE:** 55 Union Avenue; (518) 584–1558 or
(800) 398–1558; fax (518) 583–0649

**ROOMS:** 12, including 1 suite; all with private bath, air-conditioning,
telephone with dataport, television, and minirefrigerator; 2 with private
porch. Smoking in downstairs common rooms only. Pets permitted
with prior permission (small charge).

**RATES:** $205 to $250, racing season (July and August); $95 to $120,
rest of the year; double occupancy; includes continental breakfast.

**OPEN:** All year.

**FACILITIES AND ACTIVITIES:** Exercise room, tennis court, basketball
hoop, hot tub, bicycles. Nearby: National Museum of Racing and Hall
of Fame, Saratoga Harness Hall of Fame, Saratoga Spa State Park, Congress Park, Saratoga Racetrack, Skidmore College, National Museum of
Dance, boat rentals on Saratoga Lake, music and ballet at Saratoga Performing Arts Center.

**BUSINESS TRAVEL:** Telephone with dataport and television in room;
meeting space, fax, copier, overhead projector available.

*T*his elaborate 1901 Victorian mansion sits on Saratoga's most gracious street—a wide boulevard lined with trees and other stately
mansions. Furness House, as it was long known, was used for years
as a dormitory for students at nearby Skidmore College. When it was no
longer needed by the college, it
was purchased by local realtor
Tom Roohan and his wife, Jody.
Following a massive renovation
that created bathrooms for each
of the bedrooms, the house
became a showcase for local
designers. Only then did Tom and
Jody feel they were ready to open
it as a bed-and-breakfast.

# Saratoga—Queen of the Spas

In the late nineteenth century, when Saratoga Springs was the nation's most fashionable resort, elegantly dressed ladies and gentlemen arrived in their grand horse-drawn carriages to gamble at the beautiful Casino, enjoy the restorative powers of the mineral water at the Saratoga Spa, and watch the races at the Saratoga Flat Track or Raceway. There was really nothing like it anywhere in the world. The Raceway rivaled England's famous Ascot for glamour; the spa might have been compared to those at Bath, England, or to some of Germany's famous mineral spas. It was true that the Casino in Monte Carlo was more opulent than Saratoga's, but where else were all these attractions found in such close proximity? And all activity converged in August, when the Races took place. Whitneys, Vanderbilts, and Astors were all in residence then.

The 1940 WPA guide to New York State speaks nostalgically about the 1890s, when the resort was in its prime. "It stirs with anticipation in June, swings into preparatory activity in July, and rushes headlong into the full tumult of its summer season in August." It was especially in August that the grand hotels were host to fabulous balls and dinners and the Casino was filled with the notables and the notorious of the day.

Much of the decor created by local interior designers is incorporated into the guest rooms. I particularly like the dramatic Cindy (each of the rooms is named for a family member), which has navy-blue walls and white moldings. A massive pine cannonball bed sits on inlaid oak floors. The private porch is a lovely spot on which to read in the afternoons. Kate has a horsey theme, with plaid walls and bedspread and a hand-painted dresser featuring the Victorian houses of Saratoga. A mirror over the sink in the bath is made from a leather horse yoke.

The main-floor rooms are welcoming and comfortable, and this is where one of the most unique features of the house is found. Beneath layers of paint in the turret room, the Roohans found walls and moldings made of golden curly maple, richly trimmed with bamboo. The living room also has door and window moldings in curly maple. This spacious room has a carved fireplace as well. A baby grand piano is often used by guests, as is the chess set in the living room turret. But the favorite sitting room in the summer is the grand wraparound porch, which is filled with pretty wicker tables and chairs and offers a viewing platform of the gardens and the activity on the street.

Breakfast is served in the dining room, which has another elegant fireplace with a carved mahogany mantel and lincresta ceiling trim.

**HOW TO GET THERE:** From I-87 (Adirondack Northway) take exit 14. At the end of the ramp turn right onto Union Avenue (Route 9P). Traveling west follow Union Avenue for about 1 mile to the inn, which is on the right on the corner of Court Street.

# Chequit Inn

## Shelter Island, New York 11965

**INNKEEPERS:** James and Linda Eklund; Peter McCracken, manager

**ADDRESS/TELEPHONE:** 23 Grand Avenue (mailing address: P.O. Box 292, Shelter Island Heights); (516) 749-0018; fax (516) 749-0183

**WEB SITE:** www.case-web.com/chequit

**ROOMS:** 35, all with private bath and telephone; 21 with air-conditioning. Wheelchair accessible. Smoking permitted in the lounge or outside only.

**RATES:** $80 to $175, double occupancy; includes continental breakfast. Two-night minimum weekends; three-night minimum holiday weekends.

**OPEN:** All year.

**FACILITIES AND ACTIVITIES:** Restaurant serving lunch and dinner (entrees $16 to $20), bar serving lighter menu. Pool table in bar, guests may use all the sports and beach facilities of the Ram's Head Inn. Nearby: located in the charming village of Shelter Island Heights with shops, bicycle and boat rentals, ferry to North Fork to visit wineries.

**BUSINESS TRAVEL:** Telephone in all rooms; meeting room, audiovisual equipment, fax, and copier available.

*S*helter Island Heights, a steeply hilled enclave of Victorian homes on the northern tip of Shelter Island, came into its own in the 1870s when the Methodist Episcopal Church established the Grove and Camp Meeting Association here. Elaborate Victorian mansions were built to house the famed orators and lecturers who came to preach and teach, and many of these mansions have survived. Meals were often eaten communally, and parts of the original 1870s dining hall are contained in the building that is now the Chequit Inn.

The Chequit has been owned since 1996 by James and Linda Eklund, who also own the lovely Ram's Head Inn located on another part of the island. Since their purchase they have given the old inn new life by upgrading the mechanical systems and creating a lovely dining room. The large lobby/common room also serves as a waiting room for the restaurant. It is furnished with a huge oak library table, interesting old wicker chairs, and a handsome fireplace. A wide porch circles the second floor, and this is often used for dining in the evening.

The guest rooms offer a variety of choices in three different buildings. The rooms on the third floor of the main building were fully renovated in 1996 and are very pretty. They have carpeted floors, bright new baths, and amusing touches such as an old sled that has been put to use as a coffee table. The Summer Cottage behind the main inn has rooms with quirky little alcoves and interesting, brightly painted used furniture. There are additional rooms across the street in Cedar House.

Just as the rooms offer choices, so does the dining. The stylish formal dining room is located on the second floor of the inn, just off the lobby, and in summer the porch offers additional space. The menu includes grilled tuna, flounder, and salmon, as well as a sirloin steak. For lunch a table on the first-floor terrace under the trees can't be beat. There's a lounge where a lighter bar menu includes pizza, burgers, and fish and chips. There's a pool table here, and on weekend nights in summer a band plays rock and roll or blues for dancing.

HOW TO GET THERE: From New York City take I-495 (Long Island Expressway) east to exit 73, where it terminates. Follow County Road 58 east to Route 25, then follow that east for about 30 miles to Greenport. Once in Greenport follow the signs for the Shelter Island Ferry. After exiting the ferry on Shelter Island, you will be on Route 114, which becomes Grand Avenue. The inn is located on the corner of Waverly Place in the center of the village.

# Olde Country Inn ⓒⓒⓒ
## Shelter Island, New York 11965

**INNKEEPERS:** Jeanne and Franz Fenkl; Kristen Fenkl, manager

**ADDRESS/TELEPHONE:** 11 Stearns Point Road (mailing address: P.O. Box 590, Shelter Island Heights); (516) 749–1633

**E-MAIL:** oldcntryin@aol.com

**ROOMS:** 13, including 1 suite and 1 cottage; all with private bath and air-conditioning; 2 with whirlpool tub. No smoking inn. Children over the age of 12 welcome.

**RATES:** $75 to $105 from October to April; $115 to $215 from May to September; double occupancy; includes full breakfast. Two-night minimum May through September weekends; three-night minimum summer holiday weekends.

**OPEN:** All year.

**FACILITIES AND ACTIVITIES:** Restaurant serving dinner (entrees $18 to $25); garden, parking. Nearby: Crescent Beach (short walk), golfing, boating, Mashomack Preserve, historic houses.

As ship shape as a newly polished cruiser, the Olde Country Inn is old in name only. Originally known as Shelter Island House when it was built as a hotel in 1886, the inn is located on a quiet dead-end street shrouded by trees. It was renovated and opened by Jeanne and Franz Fenkl as a bed-and-breakfast in 1994, and they've done a fabulous job.

The lobby has polished oak floors and pretty Victorian furniture. The comfortable sitting room includes a fireplace and a piano, as well as Victorian sofas and chairs. The guest rooms are furnished with iron and brass beds and other typical Victorian furniture such as marble-topped dressers, upholstered chairs, and, in one room, an exquisite Victorian coatrack. The tiled baths have pedestal sinks and shelves that are cleverly placed within little niches to provide additional space.

A lovely dining room was added in 1997, and in the summer a pavilion and arbor hold additional tables. Chef Marcel Iattoni changes the menu regularly; one spring day the menu included a crispy Long Island duckling served with mashed potatoes and fresh apple cider sauce and a rack of lamb served with gratin dauphinois and ratatouille Provençal.

**HOW TO GET THERE:** From New York City take I–495 (Long Island Expressway) east to exit 73, where it terminates. Follow County Road 58 east to

Route 25, then follow that east for about 30 miles to Greenport. Once in Greenport follow the signs for the Shelter Island Ferry. After exiting the ferry on Shelter Island, you will be on Route 114, which becomes Grand Avenue. Stay on Grand, which then becomes New York Avenue. At the end of the golf course, turn right onto West Neck Road and go up the hill. At the intersection with Shore Road, turn right onto Shore Road. Take the second left onto Stearns Point Road. The inn is the second building on the left.

# The Ram's Head Inn
## Shelter Island, New York 11965

**INNKEEPERS:** Linda and James Eklund; Jeanne Lamar, manager

**ADDRESS/TELEPHONE:** 108 Ram Island Drive (mailing address: P.O. Box 638); (516) 749–0811; fax (516) 749–0059

**WEB SITE:** www.case-web.com/ramshead

**ROOMS:** 17, including 8 suites; 9 with private bath; all with air-conditioning and telephone; 2 with television and/or balcony. No smoking inn.

**RATES:** $80 to $230, double occupancy; includes continental breakfast. Two-night minimum weekends; three-night minimum some holiday weekends.

**OPEN:** All year.

**FACILITIES AND ACTIVITIES:** Restaurant serving lunch and dinner (entrees $20 to $25), bar; sunroom, sailboats, kayaks, 800 feet of private beach, exercise room, sauna, tennis, thirteen mooring slips. Nearby: bicycling, golfing, swimming, boating, fishing, hiking.

*W*e played tennis in the early morning light, read a book in the hammock under the trees, sailed a sloop in Coecles Harbor in the heat of the afternoon sun, and rested in wicker chairs on the broad porch of the inn in the late afternoon with a refreshing glass of lemonade in hand. This is my idea of a perfect little waterfront inn. We were left to our own devices. There were plenty of activities if we wanted them but no pressure to do anything at all. We felt totally relaxed and refreshed.

The handsome 1920s weathered-shingle building with white trim is a typical Hamptons-style structure, but Shelter Island is as different from the

Hamptons as Ethel Merman was from Audrey Hepburn. Quiet, unassuming, and captivating, the island has no glitzy resorts or nightclubs. Numerous celebrities live here, but they prefer their privacy to the steady stream of press courted by their colleagues on the South Fork.

From the pretty lobby with its fireplace to the broad front porch, this is a classy inn. At one end of the building there's a lovely brick-floored sunporch with green wicker furniture with floral cushions and a woodstove for warmth in the winter. Here you'll find games, puzzles, books, and magazines.

The guest rooms are furnished with wicker and white-painted furniture, interspersed with some antiques. Many of the rooms have striped wallpaper and floral fabrics on the beds. Be forewarned, however, although the Eklunds are upgrading the existing baths and adding new ones gradually, at present only nine rooms have private baths. All the rest share.

A meal in the dining room is one of pure romance. At one end there's a large fireplace that lends its soft glow in the winter. There are high ceilings, polished oak floors covered by Oriental rugs, and handsome oil paintings on the walls. Candles glow on linen tablecloths. The menu changes frequently; recently it included a maple and rum–glazed loin of pork with lemon-ginger sauce and spicy shrimp toast and a seared Atlantic salmon with horseradish-caper cream and roast beets.

This is one little inn that I enjoy going back to again and again.

HOW TO GET THERE: From New York City take I–495 (Long Island Expressway) east to exit 73, where it terminates. Follow County Road 58 east to Route 25, then follow that east for about 30 miles to Greenport. Once in Greenport follow the signs for the Shelter Island Ferry. After exiting the ferry on Shelter Island you will be on Route 114. Follow Route 114 south toward South Ferry. At George's IGA market continue straight ahead onto Manwaring Road instead of making a right turn onto Route 114. At the three-way stop take Ram Island Road, which will angle to the left. Continue on Ram Island Road to the sign for Ram Island. Turn right onto Ram Island Drive and continue for almost 2 miles to the inn, which is on the right.

# Hobbit Hollow Farm

## Skaneateles, New York 13152

**INNKEEPER:** Richard Fynn

**ADDRESS/TELEPHONE:** 3061 West Lake Road; (315) 685–2791;
fax (315) 685–3426

**WEB SITE:** www.hobbithollow.com

**ROOMS:** 5, including 4 suites; all with private bath, air conditioning,
radio, hair dryer, and robes; 4 with telephone and desk, 2 with fireplace
and whirlpool tub, 1 with balcony. Smoking permitted on porch only.
Children over the age of 16 welcome.

**RATES:** $150 to $250, double occupancy; includes full breakfast and
wine and cheese in the afternoon.

**OPEN:** All year.

**FACILITIES AND ACTIVITIES:** On 400 acres, indoor tennis court.
Nearby: wineries, Skaneateles Lake, Song Mountain for downhill skiing,
golfing, fishing.

Hobbit Hollow Farm was one of those wonderful surprises on a
recent trip through the Finger Lakes region. Hearing about an inn
that had opened in 1997, I decided to see it for myself. What a find!
The inn is on 400 acres of farmland that still produces crops such as corn.
The 1820s mansion has been so flawlessly restored that you feel as though
you're in the home of a friend
rather than in a commercial
establishment. But this friend
has impeccable taste—the inn
could be featured in the pages
of *Architectural Digest*. A lovely
reception hall has a mural of
the farm and its outbuildings
painted on the wall. This leads
to a cozy library where a TV is
located, as well as lots of books

and magazines and overstuffed chairs in which to read them in relaxed comfort. The dining room, where breakfast is served, has bright yellow walls and a bay window with a fabulous view of the fields. The living room, which is separated from a hallway by pillars, has a fireplace and is decorated in green and peach. Wine and cheese are served to guests in the evening here. A game room has a pumpkin suede couch and wing chairs. You will want to begin the day on the porch to marvel at the rising sun playing on the golden waters—and to end it while watching the lake glimmer in the fading light.

The guest rooms are spacious and furnished with lovely furniture. They are decorated with equal panache. Leon has a fabulous French bed decorated with ormolu and a sink in an antique cabinet in the room. There's a lovely tile bath. Chanticleer has a red four-poster bed and drapes that feature horses. The Master Suite includes a sunroom surrounded by columns and is furnished with wicker furniture. The bed is ornately carved. Lakeview Room is the most masculine. It has a gas fireplace and a fabulous, ornately carved bed dressed with a red matelassé spread. The bath includes a whirlpool tub.

Service and amenities are just as close to perfection as the decor. The bed linens are Italian cotton, as are the towels. Turndown at night includes a truffle on the pillow. Breakfast is served on Wedgwood china with Waterford crystal and Reed and Barton silver. If you visit on a Thursday, you will have French toast. Sunday's entree will be a western egg roulade with breakfast potatoes. All will be accompanied by fresh seasonal fruit, juice, breakfast breads, and coffee.

HOW TO GET THERE: From I-90 (New York State Thruway) traveling west, take exit 34A and go south on I-481 to I-690. Go west on I-690 to exit 6 at the fairgrounds and take Route 5 west toward Auburn. At the traffic light turn left onto Route 321 and follow this for 8 to 9 miles to Skaneateles. Turn right onto Route 20 (Genesee Street). Turn left onto Route 41A (West Lake Road). Drive approximately 2 miles. The inn is on the right. Watch for the stone pillars at the entrance. From I-90 traveling east take exit 42 (Geneva/Route 14). Go straight through the traffic light at the end of the ramp onto Route 318. Continue on Route 318 until it dead ends at Route 20. Turn left (east) and follow Route 20 to Skaneateles, then follow directions above.

# Sherwood Inn 🎴 💲

## Skaneateles, New York 13152

**INNKEEPERS:** William B. Eberhardt

**ADDRESS/TELEPHONE:** 25 West Genesee Street; (315) 685–3405 or
(800) 3–SHERWOOD; fax (315) 685–8983

**ROOMS:** 20, including 6 suites; all with private bath, air-conditioning,
television, telephone, radio, and desk; 6 with fireplace, 3 with whirlpool
tub. No smoking inn.

**RATES:** $90 to $160, double occupancy; includes continental breakfast.

**OPEN:** All year.

**FACILITIES AND ACTIVITIES:** Restaurant serving lunch and dinner
(entrees $18 to $23), tavern; on three acres across from lake. Nearby:
Clift Park and beach across street, sight-seeing cruises, wineries,
Skaneateles Festival, Merry Go Round Playhouse in Auburn.

*S*kaneateles is one of those picture-postcard towns with beautifully renovated turn-of-the-century brick buildings lining one side of Main
Street. The other side arcs in a crescent around the head of Skaneateles Lake (the name means "long lake" in Iroquois), with parks edging the
water. The Sherwood Inn stands in the heart of the village, directly across
from Clift Park, where the sight-seeing cruises take place. Built in 1807 as a
stagecoach stop, the inn has been welcoming visitors ever since.

We walked into the welcoming lobby that contains a fireplace, lovely
wing chairs in blue and rose, and an extensive gift shop. On one side there's
a convivial tavern, and on the other a bright and elegant dining room in
two rooms—one a glass-enclosed porch with a stone floor and lovely views
of the lake.

The guest rooms are on the second and third floors, with the nicest
rooms on the third floor. Room 32 is my favorite. It has a lovely antique Victorian walnut bed, smart green-and-cream–striped paper on the walls, a gas
fireplace, and a bath with a whirlpool tub. The views of the lake are mesmerizing. Room 38 also has lovely views of the lake and of the village, and it has
a steam shower in the bath. The baths are well designed and new with tile
floors. Wide hallways lead to the guest rooms and also to a library, where
guests may borrow books, play games, or watch television.

Dinner on the porch is a special treat, especially on sunny days when the emerald waters of the lake sparkle in the setting sun. The inn is noted for two dinner specialties: Scrod Christopher is baked in a cracker-crumb crust and served with a lemon-parsley butter. The herb-crusted prime rib is slow roasted and served with garlic mashed potatoes. A lighter menu is offered in the tavern. The inn is also noted for its desserts, and they should not be passed up. One night we had a luscious Swiss Alps Torte, which combined layers of rich butter cake, fresh raspberries, and liqueur. It was topped with a white chocolate butter cream that was drizzled with dark chocolate.

One of the nicest times to come to Skaneateles is during the holidays, when the entire town gets dressed up in Victorian garb for the annual, month-long Dickens Christmas Festival. There are carolers, horse-drawn carriage rides, strolling characters straight from *A Christmas Carol,* and numerous events.

HOW TO GET THERE: From I–90 (New York State Thruway) traveling west, take exit 34A and go south on I–481 to I–690. Go west on I–690 to exit 6 at the fairgrounds, and take Route 5 west toward Auburn. At the traffic light turn left onto Route 321 and follow this for 8 to 9 miles to Skaneateles. Turn right onto Route 20 (Genesee Street). The inn is on the right in about 200 yards. From I–90 traveling east take exit 42 (Geneva/Route 14). Go straight through the traffic light at the end of the ramp onto Route 318. Continue on Route 318 until it dead-ends at Route 20. Turn left (east) and follow Route 20 to Skaneateles, then follow directions above.

# The 1708 House
## Southampton, New York 11968

INNKEEPERS: Lorraine and Skip Ralph; Bernadette Meade and Peter Reyer, managers

ADDRESS/TELEPHONE: 125 Main Street; (516) 287–1708; fax (516) 287–3593

ROOMS: 12, including 3 suites and 3 cottages; all with private bath, air-conditioning, television (some have two), and telephone; 9 with desk;

2 with minirefrigerator and coffeemaker, 1 with VCR. No smoking inn. Children over the age of 12 welcome.

**RATES:** $175 to $350, double occupancy; includes continental breakfast. Two-night minimum weekends May, June, September, and October; three-night minimum weekends July and August; four-night minimum holiday weekends.

**OPEN:** All year.

**FACILITIES AND ACTIVITIES:** On one acre with lovely gardens; wine cellar, discount available to nearby health club. Nearby: Parrish Art Museum, Southampton Historical Museum, Bay Street Theatre.

**BUSINESS TRAVEL:** Television and telephone with answering machine in guest rooms, desk in most rooms, fax available, space for small meetings.

My heart and soul are in historic houses and their preservation (I've restored several myself), but I don't believe I have ever seen a building restored to such perfection as The 1708 House. We watched for years as the white-shingled Colonial in the heart of Southampton's business district became more and more derelict. The roof was falling in, the foundation was crumbling, the weeds threatened to choke out the sun, and there were squatters living in the cottages. After Lorraine and Skip Ralph purchased the property in 1993, I visited them every few months, and I am familiar with the incredible odds they overcame to bring this project to fruition.

It took three years of painstaking work, but the Ralphs now own Southampton's finest bed-and-breakfast. Although the present house was built in 1708, it actually rests on a cellar that dates to 1648. The stone walls and brick fireplace have been lovingly restored and a brick floor installed. There's a little bar at one end and wing chairs for seating. It's a favorite spot for a glass of wine in the evening before going out to dinner.

This jewel of an inn is welcoming and inviting. On the main floor one enters a spacious parlor with a fireplace. Chairs (including, on one visit, an incredible English throne chair upholstered with tapestry and with fine fringe hanging down) and sofas are conveniently paired with antique tables to form conversation areas. The Malachite Room is the most historic main-floor room. It has raised pine paneling, a lovely built-in corner cupboard, and a brick fireplace. Skip has exposed the heavy beams and the underside of the lovely pine floors to create the ceiling. A dining room with a wall of windows looking out on the yard is a bright and pleasant place for breakfast, which is set out every morning on a handsome antique buffet.

The guest rooms include numerous historic details and antique furnishings, but they also incorporate thoroughly updated baths. There are elegant silk damasks on the beds, chairs, and windows, and Ralph Lauren sheets on the beds.

We stayed one night in Room 8, which has a wonderful tall four-poster wheat-carved bed and a fabulous antique Governor Winthrop slant-top desk

## If the Walls Could Talk

The villages of the Hamptons possess a proud heritage. The first settlers came to Southampton from Connecticut in 1640, and several local families trace their lineage to those original settlers. Skip and Lorraine Ralph have sketched the history of their 1708 inn through its various ownerships and found that the 300-year-old house has actually passed through the hands of only three families.

The original house was one of the first in Southampton, dating to 1648. It was built by Isaac Bower, who retained it for fifty years until 1698. The exposed stone walls and brick fireplace in the wine cellar date to this period. The house was purchased by the Rodgers family, who have family members still living in Southampton, in 1698. They retained it for about eighty years until they sold it to the Huntting family, one of the most successful local whaling families. During the heyday of whaling the Hunttings were noted for their exploits and adventures, which are chronicled in many books about whaling.

The Hunttings and their descendants owned the house from 1770 to 1993, a remarkable period of 220 years. It was a Huntting descendant who eventually sold the house to the Ralphs.

with a serpentine front and hidden compartments. One contained a note that a previous owner had written. It said, "Purch May, 1956. $91.90." The Ralphs own a beautiful antiques shop specializing in fine American and English furniture and decorative objects, just behind the inn. All the antiques in the inn are for sale, and this particular piece is now $1,050.

My favorite rooms are the two in the front part of the oldest section of the house, although occupants of these may hear more street noise than those in the back. Room 2 is a two-bedroom suite that includes the original paneled walls and beamed ceiling. There's a needlepoint rug on the polished pine floor. The paneling in the second bedroom is painted with a garden of wisteria, pansies, tulips, and daffodils. Room 1 has a paneled wall that includes a green-pigment paint original to the early eighteenth century. In the bath the original knee braces have been exposed.

The three cottages, which are located behind the main inn, are equally charming. They all have two bedrooms and a living room; the West Cottage and East Cottage also have a small eat-in kitchen.

**HOW TO GET THERE:** From New York City take I–495 (Long Island Expressway) east to exit 70 (Manorville) and follow Route 111 south for 4 miles to Highway 27 (Sunrise Highway). Take Highway 27 (which becomes Montauk Highway) for approximately 18 miles to the traffic light in Southampton at North Sea Road (you'll see a 7-11 across the street and several gas stations). Turn right onto North Sea Road and proceed through three traffic lights. You are now on Main Street. The inn is on the left at #126, just before Saks Fifth Avenue. Drive down the Belgian-block driveway to the parking lot in back.

# Lakehouse Inn
# ... On Golden Pond 🏠 ♥
## Stanfordville, New York 12581

**INNKEEPERS:** Judy and Richard Kohler

**ADDRESS/TELEPHONE:** Shelly Hill Road; (914) 266-8093; fax (914) 266-4051

**E-MAIL:** judy@lakehouseinn.com

**ROOMS:** 7; all with private bath, air-conditioning, telephone, television, VCR, stereo, CD player, minirefrigerator, wet bar, coffeemaker, balcony or deck, fireplace, and Jacuzzi. VCR and CD libraries in each room. No smoking inn. Children welcome in The Boathouse.

**RATES:** $350 to $550, double occupancy; includes full breakfast. Two-night minimum some weekends; three-night minimum holiday weekends.

**OPEN:** All year.

**FACILITIES AND ACTIVITIES:** On twenty-two acres; rowboats, paddleboats, hiking. Nearby: historic Hyde Park home of Franklin Roosevelt, Wilderstein, Montgomery Place.

**BUSINESS TRAVEL:** Fax, computer, and copy machine available.

**RECOMMENDED COUNTRY INNS® TRAVELERS' CLUB BENEFIT:** Stay two nights, get third night free; Monday to Thursday.

*J*udy and Richard Kohler owned a Victorian gingerbread house that they called the Village Victorian Inn in Rhinebeck for many years, but when they built this contemporary home overlooking tiny Golden Pond in 1991, they created a thoroughly sophisticated and elegant retreat, as different from the fussy Victorian as Jekyll is from Hyde.

At first sight the cedar-sided house appears modest and unremarkable; even when we walked along the flying-bridge entrance to the house, we were unprepared for the gracious and urbane interior. The house envelops its guests in country charm but also offers luxurious and spacious private retreats. For a total getaway from the fast-paced city, I can't imagine a more relaxing sanctuary.

The living room is decorated with flair in gentle earth tones. The vaulted, rough-sawn pine ceiling and the wall of view windows toward the lake give

the room a warm, inviting glow. It's furnished with antiques, Oriental rugs on oak floors, twig furniture, comfortable sofas, piles of magazines and books, and an ornately carved oak English bar on which Victorian flow blue china is displayed. It's surrounded by a wraparound deck overlooking the lake.

Lakehouse Inn is the ultimate romantic retreat. The Casablanca Suite, for example, has its own fireplace, laid with logs and ready to be lighted, and a private deck. There's a pink damask sofa on which to watch the flames with a loved one while sipping a glass of wine chilled in the refrigerator. The canopy bed is swathed in lace. A television, VCR, and CD player hide in a pine armoire. In the bath a Jacuzzi for two has a serene view and is surrounded by a lip holding an array of fat candles.

The equally spacious Master Suite, located downstairs, has a private deck offering a view of the lake. Oriental rugs cover oak floors, another lace canopy decorates the bed, fat shutters shield the windows, and the pink-tile bath has another Jacuzzi. Each of the rooms is so large and so well equipped that it's possible to spend an entire weekend in the room and never feel claustrophobic. Two new rooms were added in 1997 in a building across the lake called The Boathouse.

Every possible amenity is provided. As Judy explained, "We just want our guests to be comfortable. We're too far from a town for them to run out for a soft drink, so we provide all of that in the room. We have soft drinks, wine, cookies, appetizers such as smoked salmon, truffles, and even Baby Watson cheesecakes in the refrigerator in case someone has a late-night sweet-tooth craving."

In the morning our breakfast was delivered to our room in a covered basket. One day it included an individual quiche with fresh fruit and breads. Another day we had cheese blintzes and chicken Chardonnay.

If guests do venture forth, they will find rowboats and paddleboats for use on the lake, hammocks, trails through the twenty-two-acre property, and a VCR library that includes almost 150 selections. Historic mansions, local wineries, and superb restaurants are located nearby.

HOW TO GET THERE: From New York City take the Henry Hudson Parkway north to the Saw Mill River Parkway, and then travel north on the Taconic Parkway to the Rhinebeck/Route 199 exit. Turn right onto Route 199 and go ½ mile. Take the first right onto Route 53 (South Road). Go 3½ miles. Turn right onto Shelly Hill Road and go exactly 9/10 mile. Turn into paved driveway. The Lakehouse Inn is at the end of the road.

# Three Village Inn 🖼️ 📠
## Stony Brook, New York 11790

**INNKEEPERS:** Jim, Lou, and Joan Miaritis; Daniel Laffitte, general manager

**ADDRESS/TELEPHONE:** 150 Main Street; (516) 751-0555; fax (516) 751-0593

**WEB SITE:** www.threevillageinn.com

**ROOMS:** 26; all with private bath, air-conditioning, telephone, and television; 3 with fireplace; VCR available. No smoking inn. Children welcome.

**RATES:** $105 to $165, double occupancy.

**OPEN:** All year except Christmas Day.

**FACILITIES AND ACTIVITIES:** Restaurant serving breakfast, lunch, and dinner (table d'hôte $26 to $34) and Sunday brunch; Sand Bar Tap Room. On ten acres with landscaped gardens, across from Stony Brook harbor. Nearby: The Museums of Stony Brook, harbor cruises on the *Discovery,* fishing expeditions, charming village of shops, Staller Center, Javits Lecture Center, antiquing, golfing, bicycling, nature walks, tennis.

**BUSINESS TRAVEL:** Corporate rates. Telephone and television in all rooms; desk in most rooms; conference and meeting rooms; copier, fax, computer hookups, and audiovisual equipment available.

As with so many of today's country inns, the Three Village Inn began life as the home of an important local resident. In this case that person was Richard Hallock, who built his gracious home in 1751. For years it was known as "The Old Homestead." Hallock was a farmer of substantial means, and his son George became the town's first major ship-builder. In 1835 the house was purchased by Jonas Smith, who owned a fleet of twenty-one sailing vessels. By 1907, however, the house had been purchased by the Stony Brook Assembly, a Presbyterian retreat organization that built the cottages as additional housing and turned the downstairs of the main house into their dining hall. Eventually, in 1929, the buildings were purchased by Mrs. Frank Melville, who organized a Women's Exchange here to sell homemade preserves, baked goods, and handcrafted items. The shop became so popular that she also opened a "tearoom," and in 1939 the tearoom was expanded into a first-class restaurant.

Many of the original features of The Old Homestead remain. The brick fireplace and beehive oven may still be found beside a romantic table in the Sand Bar Tap Room, and the original pine-paneled walls, hand-hewn beams, fireplace, and bookcases grace the Sitting Room.

The dining room has an old-fashioned ambience that suits most of the regular diners just fine. Glass-enclosed cases hold old commemorative plates illustrating local houses and scenes, as well as old lamps and lanterns. There are beamed ceilings, flowered carpeting, and a wall of windows that look toward the harbor. In the foyer a table is stacked high with freshly baked bread for guests to take home.

The guest rooms range from tiny and spartan to delightful cottages with a Ralph Lauren look. The baths are fine if you don't mind Formica counter-tops and acoustic-tile ceilings.

Stony Brook is a charming little village that offers something for every-one. The Museums at Stony Brook are really three museums in one. The History Museum has changing exhibits that recently included a wonderful exhibition titled "Stanford White on Long Island." The Art Gallery also has changing exhibits, but the Carriage Museum has a permanent collection of carriages on display. For shoppers there are charming shops ranging from Laura Ashley to The Nature Company.

**HOW TO GET THERE:** From New York City, take I–495 (Long Island Express-way) to exit 56 and make a left at the end of the ramp onto Route 111 north. Follow this until you reach Route 25A in Smithtown. Continue straight onto Route 25A and follow this into Stony Brook village. Bear left onto Main Street. The inn is ½ mile ahead on Main Street.

---

# The Castle at Tarrytown
Tarrytown, New York 10591

**INNKEEPERS:** Steffi and Hanspeter Walder; J. Philip Hughes, manager
**ADDRESS/TELEPHONE:** 400 Benedict Avenue; (914) 631–1980; fax (914) 631–4612
**WEB SITE:** www.castleattarrytown.com

**ROOMS:** 31, including 10 suites; all with private bath, air-conditioning, television, VCR, desk, telephone with dataport, minibar, radio, hair dryer, robes, iron, and ironing board; 10 with CD player, 5 with fireplace. Smoking permitted; designated nonsmoking rooms. Wheelchair accessible.

**RATES:** $175 to $675, double occupancy. Two-night minimum on weekends.

**OPEN:** All year.

**FACILITIES AND ACTIVITIES:** Restaurant serving breakfast, lunch (entrees $15 to $20), and dinner (entrees $21 to $32); on ten acres that include extensive gardens, a swimming pool with a grotto, a bocci court, and a life-sized chessboard. Exercise room includes treadmills, bicycles, stairs, weights, and more. Nearby: golfing, historic Hudson River mansions, museums, and cultural events.

**BUSINESS TRAVEL:** Desk, television, VCR, telephone with dataport, coffeemaker, iron, ironing board, and minibar in room. *Wall Street Journal* or *The New York Times* provided daily; fax and copy services available; exercise room; meeting rooms.

*I*magine men on charging steeds in suits of armor, ladies wearing flowing velvet dresses, and places called Camelot—and in that frame of mind you still won't be prepared for the medieval grandeur of the Castle at Tarrytown. There are crenelated towers and stone battlements and a twisty-turny road that climbs the ramparts to this gray stone mountaintop extravaganza.

Built between 1897 and 1910 and opened as an elegant country inn in 1997, the incredible stone building is the Hudson River Valley's most fashionable country inn. Designed by New York architect Henry Kilburn, the inn has elements of several notable Norman castles in Wales, Scotland, and Ireland in the architecture, but it is not a copy of any particular one.

From the grand reception hall we entered the Generals Bar, which has an ornate frieze on the ceiling and a brass chandelier. This intimate and romantic room has a round marble table in the turret, and it also leads to the terrace where drinks, lunch, and dinner are served on nice days. The view from this elevated perch of the lovely gardens and the Hudson River beyond is breathtaking.

The Oak Room, where we had dinner one evening, was transported by General Howard Carroll from his town house in Paris. It includes incredible oak paneled walls and a massive granite fireplace mantel with boars' heads carved into the surface. There are two additional dining rooms: The Tapestry Room has tapestries on the walls; the Garden Room has a tile floor and arched Gothic windows on three sides.

Dinner started with a lovely savory of spicy mushrooms on toast, followed by a dense mushroom soup that included a beggar's purse of mushrooms in the center. My dinner of swordfish included a tomato purée and was topped with eggplant and tomato. For dessert we shared a lovely pumpkin crème brûlée. After this perfect dinner in this fabulous setting, we climbed the stairs to our room.

We had the pleasure of staying in one of the suites in the main house shortly after they opened. What a fabulous experience! The St. Germain Suite is one of the most luxurious suites I have ever stayed in. It would be impossible to describe every detail, but there are elegant antiques throughout, oil paintings on the walls, rich silk damasks on the windows and on the huge puffy sofa, several fireplaces, and marble baths. The bedroom contains a huge carved canopy bed. There are Egyptian cotton sheets on the featherbeds and, at turndown, a handmade truffle. The views include the gardens, the Hudson River in the distance, and even the Manhattan skyline. We arrived to find an antique table set with a plate of fruit, cheeses, and bread. Everything about the inn is in the utmost of good taste and style.

In addition to the rooms and suites in the main inn, there are twenty-four equally beautiful rooms in the adjoining wing. Using Fortuny fabrics, elegant antiques, and oil paintings on the wall, every room is distinctive and elegant.

HOW TO GET THERE: From New York City take the Henry Hudson Parkway north to the Saw Mill River Parkway. Follow that north to exit 21W (Tarrytown) to Route 119 west. Turn right onto Route 119 and go to the fifth traffic light. Turn right onto Benedict Avenue. At the second traffic light turn left onto 400 Benedict Avenue (opposite the Hackley School). Continue up the hill to the castle, which is at the top.

# Taughannock Farms Inn
## Trumansburg, New York 14886

**INNKEEPERS:** Susan and Tom Sheridan

**ADDRESS/TELEPHONE:** 2030 Gorge Road; (607) 387–7711 or
(888) 387–7721; fax (607) 387–7721

**WEB SITE:** www.t-farms.com

**ROOMS:** 13, including 3 cottages; all with private bath, air-conditioning,
and radio; 3 with telephone, 2 with television, 2 with patio. No smoking
inn. Cottages wheelchair accessible.

**RATES:** $110 to $320, double occupancy; includes continental breakfast.
Two-night minimum some weekends.

**OPEN:** April to December.

**FACILITIES AND ACTIVITIES:** Restaurant serving dinner (entrees $19 to
$25), open April to November; private parties only in December; small
bar; on twelve acres with gardens. Across street from Cayuga Lake and
Taughannock Falls State Park, which offers boating, fishing, swimming,
hiking, and cross-country skiing. Nearby: wineries (inn is on the Finger
Lakes Wine Trail), bicycling, golfing, tennis, Cornell University (Ithaca is
9 miles south).

*I*f I were grading views, I would give Taughannock Farms Inn an A+.
From the bay window in the pretty Victorian parlor, which has clouds
painted on the ceiling, and from the tiered dining room with its wall
of ceiling-high windows, the views are breathtaking.

When John Jones built his white clapboard Victorian summer estate on a
hilltop overlooking Cayuga Lake in 1873, he owned 600 acres that included
most of the land that is now Taugh-
annock Falls State Park, including
the spectacular, roaring falls that
plunge from a height of 215 feet.
He and his wife, Molly, enjoyed the
inn for the next seventy-two years,
and during that time they deeded
all but twelve acres of the farm to
the state for the park. Molly eventually sold the home in 1945 to Mer-

ritt and Maude Agard, who converted the estate to an inn. Remarkably, the inn remained in the Agard family until 1996.

Susan and Tom Sheridan purchased the inn in 1997, and the place has been a beehive of activity ever since. But, Susan is quick to point out, "We were careful not to make too many changes." She was raised in Ithaca and fondly remembers accompanying her family here for dinner many times. She and Tom are intent on keeping that tradition alive.

They were fortunate that most of the former staff remained at the inn, including the chef and his wife, the inn's pastry chef, so such dining room favorites as chilled strawberry soup and roast turkey with all the trimmings are still on the menu. Since the Sheridans bring a combination of forty years of hotel and restaurant experience to their new enterprise, they have added new dishes as well.

Many of the lovely antiques the Jones family enjoyed in their home still reside at the inn. All the original parlor furniture remains. There's a gorgeous walnut china cabinet with glass doors, a massive mirror, and beautiful antique chairs upholstered in a rich blue velvet. A diminutive Victorian pub is to one side.

The guest rooms in the mansion are also furnished with Victorian antiques. There are high-headboard, carved-walnut Victorian beds, antique nightstands, and lovely views from three of the rooms. In addition to the five rooms in the mansion, two guest houses offer an additional seven rooms. The Sheridans have upgraded the decor and baths in both the Parkview and the Lakeview houses. Overnight guests enjoy a breakfast of freshly baked breakfast breads, fruit, juices, and coffee.

HOW TO GET THERE: From I–90 (New York State Thruway) take exit 41 onto Route 318 east. Follow this for 4 miles. Turn south onto Route 89 and continue on Route 89 for about 34 miles. The inn is on the right, high on a hill across from Taughannock Falls State Park. Climb the steep drive up the hill to the inn.

# The William Seward Inn
## Westfield, New York 14787

**INNKEEPERS:** Jim and Debbie Dahlberg

**ADDRESS/TELEPHONE:** 6645 South Portage Road (Route 394);
(716) 326–4151 or (800) 338–4151; fax (716) 326–4163

**ROOMS:** 12; all with private bath and air-conditioning; 4 in carriage
house with Jacuzzi, 2 with fireplace; telephones available. Wheelchair
accessible. No smoking inn.

**RATES:** $80 to $180, double occupancy; includes full breakfast. Corporate rates available. Request special package brochure. Two-night minimum if Saturday stay included and on holiday weekends.

**OPEN:** All year.

**FACILITIES AND ACTIVITIES:** On one and one-half acres, dinner for
guests Wednesday to Sunday by reservation ($40). Nearby: Chautauqua
Institution (7 miles), sailing, Cockaigne Ski Area in Cherry Creek, cross-
country skiing in county parks, Panama Rocks trail, wineries, antiquing,
country drives.

*I*f your idea of a lovely country inn is one that has a history and yet is
impeccably furnished with the finest furniture, fabrics, and amenities—and also offers an excellent restaurant—look no further. Jim
and Debbie Dahlberg have lavished attention on their perfect little inn ever
since they bought it in 1991, and all their hard work has paid off handsomely.

The oldest part of the inn was built in 1821, and it was still relatively new
when Williams Seward, the agent for the Holland Land Company, located in
Westfield, purchased it. He was later to gain fame as Secretary of State to
Abraham Lincoln and Andrew Johnson, especially after he purchased Alaska
from Russia—an act that was called "Seward's Folly." He added on to the

house several times and is responsible for the unique Greek Revival pillars and porch across the front. The house was located in the village of Westfield until the early 1970s, when it was moved to its current position on a hill outside town.

The interior of the house is handsome but uncluttered; the rooms are bright and light. The parlor has oak floors covered by Oriental rugs and a wood-burning fireplace with a white-painted mantle. A rose-covered Victorian love seat sits beside it. A library has a wall of built-in bookcases filled with books behind leaded-glass doors.

The Dahlbergs have left as many of the interesting old features in their house as they can. In the Wood Room, for example, the bath has its original marble sink with brass fittings. The room includes a mint-green carpet and a bed with a green-striped skirt. A lovely antique chest is in the room. The nicest room in the main building is the William Seward Room, which has a gas fireplace and a private balcony and is decorated in peach, apricot, and rose. This room has a large bath, but several other rooms have much smaller ones. In 1991 the Dahlbergs built a carriage house in the same style as the other buildings. It contains four guest rooms with double whirlpool tubs in the baths.

Dinner is served in two beautiful rooms at the inn to overnight guests as well as others. One of the rooms has a wine carpet and a lovely antique buffet; the other has a blue carpet and yellow walls. You will receive a menu with your room reservation, asking that you select your appetizer and entree and return it promptly. You might choose an appetizer of pan-seared scallops in champagne sauce or quail stuffed with veal mousse and napped with a wild grape sauce. Entree choices include pan-seared salmon with two sauces and rack of lamb with hazelnut crust.

HOW TO GET THERE: From I–90 take exit 60 to Route 394 and drive east to intersection with Route 20 in Westfield. Continue another 3½ miles on Route 394 to the inn, on the right.

# Albergo Allegria
# Bed & Breakfast 🎞 📱 ¢¢
## Windham, New York 12496

**INNKEEPERS:** Lenore and Vito Radelich; Leslie and Marianna Leman, managers

**ADDRESS/TELEPHONE:** Route 296 (mailing address: Box 267); (518) 734–5560 or (800) 6–ALBERGO; fax (518) 734–5570

**E-MAIL:** albergo@aol.com

**WEB SITE:** www.albergoUSA.com

**ROOMS:** 21, including 6 suites; all with private bath, telephone, television, and VCR; 8 with fireplace, 7 with balcony or patio, 6 with whirlpool tub, 5 with air-conditioning, radio, minirefrigerator, CD player, iron, and ironing board. Wheelchair accessible. No smoking inn.

**RATES:** $75 to $235, double occupancy; includes full breakfast. $25 each additional person. Two-night minimum weekends, three-night minimum most holiday weekends; four-night minimum on school holiday weekends.

**OPEN:** All year.

**FACILITIES AND ACTIVITIES:** On two acres overlooking Batavia Kill Creek, with fishing. Nearby: restaurant, eighteen-hole public golf course, tennis courts, swimming hole, Ski Windham, Catskill hiking, biking, ethnic festivals.

**BUSINESS TRAVEL:** Television, VCR, telephone in all rooms; desk in 12 rooms; fax, copier, and dataport available; laundry facilities; early checkout available with a "breakfast in a basket" to go.

*D*o coincidences intrigue you? This one revolves around years ending in "6." First Vito and Lenore Radelich moved from Long Island in 1976 and opened their restaurant La Griglia, which soon gained a reputation for its fine dining. In 1986, however, they decided to purchase several 1876 Victorian buildings across the street from their restaurant to restore and convert to a bed-and-breakfast. They did a wonderful job, and soon the inn was full. They decided in 1996 to restore the former horse stables on the property to create five additional suites. Through all of this they were assisted by their daughter and her husband, Leslie and Marianna Leman, who are also the innkeepers. I wonder what new adventure they'll take on in 2006?

This is a gem of an inn—one that is thoroughly Victorian from its golden oak antiques to its stained glass, but it has none of the dark rooms or the fussiness the Victorians seemed to adore. The innkeepers named their inn Albergo Allegria, which is Italian for the Inn of the Happiness. It would take a confirmed sourpuss not to be happy here.

There are two sitting rooms for guests to relax in. The main lounge has a polished cherry fireplace mantel and comfortable sofas and chairs. The other lounge is located upstairs, where there is another fireplace and a selection of 240 videos. Don't miss the gift shop with its wide selection of gifts.

The guest rooms are furnished with Victorian antiques that include oak wardrobes and chests, lace curtains, pine dressers, and stained glass. Every room has a television, VCR, and telephone, and the baths are tiled. The Master Suite is the nicest and is often chosen for honeymoons. It has a gas fireplace, a king-sized featherbed, and a Jacuzzi in the bath. The rooms in the carriage house are equally luxurious, but they also have the advantage of offering more privacy and seclusion than those in the main house.

As one might imagine from an award-winning chef, breakfast is delicious. In addition to the fruits, juices, and breakfast breads you expect to find, Vito may also prepare stuffed French toast, crepes, or an omelette that might be accompanied by a sliced turkey breast with a light apricot sauce.

HOW TO GET THERE: From I–87 (New York State Thruway) take exit 21 (the Catskills). At the first stop sign turn left and then make the first right onto Route 23 west. Follow Route 23 for just over 23 miles and then turn left onto Route 296. The inn is $\frac{1}{10}$ mile farther on the left.

# Select List of Other Inns in New York

## The Gansett Green Manor

273 Main Street
Amagansett, NY 11930
(516) 267–3133

*14 rooms; all with private bath and kitchen; in interesting cottages in the Hamptons.*

## The Hedges

Blue Mountain Lake, NY 12812
(518) 352–7325

*Rustic Adirondack camp with simple clean decor on beautiful lake; all rooms with private bath. All meals included.*

## Hemlock Hall

Route 28N
Blue Mountain Lake, NY 12812
(518) 352–7706

*22 rooms; private and shared baths; clean but old-fashioned decor in rustic Adirondack camp on lovely lake. All meals included.*

## Onteora, The Mountain House

96 Piney Point Road
Boiceville, NY 12412
(914) 657–6233

*5 rooms; 1 with private bath; in former estate of Richard Hellmann of mayonnaise fame.*

## 10,000 Delights

1170 West Lake Road
Branchport, NY 14418
(607) 868–3731

*11 rooms; 2 with private bath; in hilltop house overlooking Keuka Lake in Finger Lakes regions.*

## The Inn at Silver Maple Farm

Route 295
Canaan, NY 12029
(518) 781–3600

*10 rooms; all with private bath; in delightful new B&B in Hudson River Valley.*

## Habersham Country Inn B&B

6124 Route 5N 20
Canandaigua, NY 14424
(716) 394–1510

*4 rooms; all with private bath; in ivory clapboard B&B in Finger Lakes region.*

## Sutherland House B&B

3179 State Route 21 South
Canandaigua, NY 14424
(716) 396–0375 or (800) 396–0375

*5 rooms; all with private bath; in lovely B&B in Finger Lakes region.*

## Glen Iris Inn

7 Letchworth State Park
Castile, NY 14427
(716) 493–2622

*15 rooms; in 1828 Federal house overlooking waterfalls in "Grand Canyon of the East"; restaurant.*

## Athenaeum Hotel

Chautauqua, NY 14722
(716) 357–6269 or (800) 821–1881

*Grand 160-room hotel on lake in heart of Chautauqua Institution; restaurant*

## Plumbush

Chautauqua-Stedman Road
Chautauqua, NY 14722
(716) 789–5309

*5 rooms; all with private bath; in pink Victorian about 1 mile from Chautauqua Institution.*

## Pig Hill Inn

73 Main Street
Cold Spring-on-Hudson, NY 10506
(914) 265-9247

*8 rooms; 4 with private bath, 4 sharing 2 baths; in brick building on Main Street of village in the Hudson River Valley.*

## The J. P. Sill House

63 Chestnut Street
Cooperstown, NY 13326
(607) 547-2633

*8 rooms; 4 with private bath; in elegant and beautifully decorated Victorian in village.*

## Thistlebrook

County Road 28
Cooperstown, NY 13326
(607) 547-6093

*6 rooms; all with private bath; in converted barn in the country.*

## Rosewood Inn

134 East First Street
Corning, NY 14830
(607) 962-3253

*7 rooms; all with private bath; in Victorian house.*

## Alexander Hamilton House

49 Van Wyck Street
Croton-on-Hudson, NY 10520
(914) 271-6737

*7 rooms; all with private bath, in Victorian house in Hudson River Valley.*

## Crown Point Bed & Breakfast

Route 9N
Crown Point, NY 12928
(518) 597-3651

*6 rooms; all with private bath; in B&B on Lake Champlain.*

## Chestnut Inn at Oquaga Lake

498 Oquaga Lake Road
Deposit, NY 13754
(607) 467-2500 or (800) 467-7676

*24 rooms; 10 with private bath, the rest shared; in lakeside resort near Binghamton.*

## Centennial House

13 Woods Lane
East Hampton, NY 11937
(516) 324–9414

*4 rooms; all with private bath; in beautifully decorated shingle-style house in the Hamptons.*

## Lysander House

132 Main Street
East Hampton, NY 11937
(516) 329–9025

*3 rooms; all with private bath; in charming B&B filled with folk art in the Hamptons.*

## Mill House Inn

33 North Main Street
East Hampton, NY 11937
(516) 324–9766

*8 rooms; all with private bath; overlooking windmill in Hamptons.*

## The Pink House

26 James Lane
East Hampton, NY 11937
(516) 324–3400

*6 rooms; all with private bath; overlooking Town Pond in the Hamptons.*

## Treasure Island Bed & Breakfast

14909 Main Road
East Marion, NY 11939
(516) 477–2788

*3 rooms; 1 with private bath; on six acres of waterfront on Long Island's North Fork.*

## Bartlett House Inn

503 Front Street
Greenport, NY 11944
(516) 477–0371

*9 rooms; all with private bath; in shingled house on Long Island's North Fork.*

## Benn Conger Inn

206 West Cortland Street
Groton, NY 13073
(607) 898–5817

*5 rooms; all with private bath; in mansion on lovely grounds; restaurant.*

## Ruah B&B

34 Lake Shore Drive (Route 9N)
Hague, NY 12836
(518) 543–8816 or (800) 224–7549

*4 rooms; all with private bath; in 1890s house with spectacular views of Lake George.*

## Bykenhulle House

21 Bykenhulle Road
Hopewell Junction, NY 12533
(914) 221–4182

*5 rooms; all with private bath; in gracious manor house in the Hudson River Valley.*

## The Inn at Blue Stores

2323 Route 9
Hudson, NY 12534
(518) 537–4277

*5 rooms; 3 with private bath; in 1908 Spanish-style house in Hudson River Valley.*

## Adirondack Loj

East Shore Drive
Lake Placid, NY 12946
(518) 523–3441

*Adirondack hideaway with rooms ranging from those with queen-sized beds and private bath to dormitory rooms with shared bath. Great for hikers; group dinner nightly.*

## Mirror Lake Inn

5 Mirror Lake Drive
Lake Placid, NY 12946
(518) 523–2544

*124 rooms and suites; all with private bath; in elegant in-town hotel on shores of Mirror Lake.*

## The Federal House B&B

175 Ludlowville Road
Lansing, NY 14852
(607) 533-7362 or (800) 533-7362

*B&B in tiny little village in Finger Lakes region, near Ithaca.*

## Simmons Way Village Inn

33 Main Street
Millerton, NY 12546
(518) 789-6235

*11 rooms; all with private bath; in white clapboard house; restaurant.*

## Peri's Bed & Breakfast

206 Essex Street
Montauk, NY 11954
(516) 668-1394

*3 rooms; all with private bath; in Tudor-style home in the Hamptons.*

## Lighthouse on the Bay

North Haven, NY 11963
(516) 725-7112

*3 fabulous rooms; 2 with private bath; in newly built inn with tower that looks like a lighthouse; overlooks marshes and bays. In private community; must call for address and directions.*

## Garnet Hill Lodge

Thirteenth Lake Road
North River, NY 12856
(518) 251-2444

*28 rooms; most with private bath; in rustic Adirondack lodge.*

## Northbrook Lodge

Osgood Lake
Paul Smiths, NY 12970
(518) 327-3379

*16 rooms; all with private bath; on former estate in Adirondacks.*

## Finton's Landing B&B

661 East Lake Road
Penn Yan, NY 14527
(315) 536-3146

*4 rooms; all with private bath; B&B in Finger Lakes region overlooking Keuka Lake.*

## Rufus Tanner House

60 Sagetown Road
Pine City, NY 14871
(607) 732-0213

*4 rooms; all with private bath; in 1864 Victorian farmhouse near Elmira.*

## The Golden Pineapple

201 Liberty Avenue
Port Jefferson, NY 11777
(516) 331-0706

*3 rooms; all with private bath; in charming newly built inn on Long Island's North Shore.*

## Sagamore Lodge

Raquette Lake, NY 13436
(315) 354-5311

*Fabulous lakefront Adirondack Great Camp specializing in weeklong or weekend retreats.*

## Veranda House

82 Montgomery Street
Rhinebeck, NY 12572
(914) 876-4133

*4 rooms; all with private bath; in village in Hudson River Valley.*

## Whistle Wood Farm

51 Pells Road
Rhinebeck, NY 12572
(914) 876-6838

*6 rooms and cottages; all with private bath; on thirteen-acre horse farm in Hudson River Valley.*

## The Mansion Inn

801 Route 29
Rock City Falls, NY 12863
(518) 885-1607

*7 rooms; all with private bath; in fabulous Venetian villa near Saratoga Springs.*

## Rock Stream Bed & Breakfast

524 Rock Stream Road
Rock Stream, NY 14878
(607) 243-5898

*4 rooms; all with private bath; in brick house high on hill in Finger Lakes region.*

## Pickwick Lodge

Winter Clove Road
Round Top, NY 12473
(518) 622–3364

*45 rooms; all with private bath; resort in the Catskill Mountains.*

## Winter Clove Inn

Winter Clove Road
Round Top, NY 12473
(518) 622–3267

*52 rooms; all with private bath; resort in the Catskill Mountains.*

## Schroon Lake Bed & Breakfast

Route 9
Schroon Lake, NY 12870
(518) 532–7042

*4 rooms and 1 suite; 3 with private bath, 2 that share; in pretty clapboard bed-and-breakfast in the Adirondacks.*

## The Silver Spruce Inn Bed and Breakfast

Route 9
Schroon Lake, NY 12870
(518) 532–7031

*8 rooms; all with private bath; in a lovely B&B with fascinating architecture and history in the Adirondacks.*

## Sunset Beach Inn

35 Shore Road
Shelter Island Heights, NY 11965
(516) 749–3000

*20 rooms; all with private bath; in upscale boutique motel across from Crescent Beach; restaurant.*

## Stearns Point House

7 Stearns Point Road
Shelter Island Heights, NY 11965
(516) 749–4162

*4 rooms; all with private bath; in B&B on quiet country road.*

## Lady of the Lake

2 West Lake Street
Skaneateles, NY 13152
(315) 685–7997 or (800) 685–7997

*B&B in Queen Anne Victorian across street from Skaneateles Lake in Finger Lakes region.*

## Evergreen on Pine

89 Pine Street
Southampton, NY 11968
(516) 283–0564

*5 rooms; all with private bath; in Southampton village in the Hamptons.*

## The Ivy

244 North Main Street
Southampton, NY 11968
(516) 283–3233

*4 rooms; all with private bath; in charming B&B with pool in the Hamptons.*

## Mainstay Inn

579 Hill Street
Southampton, NY 11968
(516) 283–4375

*8 rooms; 5 with private bath; in B&B with pool in the Hamptons.*

## The Wawbeek on Upper Saranac Lake

553 Panther Mountain Road
Tupper Lake, NY 12986
(518) 359–2656 or (800) 953–2656

*Adirondack Great Camp with 19 rooms; all with private bath.*

## Westhampton Country Manor

28 Jagger Lane
Westhampton, NY 11977
(516) 288–5540

*6 rooms; all with private bath; in B&B on two and one-half country acres in the Hamptons.*

# Pennsylvania

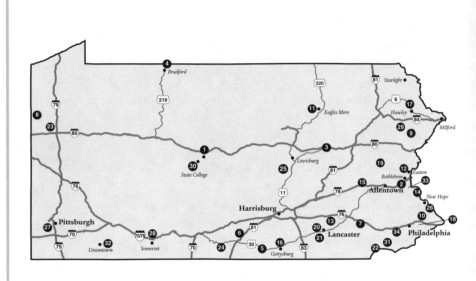

Bradford 4

220

81 Starlight

219

11 Eagles Mere

6

17

79

Hawley

8

84

23

80

29

9

Milford

1

3

80

30

25

19

12

State College

Lewisburg

Easton

33

81

Bethlehem

15

Allentown

14

11

78

New Hope

Harrisburg

26

13

76

10

27 Pittsburgh

20

7

18

70

81

6

2

34

79

28

24

30

5

16

21 Lancaster

31

32

70 76

70

83

22

Uniontown

Somerset

Gettysburg

# Pennsylvania

*Numbers on map refer to towns numbered below.*

1. Bellefonte, The Reynolds Mansion* ......................... 248
2. Bethlehem, The Sayre Mansion Inn ...................... 251
3. Bloomsburg, The Inn at Turkey Hill ...................... 252
4. Bradford, Glendorn, A Lodge in the Country* .............. 254
5. Cashtown, Cashtown Inn ................................ 257
6. Chambersburg, The Ragged Edge Inn* .................... 259
7. Churchtown, The Inn at Twin Linden* .................... 261
8. Clark, Tara—A Country Inn .............................. 264
9. Cresco, Crescent Lodge and Country Inn .................. 266
10. Doylestown, Sign of the Sorrel Horse .................... 268
11. Eagles Mere, Eagles Mere Inn ............................ 269
12. Easton, The Lafayette Inn ............................... 271
13. Ephrata,
    Historic Smithton Inn ................................ 272
    The Inns at Doneckers* ............................... 274
14. Erwinna,
    EverMay On-the-Delaware ............................. 276
    Golden Pheasant Inn ................................. 277
15. Fogelsville, Glasbern* ................................. 279
16. Gettysburg, The Gaslight Inn ........................... 281
17. Hawley, The Settlers Inn ............................... 283
18. Holicong, Barley Sheaf Farm ........................... 285
19. Jim Thorpe, The Inn at Jim Thorpe ..................... 287
20. Lancaster, The King's Cottage .......................... 289
21. Lititz, Swiss Woods Bed & Breakfast .................... 290
22. Mendenhall, Fairville Inn* ............................. 293
23. Mercer, The Magoffin Inn .............................. 295
24. Mercersburg, The Mercersburg Inn* ..................... 296
25. New Berlin, The Inn at Olde New Berlin ................. 299
26. New Hope,
    The Fox & Hound Bed & Breakfast of New Hope ......... 301
    Holly Hedge Estate Bed & Breakfast ................... 303
    The Inn at Phillips Mill .............................. 305
    The Mansion Inn* ................................... 307
27. Pittsburgh, The Priory—A City Inn ..................... 309
28. Somerset, The Inn at Georgian Place* ................... 311
29. South Sterling, The French Manor ...................... 313
30. State College, Carnegie House ......................... 315
31. Thornton, Pace One Country Inn ....................... 317
32. Uniontown, B&B Inn of the Princess and European Bakery ... 318
33. Upper Black Eddy, Bridgeton House on the Delaware* ..... 320
34. West Chester, Whitewing Farm Bed & Breakfast* .......... 322

*A Top Pick Inn

# The Reynolds Mansion 🖤
## Bellefonte, Pennsylvania 16823

**INNKEEPERS:** Joseph and Charlotte Heidt

**ADDRESS/TELEPHONE:** 101 West Linn Street; (814) 353–8407 or (800) 899–3929; fax (814) 353–1530

**E-MAIL:** jheidt@bellefonte.com

**WEB SITE:** www.bellefonte.com/rmbb

**ROOMS:** 6; all with private bath and air-conditioning; 5 with whirlpool tub and fireplace, 1 with steam shower. No smoking inn. Children over the age of 12 welcome.

**RATES:** $95 to $175, double occupancy; includes full breakfast; $5.00 less per couple for continental breakfast; $10.00 less per couple without breakfast; $8.00 additional for extra guests at breakfast. Two-night minimum during Penn State football and other special event weekends.

**OPEN:** All year.

**FACILITIES AND ACTIVITIES:** On one acre; slate billiards table, garden, croquet; treadmill available. Nearby: Penn State University, downhill skiing at Tussey Mountain, Garman Opera House.

**RECOMMENDED COUNTRY INNS® TRAVELERS' CLUB BENEFIT:** 10 percent discount, Monday to Thursday.

*J*oe and Charlotte Heidt graduated from Penn State. As with most Penn State alumni, they are avid football fans who have rarely missed a game in more than two decades. As one might imagine they became exceedingly familiar with State College and the surrounding towns—especially Bellefonte, the captivating historic Victorian village with its wealth of elaborate mansions—a legacy of its rich iron ore days.

One particular stone mansion especially caught their eye, and they watched with fascination as it went from being a private home to being a church. One day in 1990 their daughter, Andi (who was attending Penn State), happened to notice that the mansion was for sale again—and the rest is history. They opened the house as an inn in 1994.

The twenty-seven-room 1893 high-Victorian home is constructed of red sandstone and exhibits a combination of Gothic, Italianate, and Queen Anne styles. A circular extension was added to the back in 1901. Built by Major William Frederick Reynolds and inherited by his nephew, Colonel W. Frederick Reynolds, the mansion was the home of the family until 1941. The woodwork in the main-floor rooms is some of the finest I have seen and the remarkable thing is that it has never been painted or adulterated in any way. The ceilings reach to 12 feet on both the first and second floors. There's a hand-carved stairway with a brass lamp on a newel post, a marble fireplace mantel, and a paneled hall with a coffered walnut ceiling. But the floors are absolutely amazing. Each is intricately inlaid with a variety of woods and in a variety of patterns. They are truly remarkable.

Joe and Charlotte have decorated the inn and its guest rooms with whimsy and flair. In the center hall there's a charming teddy bear collection, and interesting old hats hang on the walls. The Billiard Room has massive pocket doors, a tiled fireplace, and a coffered ceiling in a Chippendale style. The intimate and charming Snuggery, with yet another fireplace, however, is my favorite retreat.

The guest rooms are equally engaging. The Heidts opened the inn with three rooms on the second floor. In 1998 they added three more rooms on the third floor. The Colonel's Green Room has a king-size iron canopy bed elaborately dressed in green and brown Ralph Lauren fabrics. There's a gas fireplace, a black whirlpool tub in the room, and a separate bath. For those who adore a romantic setting, there's a mural of cherubs painted on the ceiling in Louise's Cherub Room, a heart-shaped whirlpool tub in the room, and a fireplace. An elaborately inlaid parquet floor underscores the iron bed.

We had dinner one night at the delightful and historic Gamble Mill, a 1786 stone mill that still has water coursing through a raceway that flows beneath the building. The food was fabulous. We started with an appetizer of wild mushroom duxelle laced with port wine and baked in phyllo and spinach ravioli filled with butternut squash and served in a mushroom cream sauce. For dinner I had Kirshwasser pork, a pork loin marinated in juniper berry and cherry liqueur and served with pork demiglace and dried sour cherries; my husband had a seafood strudel, which consisted of a moist filling of shrimp, scallops, and crab encased in layers of phyllo and draped in a sour cream and Mornay sauce. Need I say more?

A full breakfast is served unless guests request less. Charlotte sets out freshly baked muffins, coffee, and tea in the upstairs hallway for early birds, but it would be a shame to miss the full treatment. It's served in the Dining Room, which has a parquet floor of maple, mahogany, and walnut. There are beautiful antiques and lovely heirloom china and glassware. The meal might start with poached pears with raspberry sauce. A typical breakfast entree is the baked stuffed French toast accompanied by sausage and miniature danish.

HOW TO GET THERE: From I–80 traveling east take exit 24. Follow Route 26 toward Bellefonte until it reaches Route 550. At the junction with Route 550, turn right. Follow Route 550 to the third light and turn right onto Allegheny Street. Go to the second light and turn left onto Linn Street. Enter through the iron gates on the right to the inn's parking lot.

## A Coincidental Friendship

Since Bellefonte is merely 10 miles from Penn State, it is natural for The Reynolds Mansion to frequently be filled with Penn State alumni, especially on football weekends. One crisp fall football Saturday, after serving breakfast, Joe and Charlotte Heidt rushed to finish their innkeeping duties to get to the game for kickoff. As they raced to the seats they had occupied for the last two decades, imagine their surprise to see several of their inn guests sitting directly across the narrow aisle from them. It turns out they had been sitting across from one another for more than seventeen years.

# The Sayre Mansion Inn 🖼 📱
## Bethlehem, Pennsylvania 18015

**INNKEEPERS:** John and Norah Cappellano; Tom Collins and
Jean Fattell, managers

**ADDRESS/TELEPHONE:** 250 Wyandotte Street; (610) 882–2100;
fax (610) 882–1223

**ROOMS:** 19, including 2 suites; all with private bath, air-conditioning,
telephone, television, desk, and radio; 2 with fireplace. Wheelchair accessible. Smoking permitted; designated nonsmoking rooms.

**RATES:** $100 to $125, double occupancy; includes continental breakfast.

**OPEN:** All year.

**FACILITIES AND ACTIVITIES:** On two acres; gardens, in the Fountain
Hill National Register Historic District; discount passes to excellent
twenty-four-hour health club. Nearby: Moravian Museum of Bethlehem,
Lehigh University, Zoellner Arts Center, Fountain Hill Opera House.

**BUSINESS TRAVEL:** Desk, telephone, and television in room. Conference
room, fax, copier, audiovisual equipment, and catered meals available.

The Sayre Mansion Inn sits high on a hill, majestically surveying the
landscape created by its builder, Robert Heysham Sayre. This
impressive brick mansion, embellished with a multitude of gables
and porches, was built in 1858 by the chief engineer of the Lehigh Valley Railroad and one of the founders of Bethlehem Steel. He was also primarily
responsible for the creation of Lehigh University, St. Luke's Hospital, The
Episcopal Cathedral Church of the Nativity, and Fountain Hill Opera House.
All are either located nearby or in the valley just below.

John and Norah Cappellano, restoration contractors, purchased the mansion and converted it to an inn in 1993. The common rooms of the inn are
grand and magnificent. The front parlor has oak floors and huge double-
hung Jeffersonian windows that open to a spacious veranda filled with wicker
chairs that offer lovely views of the valley. Elaborate moldings outline the ceiling and frame the doorways. A marble mantel surrounds the gas fireplace.

The guest rooms are equally lovely. The grandest are located in a wing of
the mansion that served as Mr. Sayre's library. This scholarly man delighted
in collecting and reading rare books, and at one time his library must have
been one of the most extensive in the East. The room created to house it has
high coffered gilt ceilings. Suite 10 has a fabulous living room with a fireplace

and a gilded domed ceiling with a crystal chandelier in its center. Books fill the shelves that climb to the ceiling. The bedroom contains an antique carved walnut bed and armoire. Suite 21 includes much of the amazing gilded library ceiling, as well as antique furniture and gold mirrors. All the guest rooms have period reproduction furniture and spacious and modern baths with tile floors.

The continental breakfast is served in the dining room, which has a huge maple table, Oriental rugs on oak floors, oil paintings, and an antique breakfront. Black tapestry placemats hold gold-rimmed china and antique silver. There will be freshly baked breakfast breads, fresh fruit, cereal, bagels, and juices.

**HOW TO GET THERE:** From I–78 take exit 21 (Route 412 Hellertown/Bethlehem) and turn right at the end of the ramp onto Route 412 north. Turn left at the first light onto West Third Street. Go straight up the hill (do not bear right) and cross over Wyandotte Street (Route 378). The Sayre Mansion Inn is on the right.

# The Inn at Turkey Hill 🎛 📱
## Bloomsburg, Pennsylvania 17815

**INNKEEPER:** Andrew Pruden

**ADDRESS/TELEPHONE:** 991 Central Road; (717) 387–1500; fax (717) 784–3718

**E-MAIL:** turkyinn@prolog.net

**WEB SITE:** www.enterpe.com/turkeyhill

**ROOMS:** 23, including 7 suites; all with private bath, air-conditioning, telephone with dataport, television, desk, radio, iron, and ironing board; suites also with coffeemaker, minirefrigerator, fireplace, whirlpool tub, and robes. Smoking permitted; designated nonsmoking rooms. Pets permitted in 16 rooms.

**RATES:** $100 to $200, double occupancy; includes continental breakfast.

**OPEN:** All year.

**FACILITIES AND ACTIVITIES:** Restaurant serving dinner (entrees $18 to $25); on four acres with duck pond and gazebo; 13 farming acres adjacent; $5.00 use fee to guests at local health club. Nearby: Bloomsburg

Fair, Bloomsburg Theatre Ensemble, Bloomsburg University, Kneobals Amusement Resort, Ricketts Glen State Park, golfing.

**BUSINESS TRAVEL:** Desk, telephone with dataport, television in all rooms; meetings rooms; fax and copier available; twenty-four-hour front-desk service.

ndrew Pruden's grandfather was a newspaper publisher who loved to farm. His haven was his farm at Turkey Hill, where Andrew can remember selling sweet corn from a roadside stand as a boy. After the interstate came along, which his grandfather supported, Andrew can remember him musing about what a nice inn his grand old home would make. Andrew's grandmother had visions of others enjoying the stately rooms and spacious grounds as much as they did. So in 1984 they built a wing adjacent to their 1839 house that contained sixteen guest rooms, and although Andrew's "Pappy" passed away shortly before construction began, his grandmother became the first innkeeper. It wasn't until Andrew took over the property, however, that it took on its current cachet. He's the one who added the whirlpool tubs and the fireplaces; he added five new rooms in 1996 as well.

The guest rooms are spacious and absolutely charming. Each of the rooms is furnished with folk art and adorned with folk murals that were painted by a local artist. Even the room numbers are whimsical and charming. Each number is painted on a different cutout of a farm animal. The furniture consists of high-quality Shaker-style reproductions. Although all the rooms are nice, I believe The Editor's Choice is my favorite. It has a green carpet, a gas fireplace, and a beautiful bath.

The common rooms include a lobby with a fireplace and a library of books, sage-green walls, an Oriental rug, and wing chairs upholstered in a floral fabric. The Tavern Room has a cabinet with a stained-glass door behind the bar.

One of the advantages of an overnight stay at The Inn at Turkey Hill is that you need not go far for dinner. The lovely dining rooms offer an ideal setting for a relaxed meal. The Mural Room has oak floors and a pretty mural that encircles the room and features a country farm scene that includes a barn, farm buildings, and a pond enclosed by a fence. The Stencil Room has stenciled designs on the walls.

Dinner may begin with crabcakes Dijonaise, a lovely combination of lump crabmeat, Parmesan cheese, and bread crumbs laced with Dijon and tarragon tartar sauce or, perhaps, a crab-asparagus soup. For an entree you might choose a crisped half duckling accompanied by an apple-cranberry sauce or a veal cutlet coated with toasted almonds, breadcrumbs, and brown sugar and served with a raspberry-champagne cream sauce.

**HOW TO GET THERE:** From I–80 traveling west, take exit 35A (Bloomsburg University). At the first light turn left; the inn is on the left. From I–80 traveling east, take exit 35 and follow directions above.

# Glendorn, A Lodge in the Country
## Bradford, Pennsylvania 16701

**PROPRIETORS:** The Dorn Family; Linda and Gene Spinner, managers

**ADDRESS/TELEPHONE:** 1032 West Corydon Street; (814) 362–6511 or for reservations (800) 843–8568; fax (814) 368–9923

**E-MAIL:** glendorn@penn.com

**WEB SITE:** www.glendorn.com

**ROOMS:** 10, including 2 suites and 6 cabins; all with private bath, telephone with dataport, television, radio, hair dryer, CD player, robes, iron, and ironing board; 9 with desk, 8 with fireplace and/or patio or porch, 6 with minirefrigerator and coffeemaker, 3 with VCR (available for other rooms on request), 2 with air-conditioning. Children over the age of 12 welcome. Smoking permitted.

**RATES:** $475 to $645, double occupancy; includes all meals and recreational activities. Two-night minimum for cabins throughout the week and for all rooms on weekends. Three-night minimum some holidays.

**OPEN:** February to New Year's Day.

**FACILITIES AND ACTIVITIES:** Tennis, skeet and trap shooting, canoes, fishing, bicycling, swimming, hiking, cross-country skiing, snowshoeing, billiards and pool. Massages and facials arranged by appointment. Nearby: golf, downhill skiing, the Allegheny National Forest.

**BUSINESS TRAVEL:** Desk, telephone with dataport, television in room; fax, copier, audiovisual equipment available; conference center.

Imagine yourself on the private porch of a secluded stone cabin tucked away among stands of hemlock and maple. In the hush of this misty morning, you've already watched several deer graze on the lawn, and you scarcely breathed when you saw a red fox dart from the woods to race across the clearing. A family of rabbits is still nibbling on the flowers in the beds. Just beyond a stone bridge crosses a gentle stream, and you believe you saw several trout hugging the shady waters under the overhanging bank. It's this seamless communication with nature that we experienced on our visit to Glendorn.

Once the family retreat of the Dorn family, founders of Forest Oil Corporation, the family converted their 1,280-acre estate into a country inn in 1995. Clayton Glenville Dorn began building the complex in 1929 with the con-

struction of the Big House, a remarkable all-redwood structure that contains a 27-by-45-foot great room with a 20-foot-high cathedral ceiling and a massive two-story sandstone fireplace. The dining room is now located at the end opposite the fireplace. Additional cabins with fireplaces (one even has three fireplaces) were added for family members over the years. These and the Big House now contain guest rooms.

The guest rooms at Glendorn are far from ordinary. Reminiscent of the style that the Dorns enjoyed in the 1930s and 1940s, they are spacious and elegant. They feature butternut- or chestnut-paneled walls; oil paintings; and beds, chairs, and sofas covered in floral prints and checks. The rich, warm woods give the rooms a soft glow, and even in the Big House, most have stone fireplaces. We loved the Dorn Suite in the Big House, which has a fireplace in both the living room and the bedroom as well as a private sunroom. We had both a tub and a shower in the bath.

All meals are included in the room price, as is the use of all the recreational facilities, which are extensive. Indeed, it would take weeks to sample them all. There are fishing streams, three stocked lakes for fishing, 20 miles of marked trails for hiking and cross-country skiing with promontories offering romantic picnic sites with views (the inn will pack a lunch), three tennis courts, skeet and trap shooting (guns, clay pigeons, and instruction provided), canoes, and bicycles; a gymnasium with a NordicTrack, vertical ascent climber, weights, a treadmill, and a half-basketball court; a 60-foot outdoor swimming pool, snowshoeing, and a game room with billiards and pool.

Few places in America offer an escape from the workaday pressures in such a serene setting. The Dorns have long known that their retreat offered a unique, environmentally sensitive sanctuary that had an ability to restore the spirit and renew the psyche. Now we are able to share it.

HOW TO GET THERE: From I–80 exit onto Route 219 at DuBois. Go north on Route 219 to Bradford. At South Avenue intersection, follow South Avenue to Corydon Street. Turn left onto Corydon. Travel for 4³⁄₁₀ miles to the Glendorn gate, which is just after a bright red barn. The complex is 1½ miles farther on a private paved road.

## The Raven and the Frog

The first thing visitors to Glendorn notice as they approach the Big House is the spectacular totem pole. The pole is more typical of the Pacific Northwest and Alaska than the East Coast, and it was probably purchased by Forest Dorn on one of his many fishing expeditions to the Pacific Northwest.

The design of the pole is derived from the famous Seattle Totem Pole. It uses characters designed originally in the Tlingit village of Tongass in Southeastern Alaska and draws primarily from the Tlingit Raven myth series.

The Glendorn totem pole features the culture hero and trickster, Raven, who sits atop the pole and holds a crescent moon in his beak. This represents the story about his theft of the sun, moon, stars, and daylight from their owner, Nass-shu-ki-yehl, who is represented as a bird with a humanoid face featuring a fiercely hooked nose. He sits at the bottom of the pole. Just under Raven sits a woman who married a frog; her frog husband sits just below her. This image is followed by Mink, who, with his companion Raven, entered a whale's mouth and cooked his fat and heart. When they emerged, they were covered with oil, which gives them shiny coats. They sit on the whale, and his image is next to the bottom, just above Nass-shu-ki-yehl.

This unique form of Indian art is rarely seen outside the Pacific Northwest and Alaska, yet in this serene setting of first-growth evergreen trees and natural redwood buildings, the totem pole seems perfectly at home.

# Cashtown Inn 🏨
## Cashtown, Pennsylvania 17310

**INNKEEPERS:** Dennis and Eileen Hoover; Jason Hoover, assistant innkeeper

**ADDRESS/TELEPHONE:** 1325 Old Route 30 (mailing address: P.O. Box 103); (717) 334–9722 or (800) 367–1797; fax (717) 334–1442

**E-MAIL:** cashtowninn@mail.cvn.net

**WEB SITE:** www.Gettysburg.com/cashtowninn

**ROOMS:** 7, including 3 suites; all with private bath, air conditioning, radio, and robes; 3 with television, 2 with deck or patio. Smoking permitted in Tavern only. Children welcome in two family suites only.

**RATES:** $95 to $145, double occupancy; includes full breakfast. Two-night minimum weekends from May to November.

**OPEN:** All year.

**FACILITIES AND ACTIVITIES:** Restaurant serving lunch Tuesday to Sunday and dinner Tuesday to Saturday (entrees $15 to $18); tavern; on three acres with gardens. Nearby: Gettysburg National Military Park, antiquing, golfing, downhill skiing at Ski Liberty.

**RECOMMENDED COUNTRY INNS® TRAVELERS' CLUB BENEFIT:** 10 percent discount, Monday to Tuesday, May to October. Stay two nights, get third night free, November to April, excluding holidays.

*S*teeped in Civil War history the Cashtown Inn should be on the itinerary of every Civil War buff. The first stagecoach stop west of Gettysburg, the brick tavern with its broad porch across the front and side was built in 1797. Peter Marks knew that a new turnpike was about to pass this spot, so he built a substantial building where he could offer meals and overnight accommodations to travelers, as well as an adjacent barn to stable forty horses. A frugal individual, he refused to accept credit for the food or liquor he served, for the toll he collected on the road, or for the overnight lodging he offered to man and horse. Soon riders up and down the pike would shout as they passed one another, "Don't forget that CASH TOWN ahead." Eventually, the name stuck.

In 1863, as the battle at nearby Gettysburg raged, Confederate troops used the Cashtown Inn as a staging area and later for the care of many of their wounded. It was from this point that the 17-mile-long wagon train of wounded and dying left for the security of northern Virginia. The inn was featured in the movie *Gettysburg*, and it is filled with authentic Civil War memorabilia.

Dennis and Eileen Hoover, who purchased the inn in 1996, are the ideal keepers of this piece of history. Eileen has a master's degree in American history, and she has thoroughly researched the stories about the inn and the surrounding farms and families. Furthermore, the couple appreciate the unique ambience of their inn and have decorated it with all the appropriate furnishings.

The formal dining room has a wonderful folk-art wall mural depicting the inn; an oil painting of General Robert E. Lee and General A. P. Hill meeting at the inn hangs on the wall in the lobby, and prints are available for sale in the extensive gift shop. In the cozy tavern, which has a huge brick fireplace, there's an old Civil War flag hanging over the mantel.

The guest rooms are decorated with four-poster and canopy beds as well as quilts, antique chests, and tables. I stayed one rainy night in the General Lee Suite on the third floor, where I imagined the rainy night in 1863 on which the exodus of wounded troops took place. I could hear the rain pattering on the tin roof above the beamed ceiling as I snuggled beneath my quilt. A separate living room contains a television and sofas upholstered in a pretty, soft plaid.

The Cashtown Inn has a wonderful chef who graduated from the Culinary Institute of America. George Keeney has a repertoire that includes pork chops in a sweet-and-sour raspberry sauce and crumbled blue cheese medallions of beef tenderloin. For dessert you might choose a peach trifle or, perhaps, bananas Foster.

HOW TO GET THERE: From I–81 take Pennsylvania exit 6 (Chambersburg) onto Route 30 east (Lincoln Way). Travel 17 miles on Route 30, and then turn right at the flashing yellow light at the Cashtown branch of the Adams County Bank. You will be on High Street. At the end of the street, turn right. The inn is just ahead on the right.

# The Ragged Edge Inn
## Chambersburg, Pennsylvania 17201

**INNKEEPER:** Darlene Elders

**ADDRESS/TELEPHONE:** 1090 Ragged Edge Road (mailing address: P.O. Box 482); (717) 261–1195 or (888) 900–9555; fax (717) 263–2118

**E-MAIL:** raggededge@innernet.net

**WEB SITE:** www.innernet.net/raggededge

**ROOMS:** 10, including 4 suites; all with private bath, air-conditioning, television, and radio; 9 with telephone; 8 with CD player; 4 with whirlpool tub, minirefrigerator, and coffeemaker; 3 with fireplace, VCR, iron, and ironing board. Smoking outside on veranda only. Children over the age of 6 welcome.

**RATES:** $89 to $179, double occupancy; includes full breakfast; $69 travelers special Monday to Thursday with continental breakfast. Two-night minimum weekends in October and all holidays.

**OPEN:** All year.

**FACILITIES AND ACTIVITIES:** On six and one-half acres with gardens, trails through the woods. Nearby: Totem Pole Playhouse, golfing, cross-country ski trails in the Gettysburg National Battlefield Park, downhill skiing at Whitetail Ski Resort.

**BUSINESS TRAVEL:** Telephones with multiple lines in all but two rooms (these share one telephone), television, conference room; fax and copier available.

**RECOMMENDED COUNTRY INNS® TRAVELERS' CLUB BENEFIT:** 10 percent discount, subject to availability. Holidays and special-event weekends excluded.

When Moorhead Kennedy called on Frank Furness's renowned Philadelphia architectural firm to design his palatial 13,000-square-foot brick mansion in the 1900s, it was meant to impress—and it does. Kennedy was president of the Cumberland Valley Railroad and so, naturally, he built a railroad spur to his house. He entertained on a lavish scale and often brought guests to his home in his private railroad car, which was luxuriously upholstered in velvet. For these parties Mr. Kennedy would transport caterers from Philadelphia and import an entire orchestra to provide dance music.

In the meticulously restored mansion Darlene Elders provides an equally inspired party every night. There may not be an orchestra and catered events (Darlene is such a fabulous cook that no outside caterers are needed), but she does often provide entertainment in the form of murder mystery weekends that include a plot and script that she writes herself. But whether planned entertainment is on the schedule or not, guests can always celebrate Christmas at the Ragged Edge. A magnificent, fully decorated tree is on display throughout the year, and there are more than 1,000 various Christmas items tucked throughout the inn.

The inn is decorated with superb antiques that Darlene has been collecting all her life. I could scarcely take my eyes off the hand-carved French oak sideboard and table in the dining room; and the sofas, chairs, and mahogany china cabinet in the living room offer just the right note of comfort to a room that has rich mahogany walls, an oak floor laid on the diagonal, heavy oak doors, and a marble mantel over the fireplace.

The guest rooms are also furnished with wonderful antiques. The Kennedy Suite has a brass bed and wing chairs beside the fireplace, but the room that generates the most comments is the Honeymoon Suite. It has a trellis headboard and a whirlpool tub set under a skylight in the room. The bath includes a real throne and another skylight.

During the week Darlene fixes a continental breakfast unless guests indicate they want more. On weekends, however, she pulls out all the stops. The lavish brunch will include a variety of courses that this creative and talented artist and cook will prepare based on the bounty of the season and the whims of the day.

HOW TO GET THERE: From I–81 take Pennsylvania exit 6 (Chambersburg) onto Route 30 east (Lincoln Way). Follow Route 30 toward Gettysburg for 2½ miles to Ragged Edge Road. Turn left (north) onto Ragged Edge Road. The inn is in 1 mile on the right.

# *Who Done It?*

When Darlene Elders, the innkeeper of The Ragged Edge Inn, started writing murder mysteries for her guests to perform, little did she suspect that she would actually star in one herself. But that's exactly what happened

Shortly after she opened the inn, two gentlemen came to stay. They had come to see a mystery performed at the nearby Totem Pole Playhouse, since one was a theater critic for a newspaper. They were fascinated to learn about Darlene's Murder Mystery weekends. So, immersed in murder mysteries, on the way back home they developed the plot for a murder mystery of their own.

You can imagine Darlene's surprise several years later to receive in the mail a copy of a book titled *1 Ragged Ridge Road*. The plot weaves a tale of an innkeeper who restores a magnificent mansion that becomes a bed-and-breakfast inn called "The Christmas Inn" and the murder of the mansion's original owner. Yes, even though the murder took place more than seventy years earlier, it is solved.

Book signings have taken place at the inn, and several national articles have been written about this inn that inspired a book.

# The Inn at Twin Linden
## Churchtown, Pennsylvania 17555

INNKEEPERS: Bob and Donna Leahy

ADDRESS/TELEPHONE: 2092 Main Street (Route 23) (mailing address: 2092 Main Street, Narvon, PA 17555); (717) 445-7619; fax (717) 445-4656

ROOMS: 7, including 1 suite; all with private bath, air-conditioning, and television; 3 with fireplace, 2 with Jacuzzi, desk, VCR, radio, and CD player. No smoking inn. Children welcome Sunday to Thursday.

RATES: $100 to $210, double occupancy; includes full breakfast and afternoon tea. Two-night minimum if Saturday stay included and on holidays.

**OPEN:** All year except January.

**FACILITIES AND ACTIVITIES:** Dinner served Saturday ($48 fixed price) by reservation; BYOB; garden, outdoor hot tub, and gift shop. Nearby: The People's Place and Old Country Store in Intercourse, Railroad Museum in Strasbourg, country quilt shops, factory outlets, Artworks Complex, farmer's markets.

ob and Donna Leahy are truly an amazing couple. Bob, a professor at Temple University and a world-recognized underwater photographer, and Donna, who has prepared gourmet meals at the James Beard House in New York City and on NBC's *Today* show, somehow find time to add new improvements to their already fabulous inn and to collaborate on books. First they wrote and photographed a beautiful coffee-table cookbook called *Morning Glories,* and now they have produced a new book, *Wisdom of the Plain Folk,* which features Amish and Mennonite songs and prayers combined with Bob's eloquent photographs.

When Donna and Bob purchased their inn, located in a little town in the heart of the Amish and Mennonite countryside, they had the task of reno-

vating a dilapidated farmhouse. What they have created is truly remarkable. The pine floors gleam, the huge fireplace in the living room is flanked by inviting wing chairs, and the walls are decorated with stencils that Donna painted herself and with Bob's beautiful photographs. On a table sit decanters of brandy and sherry with stemmed glasses. What could be more appealing?

The guest rooms contain four-poster, sleigh, and canopy beds splashed with blue, yellow, and white hues in Waverly and Laura Ashley fabrics. The grandest is the Palladian Suite, which has numerous skylights and a huge Palladian window offering picturesque views of a Mennonite farm below. There's a pellet-burning stove, a wet bar, and a Jacuzzi in the black-tiled bath. All the rooms are decorated with Bob's photographs, stenciling, fabulous dried flower arrangements, and brilliantly colored hand-made quilts. The baths are smart and modern and finished with tile.

One of the glories of The Inn at Twin Linden is its gardens. From the earliest misty spring days to the finale of autumn, they bloom with a kaleidoscope of colors. Wind chimes softly play a melody in the breeze as a backdrop

# Plainly Speaking

Bob and Donna Leahy's book *Wisdom of the Plain Folk, Songs and Prayers from the Amish and Mennonites* is a reflection of the couple's appreciation for their neighbors in their adopted home. The Inn at Twin Linden is located in the heart of Pennsylvania's Amish and Mennonite region.

When you enter Churchtown you may feel as though you've stepped back in time. Horse-drawn buggies driven by men and women in traditional "Plain Folk" garb share the road with cars driven by people wearing modern-day dress. That these two diverse groups live so compatibly side by side can be attributed to the attitude of the Amish and Mennonites. Their philosophy inspired the Leahys to write this book.

The beautiful book is a compilation of Bob's gloriously luminous photographs, which capture local scenes such as Amish buggies and covered bridges, matched by Donna with Amish and Mennonite proverbs, songs, and maxims. Examples follow:

## On How to Be Rich and Beautiful

If any of you are dissatisfied because you are poor and plain looking, let me tell you how to be rich and beautiful. Have a heartful of love and goodness and a soul beautiful with the beauty of holiness and you will be rich.

## On Forgiveness

If anyone wrongs you, exercise forgiveness and patiently dismiss the matter. For if you take the wrong to heart, you hurt no one but yourself.

## Bedtime Contemplations

Never go to sleep without considering how you have spent the day just past and what you have accomplished for good or evil.

for folks using the outdoor hot tub. A family of rabbits watch all the goings on from their cage.

If your stay includes a Saturday night, you should definitely plan to have dinner at the inn, but don't forget to bring your own wine. Tables are set on several porches that have French doors offering beautiful garden vistas. Donna may start the meal, as she did one March weekend, with a grilled quail served with sautéed wild mushrooms garnished with watercress and a ginger-soy sauce. This was followed by a salad of endive and mesclun tossed with imported Stilton in a fresh herb vinaigrette and served with thin slices of pear and toasted walnuts. For an entree we had a rack of lamb with fresh rosemary and pecans served over a ginger-apple sauce. But it was the dessert that I will never forget. We had a superb white-chocolate-and-macadamia-nut bread pudding served with chocolate sorbet and drizzled with bittersweet chocolate sauce. It was to die for! Breakfasts are as sophisticated and as luscious as dinner, and the joy for me was being able to purchase Donna's cookbook and to recreate some of the meals at home.

HOW TO GET THERE: From I–76 (Pennsylvania Turnpike) take exit 22 (Morgantown) to Route 23 (less than 1/10 mile) and proceed west 4 miles into Churchtown. Inn is on the left, in the center of village.

# Tara—A Country Inn
Clark, Pennsylvania 16113

INNKEEPERS: James E. and Donna N. Winner; Deborah A. DeCapua, manager

ADDRESS/TELEPHONE: 2844 Lake Road; (714) 962–3535 or (800) 782–2803; fax (714) 962–3250

ROOMS: 27, including 3 suites; all with private bath, air-conditioning, telephone, television, VCR, fireplace, radio, hair dryer, and robes; 21 with whirlpool tub, 3 with patio or porch. Wheelchair accessible. Children over the age of 12 welcome. No smoking inn; $100 charged for smoking violations.

RATES: $150 to $355, double occupancy; includes full breakfast, afternoon tea, and a tour of Tara; $180 to $430, double occupancy; includes full or continental breakfast, dinner, afternoon tea, and tour of Tara.

OPEN: All year except Christmas Day.

**FACILITIES AND ACTIVITIES:** Ashley's Restaurant serving dinner (prix fixe $75), Stonewall's Tavern serving lunch and dinner (entrees $22 to $40). On four acres with gardens, gazebo, patios, croquet, bocci courts; outdoor pool, mineral baths; Red Petticoat Treasures gift shop. Nearby: Shenango Lake with marina for pontoon boat rides, fishing and swimming, golfing.

**BUSINESS TRAVEL:** Telephone, television, and VCR in room; six rooms with desks; computer hookups available. Express checkout; complimentary newspaper. Two meeting rooms with complete audio-visual capabilities.

*I*f you have ever longed to spend the night on a movie set, or to play make-believe with Rhett and Scarlett, then you should definitely come to Tara. The place is absolutely amazing.

In a little village almost on the Ohio border and high on a hill overlooking Shenango Lake, Tara seems like a grown-up dollhouse of gigantic proportions. The Greek Revival mansion, built in 1854 by Charles Koonce, has massive classical columns that rise several stories to a pedimented roof. Wings that overlook the formal gardens stretch on both sides. The structure is bigger and grander than Hollywood ever could have imagined.

The entire inn is themed after the movie *Gone with the Wind*. In the common rooms there are a variety of antiques and paintings that include John Brown's bible, the dining room table that President Buchanan used when he was in the White House, and much more. It would take days to absorb all the memorabilia in Scarlett's Room, a little museum that can be viewed from the roped off doorway. There's the yellow bed jacket trimmed in ermine that Scarlett wore. Over here is a photograph of a scene from the movie, and there's a dressing robe given to Rhett (or was it Clark Gable?) by his wife Carole Lombard. A fainting couch used in the movie and a fabulously carved walnut high-Victorian bed that includes a bust of Jenny Lind in the headboard are here, too.

The guest rooms are as theatrical as the rest of the inn. Fiddle Dee Dee is quite feminine with crisp blue and white fabrics used lavishly throughout. There's a canopy bed, a gas fireplace, and a whirlpool tub in the room. The Butler's Bedroom is strictly masculine, however. There's a brass and black-iron king-size bed, an elaborately painted armoire, and a black whirlpool tub in the room. The Garden Suite is in the original master bedroom of the mansion. It has a brass bed, a fireplace, and a porch overlooking the herb garden. There's a two-person whirlpool tub in the bath.

The inn offers a package that includes an overnight stay for two with a welcome basket of fresh fruit, wine and cheese, plus many extras. First-time visitors would benefit from a tour of the common rooms to acquaint themselves with the various rooms and their furnishings. Afternoon tea is served on the veranda accompanied by finger sandwiches and pastries. On Friday and Saturday the owners also meet with their guests for a hospitality hour. Those on a package have the option of eating a seven-course dinner in Ashley's, the inn's elegant dining room. The intimate room is utterly romantic. There's a crystal chandelier hanging from the high ceiling, an Oriental rug on the floor, and a fabulous mural painted on all the walls that depicts scenes from *Gone with the Wind*. Should guests prefer a more informal setting, they can eat in Stonewall's Tavern, three rooms that have low-beamed ceilings, wooden booths, brick or stone walls, and antique oak furniture.

On the grounds guests will find an outdoor swimming pool and spacious formal gardens.

**HOW TO GET THERE:** From I–80 take exit 1 (Sharon/Hermitage) onto Route 18 north. Follow this for 7 miles through Hermitage to Route 258. Tara is at the junction of Routes 18 and 258.

# Crescent Lodge and Country Inn
## Cresco, Pennsylvania 18326

**INNKEEPER:** Robert Dunlop

**ADDRESS/TELEPHONE:** Route 191, Paradise Valley; (717) 595-7486 or (800) 392-9400; fax (717) 595-3452

**ROOMS:** 30, including 18 cottages; all with private bath, air conditioning, television, telephone, radio, minirefrigerator, hair dryer, iron, and ironing board; 15 with VCR and fireplace, 12 with deck or patio, 11 with whirlpool tub and robes, 4 with CD player. Not appropriate for children. Smoking permitted in cottage rooms; main inn rooms designated nonsmoking.

**RATES:** $115 to $325, double occupancy; includes continental breakfast weekdays; no breakfast weekends; two-night minimum weekends.

**OPEN:** All year.

**FACILITIES AND ACTIVITIES:** Restaurant serving dinner (entrees $17 to $26); on twenty-eight acres with beautiful gardens, pool, tennis court, horseshoes, volleyball, badminton, shuffleboard, fitness trail. Nearby: Camelback Ski Area; Delaware Water Gap Recreation Area; numerous lakes, streams, and waterfalls in the Pocono Mountains.

**BUSINESS TRAVEL:** Telephone, television, and VCR in rooms; meeting rooms.

*J*ack and Minerva Dunlop purchased a nine-bedroom tourist house in this bucolic Poconos Mountain hideaway spot in 1947. Over the years the old house was expanded, and in 1962 it was winterized and opened as a year-round facility. It became especially popular with skiers at the newly opened Camelback Ski area. In 1992, however, the lodge underwent another transformation when Jack and Minerva's son, Bob, who had managed the lodge with his parents since 1962, put in canopy beds and romantic whirlpool tubs and lavishly decorated with floral chintz and striped fabrics. Today, although it retains some of its lodge-like appeal, one can legitimately call it a country inn.

It's hard to imagine a neater and more groomed inn. Every blade of grass seems perfectly placed; the flower beds haven't a weed in sight. One March day I arrived to find all the carpets undergoing a thorough shampooing. The lobby has the feel of a country living room, with a pretty floral carpet, a fireplace, a wagon-wheel chandelier, and comfortable seating areas that encourage reading, card playing, or friendly conversation. The Starting Post, an old world–style tavern to one side, has an old brass cash register and a television.

The dining room is equally attractive, with paneled walls and a green carpet. A buffet breakfast is served to house guests every morning. Bob's son, Wayne, is the chef, and he's put together an adventurous menu for dinner. You might start a meal with tender batter-dipped, deep-fried alligator strips that you can dip in a chilled curry sauce. Dinner entrees range from bouillabaisse to beef Wellington to grilled pork calvados. For dessert there is a wonderful array of ice cream desserts and home-baked pies.

The guest rooms are beautifully decorated. Room 301, in the Chalet, has a bed with a fishnet canopy and a rose floral spread. A plaid sofa and wing chairs sit on a ruby carpet, there's an armoire hiding the television, and the bath has emerald Formica countertops. The most lush accommodation, the Mountain Jacuzzi, is also the most romantic. In a private secluded mountain setting, this cottage has a canopy bed, a fireplace, a balcony, sundeck, VCR, and a sunken Jacuzzi tub.

**HOW TO GET THERE:** From I–80 traveling west take exit 52 (Marshalls Creek) and travel north on Route 447 to Route 191. Then follow Route 191 north to Paradise Valley. The inn is on the right.

# Sign of the Sorrel Horse
## Doylestown, Pennsylvania 18901

**OWNER:** Chef Jon Atkin; Monique Gaumont-Lanvin and Christian Gaumont-Lanvin, managers

**ADDRESS/TELEPHONE:** 4424 Old Easton Road; (215) 230–9999; fax (215) 230–8053

**ROOMS:** 5, including 2 suites; 3 with private bath; all with air-conditioning, 1 with fireplace or whirlpool tub. Children over the age of 12 welcome. No smoking inn.

**RATES:** $85 to $175, double occupancy; includes continental breakfast. Two-night minimum spring, fall, and holiday weekends.

**OPEN:** All year except two weeks in March.

**FACILITIES AND ACTIVITIES:** Restaurant serving dinner (entrees $15 to $26). On four acres with millrace, stream for fishing. Nearby: Pearl Buck's former home, James A. Michener Art Museum, Mercer Museum, Moravian Pottery and Tile Works, golfing, antiquing, tennis, bicycling.

**RECOMMENDED COUNTRY INNS® TRAVELERS' CLUB BENEFIT:** Stay two nights, get third night free, Wednesday to Friday.

*L*ocated in a charming 1714 stone gristmill, in a minuscule hamlet known as Dyerstown, the Sign of the Sorrel Horse occupies a building that has served food and offered lodging to weary travelers since 1900. Remarkably, although the hustle and bustle of used-car lots and fast-food eateries are merely minutes away, this little enclave of stone houses anchored by the mill seems to be tethered to the horse-and-buggy days.

The stone exterior of the mill is now partly sheathed in creamy clapboard, but the mill race continues to course underneath just as it did when it powered a waterwheel. The outstanding restaurant of the inn occupies most of the first-floor rooms. There's a lovely common room for guests to use and an atmospheric bar with a stone fireplace. Cozy tables invite players of chess or readers who wish to curl up in this warm setting to read one of the books from the shelves.

The restaurant is divided into several rooms. The most romantic one features lacy cages of doves, candles in tall hurricanes, and an abundance of plants—all offering an intimate and alluring setting. There's also a pretty garden dining room and a more masculine room with tapestries hanging on rust walls and another fireplace.

You will dine on such entrees as nut-encrusted venison chops with lingonberries and cassis sauce or a combination of roast swordfish and salmon with blue cheese polenta and whole-grain mustard sauce. For dessert you might try the Sorrel Horse Deadly Sin, a combination of several specialty desserts.

The emphasis at the Sign of the Sorrel Horse is clearly on the restaurant and not on the guest rooms. Although the Pearl S. Buck Room has some antiques, the bath, which is located up several stairs, is not terrific and the hall baths are very tiny. The Edward Hicks Room has a peach velvet sofa in the sitting area and a floral canopy and spread on the bed. The bath is in the hall.

**HOW TO GET THERE:** From I–78 in New Jersey take exit 29 onto I–287 south. Then take exit 13 onto Route 202 south. Follow Route 202 across the Delaware River and continue for about 10 miles to Doylestown. From Route 202 in Doylestown take Route 313 west (Swamp Road) for 1 mile. Turn right at the second road onto Old Easton Road. The inn is on the left in 1 mile.

# Eagles Mere Inn
## Eagles Mere, Pennsylvania 17731

**INNKEEPERS:** Susan and Peter Glaubitz

**ADDRESS/TELEPHONE:** Mary and Sullivan Avenues (mailing address: Box 356); (717) 525–3273 or (800) 426–3273

**E-MAIL:** eminn@epix.net

**WEB SITE:** www.eaglesmereinn.com

**ROOMS:** 18, including 3 suites; all with private bath and ceiling fan; 13 with air-conditioning, 1 with Jacuzzi. One room wheelchair accessible. No smoking inn.

**RATES:** $139 to $225, double occupancy; includes full breakfast and dinner; $30 less if B&B arranged in advance. Two-night minimum some weekends.

**OPEN:** All year.

**FACILITIES AND ACTIVITIES:** Restaurant serving dinner (prix fixe $18 to $24), pub/tavern; on one-half acre with gardens. Nearby: Tobagganing, hiking, cross-country skiing, horseback riding, country club golf, and lake swimming; Wyoming and Tiadaghton State forests surround Eagles Mere.

*E*agles Mere is a remote but engaging little town in the Endless Mountains of Sullivan County Pennsylvania—a summer resort created in the late 1880s by wealthy "Main Line" Philadelphians who wished to retreat to the fresh, clean mountain air and the cool clear waters of Eagles Mere Lake in the summer. They built magnificent Victorian cottages for their families on the hills with lovely views of the mountains and the lake. Six huge hotels catered to visitors and transient travelers. The passage of time has been gentle here. Sullivan County still has only one traffic light, and the land remains 94 percent forested.

The Eagles Mere Inn was built in 1887 to house the workers and artisans who were building the mansions and hotels. Now, although many of the "cottages" remain, the hotels are gone. Nevertheless, the Eagles Mere Inn lives on. It's a winsome village hostelry with bright and spotlessly clean facilities.

You can sit in the living room and read a book on the sofa before the fireplace. My favorite spot, however, is downstairs in the pub, where a shale fireplace is surrounded by a mural depicting the village of Eagles Mere. There's a nice piano bar here and cabinets loaded with fine wines.

The guest rooms are charming. You might stay in Room 3, which has a red-and-white quilt on a four-poster bed, or in Room 2, which has an iron-and-brass bed topped by another pretty quilt. Room 10 has a bed with a pine headboard and a separate sitting room with a lovely rug.

If you come in the winter, you may want to coordinate your visit with the famous Eagles Mere toboggan slide. This unique form of recreation was created in 1904. When the lake is decidedly frozen, the local townsfolk create an ice slide down Lake Avenue. Riders zip down the slide on their toboggans, reaching speeds of up to 60 miles per hour and then skim across the icy lake, stopping at the far side. It's absolutely exhilarating.

HOW TO GET THERE: From I–80 take exit 34 (Buckhorn) onto Route 42. Travel 33 miles north to Eagles Mere. In the village pass the shops and clock and turn right at the second street onto Mary Avenue. The inn is on the corner of Mary and Sullivan Avenues.

# The Lafayette Inn

## Easton, Pennsylvania 18042

**INNKEEPERS:** Scott and Marilyn Bushnell

**ADDRESS/TELEPHONE:** 525 West Monroe Street; (610) 253–4500;
fax (610) 253–4635

**E-MAIL:** lafayinn@fast.net

**WEB SITE:** www.lafayetteinn.com

**ROOMS:** 16, including 2 suites; all with private bath, air conditioning,
television, and telephone with dataport; 15 with desk, 3 with fireplace,
2 with deck, 1 with whirlpool tub. Children welcome. Smoking permitted in two rooms; the rest are designated nonsmoking.

**RATES:** $95 to $150, double occupancy; includes continental breakfast.

**OPEN:** All year.

**FACILITIES AND ACTIVITIES:** On one acre; gardens, patio with fountain
and waterfall. Nearby: Crayola Factory and Store, National Canal
Museum, Lafayette College, live entertainment at State Theatre Center
for the Arts.

**BUSINESS TRAVEL:** Desk, telephone with dataport, television in rooms;
fax and copier available; two conference rooms.

Although the handsome brick house on the corner of Cattell and
Monroe Streets has been an inn since 1986, it's become a warm
and inviting hostelry since Scott and Marilyn Bushnell purchased it in 1997. Scott greeted me at the door as he deftly seated guests in
the sun-splashed breakfast room. A spread of fresh fruit salad, breads, coffee
cakes, croissants, etc., was preparing guests for their day.

The handsome brick mansion was built originally in 1895 and then
expanded extensively in the 1910s, when it was owned by the superintendent
of Ingersoll Iron Works (this became Ingersoll Rand). Through the years the
Depression and a stint as a frat house left their marks, but in 1986 a group
of local businessmen invested almost a million dollars in its restoration into
a country inn. Today its broad front porch contains antique wicker, and
there's a lovely living room with an elaborately patterned wood floor, floor-
to-ceiling columns, a fireplace, and a baby grand piano.

The Bushnells have completed a renovation of their own, adding gas
woodstoves to several of the guest rooms and a whirlpool tub to one. Room
10, for example, has a woodstove and a whirlpool tub as well as a four-poster

bed. Antiques are used throughout. In Room 12 there's a lovely armoire, a marble-topped chest, and an antique burl table. Best of all they've installed a secluded flagstone courtyard that contains a waterfall and a fountain beside the house and furnished it with Adirondack chairs and benches. It's a wonderfully relaxing spot.

The Bushnells are gracious and charming hosts. They have a refrigerator stocked with beer, wine, and soft drinks for their guests, as well as fresh fruit, candies, and pastries. At turndown, they provide both chocolates and warm cookies.

HOW TO GET THERE: From I–78 take exit 3 (Phillipsburg, NJ). Follow Route 22 west through Phillipsburg to the toll bridge over the Delaware River, crossing into Pennsylvania. Take the second exit after the bridge (Easton) and turn north onto Third Street. The road curves right and ascends a steep hill. At the top of the hill the road curves left and the name changes to Cattell Street. Turn left at the first light onto Monroe Street and then take an immediate right into the driveway of the inn.

# Historic Smithton Inn
## Ephrata, Pennsylvania 17522

INNKEEPER: Dorothy Graybill

ADDRESS/TELEPHONE: 900 West Main Street; (717) 733–6094

ROOMS: 8, including 1 suite; all with private bath, air-conditioning, and fireplace; 6 with small refrigerator, 3 with whirlpool bath. One room wheelchair accessible. Pets by prior arrangement. No smoking inn.

RATES: $75 to $170, double occupancy; includes full breakfast. Children, no charge up to 18 months, $20 up to 12. $35 additional person. Two-night minimum if Saturday stay included and on holidays.

OPEN: All year.

FACILITIES AND ACTIVITIES: Gardens; on almost one acre. Nearby: restaurants, Ephrata Cloister, Artworks Complex, museums, Adamstown Antiques Market, farmer's markets, factory outlets.

If you arrive at Historic Smithton Inn in the summer, you will marvel at the amazing display of dahlias that line the fence. Their brilliant hues of pink, yellow, burgundy, and white are truly spectacular. But that is only a preview to this amazing inn.

Dorothy Graybill is indefatigable, and she never stops thinking of new ways to improve her already excellent inn. She's owned the handsome 1763 fieldstone house that began life as a stagecoach stop and tavern since 1983. Her most recent embellishments include beautiful raised frescoes on the outside gabled walls on the west and the northwest sides. One depicts the sun, moon, and stars with doves raining love and peace on the world below in the form of heart-shaped raindrops. The other is the inn's logo, a combination of doves and wildflowers similar to the book illustrations painted at the Ephrata Cloister.

The private gardens behind the inn include a pretty white bench beside a little fountain, garden furniture placed in solitary spots, and a spacious cage where Peter, Jr., the black flop-eared rabbit, can gambol about waiting for a vegetable from a guest.

The wide-plank pine floors of the inn are burnished and covered with braided rugs. There are painted chests, oil paintings on the walls, and a great

stucco fireplace in the common room. The furnishings are typical of the Pennsylvania Dutch countryside that surrounds Ephrata. Dorothy is a great proponent of the Amish, Mennonite, and Brethren lifestyles, which she will be happy to describe to you; she can even make arrangements for you to visit a family. She appreciates the lovely crafts that are produced locally and has made her inn a showcase for them.

The guest rooms are charming but include thoroughly modern amenities. There are beds with handwoven canopies covered with handmade quilts, and each room has its own fireplace. In the baths locally made tiles surround the tubs, several of which are whirlpools. The South Wing Suite even includes a small snack kitchen as well as its own private porch.

HOW TO GET THERE: From I–76 (Pennsylvania Turnpike) take exit 21 and follow Route 222 south. At the Ephrata exit, turn west onto Route 322 (Main Street) and travel 2½ miles, passing through the town of Ephrata. After passing the Ephrata Cloister you will climb a long hill. At the traffic light at the top of the hill, turn left onto Academy Drive and then immediately turn right into the inn's parking lot. The inn is on the corner of Academy Drive and West Main Street.

# The Inns at Doneckers
Ephrata, Pennsylvania 17522

**INNKEEPER:** Amy Gorham; Bill Donecker, proprietor

**ADDRESS/TELEPHONE:** 318-324 North State Street; (717) 738–9502; fax (717) 738–9554

**WEB SITE:** www.doneckers.com

**ROOMS:** 40, including 12 suites and 2 cottages; all with air-conditioning, radio, and telephone; 38 with private bath, 14 with whirlpool tub, 8 with patio or porch, 6 with fireplace, television, and/or minirefrigerator. Wheelchair access. Children welcome. Smoking permitted; some designated nonsmoking rooms.

**RATES:** $69 to $210, double occupancy; includes continental buffet breakfast. $10 for rollaway; $8 for crib. Two-night minimum on holiday weekends.

**OPEN:** All year.

**FACILITIES AND ACTIVITIES:** The Restaurant serves dinner nightly except Wednesday and Sunday (entrees $17 to $29); The Hearthside Cafe Bistro serves lunch and dinner except Wednesday and Sunday (entrees $7.50 to $17.00); full beverage license; shopping, Artworks Complex, farmer's market. Nearby: Ephrata Cloister, Amish country, Adamstown Antique Market.

**BUSINESS TRAVEL:** Telephone, fax, and desk available; conference room.

*I*t all started in 1961 with a very successful retail fashion store that became such a destination for its quality merchandise that Bill Donecker decided to open a restaurant so that people could make a day of it. But when that became so renowned for its food, he felt he should provide a place for people to stay so that they didn't feel rushed. Now the guest rooms attract people for their style and comfort also.

Bill Donecker has created his collection of guest accommodations by restoring several of this historic town's best-loved buildings. The Guesthouse, built in 1918, is located just across the street from the restaurant. It contains twenty rooms that range from the Franklin and the Marshall Rooms, which share a bath, to several spacious suites. The Gerhart House— built in 1926 by a local builder who prided himself on the chestnut doors and trim, pine floors, and frosted and beveled or stained glass he used—contains five rooms. The Homestead was the former residence of Bill Donecker's mom; it now contains four rooms, each with a fireplace and a whirlpool tub.

My favorite is The 1777 House, which is down the street from the rest. It was built originally by Jacob Gorgas, a member of the Ephrata religious community who became an acclaimed clockmaker. An example of his fine craftsmanship, a lovely tall-case clock, is displayed in the center hallway. The house has been restored to feature its original stone walls and tile floors and includes walls embellished with hand-cut stenciling. A carriage house beside the 1777 House contains the two finest suites in the complex. These have

fireplaces, Jacuzzis, cathedral ceilings, and antique furnishings on multiple levels.

Breakfast is served in each of the individual homes. The breakfast room at the 1777 House is in keeping with the age of the house and includes a fireplace and old wooden tables. You may have juice, baked fruit, cheese, muffins, croissants, and cereal.

There are two restaurants now in the Donecker complex. One, a fine-dining restaurant, includes such entrees as rack of lamb with minted rosemary demiglace served with truffled mousseline potatoes and seared medallions of swordfish with a compote of lobster, lump crabmeat, and leeks served with saffron potatoes and shrimp dill sauce. The Hearthside Cafe Bistro is more casual and features a variety of salads, sandwiches, and pasta dishes, as well as such entrees as pork tenderloin with fire-roasted walnuts and Eastern Shore crab cakes with tomatoes and basil.

In addition to the lovely clothing stores that still attract visitors to Donecker's, you won't want to miss the outlet store where merchandise is discounted from 20 percent to 50 percent. Next door The Artworks is a four-story building filled with artist studios and galleries. You can buy jewelry, pottery, fine paintings, and collectibles here. Locally grown vegetables and fruits and locally made gourmet foods are sold at the farmer's market that's included in The Artworks on Thursday through Saturday.

HOW TO GET THERE: From I–76 (Pennsylvania Turnpike) take exit 21 and follow Route 222 south to the Ephrata exit. Follow Route 322 west into Ephrata, where it becomes Main Street. Turn right onto North State Street and proceed 4 blocks to the inn, which is on the left.

# EverMay On-the-Delaware
Erwinna, Pennsylvania 18920

**INNKEEPERS:** William and Danielle Moffly; Dawn M. Smigo, manager

**ADDRESS/TELEPHONE:** 889 River Road (mailing address: P.O. Box 60); (610) 294–9100; fax (610) 294–8249.

**E-MAIL:** moffly@evermay.com

**WEB SITE:** www.evermay.com

**ROOMS:** 15, including one suite and one cottage; all with private bath, air-conditioning, telephone with dataport, and hair dryer. Children over the age of 12 welcome. No smoking inn.

**RATES:** $120 to $290, double occupancy; includes continental breakfast, afternoon tea, and evening sherry. Two-night minimum if stay includes a Saturday.

**OPEN:** All year except Christmas Eve and Christmas Day.

**FACILITIES AND ACTIVITIES:** Restaurant serving six-course dinner Friday, Saturday, and Sunday (prix fixe $62); on twenty-five acres with formal gardens, walking paths, pasture with sheep, chickens, geese. Nearby: bicycling, canoeing, tubing on the Delaware River, walking along the canal tow paths, horseback riding, Bucks County Playhouse.

**BUSINESS TRAVEL:** Telephone with dataport in room; fax and copier available.

Route 32, otherwise known as River Road, meanders along the lip of the Pennsylvania side of the Delaware River, wandering over bridges that cross the canal and passing beside craggy stone walls and beneath overhanging trees. In several places the road twists wildly off course to miss stone houses that have nevertheless been sheared by a few cars passing too closely. In my opinion it's one of the prettiest roads in America— one that requires us to slow down and enjoy the wonderful views.

EverMay occupies a bucolic spot across the street from the river with spacious lawns, a circular driveway, and a courtyard behind that overlooks the fields and pastures. The house was built in the 1700s and extensively enlarged in 1871. The handsome parlor is inviting with its tall ceilings and lovely burnished wood floors covered by Oriental rugs. On weekend evenings elegant tables are set up in the formal dining room, on the porch, and in the garden room for the lovely six-course prix fixe dinner that is the highlight of any stay here. Dress in your finest and plan to spend several hours at your table, because this is a leisurely and relaxed gourmet dinner. You will start with a soup (perhaps a shrimp bisque), then have an appetizer (a wild mushroom and goat cheese strudel is wonderful); a salad course of seasonal greens will follow. Your choice of entree may be a panko-breaded Chilean sea bass or a roast loin of veal with red onion marmalade. A lovely selection of cheeses and fresh fruits is presented next. For dessert you might have asked for a warm chocolate mousse cake or a lemon custard tart.

After a repast of this magnitude, you may wish to take a stroll, but when you return you will find lovely guest rooms filled with antiques waiting for you. The Mercer Room, for example, has a beautiful Victorian, highly carved walnut bed with a matching dresser as well as a fireplace.

William and Danielle Moffly have owned EverMay on-the-Delaware since 1996, and every year they make more improvements. In the first two years they repainted most of the rooms and lavished considerable attention on the gardens. Now they are turning their attention to upgrading the bathrooms.

HOW TO GET THERE: From I–78 take exit 15 (Pittstown). Go through Pittstown following Route 513 south and continue to Frenchtown, New Jersey. Cross the bridge at Frenchtown to Pennsylvania. Turn left onto Route 32 (River Road). The inn is 1½ miles south on the right.

# Golden Pheasant Inn
Erwinna, Pennsylvania 18920

INNKEEPERS: Barbara and Michel Faure

ADDRESS/TELEPHONE: 763 River Road; (610) 294–9595 or (800) 830–4GPI (474); fax (610) 294–9882

WEB SITE: www.goldenpheasant.com

ROOMS: 6, including 1 cottage suite; all with private bath, air-conditioning, radio, hair dryer, and robes; cottage suite with private porch, minirefrigerator, coffeemaker, and desk. Children and pets permitted in Cottage Suite. No smoking inn.

RATES: $75 to $165, double occupancy; includes continental breakfast. Two-night minimum weekends.

OPEN: All year.

FACILITIES AND ACTIVITIES: Restaurant serving dinner (entrees $18 to $25) and Sunday brunch; on five acres bordering the Pennsylvania

Canal and across the street from the Delaware River. Nearby: Sand Castle Winery, numerous covered bridges, walks along the tow path.

**RECOMMENDED COUNTRY INNS® TRAVELERS' CLUB BENEFIT:** Stay two nights, get third night free, Monday to Thursday.

*W*ere you to walk along the tow path bordering the Pennsylvania Canal south of Uhlerstown, you would pass right behind The Golden Pheasant Inn. In fact the handsome fieldstone inn was built in 1857 to offer accommodations and meals to the bargemen who were plying the newly built canal, as well as to stagecoach travelers. Today it offers food and lodging to wayfarers who most often arrive by car.

The restaurant of this inn has always had my vote as one of the most romantic in Bucks County, partly because my husband and I had an utterly romantic dinner here early in our courtship and shortly after Michel and Barbara became owners of the inn. We have had many meals here since, and we especially like the old tavern room with its wood-burning fireplace, worn pine floors, hewn-beamed ceiling, and fieldstone wall for winter meals. But it's the Greenhouse, with its glass ceiling and wall of windows overlooking the canal, that we ask for in warm weather. We come early enough to watch the light fade on the canal and to watch the ducks and geese wander by. But the magical time is when darkness descends and the lights illuminate the canal, casting their romance over us.

The thoroughly French food reflects Michel's roots (he was raised in Grenoble and trained at some of the finest restaurants in France and the United States). We have had fabulous meals here and some that were not so wonderful, I must sadly report. On our last adventure I had a marvelous dish of roasted duck with a raspberry, ginger, and rum sauce, but my husband's bass dish was dry and overcooked. Don't miss the Belgian white chocolate mousse, however.

On a visit in 1998 we found that Barbara had spectacularly redecorated the guest rooms, and so it is with pleasure that I feel I am now able to recommend the inn as a place to stay as well as a place to eat. As you ascend the stairs from the dining rooms, you pass walls beautifully painted with roses and ribbons. Room 5 has a stone wall and a charming bed with a fishnet canopy and green bed dressings. The bath for this room is in the hallway, but it is delightful. It is finished in tile and has modern fixtures, and there are flowers painted on the mustard-colored sponged walls. The nicest and most romantic room is the Cottage Suite, which has a porch overlooking the canal and a bed that is lavishly canopied and skirted in pink, cream, and green floral and striped fabrics. There's a sitting room and a small kitchen as well. All the rooms have private baths and canal views.

**HOW TO GET THERE:** From I–78 take exit 15 (Pittstown). Go through Pittstown following Route 513 south and continue to Frenchtown, New Jersey. Cross the bridge at Frenchtown to Pennsylvania. Turn left onto Route 32 (River Road). The inn is 1¾ miles south on the right.

# Glasbern 🎞 📱 💟
Fogelsville, Pennsylvania 18051-9743

**INNKEEPERS:** Al and Beth Granger; Erik Sheetz, manager

**ADDRESS/TELEPHONE:** 2141 Pack House Road; (610) 285–4723; fax (610) 285–2862

**E-MAIL:** innkeeper@glasbern.com

**WEB SITE:** www.glasbern.com

**ROOMS:** 25, including 17 suites and 1 cottage; all with private bath, air-conditioning, television, VCR, desk, telephone with dataport, radio, minirefrigerator, hair dryer, iron, and ironing board; 20 with whirlpool tub and robes, 14 with fireplace. Wheelchair accessible. Children permitted in several rooms. Smoking permitted in some rooms; other rooms designated nonsmoking.

**RATES:** $145 to $355, double occupancy, weekends; $125 to $215, double occupancy, weekdays; $100 to $155, single occupancy Sunday to Thursday; all include full breakfast. Two-night minimum if Saturday stay included.

**OPEN:** All year.

**FACILITIES AND ACTIVITIES:** Dinner nightly (entrees $25 to $38), service bar. Outdoor swimming pool, pond, on 200+ acres; fitness center including treadmill, exercise bikes, universal weights; hot-air balloon rides, sixteen acres farmland. Nearby: Hawk Mountain Sanctuary, antiquing in Kutztown and Adamstown, ski Blue and Doe mountains, wineries, historic Bethlehem.

**BUSINESS TRAVEL:** Desk, telephone with dataport, television, VCR, minirefrigerator, radio, iron, and ironing board in every room; some rooms with coffeemaker, and/or fax. Fax, copier available; conference rooms; corporate rates.

*B*uilt as a farm more than 150 years ago, Glasbern combines the best of rural and urban living. The oldest part of the farm is the Pennsylvania German bank barn, built into the bank of the hillside, with a ceiling that rises 26 feet to hand-hewn beams punctuated by skylights. In this Great Room rough shale walls contrast with the smooth, clean lines of the plaster fireplace and chimney. The corn crib remains from the days when this was a working barn, as do the ladders that lead to where the hayloft used to be. One wall consists almost entirely of windows and gave the inn its name. (Glasbern is a Middle English word meaning "glass barn.")

Beth and Al Granger purchased the farm in 1985 and have never stopped making improvements. The guest rooms are distributed among the original farm buildings, which include the barn, the original farmhouse, the carriage house, the gatehouse, the garden cottage, and the newest addition, the stables. Room 42, which is in the carriage house, for example, is delightful. It has barnwood walls, a beamed ceiling, and a double Jacuzzi, as well as a brass bed, a fireplace, and a wonderful antique marble-topped dresser. The bath has barnwood wainscoting, plank floors, and exposed beams. The Garden Cottage has a huge stone fireplace wall with a leather sofa in front. Flagstone floors are topped with Oriental rugs. Upstairs there's a bedroom with an iron bed and a Jacuzzi in the corner where it catches the light from another stone fireplace. There's a television hidden in a barnwood cabinet. A private deck with a fountain in the center of a pool is in back.

Dinner is a wonderful event at Glasbern. In a setting of stone walls, a fireplace, and mint-colored carpeting covered by Oriental rugs, guests eat either in the Great Room, the Granary, or the Harvest room. There will be herbs and vegetables organically grown on the farm folded into the meal, and the fresh flowers in the Great Room and on the tables are all grown on the premise. Dinner might include roast pheasant stuffed with wild mushrooms, foie gras, and risotto or, perhaps, jumbo lump crab cakes served with a coconut and raisin remoulade sauce. Among the wonderful desserts our favorites are the baked bananas Foster and the crème brûlée napoleon.

There are walking or cross-country skiing trails throughout the property, or you can feed the horses in the field or take a dip in the pool. It's all there for guests of this very special inn to use.

**HOW TO GET THERE:** From I–78 traveling west take exit 14B north (Fogelsville) and get into the left lane. Turn left at the first traffic light onto Main Street. Follow this for $^3/_{10}$ mile to Church Street. Turn right and continue on Church Street for $^8/_{10}$ mile. Turn right onto Pack House Road; the inn is on the right $^8/_{10}$ of a mile down.

# The Gaslight Inn 📱
## Gettysburg, Pennsylvania 17325

**INNKEEPERS:** Denis and Roberta Sullivan

**ADDRESS/TELEPHONE:** 33 East Middle Street; (717) 337–9100

**E-MAIL:** gaslight@mail.cyn.net

**ROOMS:** 9; all with private bath, air-conditioning, telephone with dataport, television, and radio; 5 with fireplace and whirlpool tub or steam shower, 4 with balcony or patio, 3 with VCR. Wheelchair access. Children over the age of 10 welcome. No smoking inn.

**RATES:** $100 to $173, double occupancy; includes full breakfast. Two-night minimum or $15 surcharge April to mid-November if stay includes Saturday except on holiday weekends.

**OPEN:** All year except Christmas Eve and Christmas Day.

**FACILITIES AND ACTIVITIES:** Dinner served to inn guests with twenty-four-hours' advance notice; passes are available to YWCA fitness center and pool. Nearby: Gettysburg National Military Park, Eisenhower farm, tennis, bicycling, horseback tours, Ski Liberty.

**BUSINESS TRAVEL:** Telephone with dataport and television in all rooms, VCR in some; scanner and fax available.

**RECOMMENDED COUNTRY INNS® TRAVELERS' CLUB BENEFIT:** 10 percent discount, Monday to Thursday.

*C*risp, fresh, and very, very pretty, the Gaslight Inn was originally built in 1872 as the family home of a prosperous local carriage maker. Over the years it had been expanded and eventually became an apartment house. And that's the condition in which Denis and Roberta Sullivan found it in 1994. Today, after a thorough renovation, the creamy brick building is as welcoming and comfortable as the carriage maker's family home once was.

We love the front parlor with its pale buff walls and lincresta borders. Oriental rugs grace narrow-width oak floors. But we are always drawn first to the dining room, with its beautiful stained-glass windows that were rescued from an old church. Along one wall there's a buffet that holds a delectable array of cookies, candies, nuts, and tea accoutrements. From a little refrigerator we can choose a beer or a soft drink or bottled water. Roberta is also a caterer, and her recipes and goodies are fabulous. (We wish she'd do a cookbook.)

The guest rooms, which are named for flowers, are serene and luxurious. All of them are beautifully decorated and have fresh tile baths. My favorites are the Astor Room, which has a brass bed, a gas fireplace, and a large private deck, and the Sweet William, which is done in burgundy colors and also has a brass bed, a gas fireplace, and a deck.

Roberta fixes a full breakfast that will start with fresh fruit and juice as well as gourmet coffees. If it's summer she may also serve iced moccachinos. She may offer her fabulous bubble loaf (you'll have to stay here to learn what it is) or cream cheese–strawberry puff pastries. For an entree you may have banana rum crepes or fried apricot bread pudding with apricot brandy sauce. In the summer breakfast is served outside on the courtyard that is surrounded by beautiful flower beds. But in the winter guests are seated at the polished cherry dining room table.

If you plan ahead you can ask Roberta to prepare a special dinner for you, or you might plan your stay for one of her special-event dinners. She offers a Thanksgiving, Valentine's Day, and Battle of Gettysburg Anniversary Weekend dinner, but you might ask about other weekends as well.

HOW TO GET THERE: From I–76 (Pennsylvania Turnpike) take exit 17 (Gettysburg) and go south on Route 15. Proceed for about 30 miles to the Hanover Street exit (Route 116). Follow Route 116 for 1½ miles toward Gettysburg. Turn left onto Third Street. Go 1 block and turn right onto East Middle Street. The Gaslight Inn is 2½ blocks farther on the left.

# Anchors Away

Since President and Mrs. Eisenhower's former home is located in Gettysburg, the town has a special relationship with the nuclear aircraft carrier *USS Eisenhower*. When the ship is in port in Norfolk, Virginia, the officers and crew members often volunteer their time to assist with maintenance at the Eisenhower Farm. They clear brush, scrape and paint the buildings, and do whatever they can to augment the limited resources provided by the federal budget.

In return Gettysburg residents and businesses participate in the "Adopt a Sailor" program to provide lodging and meals to the volunteers. The Gaslight Inn is often host to the captain and other chief officers. To say "thank you" the captain has invited the town participants for a family-day sail on the massive ship, complete with an airshow. Denis and Roberta Sullivan, innkeepers of The Gaslight Inn, have been invited to participate.

The greatest thrill, however, was reserved for Denis, who was also invited to fly in one of the planes. They were catapulted off and then returned for a tailhook landing—and he has a certificate to prove it! Mention the experience to him and you'll get a full minute-by-minute account.

# The Settlers Inn
Hawley, Pennsylvania 18428

INNKEEPERS: Grant and Jeanne Genzlinger

ADDRESS/TELEPHONE: Four Main Avenue; (717) 226–2993 or (800) 833–8527; fax (717) 226–1874

E-MAIL: settler@ptdprolog.net

ROOMS: 18, including 2 suites; all with private bath, air-conditioning, telephone with dataport, television, radio, and hair dryer; 1 with VCR, kitchen, and whirlpool tub. No smoking inn.

**RATES:** $100 to $160, double occupancy; includes full breakfast. Two-night minimum weekends July to October.

**OPEN:** All year.

**FACILITIES AND ACTIVITIES:** Lunch, dinner (entrees $14 to $27), Sunday brunch, tavern; private guest parlor; on 6 acres; fishing in river on property; opposite park with tennis courts. Nearby: Lake Wallenpaupack for fishing, boating, beach swimming; Satellite Station Tour, Zane Grey Museum, steam train rides, The Ritz Company Playhouse, skiing at Tanglewood and Mast Hope, cross-country skiing, Promised Land State Park, hiking, antiquing.

**BUSINESS TRAVEL:** Thirty-five miles to Scranton. Telephone and data-port in all rooms; desk in 4 rooms; copy machine, computer, fax, audio-visual equipment available; conference room.

**RECOMMENDED COUNTRY INNS® TRAVELERS' CLUB BENEFIT:** Stay two nights, get third night free.

We arrived one wintery day as the snow gently sifted down, leaving a light cover on the bushes and parking lot. The lights of the inn twinkled a welcome as we approached.

When the huge hydroelectric plant was being built nearby, Lake Wallenpaupack was created by the dam and it became a natural recreational magnet. The fact did not go unnoticed by local businessmen who realized that if there was a nice restaurant and place to stay in Hawley, the town would reap the benefits of tourist dollars. They raised funds (often by selling shares door-to-door) for a grand hotel. It was 1927 and they envisioned a magnificent Tudor-style edifice of stucco and stone. Then the stock market crashed and the Great Depression hit, and then World War II engulfed the country. The hotel remained unfinished until 1947.

Jeanne and Grant Genzlinger met at high school boarding school. Grant studied Chinese in college, but Jeanne had summered in the Poconos and she and Grant came back one summer. That was when they became hooked on the big old hotel.

The inn has a distinctly Arts and Crafts feel to it. The Great Room has a wonderful stone fireplace and lots of oak. There are green tapestry chairs and sofas, lamps with stained-glass shades, and a whimsical frog and turtle chess set. The dining room includes a massive oak buffet, boxed pillars, and oak chairs rescued from a cathedral in Philadelphia that include a pocket for a hymnal. Leafy William Morris–style fabric hangs from the windows, and a homespun linen-like fabric covers the tables. Votives are in brown pottery pots. Grant is the chef and we had a fabulous meal one night.

As much attention has been given to the guest rooms as to the common rooms. The rooms continue the Arts and Crafts theme. Room 14 has a leafy verdigris canopy bed covered with a matelassé spread and an oak dresser with a television; the bath is huge. Room 2 has a green wicker sofa with pink striped cushions; Room 21 has a white iron bed and green tapestry arm chairs.

On my last visit Grant proudly showed me the new tavern that he paneled in wormy chestnut. French doors lead to the huge back porch and the beautiful gardens. You can sit on benches to admire the herb garden, walk down to the Lackawaxen River, or visit The Potting Shed and attached greenhouse—the inn's unique gift shop, located in a little building in the garden.

**HOW TO GET THERE:** From I–84 take exit 7 (Promised Land) and travel north on Route 390. In about 8 miles turn right onto Route 507 north. In 1 mile turn left at the traffic light onto Route 6 west. Take Route 6 for 2½ miles through the town of Hawley and continue to the inn, which is on Route 6, across from Bingham Park.

# Barley Sheaf Farm
## Holicong, Pennsylvania 18928

**INNKEEPERS:** Peter and Veronika Süess

**ADDRESS/TELEPHONE:** 5281 York Road (Route 202) (mailing address: Box 10); (215) 794–5104; fax (215) 794–5332

**E-MAIL:** barleysheaf@netreach.net

**ROOMS:** 12, including 4 suites; all with private bath and air-conditioning; 9 with telephone, 3 with fireplace. One room wheelchair accessible. No smoking inn.

**RATES:** $105 to $255, double occupancy; includes full breakfast. Two-night minimum, three-night minimum holidays.

**OPEN:** All year.

**FACILITIES AND ACTIVITIES:** Outdoor swimming pool, pond, fishing, walking trails, volleyball, badminton, croquet, horseshoes, sheep in pasture, thirty acres. Nearby: restaurants, antiquing, bicycling, barge rides, mansions along the Delaware, Mercer Mile in Doylestown, Peddler's Village.

**BUSINESS TRAVEL:** Dataport in 9 rooms; desk in 5 rooms; meeting rooms for small conferences with full audiovisual capabilities and telephone hookups.

**RECOMMENDED COUNTRY INNS® TRAVELERS' CLUB BENEFIT:** Stay one night, get second night free, Sunday to Thursday.

Oscar Hammerstein lived just down the street when playwright George S. Kaufman lived here in the 1920s and 1930s. One can only imagine the visits these two may have had. Certainly Mr. Kaufman worked on many of his plays here, although *Guys and Dolls* came later.

When the pretty farmhouse opened as a bed-and-breakfast in 1976, it was one of the first in Bucks County. We love what Veronika and Peter Süess, a friendly Swiss/German couple who purchased the inn in 1994, have done to the guest rooms. The baths are thoroughly upgraded with sparkling tile, and some retain claw-footed tubs and pedestal sinks. The rooms have all been painted in light, soothing colors, and spritely floral fabrics are used liberally. There are iron beds, sleigh beds, brass beds, and four-posters. I've always loved the cozy little cottage rooms—with beamed ceilings, a brick floor, a window seat overlooking the meadow, a fireplace, and reached along a stone path between waist-high tiger lillies—but now there are also two spacious suites in the barn, one with a woodstove.

Adjacent to the barn, a multilevel conference center, complete with private interview offices, overlooks the grazing sheep. It seems to me that only congenial decisions could be made in such a relaxed setting.

A large breakfast is served at the tables that fill the brick-floored dining room. It usually begins with freshly squeezed orange juice; a fruit course precedes fresh farm eggs in one form or another or waffles and a sweet roll or muffins, as well as country sausage. If fresh honey is served, it's been combed right here on the farm. Everyone enjoys a chat around the long tables in this setting filled with plants. In the winter a wood-burning stove is well stoked for the final touch.

Barley Sheaf is appropriate whether you're newly married, a high-powered pair of professional talents, or celebrating your fortieth anniversary. Next time I'd like to be there for Peter and Veronika's bread-making or wine-tasting events.

**HOW TO GET THERE:** From I-78 in New Jersey take exit 29 onto I-287 south. Then take exit 13 onto Route 202 south. Follow Route 202 across the Delaware River into Pennsylvania and continue for about 6 miles. Route 202 is called York Road in Holicong. Watch for the B&B sign at a driveway on the left.

# The Inn at Jim Thorpe
## Jim Thorpe, Pennsylvania 18229

**INNKEEPER:** David Drury; John, Jr., Dale, and David Drury, owners

**ADDRESS/TELEPHONE:** 24 Broadway; (717) 325-2599 or (800) 329-2599; fax (717) 325-9145

**E-MAIL:** innjt@ptd.net

**WEB SITE:** www.innjt.com

**ROOMS:** 33, including 8 suites; all with private bath, air-conditioning, telephone, television, and access to a balcony; 12 with VCR, hair dryer, and minirefrigerator; 10 with coffeemaker, 8 with whirlpool tub; 6 with fireplace. Wheelchair accessible. Smoking permitted; designated non-smoking rooms.

**RATES:** $70 to $250, double occupancy; includes continental breakfast. Two-night minimum weekends.

**OPEN:** All year.

**FACILITIES AND ACTIVITIES:** The Emerald Restaurant open for lunch and dinner (entrees $11 to $22); exercise room with stationary bike, treadmill, step machine. Nearby: Asa Packer Mansion, Mauch Chunk Opera House, the Jim Thorpe Mausoleum, Lehigh River, mountain biking, hiking, whitewater rafting.

**RECOMMENDED COUNTRY INNS® TRAVELERS' CLUB BENEFIT:** 25 percent discount, Sunday to Thursday.

*L*et's set the record straight right away. Jim Thorpe was not raised in the town named for him (he was from Oklahoma), but he did go to school nearby at Carlisle Academy. Although he won numerous gold medals at the 1912 Olympics games in Stockholm, Thorpe died a pauper in 1953, and his widow eventually appealed to the State of Pennsylvania for a final resting place for her husband. By coincidence, shortly after the great Native American sports hero died, local natives thought the current name of Mauch Chunk didn't sound very grand and that a new name might spur the town's rebirth. So the Victorian ghost town built a mausoleum to Jim Thorpe and named their town for him. Soon Burt Lancaster starred in a movie about the man, and the town that bears Thorpe's name has been gradually improving ever since.

The interesting and unusual town was founded in 1816 on a steep hillside that slides down to the Lehigh River. Back in the late 1800s the town's narrow, steep, twisting main street earned the town the nickname "The Switzerland of America," and it was the most popular honeymoon destination after Niagara Falls.

The Inn at Jim Thorpe was built in 1833 during the apex of the town's prosperity as a coal and railroad town. It was an era of extreme wealth, fabulous mansions, gaslights, and horse-drawn carriages. Originally made of wood the hotel burned in 1849 and was rebuilt in a more durable brick. The elaborate New Orleans–style iron-lace balconies that grace two floors distinguish it from all other buildings. It reopened as a hotel in 1990, and every year the Drury family add additional rooms or amenities. (By the way, do ask David about his days as a rock and roll musician.)

The Victorian lobby has a gas fireplace fronted by Victorian chairs in wine velvet and green tapestry. Although the hallways were still dreary on my last visit and the reproduction furniture was commonplace, improvements are constantly under way. Three suites and one room were remodeled in February 1998, and five more were redone in July. A game room and an exercise room were also added.

The adjacent restaurant looks like a page from a Victorian book. There are old hexagon tiles on the floor and a tin ceiling and walls. Victorian lights illuminate the room. The restaurant is leased to the Behan family, who hark from County Dublin, Ireland, and the fare is typically Irish. You might have Bubble and Squeak, Dublin-style fish and chips, or filet mignon with jumbo shrimp.

**HOW TO GET THERE:** From I–476 (northeast extension of Pennsylvania Turnpike) take exit 34 and travel south on Route 209 through Lehighton to Jim Thorpe. Turn left at the first light; the inn is in 100 yards on the right.

# The King's Cottage

## Lancaster, Pennsylvania 17602

**INNKEEPERS:** Karen and Jim Owens

**ADDRESS/TELEPHONE:** 1049 East King Street; (717) 397–1017 or (800) 747–8717; fax (717) 397–3447

**ROOMS:** 9, including 1 cottage; all with private bath, and air-conditioning; 1 with fireplace, 1 with whirlpool, 1 with television. One floating telephone for all guests. One room wheelchair accessible. No smoking inn.

**RATES:** $100 to $195, double occupancy; includes full breakfast and afternoon tea. Two-night minimum weekends; three-night minimum holidays.

**OPEN:** All year.

**FACILITIES AND ACTIVITIES:** Television in parlor. Nearby: restaurants, Lancaster sites, Visitor's Center, antiquing, Landis Farm Museum, biking, golfing, tennis, factory outlets.

**BUSINESS TRAVEL:** Desk in 7 rooms; telephone and fax available; meeting room.

**RECOMMENDED COUNTRY INNS® TRAVELERS' CLUB BENEFIT:** 10 percent discount, Monday to Thursday, November to June, subject to availability; excludes holidays and special events.

We had spent the day visiting the many attractions that Lancaster offers an Amish quilt maker, the Lancaster Central Market, and President James Buchanan's home, Wheatland. Now we eagerly anticipated some quiet time before dinner and a play at the American Music Theater.

The King's Cottage offers a royal welcome to its guests, who are often surprised by its variety of styles. It was built in 1913 and is on the National Register of Historic Places. The golden stucco exterior is topped by a red tile roof in a Spanish Mission Revival style. Inside there are numerous

spots for relaxation. In the parlor there are comfortable sofas near a marble Georgian fireplace; the Library has a brick Art Deco fireplace and Victorian stained glass. We chose to have a glass of iced tea in the wicker chairs on the tile-floored sunporch, where we could also admire the selections the gift shop has to offer.

I do have a favorite guest room, but each of them has its own charms. The cozy Baron on the top floor, under the eaves, has a window seat for reading; the Contessa, on the first floor, a private porch and a grand antique cherry secretary and bookcase. I have luxuriated in the antique cherry four-poster in Princess, and I love to stand on the balcony and watch the koi in the pond. But my favorite is the utterly private and thoroughly romantic Carriage House, with its canopy bed, fireplace, and Jacuzzi.

Breakfast will begin with freshly squeezed orange juice and coffee and is served in the formal dining room. You may take a bite of the heavenly peaches-and-cream French toast while you discover why you simply must purchase the inn's cookbook.

**HOW TO GET THERE:** From I–76 (Pennsylvania Turnpike) take exit 21 and follow Route 222 south for 15 miles to Lancaster. Turn east onto Route 30 and follow this to Route 23 west (Walnut Street), traveling to King Street. Turn right at the end of the exit ramp. At the second light turn left onto Ranck Avenue. At the second stop sign turn left onto East Orange Street. Follow East Orange Street for 1 block to Cottage Avenue and turn right. The B&B is the last building on the right, on the corner of East King Street and Cottage Avenue. Turn right into the lane just before the B&B and then turn left into the parking area.

# Swiss Woods Bed & Breakfast
Lititz, Pennsylvania 17543

**INNKEEPERS:** Werner and Debrah Mosimann

**ADDRESS/TELEPHONE:** 500 Blantz Road; (717) 627–3358 or (800) 594–8018; fax (717) 627–3483

**E-MAIL:** swisswoods@prodigy.net

**WEB SITE:** www.swisswoods.com

**ROOMS:** 7, including 1 suite; all with private bath, balcony or patio, and air-conditioning; 2 with whirlpool bath, 1 with television. No smoking inn.

**RATES:** $105 to $170, double occupancy; includes full breakfast. $15 for each additional person or child. Two-night minimum on weekends, mid-March to December; three-night minimum holidays. Corporate rates and off-season discounts available.

**OPEN:** All year except Christmas.

**FACILITIES AND ACTIVITIES:** Guest kitchenette, thirty acres, extensive gardens, hiking trails, lake, canoe. Nearby: restaurants, Landis Farm Museum, chocolate and pretzel factories, Ephrata Cloister, antiques markets, farmer's markets, country roads, Lancaster sites, Hershey Chocolate World.

*S*wiss Woods B&B blooms among the glorious gardens that surround it, cultivated as tenderly as the daffodils, tulips, dahlias, zinnias, and daisies. Its contemporary, natural cedar exterior has shutters embellished with heart cutouts and cascading planters of flowers. Aptly named for the country of Werner Mosimann's ancestry and where he and Debrah used to live, the fields bloom more brilliantly than an Alpine meadow. The lush gardens are the particular pride of Werner, who obtained a degree in agronomy in Switzerland.

Throughout the thirty-acre property guests will find walking trails and benches. Don't miss the opportunity to walk the property to savor the sweet fragrances, admire the brilliant flowers, watch the birds flit from bird houses to perches, and observe the unrehearsed ballet of the bees and butterflies as they glide from flower to flower. Meander down the path to Speedwell Forge Lake and take a quiet canoe journey to extend the peaceful interlude.

The heart of the inn is the Great Room or "Anker Stube" with its magnificent sandstone wall and fireplace mantel hand-hewn by Debrah's father. There's a fountain at the entrance, rag rugs on pine floors, and tables and chairs beside a wall of windows at which guests often sit in the afternoon to enjoy freshly baked cookies and tea.

The guest rooms are furnished in a restful and spare style, much as they are in Switzerland, except that the beds are exceptionally beautiful. There are several four-poster, locally made cherry beds and some pine sleigh beds, but my favorites are the beautiful twisted-spindle pine and wrought-iron canopy beds. Most of the baths include floor and wall tiles in brilliant colors, and two have whirlpool tubs. Although there are no telephones in the guest rooms, every room is equipped with a jack to which a telephone can be connected.

Unlike many inn gift shops, the one at Swiss Woods features beautiful locally made craft items. There are quilted potholders and tote bags, mugs, pinafores in colorful floral fabrics, books, soaps, and jams.

Debrah puts her home economics degree to good use at breakfast time. She may prepare eggs Florentine or, perhaps, her raisin-bread French toast stuffed with strawberry or chocolate cream cheese.

HOW TO GET THERE: From I–76 (Pennsylvania Turnpike) take exit 21 and follow Route 222 south about 1 mile to the exit for Route 322 west (Ephrata). Follow Route 322 until it intersects with Route 501 in Brickerville. Turn left onto Route 501 and travel south to the first crossroads, which is Brubaker Valley Road. Turn right and go 1 mile toward the lake. Just before the lake turn right onto Blantz Road. The inn is the first property on the left.

# Fairville Inn 📱
## Mendenhall, Pennsylvania 19357

**INNKEEPERS:** Ole and Patricia Retlev

**ADDRESS/TELEPHONE:** 506 Kennett Pike/Route 52 (mailing address: P.O. Box 219); (610) 388–5900; fax (610) 388–5902

**ROOMS:** 15, including 2 suites; all with private bath, air-conditioning, telephone, and television; 8 with fireplace, 11 with private deck. One room limited wheelchair accessibility. No smoking inn. Children over the age of 10 welcome.

**RATES:** $150 to $200, double occupancy; includes continental breakfast and afternoon tea. Two-night minimum weekends; three nights some holiday weekends.

**OPEN:** All year.

**FACILITIES AND ACTIVITIES:** On three and one-half acres. Nearby: restaurants (five-minute drive), Winterthur, Longwood Gardens, Chadds Ford and Brandywine River Museum, antiquing, golf, Wilmington, Delaware.

**BUSINESS TRAVEL:** Thirty miles to Philadelphia and 8 miles to Wilmington. Telephone in room; desk in 13 rooms; fax available; corporate rates.

Ole and Patricia Retlev were ski instructors when they met, and after marrying they traveled the globe for five years, skiing, sailing, and exploring numerous countries together. With the arrival of their first child, however, they settled down and became innkeepers in Vermont (Patti's relatives own Vermont's acclaimed Inn at Saw Mill Farm). Patti had been raised in the Brandywine Valley, however, and in 1986, they purchased a lovely 1820s Federal-style house on three and one-half acres that included a barn and carriage house near Winterthur and Longwood Gardens.

Soon hammer, saw, and patience transformed the property into a gracious country inn. The Retlevs painted the outside of the main house in soft shades of cream and white and placed an Amish bench and Tennessee rockers on the covered veranda. In the living room a fireplace warms guests in winter, and a handsome copper coffee table holds Swedish butter cookies and tea every afternoon. An abundance of flowers grace tables and desks—all grown in the inn's gardens.

There are five guest rooms in the main house. All are decorated with a mixture of antiques and period reproduction pieces. The ten rooms in the carriage house include canopy or four-poster beds, as well as beamed ceilings, barnwood walls, spacious porches, and elegant baths. There are two more rooms in the barn. The lovely floral chintz curtains and bed coverings were all handmade by Patti. On one occasion I stayed in the carriage house, where I had a fireplace in the room and a secluded deck overlooking the gardens and a pond. The deck was filled with pots of geraniums and a huge red hibiscus that must have been deliciously sweet to the hummingbird that returned again and again to sample its nectar.

## The Oriental Teuton

Once, during the Philadelphia Flower Show, the Fairville Inn played host to a German count and his entourage. As a special welcome Patti and Ole had thoughtfully gone to a German deli to purchase Bavarian cold cuts, cheeses, and breads to supplement the breakfast buffet.

But the count had a surprise of his own. He arrived for breakfast wearing his wife's kimono and a broad-brimmed straw hat covered with dried flowers that had previously been decorating an upstairs hallway. Slowly he entered the room chanting "Bonsai, Bonsai, Bonsai."

Breakfast continued in a convivial manner as the German friends became acquainted with the other guests. Following the meal the counts and princes serenaded the inn guests with a variety of Bavarian and German songs and yodels—providing lasting memories of a pretty country inn and its guests for everyone who was there.

Patti serves a continental breakfast in the morning. She will prepare fruit, juice, and freshly baked scones, muffins, or sticky buns. Although there is no restaurant at the inn, historic Buckley's Tavern is located only minutes away. This 1817 former stagecoach stop has beamed ceilings and paneled walls. The atmosphere is casual and relaxed—a place where you might order a burger or pasta as well as chicken or steak.

The beautiful Brandywine Valley has been an inspiration to three generations of Wyeths. Backroad drives yield views of gently undulating farmland and glimpses of hidden estates.

HOW TO GET THERE: From I-95 in Wilmington, Delaware, take exit 7 and follow Route 52 north through Greenville and Centerville, crossing the state line into Pennsylvania. Fairville is the first village on Route 52 in Pennsylvania. The B&B is about 1½ miles beyond the state line.

# The Magoffin Inn
## Mercer, Pennsylvania 16137

INNKEEPER: Gene Slagle; manager: Jacque McClelland

ADDRESS/TELEPHONE: 129 South Pitt Street; (724) 662-4611 or (800) 841-0824; fax (724) 662-4611

ROOMS: 5, including one suite; all with private bath, air-conditioning, television, and fireplace. No smoking inn.

RATES: $120 to $135, double occupancy; includes full breakfast.

OPEN: All year.

FACILITIES AND ACTIVITIES: Restaurant serving dinner Thursday to Saturday (prix fixe $16 to $25). Nearby: Mercer County Historical Society Museum, summer band concerts, Grove City Factory Shops (140 outlet stores).

The handsome 1884 three-story brick Victorian mansion has a welcoming front porch and elaborate gingerbread dripping from overhanging eaves. It was built by Dr. Montrose Magoffin and housed the Magoffin family and its members' medical practice until 1946. It sits on a tree-lined street next door to the Mercer County Historical Museum and across from the impressive court house. Although the house was converted to an inn in 1986, it wasn't until it was purchased in 1988 by Gene Slagle that significant improvements were made. The building also underwent a total renovation in 1996 after it was damaged by a tornado.

One of the unique features of the house is that every room has a fireplace. This gives the three main-floor rooms, which are used as dining rooms in the evening, a warm and romantic air. Candlelight, fresh flowers, pressed-back oak chairs, and tall windows complete the immersion into the Victorian era. A four-course prix fixe dinner is offered nightly that includes an appetizer, salad, entree, and dessert. For the main course guests might order lobster tails, prime rib, roast lamb, or, perhaps, a salmon steak.

The guest rooms all have gas fireplaces, and they are furnished with lovely Victorian antiques that include elaborate beds with high head and foot-boards and matching dressers. The set in the Bridal Suite is particularly impressive and also includes a pair of Victorian nightstands, a marble-topped chest, and a pretty couch. The smart tile bath has a pedestal sink. The baths in several of the other guest rooms are still under renovation, but the two-level Amish Suite, which is located in the former slave quarters, is as impressive as the Bridal Suite. The style, as the name suggests, is not Victorian but Amish. Here the innkeepers have included an Amish-made sleigh bed, a woodstove, and folk-art decor. The bath is gorgeous. It includes a claw-foot tub, a skylight, a pedestal sink, a wonderful Amish twig bench and chair, and a separate shower.

**HOW TO GET THERE:** From I–80 take exit 2 and follow Route 19 north for 2 miles to Mercer. At the first traffic light turn right. At the first stop sign turn left. The inn is the third house on the right.

# The Mercersburg Inn 👥 📱
Mercersburg, Pennsylvania 17236

**INNKEEPERS:** Walt and Sandy Filkowski

**ADDRESS/TELEPHONE:** 405 South Main Street; (717) 328–5231; fax (717) 328–3403

**ROOMS:** 15; all with private bath, air-conditioning, and telephone; 3 with fireplace, 6 with balcony. No smoking inn. Children over the age of 7 welcome.

**RATES:** $120 to $235, double occupancy; includes full breakfast. Two-night minimum October and during ski season.

**OPEN:** All year except Christmas.

**FACILITIES AND ACTIVITIES:** Restaurant serving dinner Thursday to Saturday (prix fixe $45 or entrees $16 to $34), full wine/cocktail service, bar; game room that includes an antique pool table, TV/VCR, and darts; backgammon table; NordicTrack available; gardens with horseshoes, croquet, mountain bikes available. Nearby: Mercersburg Academy (private 105-year-old high school with a fabulous 1922 Gothic cathedral and forty-three-bell carillon), Whitetail Ski Resort (6 miles), Cowans Gap State Park, Frank Lloyd Wright's Fallingwater, outlet centers, golfing, fishing.

**BUSINESS TRAVEL:** Telephone in all rooms; desk in 4 rooms; corporate midweek rates.

**RECOMMENDED COUNTRY INNS® TRAVELERS' CLUB BENEFIT:** Stay one night, get second night free, Sunday to Thursday.

When Ione and Harry Byron built their grand estate in 1909, they spared no costs. Harry owned the local tannery, and his 20,000-square-foot brick mansion includes fabulous stained glass, a sweeping double stairway with wrought-iron balustrades, magnificent scagliola columns, elaborately inlaid oak floors, and chestnut paneling. Across the front of the three-story Georgian mansion, huge columns frame the doorway. Situated high on a hill it commands panoramic views of the Cumberland Valley and the Tuscarora Mountains beyond. Especially when the carillon in the Gothic Mercersburg Academy next door is being played, it's magical. Walt and Sandy Filkowski purchased the inn in 1996.

The public rooms are elegant but comfortable. One enters a massive tile-floored entrance that has leaded windows. The Great Room includes a fireplace, a leather backgammon table, and parquet oak floors. Daffodil-yellow

walls, a pretty yellow floral sofa, and yellow damask chairs give the room a cheerful look. Afternoon tea and scones are served here on weekends. The adjoining west porch contains green wicker tables and chairs.

The guest rooms are spacious and equally beautiful. I love Room 2, which is on the second floor in the front. It has a private balcony that projects under the roof of the two-story front porch, and it's furnished with a marble table on a cast-iron base. The bowed-top bed has a lacy canopy and peach bed coverings. Peach-colored chairs contrast with the pale green walls and ivory trim. The bath is lovely and modern. Room 8 has a pretty marble-topped counter in the bath and a view of the Tuscarora Mountains.

Breakfast and dinner are served in the formal dining room lighted by a gorgeous Tiffany lamp and warmed by a fire in the fireplace in winter. On busy days and nights tables may also be set on the huge enclosed porch with its bead board ceiling and brick wall.

Breakfast will include cereals, a fruit cup with whipped cream, and, per-haps, a hot apple and raspberry strudel, followed by delicate Swedish pan-cakes and bacon. If possible plan a stay for a night when the dining room is open. You won't be sorry.

On one recent visit I tried the prix fixe dinner and was delighted with my choices. I started with a shrimp bisque, which was followed with a hot appe-tizer of braised sweetbreads with shiitake mushrooms and vegetable polenta. A light sorbet was a prelude to the entree of grilled duck breast with pear and cranberry sauces. I enjoyed a marvelous selection of wines, with many excel-lent California offerings. I ended the meal with a luscious Grand Marnier–soaked angel food cake topped with chocolate sauce. Gourmet cooking buffs may wish to plan a trip to coincide with the quarterly weekend cooking classes taught at the inn.

Mercersburg has a nice collection of antiques and gift shops, but village life revolves around Mercersburg Academy, where concerts, plays, lectures, and events frequently take place. The Gothic stone buildings are a symphony of beautiful architecture, especially the fabulous chapel with its interior of moody, pensive, and gorgeous cobalt-blue stained glass.

HOW TO GET THERE: From I–81 take exit 3 and travel west on Route 16 for 11 miles through Greencastle to Mercersburg. The inn is at the intersection of Routes 16 and 75.

# The Inn at Olde New Berlin

New Berlin, Pennsylvania 17855

**INNKEEPERS:** John and Nancy Showers

**ADDRESS/TELEPHONE:** 321 Market Street; (717) 966–0321;
fax (717) 966–9557

**E-MAIL:** John@newberlin-inn.com

**WEB SITE:** www.newberlin-inn.com

**ROOMS:** 11, including 2 suites; all with air-conditioning, radios, robes,
and CD/tape players; 2 with fireplace and two-person soaking tub, one
with private deck or patio; telephone, TV, VCR, and hair dryer available
on request. Wheelchair accessible. No smoking inn.

**RATES:** $85 to $175, double occupancy; includes full breakfast. Two-
night minimum several university weekends.

**OPEN:** All year except first two weeks of January.

**FACILITIES AND ACTIVITIES:** Restaurant (Gabriel's) serving dinner
Wednesday to Sunday (dinner entrees $14 to $23); Sunday brunch,
extensive give shop. Nearby: Amish country, Mifflinburg Buggy
Museum, Walnut Acres Organic Farm, Slifer House Museum, Penn's
Creek Pottery, quilt, craft, and antiques shopping.

**BUSINESS TRAVEL:** Telephone, fax, dataport, TV, and desk available;
corporate rates available midweek.

**RECOMMENDED COUNTRY INNS® TRAVELERS' CLUB BENEFIT:** 10 percent discount, Wednesday, Thursday, and Sunday; subject to availability.
Mention offer at time of booking.

*J*ohn and Nancy Showers have exhibited a whirlwind of energy and
activity ever since they purchased the former Jacob Schoch house in
1993. What they have accomplished is next to miraculous and
much too extensive to itemize in every detail. Suffice it to say that their original inn of five rooms has now grown to a complex of five buildings, all
within 1 block of one another. Altogether there are eleven guest rooms,
Gabriel's Restaurant, and a separate house that contains Gabriel's Gift Collection, a fine gift shop and art gallery.

New Berlin was the home of the first Evangelical Church of America, and
its founder, Jacob Albright, also started Union Seminary here. A life-sized
depiction of the angel Gabriel, in the form of a weathervane, "flies" over the

United Church of Christ across the street from the inn, giving the inn's restaurant and gift shop its name.

John's parents operated the New Berlin general store for some thirty-seven years, so John is familiar with every detail of the town's history. The main house of the inn was built as a summer home in 1906 and served as a private home until John and Nancy purchased it.

Guests enter the pretty Victorian main house, which has an oak bench in the entry and a step-down living room with an oak floor, an organ, and a baby grand piano. A huge bowl of fresh daffodils greeted me one spring afternoon. The inn's restaurant, Gabriel's, takes up the rest of the main-floor rooms, where guests can dine on such entrees as maple and honey duckling, veal Oscar, and prime rib of pork.

Although the bath is across the hall, my favorite room in the main house is Number 1, which is located in the turret. It has stained glass and a lovely

walnut high-headboard bed. A marble-topped dresser and nightstand complete the decor. The newest rooms are located in the carriage house. Room 6 has a gas fireplace, a private bath in the room, and a king-size bed. All the rooms are decorated with local quilts and Victorian antiques.

**HOW TO GET THERE:** From I–80 take exit 30 and travel south on Route 15 to Lewisburg. At the intersection with Route 45, turn west and go as far as the Dreisbach Church sign. Turn left and continue up over the mountain and down into New Berlin. Turn right onto Market Street. The inn is the second house on the right.

# A Night to Remember

The Inn at Olde New Berlin has collaborated with numerous suitors who wish to create a memorable evening. There have been rings presented in the bottom of champagne glasses, rings tied inside scrolled menus, and rings presented inside desserts. In one case the gentleman asked John to be prepared to take a photograph right after the salad course was removed. John was, and in the midst of a restaurant, the man dropped to his knees to pop the question.

The inn has created a unique remembrance for birthday celebrations also. A special dessert is presented on a red plate that reads "You are special today." It's accompanied by a music box playing "Happy Birthday." Plus, if a guest has requested it, a gift certificate is presented so that the celebrant can purchase a red dinner plate or a music box in the inn's gift shop.

# The Fox & Hound
# Bed & Breakfast of New Hope
## New Hope, Pennsylvania 18938

**INNKEEPER:** Dennis Anthony

**ADDRESS/TELEPHONE:** 246 West Bridge Street; (215) 862–5082 (also fax) or (800) 862–5082

**E-MAIL:** foxhound@bellatic.net

**WEB SITE:** www.visitbucks.com/foxandhound/

**ROOMS:** 8; all with private bath and air-conditioning; 4 with fireplace, 2 with whirlpool tub. Children over the age of 12 welcome. Pets permitted with prior permission. Smoking permitted; designated nonsmoking rooms.

**RATES:** $65 to $165, double occupancy; includes full breakfast on weekends and continental-plus breakfast on weekdays. Two-night minimum when Saturday stay included.

**OPEN:** All year.

**FACILITIES AND ACTIVITIES:** On two acres with gardens; passes available for nearby fitness center. Nearby: Bucks County Playhouse, New Hope Mule Barge Tours, Washington Crossing State Park, golfing, hiking along the canal towpath, rafting and canoeing on the Delaware River.

**BUSINESS TRAVEL:** Conference room; fax, copier, computer, office supplies available.

*T*he impressive 1850s gray stone building with its slate mansard roof looks as welcoming and inviting as those lovely stone houses that dot the English countryside. Even the two acres of gardens, as neat and trim as they can be, have some of the random abandon we all love about a Cotswold landscape. Yet The Fox and Hound is as upscale and sophisticated (combined with a whimsical, tongue-in-cheek drollery) as an English manor house.

As you meander up the driveway, you'll be greeted by a huge cement pig on the lawn. You'll enter a graceful foyer. To the right there's a lovely breakfast room with an oak floor, green walls with white trim, and French doors leading to a terrace. A new kitchen just beyond the breakfast room is available for guests to use.

The living room has a gas fireplace and a hooked rug on the oak floor. The antique sofa and chairs are beautifully upholstered in a soft tapestry, and the walls are painted a lovely shade of green.

Each of the guest rooms is furnished with antiques also, and the baths are new and modern. Room 2, for example, has a gas fireplace and a king-size wrought-iron bed. The beautiful bath has a Jacuzzi tub and a pedestal sink. Rooms 5 and 6 are decorated with lovely stenciling. My favorite rooms are upstairs, however. Room 7 has a queen-size canopy bed and a striped sofa as well as several interesting antique pieces—one table has a carved ram's head; a game table has a harp base. There's stenciling on the walls and shutters on the windows. Room 8 has a fabulous bed that incorporates a variety of polished woods.

Breakfast is served every morning on white plates with gold rims and using pretty stemmed glasses. During the week the meal will include fruit, juice, and muffins. On weekends, this may be supplemented with the inn's fabulous French toast made with homemade Italian bread or, perhaps, with a cheese quiche.

**HOW TO GET THERE:** From I–287 in New Jersey, take exit 13 onto Route 202 south. Follow Route 202 for 26 miles and cross over the bridge into Pennsylvania. Take the first Pennsylvania exit and follow Route 32 south for about ½ mile to New Hope. At the traffic light turn right onto Bridge Street and proceed up the hill. The inn is on the right in ½ mile.

# Holly Hedge
# Estate Bed & Breakfast
## New Hope, Pennsylvania 18938

**INNKEEPER:** Mary Kay Fischer; Joe Luccaro, manager

**ADDRESS/TELEPHONE:** 6987 Upper York Road; (215) 862-3136 or (800) 378-4496; fax (215) 862-0960

**E-MAIL:** Hollyhedge@aol.com

**ROOMS:** 15, including 5 suites and 2 cottages; all with private bath, air-conditioning, and telephone; 3 with fireplace and/or balcony or porch, 2 with TV. Wheelchair accessible. No smoking inn.

**RATES:** $100 to $175, double occupancy; includes full breakfast and afternoon and evening snacks.

**OPEN:** All year.

**FACILITIES AND ACTIVITIES:** On twenty acres; pond with gazebo, formal and informal gardens, pool, tennis court, volleyball, basketball, baseball, yard games; workout room with treadmill, weights. Nearby: Delaware River for rafting, canoeing, shops in New Hope, outlet shops in Peddler's Village, walking trail along canal tow path, Bucks County Playhouse.

**BUSINESS TRAVEL:** Telephone in all rooms; meeting rooms, corporate rates, fax, copier, audiovisual, flipcharts, etc., available.

**RECOMMENDED COUNTRY INNS® TRAVELERS' CLUB BENEFIT:** Stay two nights, get third night free, Monday to Thursday.

*I*'ll never forget my first visit to Holly Hedge. As we drove up the hill from the Delaware River, the trees created a canopy and the foliage on either side of the narrow road was so dense we felt as though we were in a Maurice Sendak illustration. We turned into the inn's driveway, crossed the stream, and commented about the beauty of the pond with its gazebo, but it was the white stucco mansion that wove us under its spell.

Holly Hedge is centered around a grand manor house set majestically on a hill overlooking twenty acres of gardens and outbuildings. It was built in 1730, and from the beginning it's been welcoming guests. It was the private home of the owner of the ferry running across the Delaware River, and it was his custom to offer overnight accommodations to travelers.

We entered a charming foyer filled with books. The Living Room has a fireplace as well as a curved-glass china cabinet filled with Santas year-round. Books line the walls.

Most of the fifteen guest rooms are located in the manor house, but others are distributed in the stone summer cottage, the carriage house, and the fieldstone barn. Of those in the main house (all the rooms are furnished with antiques), I like Rooms 9 and 10—one of which has a brass bed and the other a sleigh bed. Both have fireplaces and lovely sparkling baths. A sitting room between them make them ideal for couples traveling together or for families.

The rooms in the outbuildings, however, are truly remarkable. Room 17 is located on the second floor of the fieldstone barn. It has a loft with a huge window overlooking the formal English garden. Room 11 is in the stone smokehouse, and it has hand-hewn beams, stone walls (one includes a massive stone fireplace), and a tile floor. The rooms are distinctive and utterly romantic.

Breakfast is served in the dining room of the manor house. Mary Kay may prepare a fresh fruit crepe or a puffy frittata. This will be accompanied by fresh fruit, gourmet coffee or tea, homemade breads and muffins, and juices.

Although in a secluded country setting, the inn is close to fine restaurants, sophisticated shops, antiques and art galleries, as well as a discount outlet center.

HOW TO GET THERE: From I–287 in New Jersey, take exit 13 onto Route 202 south. Follow this for 26 miles to the last exit in New Jersey (Stockton). Follow the signs to Route 29 and go north on Route 29 for 3 miles into Stockton. Turn left and go over the bridge into Pennsylvania. Continue straight for ½ mile, following Route 263 up the hill. The inn is on the right.

## From the White House to the White House

Holly Hedge Estate has an impressive 300-foot-long box-wood hedge that lines the front walkway. It has often been admired, but it nevertheless came as a surprise to Innkeeper Mary Kay Fischer when a guest at a reception one day informed her that President Truman had donated the cuttings from clippings he had taken from a White House hedge. Apparently President Truman had been friends with the owner of the farm. Mary Kay believes that the information is true, although she has been unable to verify it.

# The Inn at Phillips Mill
## New Hope, Pennsylvania 18938

**INNKEEPERS:** Joyce and Brooks Kaufman

**ADDRESS/TELEPHONE:** 2590 North River Road; (215) 862–2984

**ROOMS:** 4, including 1 cottage; all with private bath and air-conditioning; 1 with private patio. Children over the age of 7 welcome. Smoking tolerated.

**RATES:** $80 to $90, double occupancy. Two-night minimum Memorial Day and Labor Day weekends. No credit cards.

**OPEN:** February to December.

**FACILITIES AND ACTIVITIES:** Restaurant serving dinner (entrees $15 to $23), gardens, gift and antiques shop, and pool. Nearby: Bucks County Playhouse; walking along the canal towpath; outlet shopping at Peddler's Village; numerous antiques shops, art galleries, and book stores.

For those of us who love Bucks County, a special fondness dwells in our hearts for the wonderfully romantic Inn at Phillips Mill. As you twist and turn along scenic Route 32 between New Hope and Center Bridge, you must slow almost to a stop to miss the protruding corner of the inn that was carved from a great old eighteenth-century stone barn. The quaint buildings overflow with pots of flowers from spring through fall, and the picturesque, old-fashioned wrought-iron-and-brass sign featuring a well-fed porky always brings a smile to our lips. Joyce and Brooks Kaufman have owned the inn since 1974.

The main floor of the inn is composed of a multitude of charming low-ceilinged dining rooms—four have massive fireplaces; one is located on a tiled covered terrace that has a stone wall. They are furnished with tables and ladder-back chairs tied with cushions in bright country-French fabrics. In warm weather additional tables may be set up on a brick courtyard that is surrounded by pots of flowers. Gardens behind the inn overflow with flowers and little brick pathways meander about—back to the gift and antiques shop, to the pool, over to the stone cottage. I have had some fabulous meals here over the years, but do be sure to bring a bottle of your favorite wine as none is available at the inn.

The guest rooms are decorated in a manner that's as charming as the restaurant, although several of the baths could be improved. There are antique beds and furnishings and checked curtains and chair covers. The most romantic place to stay in Bucks County, however, is located here. It's a little stone cottage, located in a very private setting that's surrounded by English and American boxwoods, lilacs, and azaleas. The living room has stone walls and a beamed ceiling and includes a fireplace on the main floor and a bedroom on the second floor reached by climbing a narrow stairway.

A continental breakfast is brought to each room in a basket at a pre-arranged hour. It will include fresh muffins and croissants and coffee or tea. Don't forget to visit the charming gift shop. It may have the exact antique or gift item you're looking for.

HOW TO GET THERE: From I–287 in New Jersey take exit 13 onto Route 202 south. Follow this for 26 miles and cross over the bridge into Pennsylvania. Take the first Pennsylvania exit and follow Route 32 north for ¼ mile. The inn is on the right.

# The Mansion Inn

New Hope, Pennsylvania 18938

**INNKEEPER:** Deanna Cerwin; Keith David and Elio Filippo Bracco, proprietors

**ADDRESS/TELEPHONE:** 9 South Main Street; (215) 862–1231; fax (215) 862–0277

**E-MAIL:** mansion@pil.net

**WEB SITE:** www.themansioninn.com

**ROOMS:** 9, including 5 suites; all with private bath, air-conditioning, telephone with dataport, TV, clock/radio, robes; 5 with fireplace, whirlpool tub, and desk; 2 with porch or patio. Children over the age of 16 welcome. No smoking inn.

**RATES:** $175 to $265, double occupancy; includes full breakfast. Two-night minimum weekends; three-night minimum holidays.

**OPEN:** All year.

**FACILITIES AND ACTIVITIES:** Pool, gardens, parking area. Nearby: Parry Mansion, Washington's Crossing park, Bowman's Hill Wildflower Preserve, golf, bicycling, river rafting, antiquing, walking.

**BUSINESS TRAVEL:** Telephone with dataport, TV in all rooms; most rooms with desk; fax, copier available; corporate rates.

*T*he fanciful Victorian mansion on New Hope's main street had attracted the admiration and the dismay of passersby for many years. You could not fail to be impressed by the arched windows and entrance doors, the elaborate gingerbread fretwork, and the domed cupola, but neither could you disguise your concern about their deteriorated condition. Fortunately, in 1995 the building obtained a new lease on life.

Built in 1865 by Charles Crook in a style whimsically described as Baroque Victorian, the house was embellished with a virtual catalog of fancy wooden trim. Even the wrought-iron fence in front is far from ordinary: A tangle of grapevines marches across the front on either side of an arched gate filled with clusters of grapes.

For some sixty years the house, in the heart of New Hope, was the home and office of Dr. Kenneth Leiby, who delivered many of the area's babies here. When he decided to sell, the ideal buyers stepped up. Keith David and

Dr. Elio Bracco wanted to turn the home into an elegant bed-and-breakfast, and nothing could have pleased Dr. Leiby more.

Today the house glows in a soft buttercup yellow, and the trim is painted a sparkling white, accenting the fancy carpentry. Inside, in the parlor and drawing rooms, Oriental rugs lie atop polished pine floors, crystal chandeliers illuminate elaborate moldings, and antique tables and chests are enhanced by upholstered velvet sofas and floral linen chairs and drapes. Oil paintings hang above arched marble fireplaces, and sparkling cranberry and etched green glass are attractively displayed.

The guest rooms are equally refined, with canopy, iron-and-brass, and four-poster beds. Plush pillows are piled on top of white matelassé spreads. Starched and ironed Portault linens dress the featherbeds. Hampton Court is decorated in shades of sage and rose and has a magnificent marble bath with a bay window and an antique chandelier. Windsor has a canopy bed, a two-person whirlpool tub, a gas fireplace, antique tables and lamps, and pretty boudoir chairs upholstered in pink. All baths offer the ultimate in comfort and style. Special room amenities include a decanter of sherry and stemmed glasses; freshly baked cookies are offered bedside at night; bathrooms contain bath salts and oils.

Breakfast, served in a sunny room with linen-clad tables and wicker chairs, includes juice, fresh fruit, and baked goodies displayed on a handsome antique Dutch chest with massive brass hinges. An entree, such as an omelette or stuffed croissant toast with raspberry sauce, is served at individual tables.

Behind the house a pretty garden contains a gazebo. A swimming pool is located in a separate enclosure beside the private parking lot—a much appreciated amenity in New Hope, where crowds of tourists throng the streets in summer and parking is often at a premium.

HOW TO GET THERE: From New York City take the New Jersey Turnpike to exit 14 and take I–78 west to Route 202 south. After crossing the Delaware River, exit onto Route 32 south to New Hope. At the traffic light (Bridge Street), turn right. Turn left into the first alley on the left to reach the parking area.

# The Priory—A City Inn 🖼 📱 ¢¢
## Pittsburgh, Pennsylvania 15212

**INNKEEPER:** Mary Ann Graf; Joanie Weldon, manager

**ADDRESS/TELEPHONE:** 614 Pressley Street; (412) 231–3338; fax (412) 231–4838

**WEB SITE:** www.sgi.net/thepriory/

**ROOMS:** 24, including 3 suites; all with air-conditioning, telephone, television, radio, hair dryer, and robes. Wheelchair accessible. Smoking permitted; designated nonsmoking rooms.

**RATES:** $68 to $160, double occupancy; includes continental breakfast and wine 5:00 P.M. to midnight.

**OPEN:** All year.

**FACILITIES AND ACTIVITIES:** Complimentary wine and finger snacks in sitting room; honor cash bar for mixed drinks and beer in the library; garden courtyard. Nearby: Carnegie Science Center, The National Aviary, Andy Warhol Museum, Mattress Factory Art Gallery, Pittsburgh Public Theater, Children's Museum, and Three Rivers Stadium.

**BUSINESS TRAVEL:** Located in North End, ½ mile from downtown; parking. Complimentary weekday morning shuttle downtown. Telephone and television in room; desk in 6 rooms; conference room. Corporate rates available for multiple visits. Fax and copier available.

*Y*es, The Priory did begin life as a Benedictine monastery, and you can easily imagine the quiet contemplation and the serene spiritual peace of the monks when you walk through the hallways yourself. Built in 1888 the ornate red-brick building has 16-foot ceilings on the first floor, 14-foot ceilings on the second floor, and 12-foot ceilings on the third floor. There are massive oak doors, tin ceilings, and stained glass. A beautiful sitting room has a fireplace with a white mantel and a tin ceiling; complimentary wine and finger foods are available from 5:00 P.M. to midnight. The ornate library includes another tin ceiling and a honor cash bar for mixed drinks and beer (an appropriate use for the rooms, by the way, since it's rumored the dining room of the monastery was known as the "beer chapel" when the monks were in residence. It appears they brewed and sipped their own pilsner here). In the afternoons my favorite place to sit with a book (providing the weather is nice) is at a table in the interior courtyard.

The inn is adjacent to the former St. Mary's German Catholic Church, which is now part of The Priory as well. This fabulous building, now called the Grand Hall of The Priory, was built in 1854. Although it was abandoned and boarded up for five years, the Graf family rescued it in the mid-1990s as a reception, banquet, and wedding hall for their inn. It has a massive 30-foot center dome, brilliant mural frescoes, a huge pipe organ, impressive Corinthian columns with gold-leaf capitals, and fabulous Austrian stained-glass windows. You can imagine the grand weddings and receptions that take place here. Visitors to The Priory will enjoy reading the entire history of St. Mary's and the Graf's restoration of it in *A Story of Resurrection: Grand Hall at The Priory,* written by Stephen Graf. It can be purchased at the inn.

The guest rooms at the inn vary from small rooms with tiny baths (such as Number 207) to spacious suites (such as Number 310), which has a sitting room furnished with oak tables and Victorian chairs and a large bedroom. All the rooms have floral carpeting and antique furnishings. Room 203 has a brass-and-iron bed, an oak armoire, and a fabulous tin ceiling.

A breakfast buffet is served in the dining room every morning, allowing guests to eat at their leisure.

The inn is located in a historic but transitional neighborhood near an exit off I–279. Settled originally by German immigrants, and known as Deutschtown, it's now part of the East Allegheny Historic District. This area, near where industrialists Andrew Carnegie and Henry Phipps and composer Stephen Foster grew up and where Willa Cather lived and wrote, still has streets containing excellent German restaurants and taverns featuring bratwurst, sauerkraut, and lager.

HOW TO GET THERE: From I–79 traveling north take exit 14 to I–279 and follow the signs to Pittsburgh, traveling through the Fort Pitt Tunnel. Immediately upon exiting the tunnel, get into the far left lane and follow I–279 north. As you cross the second bridge (the Fort Duquesne) move into the far right lane, still traveling on I–279 north. Take exit 13 and follow the signs for East Ohio Street. Turn left at the light onto East Ohio Street and get into the right lane. Go through one light. At the second light turn left onto Cedar Avenue. Go 3 blocks and turn left onto Pressley Street. The Priory is at the end of the street on the left. The parking lot is across the street on the right. If arriving on I–79 from the north, take exit 21 and follow I–279 south to exit 15 (East Street). Do not go across the Fort Duquesne bridge. Follow East Street to the third traffic light and then turn right onto East Ohio Street. At the first light turn left onto Cedar Avenue. Follow remaining directions above.

# The Inn at Georgian Place
Somerset, Pennsylvania 15501

**INNKEEPERS:** Douglas Gardiner, Roger Haddon; Jon Knupp, innkeeper/manager

**ADDRESS/TELEPHONE:** 800 Georgian Place Drive; (814) 443–1043; fax (814) 445–3047

**ROOMS:** 11, including 2 suites; all with private bath, air-conditioning, telephone, television, VCR, and robes. Children over the age of 12 welcome. Pets permitted with prior permission. Smoking permitted; designated nonsmoking rooms.

**RATES:** $95 to $185, double occupancy; includes full breakfast.

**OPEN:** All year.

**FACILITIES AND ACTIVITIES:** Restaurant open for lunch (entrees $7.00 to $8.00) and afternoon tea, cocktails served 1:00 P.M. to 9:00 P.M.; tours of house daily; flower gardens, terraces, adjacent to shops at Georgian Place. Also near Lake Somerset where guests can fish and boat. Nearby: golfing, hiking on the Laurel Highlands Trail, Frank Lloyd Wright's Fallingwater in Mill Run and Kentuck Knob in Ohiopyle, rafting on the Youghiogheny River, skiing at Hidden Valley, Laurel Ridge State Park.

*S*nuggled into the Laurel Highlands, at the turn of the century Somerset was in the heart of a prosperous coal mining region. By 1907 Daniel B. Zimmerman had more than 140,000 acres devoted to coal mining, as well as 100,000 acres in ranch land that spread from North Dakota to California where he grazed cattle—so many that he (or his minions) drove more than 40,000 a year to market.

It wasn't unusual in this era of no income taxes for a coal and cattle baron to build a grand edifice as his family home, and Mr. Zimmerman was no exception. In 1918 he built a twenty-two-room brick mansion. The classic Georgian-style house has an elegant pillared entrance and two side wings. The grand marble entrance hall includes an impressive staircase supported by huge fluted columns. The ornate moldings, oak paneling, polished brass and silver wall fixtures, crystal and gold-leafed chandeliers, and nine fireplace mantels have now been elegantly restored. The inn, which opened in 1993, is on the National Register of Historic Places.

Guests may sit in the living room, which has a gorgeous grand piano, walls of bookshelves, and a fireplace, as well as on an outside terrace in nice weather. Breakfast, lunch, and afternoon tea are served in the elegant dining room or on the terrace. We love the wonderful afternoon tea, which includes a variety of tea sandwiches, freshly baked scones, lemon cake, and a variety of teas and coffees. For breakfast you might peruse a New York, Washington, Philadelphia, or Pittsburgh newspaper while munching muffins, fruit, and juice and eating eggs Benedict, stuffed French toast with orange apricot glaze, or Dutch pancakes.

The guest rooms are spacious and elegant and have wonderful baths. All the furnishings are high-quality period reproductions. The Library Suite, in the former mansion library, has oak-paneled walls, oak bookcases, and a scroll-carved fireplace mantel (alas none of the guest room fireplaces are functional). There's a king-size sleigh bed and a soft leather chair and ottoman just made for snuggling into for a good read. A sitting room is adjacent. Sally Zimmerman's (the only Zimmerman daughter) former bedroom has a four-poster rice-carved bed and a beautiful flower-carved Neoclassical mantel. Several rooms on the third floor in the former servants quarters are furnished with wicker and bright fabrics and have wonderful mountain and sunset views.

The Inn at Georgian Place is the perfect stopover between meetings in Pittsburgh and points further east and the ideal spot from which to take a Frank Lloyd Wright excursion to Fallingwater and Kentuck Knob.

**HOW TO GET THERE:** From I–76 (Pennsylvania Turnpike) take exit 10 and follow Route 601 north for ½ mile. The inn and the shops at Georgian Place are on the right.

# The French Manor  🏛

## South Sterling, Pennsylvania 18460

INNKEEPERS: Ron and Mary Kay Logan; Robin Huttie, manager

ADDRESS/TELEPHONE: Huckleberry Road; (717) 676–3244 or
(800) 523–8200; fax (717) 676–9786

E-MAIL: thesterlinginn@ezaccess.net

WEB SITE: www.thesterlinginn.com

ROOMS: 9, including 3 suites; all with private bath, air-conditioning,
and radio; 7 with desk; 3 with television; 2 with fireplace, whirlpool tub,
and minirefrigerator. Wheelchair accessible. Children over the age of
7 welcome. No smoking inn.

RATES: $150 to $250, double occupancy; includes full breakfast and
afternoon tea. Two-night minimum most weekends.

OPEN: All year.

FACILITIES AND ACTIVITIES: Restaurant serving dinner (entrees $20 to
$32); on thirty-four acres with tennis court, pool, gardens, lake, boating,
nature trails. Nearby: Pocono Playhouse, Lake Wallenpaupack for sailing, boating.

The Pocono Mountains have been attracting summer residents and
tourists seeking a getaway for many years. Most of the homes built
here are of a modest nature, attuned to the casual ambience of the
region. That was not the case, however, when Joseph Hirshhorn built his
grand summer estate in 1932. His brick manor house is a smaller replica of
his magnificent French chateau in the south of France. To build it he
brought German and Italian craftsmen to Pennsylvania to mold the exterior
from fieldstones carved out of nearby Huckleberry Mountain, to install
beautiful "pecky" cypress paneling and leaded-glass windows, and to roof the
structure with imported Spanish slate. They added a romantic stone tower
with a tiny wrought-iron balcony.

Hirshhorn, a Russian Jew, was one of the great art collectors of his day.
Concerned about the art treasures in Germany under Hitler, he imported
numerous pieces to his estate and housed them in a boxy climate-, bomb-,
and burglar-proof brick building on the property. His collection now forms
The Hirshhorn Museum and Sculpture Garden, part of The Smithsonian
complex. It's located on The Mall in Washington, D.C. Hirshhorn sold his
house to Samuel Kress (of dime-store fame), who eventually donated it to

Bucknell University. It remained vacant and unused until the mid-1980s, when it was turned into a bed-and-breakfast. Finally, in 1990 it was purchased by Ron and Mary Kay Logan, who also own the easygoing Sterling Inn just down the road. They converted the manor house to the quality country inn we enjoy today.

The Great Room of the inn sports an adobe fireplace wall that reaches to the cathedral ceiling. There are massive beams, pecky cypress walls, and a wall of bookshelves. This is where dinner is served. Downstairs there's a game room with a television and an abundance of games and books.

The dining room decor includes a variety of chairs with gingham, calico, and patchwork cushions; a Chinese screen on the wall; and little ceramic table lamps with pleated shades. We had a wonderful and romantic dinner here one night that featured a Roquefort tarte, a salad, and a lime sherbet. One of us had lamb crusted with mustard; the other had coquilles St. Jacques brulee. For dessert I had a raspberry crème brûlée, and my husband had a caramel pear tarte. A pianist played softly in the background.

The guest rooms could be as elegant as the restaurant, but on a recent visit I did note some maintenance problems. We stayed in Florence, which has a bow-top canopy bed and pecky cypress walls. The furniture has a 1940s feel, and the decanter of sherry, stemmed glasses, and fresh flowers are lovely touches. The most romantic accommodation is the Turret Suite, which has a living room with a television tucked into an armoire and a bath on the main floor, while upstairs there's a bedroom with windows on three sides offering magnificent views of the surrounding countryside. The four rooms in the Carriage House have more modern decor.

The grounds are beautiful and include flagstone terraces, an abundance of rhododendrons, and happy birds flitting among the trees and bushes.

HOW TO GET THERE: From I-80 take exit 50 and follow Route 191 north about 28 miles to South Sterling. Turn left onto Huckleberry Road. The inn is reached through stone pillars on the right in ½ mile.

# Carnegie House 📱
## State College, Pennsylvania 16803

INNKEEPERS: Peter and Helga Schmid

ADDRESS/TELEPHONE: 100 Cricklewood Drive; (814) 234–2424 or
(800) 229–5033; fax (814) 231–1299

E-MAIL: carnhouse@aol.com

WEB SITE: www.cmagic.com/ch/

ROOMS: 22, including 2 suites; all with private bath, air-conditioning,
telephone with dataport, and television; most with soaking tubs. Wheelchair accessible. Appropriate only for children old enough to have their
own room. No smoking inn.

RATES: $125 to $250, double occupancy; includes continental breakfast.
Two-night minimum some Penn State activity weekends.

OPEN: All year.

FACILITIES AND ACTIVITIES: Restaurant serving lunch and dinner
(prix fixe $32) Tuesday to Saturday and brunch Sunday; on two acres
adjacent to eighteen-hole Toftrees golf course, preferred privileges and
greens fees, plus shoe and club rentals, lessons; cross-country skiing in
winter. Nearby: Penn State University, Mount Nittany, Tussey Mountain
for downhill skiing, outlet malls, Palmer Museum of Art.

BUSINESS TRAVEL: Telephone with dataport and television in guest
rooms; some rooms with desk; conference room with full audiovisual
capabilities.

*P*eter and Helga Schmid love what they are doing so much that they
still believe themselves to be "retired." Peter had a distinguished
career with various hotel companies, and Carnegie House, of
which he and Helga are part owners, is a culmination of these years of experience and background. Although Peter and Helga are the hands-on innkeepers, the rest of the ownership team includes Philip Sieg, a local entrepreneur
and land developer, William Schreyer, chairman emeritus of Merrill Lynch,
and Joe Paterno, Penn State's head football coach for twenty-eight years.

Carnegie House is named for one of Pennsylvania's favorite sons, Andrew
Carnegie, who at one time owned the land the inn is located on. He called it
Pond Bank Farm, and the remnants of his iron-ore mining pits are still visible along the first nine holes of the adjacent Toftrees Golf Club. Scotland,
which is noted for its golf courses, and Carnegie, who emigrated to the

United States from Scotland and played some of Scotland's finest greens throughout his life, are the inspiration for the inn.

The inn is a new building that opened in 1994. It was built on a point of land overlooking the seventeenth tee of Toftrees Golf Club. It's motto *Ceud Mile Failte* (one hundred thousand welcomes) embodies the philosophy of Peter and Helga to a golf tee. They greet their guests with an open and friendly manner, proudly showing them the arched central hallways with their restful sitting areas (one with a fireplace) and the handsome library, which is paneled in golden oak, lined with book-filled shelves, and features a lovely fireplace, where a fire will be glowing in winter. The Thistle Bar, which is named for the national flower of Scotland, is cozy and warm, just like a Scottish pub should be. We had a great time looking at all the photos of Scottish golf courses on the walls.

The guest rooms are modern and exceptionally well designed. Each is distinctive and different. Room 14 is done in red and white Laura Ashley fabrics, Room 4 incorporates green and red taffeta and faille fabrics, and Room 5 is done in masculine shades of wine. There are period reproduction furnishings, cushioned window alcoves, and thoroughly impressive baths.

A buffet breakfast is served in the dining room every morning, as well as lunch and dinner Tuesday through Saturday and brunch on Sunday. The five-course table d'hôte menu includes such entrees as medallions of veal with a wild mushroom Madeira cream sauce and roasted breast of pheasant stuffed with chestnuts and arugula and served with a port wine sauce.

Before departing, do stop in the inn's wonderful gift shop, where you might purchase a piece of handcrafted beaded jewelry, a cookbook, or a T-shirt.

HOW TO GET THERE: From I–80 take exit 23 to Route 220 south and follow this for 16 miles to Route 322. Take Route 322 east toward State College. At the entrance take the Mt. Nittany Expressway (Route 322) to the Toftrees exit. Turn left onto Waddle Road and follow this north to Toftrees Avenue. Turn right and follow Toftrees Avenue to the first stop sign, which is Cricklewood Drive. The inn is on the left.

# Pace One Country Inn
## Thornton, Pennsylvania 19373

**INNKEEPER:** Ted Pace

**ADDRESS/TELEPHONE:** Glen Mills and Thornton Road (mailing address: P.O. Box 108); (610) 459-3702; fax (610) 558-0825

**WEB SITE:** www.tman/home/paceone

**ROOMS:** 6; all with private bath, air-conditioning, and telephone. Smoking permitted.

**RATES:** $75 to $95, double occupancy; includes continental breakfast.

**OPEN:** All year.

**FACILITIES AND ACTIVITIES:** Restaurant serving lunch (Monday to Friday) and dinner (entrees $17 to $24), Sunday brunch; on three acres with gardens and patio. Nearby: Longwood Gardens; Brandywine River Museum; Franklin Mint Museum; Winterthur Museum, Garden, and Library; Chaddsford Winery.

*T*ed Pace is a dreamer who makes dreams come true—at least his own. His personal goal originated when he was a child helping his dad in the family restaurant. He graduated from Penn State University in hotel and restaurant management to prepare himself for owning his own inn and restaurant. His dream took flower eighteen years ago when he serendipitously read a newspaper ad saying there was a 1740s fieldstone barn for rent for $300 a month. He impulsively signed a lease and opened a small restaurant three weeks later. And, as they say, the rest is history.

Now, after winning numerous preservation and architectural awards, the fieldstone barn, supported by hand-hewn beams, is the site of Pace One restaurant. The second floor of the barn contains private banquet rooms, and on the third floor there are six comfortable and uncluttered rooms offering overnight lodging. Furnished in a simple decor, the rooms contain pine floors, pine platforms beds with floral spreads, quilts on the walls, and neat and trim baths with pine floors.

The primary focus of Pace One is the wonderful restaurant. The decor highlights the warm stone walls and post-and-beam construction of the barn. There are pine floors and fresh flowers on the tables. The walls are decorated with Wyeth-style paintings done by the owner's wife, artist Sarah Yelman. Prints are available for purchase at the inn. A cozy bar, where numerous wines are offered by the glass, has a wood stove and a beamed ceiling.

We enjoyed a lovely dinner here one evening that started with duck ravioli, a dish of freshly made ravioli stuffed with raspberry-smoked duck and served with a Madeira sauce. My entree of char-grilled chicken was accompanied by a warm pear-and-cabbage salad. For dessert the old-fashioned chocolate fondue with fresh fruit was wonderful. The wine list is extensive and excellent. A Tuesday night prix fixe called Cork and Fork Night, which pairs innovative off-the-menu dishes with fine wines from the cellar, is exceptionally popular.

Pace One is on a peaceful country road in a tiny village surrounded by farms and estates, yet the many attractions of the Brandywine Valley are but a short drive away.

**HOW TO GET THERE:** From I–95 take exit 3 onto Conchester Road (Route 322). Follow this west for 10 miles to Route 1 (Route 322 ends here). Turn right onto Route 1 north and immediately get in the left lane. Take the first left, which is Thornton Road. The inn is on the right in 2 miles.

# B&B Inn of the Princess  and European Bakery
Uniontown, Pennsylvania 15401

**INNKEEPER:** Maryanne Meyer

**ADDRESS/TELEPHONE:** 181 West Main Street, National Heritage Road; (724) 425–0120; fax (724) 425–0124

**ROOMS:** 5; all with private bath, air-conditioning, television, telephone with dataport, radio, hair dryer, and robes; 2 with whirlpool tub. Wheelchair accessible. Pets permitted with prior permission. Smoking permitted.

**RATES:** $85 to $125; includes full breakfast.

**OPEN:** All year.

**FACILITIES AND ACTIVITIES:** Cafe serving lunch and restaurant, Chez Gerard, serving dinner (prix fixe $35); bakery cafe, large porch. Nearby: jogging trail, Christian Klay Winery, Frank Lloyd Wright's Fallingwater and Kentuck Knob, Laurel Caverns, whitewater rafting in Ohiopyle State Park.

**BUSINESS TRAVEL:** Telephone with dataport and television in all rooms, desk in 3 rooms; wake-up calls; fax and copier available; laundry service.

**RECOMMENDED COUNTRY INNS® TRAVELERS' CLUB BENEFIT:** 10 percent. Package featuring lodging with king-sized bed, full breakfast, afternoon tea, and six-course dinner with complimentary champagne for two at Chez Gerard; $200 plus tax and gratuities.

*T*his little French oasis in the heart of Pennsylvania's Laurel Highlands is no accident. It's the outcome of a happy sequence of circumstances: Girl from Uniontown becomes top model in New York and Paris. Boy from France meets girl in Paris. They fall in love, marry, and eventually return to her hometown to open a restaurant.

Gerard Meyer was no neophyte to the restaurant world. Acquainted with some of the greatest chefs of France (notably Paul Bocuse), he had helped organize a chef's award competition known as Bocuse d'Or. He established his romantic and intimate Uniontown restaurant in 1994 in a stone house that dates to 1790. There are stone fireplaces, country-French decor, and award-winning food. As a means of introducing the local area to French food and customs, he has an all-French staff—many of his "Culinary Ambassadors" have worked in top-notch French restaurants. They come here for a year to broaden their culinary education.

The inn, which is run by Maryanne, is located a few blocks up the hill from the restaurant. It also has an interesting history. A blocky brick building that dates to the 1880s, it was renovated in 1997 and opened as an inn. Its most notorious owner was a colorful local character known as Princess Lida of Thun und Taxis, the namesake of the inn.

Overnight guests enter a spacious entry hall. To the right a pretty, bright cafe has huge windows that flood the room with light and a bakery case filled with cheese, cakes, breads, and fruit. This is where breakfast is served in the morning. In addition to fruit, juice, and pastries, it might include pancakes or an omelette or eggs made to order.

There are two guest rooms on the main floor. Number Une is a huge room with a brick wall and wood shutters and is furnished with Mission-style furniture. Number Deux is my favorite. It also has Mission-style furniture and a collection of old hats decorating the wall. There's a lovely bath with a tile floor, a whirlpool tub, and a pedestal sink. The other three rooms are upstairs. All the baths are new and extremely well designed. The beds are dressed with Porthault linens and fragrant soaps are found in the baths.

There's also a nice upstairs lounge for guests that includes a wet bar, a refrigerator stocked with sodas and juices, and a tray holding a bottle of sherry and stemmed glasses.

The inn has a lovely deck, where a nice lunch is served if the weather is warm. Otherwise, lunch is served in the cafe. For Francophiles, the croque monsieur and the salade Niçoise will be reminders of France, although other sandwiches and salads are also on the menu. Dinner, *mais oui,* should definitely be taken at the restaurant, where you might end your meal, as we did, with a dessert of crepes Suzettes.

HOW TO GET THERE: From I-68 take exit 7 (Morgantown, West Virginia) onto Route 119 north. Follow this for 25 miles to Uniontown. Take the Main Street exit onto Route 40 Business (National Heritage Road). The inn is on the right at 181 West Main Street.

# Bridgeton House on the Delaware
## Upper Black Eddy, Pennsylvania 18972

INNKEEPERS: Bea and Charles Briggs

ADDRESS/TELEPHONE: 1525 River Road (Route 32); (610) 982–5856; fax (610) 982–5080

E-MAIL: bestinn1@epix.net

WEB SITE: www.bridgetonhouse.com

ROOMS: 11, including 4 suites and 1 cottage; all with private bath, air-conditioning, telephone with dataport, radio, and robes; 10 with porch or deck, 5 with television, 4 with VCR and/or fireplace, 2 with CD player and/or whirlpool tub. Children over the age of 8 welcome. No smoking inn.

RATES: $99 to $279, double occupancy; includes full breakfast and afternoon tea with cakes and sherry. Two-night minimum weekends; three-night minimum holidays.

OPEN: All year.

**FACILITIES AND ACTIVITIES:** Located on Delaware River; swimming and fishing from private dock. Nearby: restaurants, covered bridges, New Hope, Washington Crossing State Park, art galleries, theater, shopping, antiquing, tennis, river rafting.

**BUSINESS TRAVEL:** Telephone and dataport in all rooms; desk and television in 5 rooms, VCR in 4 rooms; early breakfast arranged.

Take one run-down 1836 terra-cotta apartment house overlooking the Delaware River, combine it with the creativity and entrepreneurial daring of an enthusiastic couple, and what do you get? In the case of Bridgeton House on the Delaware, a unique inn bursting with character in an imaginative/funky style.

Innkeepers Bea and Charles Briggs, working with Bea's cousin, artist Cheryl Raywood, have blended comfort and practicality with whimsy and artistry. After purchasing the building in 1981, Charles, who is a master craftsman, added windows and French doors along the back walls to bring more light into the rooms and built balconies that overlook the river.

Each guest room is painted in bold colors and decorated with imagination and flair. In one suite, for example, the top half of the walls are painted a mustard yellow and the lower half a combination of green, blue, and yellow checks. Other features include a corner fireplace and a screened porch. On our last visit, we stayed in Room 2, which has an entire palette of colors. There are magenta crown moldings stenciled in teal and framed walls of

mustard that are splash-painted in rust, ivory, brown, and seafoam-green and outlined in frames of magenta and teal. There's a high-headboard walnut Victorian bed, hooked scatter rugs, and pretty linens on the windows and bed. The room and the bath are tiny and the room's on the street, so it would

not be my number-one choice. Several of the rooms have mahogany cabinets handcrafted by Charles, and ten of the rooms have balconies or porches. My favorite room is the cozy Garrett Room on the third floor. It has pink sponged walls embellished with squiggles, a half-canopy bed, and a private and romantic porch. The top floor penthouse is fabulous and smashing in a black-and-white color scheme. It has a panoramic view of the Delaware River from huge Palladian windows and a terrific marble bath.

Although the inn is situated directly on the road, there's plenty of off-street parking behind. Guests enter the inn through a little sitting room that has white paneled walls and a dark wood floor, rustic furniture, and bird prints on the wall. There are a multitude of books, magazines, and newspapers to read. A cake or cookies and sherry are set out for arriving guests in a spacious room with a fireplace.

Breakfast is served in a heavily stenciled room containing a fireplace. Mismatched (but coordinated) painted or pine tables and chairs are set with a variety of pretty china. Breakfast selections include baked pear in a light cream sauce or baked apple with oats and walnuts. The entree might be a cheddar cheese-and-spinach omelette with Canadian bacon or orange-pecan waffles. Whichever you choose, the plate will be decorated with flowers and fruit, and a basket of lemon bread will be served with a round of butter on an ivy leaf.

Charles and Bea have been serving their own special blend of creative hospitality for eighteen years now, and there's still nothing like it that I've seen. Their sense of playfulness, whimsy, and guest comfort are unmatched.

**HOW TO GET THERE:** From I–78 take exit 15 (Clinton/Pittstown in New Jersey). Go to the light and turn left. Turn left at the end of the ramp onto Route 513 south and go for 11 miles to the New Jersey town of Frenchtown. Cross the Delaware River into Pennsylvania. Turn right onto Route 32 north and go 3½ miles to the inn, which is on the right.

# Whitewing Farm
# Bed & Breakfast
West Chester, Pennsylvania 19382

**INNKEEPERS:** Wanda and Ed DeSeta

**ADDRESS/TELEPHONE:** 370 Valley Road; (610) 388–2664; fax (610) 388–3650

**ROOMS:** 9, including 2 suites; all with private bath, air-conditioning, television, and radio; 2 with porch or patio and/or fireplace. Wheelchair accessible. No smoking inn.

**RATES:** $120 to $215, double occupancy, including full breakfast and afternoon tea. Two-night minimum weekends.

**OPEN:** All year except two weeks in February.

**FACILITIES AND ACTIVITIES:** On forty-three acres with extensive gardens including ponds, greenhouses, rose garden; tennis court, ten-hole chip-and-putt golf course, swimming pool, and Jacuzzi. Nearby: Longwood Gardens; Winterthur Museum, Gardens, and Library; Brandywine River Museum; Hagley Museum; Nemours.

"We'd never even stayed in a country inn ourselves when we decided to open one," laughed Wanda DeSeta. The gregarious couple must be possessed with an innate sense of hospitality then, because they obviously knew exactly what to do. This is one of the most gracious country inns I've ever stayed in. It's beautifully decorated, located in a quiet country setting in the Brandywine Valley with streams, ponds, gardens, and outbuildings, and yet it's utterly comfortable and unpretentious—just like the innkeepers.

We entered the spacious 1700s Pennsylvania farm house through the bright and welcoming kitchen. The aroma of a wonderful cake that was still warm from the oven wafted through the open door. It's obvious that the kitchen is where Wanda presides—unless she's in her greenhouse. All the gorgeous big orchids throughout the inn were grown by Wanda in the huge glass-enclosed building beside the former stables. You must pay the greenhouse a visit to see the pretty walls and cupboards that Wanda painted flowers and greenery on.

The house has three primary common rooms. The living room has a fireplace and an elegant reproduction of an eighteenth-century Rhode Island secretary, an original of which resides at Winterthur, as well as a huge collection of tin soldiers and papier-mâché santas. The cozy, pine-paneled den is filled with bookshelves laden with books. There's another fireplace here, and this is where the guest telephone is located. In the Pine Room, which serves as an informal living room, there are beamed ceilings, a wall of pine paneling, and an oak floor. It contains a pool table and a deep cooking fireplace, complete with the old wrought-iron

ratchets and a handsome woodstove. I'm not crazy about stuffed deer heads, but the taxidermy in the Pine Room is extraordinary—especially a leaping bobcat catching a quail. There's a television here, and the casual comfort of the room is a natural magnet. A sunroom has a flagstone floor and a wonderful view of a lily pond. Outside stone terraces oversee the sloping lawns and the ponds that are nourished by a stream that spills down the hillside, neatly contained in a stone trough.

The guest rooms are distributed throughout the property—in the carriage house, the stables, a gate house, and a cottage that overlooks the ponds. We stayed in the Paddock Room, which has green carpeting, yellow walls, a vaulted ceiling, and period reproduction furniture. A pretty blue-and-white chintz covered the bed and chairs. It was springtime and a bright bunch of daffodils sat on a table next to a dish of candy. The marble tile bath included a spacious shower for two and a counter that held another vase of fresh flowers. There were horsy prints on the walls and a beautiful leather statue of a horse—these one-of-a-kind artifacts are found in every guest room.

A formal breakfast is offered in the dining room every morning. Wanda loves to bake, and her lemon-poppyseed bread is the stuff legends are made of. We also munched on apple and blueberry breads while Ed told us about places to visit and things to do. Wanda fixed a wonderful version of stuffed French toast that she served with a blueberry sauce.

Frankly, I could describe much more, but then you really must stay here to see for yourself. Do take time to walk down to the pasture to feed a carrot to the pet cows, Mickey, Oreo, or Doublestuff. They'll come when you call. The farm is adjacent to Longwood Gardens and an easy drive to Winterthur.

HOW TO GET THERE: From I-95 in Wilmington, Delaware, take exit 7 and follow Route 52 north, crossing the state line into Pennsylvania. Continue on Route 52 for about 6 miles to Valley Road. Turn left onto Valley Road. The driveway to Whitewing Farm is on the right in ¾ mile.

# Select List of Other Inns
# in Pennsylvania

## Adamstown Inn

62 West Main Street
Adamstown, PA 19501
(717) 484–0800 or (800) 594–4808

*4 rooms; all with private bath; in brick house in Pennsylvania Dutch town called "antiques capital of the world."*

## Boxwood Inn

Diamond and Tobacco Road
Akron, PA 17501
(717) 859–3466 or (800) 238–3466

*5 rooms; all with private bath; in eighteenth-century stone farmhouse in Pennsylvania Dutch area.*

## Wydnor Hall Inn

3612 Old Philadelphia Pike
Bethlehem, PA 18015
(610) 867–6851 or (800) 839–0020

*5 rooms; all with private bath; in lovely country mansion owned by artist.*

## Brookview Manor B&B Inn

Route 447
Canadensis, PA 18325
(717) 595–2451 or (800) 585–7974

*10 rooms; all with private bath; in 1911 Victorian house in the Poconos.*

## Pennsbury Inn

883 Baltimore Pike
Chadds Ford, PA 19327
(610) 388–1435

*7 rooms; all with private bath; in stone house in Brandywine Valley owned by decorators.*

## Shultz Victorian Mansion B&B

756 Philadelphia Avenue (Route 11)
Chambersburg, PA 17201
(717) 263–3371

*9 rooms; all with private bath; in 1880s Victorian mansion.*

## The Columbian

360 Chestnut Street
Columbia, PA 17512
(717) 684–5869 or (800) 422–5869

*6 rooms; all with private bath; in Victorian mansion in Pennsylvania Dutch area.*

## Gateway Lodge

Route 36
Cooksburg, PA 16217
(814) 744–8017 or (800) 843–6862

*16 rooms; most with private bath; in rustic mountain resort; restaurant.*

## Highland Farms

70 East Road
Doylestown, PA 18901
(215) 340–1354

*4 rooms; 2 with private bath, 2 with shared bath; in Oscar Hammerstein's former home in Bucks County.*

## The Inn at Fordhook Farm

105 New Britain Road
Doylestown, PA 18901
(215) 345–1766

*7 rooms; 5 with private bath; in former home of Burpee family (Burpee seeds) in Bucks County.*

## Peace Valley B&B

75 Chapman Road
Doylestown, PA 18901
(215) 230–7711

*4 rooms; all with private bath; in stone house in Bucks County.*

## Pine Tree Farm

2155 Lower State Road
Doylestown, PA 18901
(215) 348-0632

*3 rooms; all with private bath; in stone house in Bucks County.*

## Clearview Farm

355 Clearview Road
Ephrata, PA 17522
(717) 733-6333

*5 rooms; all with private bath; in lovely farmhouse on 200 acres in Pennsylvania Dutch area.*

## Maplewood Farm B&B

5090 Durham Road
Gardenville, PA 18926
(215) 766-0477

*7 rooms; all with private bath; in country farmhouse in Bucks County decorated with pretty stencils.*

## Baldaderry Inn

40 Hospital Road
Gettysburg, PA 17325
(717) 337-1342 or (800) 220-0025

*8 rooms; all with private bath; in 1812 farmhouse used as field hospital during Battle of Gettysburg.*

## Battlefield B&B Inn

2264 Emmitsburg Road
Gettysburg, PA 17325
(717) 334-8804

*8 rooms; all with private bath; on forty-six-acre farm where guests are immersed in Civil War history.*

## The Doubleday Inn

104 Doubleday Avenue
Gettysburg, PA 17325
(717) 334-9119

*9 rooms; all with private bath; in B&B with Civil War theme.*

## The Old Appleford Inn

218 Carlisle Street
Gettysburg, PA 17325
(717) 337-1711 or (800) 275-3373

*11 rooms; all with private bath; in 1867 Victorian house in center of town.*

## Sweetwater Farm

50 Sweetwater Road
Glen Mills, PA 19342
(610) 459-4711

*11 rooms; most with private bath; on fifty acres in Brandywine Valley.*

## Nine Partners Inn

1 North Harmony Road
Harford, PA 18823
(717) 434-2233

*3 rooms; all with private bath; in Endless Mountains.*

## Harry Packer Mansion

Packer Hill
Jim Thorpe, PA 18229
(717) 325-8566

*13 rooms; 11 with private bath, 2 with shared bath; in fabulously ornate mansion—restoration still ongoing.*

## Bucksville House

Route 412 and Buck Drive
Kintnersville, NY 18930
(610) 847-8948

*5 rooms; all with private bath; in distinctive 1797 former stagecoach stop in country setting in Bucks County.*

## Lightfarm B&B

2042 Berger Road
Kintnersville, PA 18930
(215) 847-3276

*4 rooms; all with private bath; in historic B&B with architectural dig in Bucks County.*

## Gardens of Eden

1814 Eden Road
Lancaster, PA 17601
(717) 393–5179

*4 rooms; all with private bath; in beautiful stone house on banks of river with extensive gardens.*

## The Bridgetown Mill House

760 Langhorne-Newtown Road (Route 413)
Langhorne, PA 19047
(215) 752–8996

*5 rooms; 3 with private bath; fabulous restoration of eighteenth-century field-stone house on eight acres bordering stream.*

## Historic General Warren Inne

West Old Lancaster Highway
Malvern, PA 19355
(215) 296–3637

*8 rooms; all with private bath; in old hotel in Brandywine Valley.*

## Stoneymead

3719 Indian Spring Road
Mechanicsville, PA 18934
(215) 794–8081

*3 rooms; all with private bath; in beautiful stone house in rural Bucks County on fifty-three acres.*

## Mount Gretna Inn

16 West Kauffman Street
Mount Gretna, PA
(717) 964–3234 or (800) 277–6602

*9 rooms; all with private bath; in B&B that specializes in hiking and biking.*

## The Whitehall Inn

1370 Pineville Road
New Hope, PA 18938
(215) 598–7945

*6 rooms; 4 with private bath; in rural setting in Bucks County.*

## Joseph Ambler Inn

1005 Horsham Road
North Wales, PA 19454
(215) 362–7500

*28 rooms; all with private bath; on elegant country estate; restaurant.*

## The Inn at Oakmont

P.O. Box 103
Oakmont, PA 15139
(412) 828–0410

*8 rooms; all with private bath; in village just outside Pittsburgh.*

## Auldridge Mead

523 Geigel Hill Road
Ottsville, PA 18942
(215) 847–5842 or (800) 344–4171

*5 rooms; 3 with private bath; on horse farm in rural Bucks County.*

## The Gables B&B

4520 Chester Avenue
Philadelphia, PA 19143
(215) 662–1918

*10 rooms; 5 with private bath; in brick Victorian house.*

## Thomas Bond House

129 South 2nd Street
Philadelphia, PA 19106
(215) 923–8523 or (800) 845–BOND

*12 rooms; all with private bath; in brick house in historic district.*

## The Victorian Peacock Bed & Breakfast

309 East Dark Hollow Road
Pipersville, PA 18947
(215) 766–1356

*4 rooms; all with private bath; in beautifully restored Victorian house in rural Bucks County.*

## Appletree Bed & Breakfast

703 South Negley Avenue
Pittsburgh, PA 15232
(412) 661-0631

*4 rooms; all with private bath; in painted Victorian in Shady Side District.*

## Morning Glory Inn

2119 Sarah Street
Pittsburgh, PA 15232
(412) 431-1707

*5 rooms; all with private bath; in townhouse in Eastern Carson Street Historic District.*

## Shady Side B&B

5516 Maple Heights Road
Pittsburgh, PA 15232
(412) 683-6501

*8 rooms; all with private bath; in elegant Jacobean-style hilltop mansion near Shady Side District.*

## Plumsteadville Inn

Route 611 and Stump Road
Plumsteadville, PA 18949
(215) 766-7500

*Countryside inn and restaurant in Bucks County.*

## Tattersall Inn

Cafferty and River Road
Point Pleasant, PA 18950
(215) 297-8233 or (800) 297-4988

*4 rooms; all with private bath; in Bucks County.*

## Stone Pond Bed & Breakfast

5846 Durham Road (Route 412)
Riegelsville, PA 18077
(610) 346-6236

*4 rooms; all with private bath; in stone house in Bucks County countryside.*

## The Main Stay B&B

214 Main Street
Saxonburg, PA 16056
(412) 352–9363

*4 rooms; all with private bath; in historic town near Pittsburgh.*

## Foggy Mountain Lodge

RR#1 Box 190
Stahlstown, PA 15687
(724) 593–1000

*12 rooms; all with private bath; in inn located on forty-eight acres in Laurel Highlands area.*

## Liondale Farm

160 East Street Road
Unionville, PA 19375
(610) 444–7130

*4 rooms; share 2 baths; in charming B&B on farm in Brandywine Valley.*

## Thomas Lightfoote Inn

2887 South Reach Road
Williamsport, PA 17701
(717) 326–6396

*7 rooms; all with private bath; in historic former tavern dating to 1792 on Susquehanna River; restaurant.*

# Virginia &
# Washington, D.C.

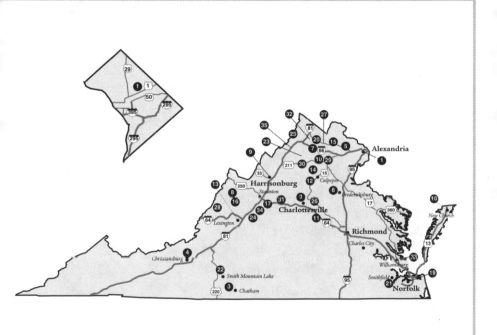

Alexandria

Harrisonburg

Staunton

Charlottesville

Richmond

Charles City

Lexington

Christiansburg

Williamsburg

Smith Mountain Lake

Smithfield

Chatham

Norfolk

New Church

Fredericksburg

Culpeper

# Virginia & Washington, D.C.

*Numbers on map refer to towns numbered below.*

## Virginia

1. Alexandria, Morrison House* .............................. 336
2. Charlottesville,
   Clifton: The Country Inn* ................................ 338
   Silver Thatch Inn ....................................... 341
   200 South Street Inn .................................... 343
3. Chatham, Eldon—The Inn at Chatham .................... 344
4. Christiansburg, The Oaks Victorian Inn* ................. 347
5. Fairfax, The Bailiwick Inn* ............................. 350
6. Fredericksburg, Richard Johnston Inn .................. 352
7. Front Royal, Killahevlin ................................ 353
8. Goshen, The Hummingbird Inn ........................... 355
9. Harrisonburg, The Joshua Wilton House ................. 357
10. Hume, The Inn at Fairfield Farm ....................... 359
11. Keswick, Keswick Hall* ................................. 361
12. Leon, The Suites at Prince Michel ...................... 363
13. Lexington, Brierley Hill Country Inn .................... 366
14. Locust Dale, The Inn at Meander Plantation* ........... 368
15. Middleburg, The Red Fox Inn .......................... 370
16. Millboro, Fort Lewis Lodge ............................ 372
17. Nellysford, The Mark Addy ............................. 374
18. New Church, The Garden and The Sea Inn .............. 376
19. Norfolk, The Page House Inn* .......................... 378
20. Paris, The Ashby Inn* ................................. 380
21. Smithfield,
    The Smithfield Inn ..................................... 382
    Smithfield Station ...................................... 385
22. Smith Mountain Lake, The Manor at Taylor's Store ......... 387
23. Stanley, Jordan Hollow Farm Inn ....................... 389

24. Steeles Tavern,

    Osceola Mill Country Inn ................................ 391

    Steeles Tavern Manor Country Inn ........................ 393

    Sugar Tree Inn* .......................................... 395

25. Stephens City, The Inn at Vaucluse Spring* ................. 397

26. Trevilians, Prospect Hill* .................................. 400

27. Upperville, 1763 Inn ....................................... 402

28. Warm Springs, The Inn at Gristmill Square.................. 404

29. Warrenton, The Black Horse Inn* ......................... 406

30. Washington,

    Bleu Rock Inn ........................................... 409

    The Inn at Little Washington* ........................... 412

31. Waynesboro, The Iris Inn* ................................. 414

32. White Post, L'Auberge Provençale ......................... 416

33. Williamsburg,

    The Cedars Bed & Breakfast ............................. 418

    Colonial Houses Historic Lodging......................... 420

34. Wintergreen, Trillium House ............................. 422

35. Woodstock, The Inn at Narrow Passage .................... 424

## Washington, D.C.

  1. Morrison-Clark .......................................... 426

*A Top Pick Inn

# Morrison House ⚄ ☎
## Alexandria, Virginia 22314

**GENERAL MANAGER:** Wanda McKeon; Stephen Beck, manager

**ADDRESS/TELEPHONE:** 116 South Alfred Street; (703) 838–8000; outside Virginia (800) 367–0800; fax (703) 684–6283

**E-MAIL:** mhsales@morrisonhouse.com

**WEB SITE:** www.morrisonhouse.com

**ROOMS:** 45, including 3 suites; all with private bath, air-conditioning, telephone with dataport, television, radio, hair dryer, and robes. Wheelchair accessible. Children welcome. Smoking permitted; designated nonsmoking rooms.

**RATES:** $150 to $295, double occupancy; rollaway in room, $20. Seasonal specials. Parking $5 a day.

**OPEN:** All year.

**FACILITIES AND ACTIVITIES:** Breakfast, lunch, afternoon tea ($19.50) dinner served in two restaurants: Elysium (three prix fixe menus offered nightly—three-course $37.50; four-course $45; five-course $55); Morrison House Grille (entrees $15 to $25); full beverage license; twenty-four-hour room service; elevator. Nearby: walking and carriage tours of Old Town Alexandria, Potomac River cruise.

**BUSINESS TRAVEL:** Located fifteen minutes from Washington, D.C. Telephone with dataport and desk in all rooms; fax and audiovisual equipment available; conference room; corporate rates.

*L*ooks can be deceiving. Morrison House looks as if it could have welcomed George Washington and Thomas Jefferson, but it was actually built in 1985.

The Federal-style brick mansion has a porticoed entrance supported by four Ionic columns. Black shutters accent the six-over-six windows, and twin staircases circle past a fountain sculpture up to the paneled front door. In the heart of old Alexandria, the inn would be equally comfortable in London.

A butler greets guests at the entrance, assists with bags, and in general performs duties similar to those of a concierge in larger hotels. Unfailing attention to English service (unobtrusive but thoughtful) extends to delivering messages to guests on silver trays.

Inside all is perfection. There's a marble floor in the foyer, oil paintings on the walls, and parquet floors covered with Oriental rugs. The intimate parlor, just off the lobby and where high tea is served every afternoon, has peach-colored damask and pale-green silk brocade sofas and chairs. The quiet mahogany-paneled library has damask drapes and elegant mahogany furniture. Baccarat crystal chandeliers and sconces enhance the feeling of being in an elegant home rather than a hotel. Fresh flowers in spectacular arrangements lend a soft accent.

Some guest rooms have four-poster or canopy beds, as well as armoires made especially for the inn. All have high-quality Federal reproductions. One bedroom has Wedgwood-blue walls with creamy white trim; another has a canopy bed on a rose carpet. The hallways are done in pale blues and yellows. Bathrooms are finished in Italian marble with brass fixtures. Each has a basket of Gilchrist and Soames amenities, as well as fluffy imported terry robes and full-length mirrors.

With soft leather chairs and a polished mahogany bar, Elysium, the inn's fine-dining restaurant, features three choices of prix-fixe menus nightly, all

under the expert direction of Chef Chris Brooks. We had a fabulous dinner here one evening with friends. Each course is accompanied by a wine suggestion appropriate for the dish, which allows you to sample wines you might not try if you were buying an entire bottle.

We started the meal with an appetizer of twice-cooked poblano peppers stuffed with crab and chevre; we enjoyed a glass of Oregon King Estate Vineyards Pinot Gris with that. Our first course was blackened bass with tomato confit, accompanied by a South African Stellenzicht Vineyards Chardonnay. Our entree was a dish of Muscovy duck breast glazed with caramelized rhubarb with foie gras and ginger noodles. The wine was a California Calera Pinot Noir. For dessert we had frozen honey almond mousse with a berry-port sauce, which was paired with Veuve Cliquot Pensardin *demi-sec* champagne. It was one of the finest dinners we've had.

For those who might prefer a more casual evening, the clubby mahogany-paneled Grille offers entrees such as pan-roasted Chilean sea bass with shaved fennel. Desserts include Tahitian vanilla crème brûlée and chocolate hazelnut tart with orange sauce.

**HOW TO GET THERE:** Ten-minute walk from Alexandria Metro Station. Ten-minute limo ride from National Airport. From I–495 south of Alexandria, exit Route 1 north and proceed to Prince Street, turn right, go 1 block, and turn left again on South Alfred. The inn is on the left.

# Clifton: The Country Inn
## Charlottesville, Virginia 22911

**INNKEEPERS:** Craig and Donna Hartman; Mitch and Emily Willey, proprietors

**ADDRESS/TELEPHONE:** 1296 Clifton Inn Drive; (804) 971–1800 or (888) 971–1800; fax (804) 971–7098

**E-MAIL:** reserve@cstone.net

**WEB SITE:** www.cliftoninn.com

**ROOMS:** 14, including 10 suites; all with private bath, air-conditioning, robes, and fireplace; 4 with porch or patio. Wheelchair accessible. Children welcome. No smoking inn.

**RATES:** $150 to $315, double occupancy; includes full breakfast and afternoon tea. Two-night minimum weekends.

**OPEN:** All year.

**FACILITIES AND ACTIVITIES:** Restaurant serving prix fixe dinner Friday and Saturday $58; Sunday to Thursday $48. On forty-eight acres with pool and waterfall, year-round heated spa, lake for fishing and tubing, croquet lawn, clay tennis court, gardens with gazebo. Nearby: Ash Lawn-Highland (home of James Monroe), Monticello (home of Thomas Jefferson), Mitchie Tavern, Montpelier (home of James Madison), Museum of American Frontier Culture, Charlottesville Ice Park, wineries.

**BUSINESS TRAVEL:** Desk in 6 rooms; telephone, dataport, fax, PC, copy machine, laser printer available; meeting rooms.

*W*e came for a post-holiday weekend getaway with friends. A winter storm had passed and daytime temperatures hovered in the 50s, while at night they dipped to below freezing. The countryside surrounding Charlottesville is laced with historic estates, often hidden away along winding country roads that pass fields of grazing cattle and horses. Just outside the town proper, Clifton is announced by a discreet sign at the entrance to a tree-shrouded drive. The driveway leads through a historic forty-eight-acre estate where Thomas Jefferson and other American luminaries were frequent visitors.

The manor house, a combination of Federal and Colonial Revival styles with a series of boxed columns across the front, was built in 1799 by Thomas Mann Randolph, who married Martha Jefferson, Thomas Jefferson's daughter. Randolph eventually became Governor of Virginia, a member of the Virginia House of Delegates, and a member of the U.S. Congress.

His grand house has been enlarged and embellished numerous times throughout the years, yet it retains its colonial ambience. The polished pine floors and the simple Federal fireplace mantels date to the late 1700s, while the fan- and side-lights are more recent additions. For comfort and style, however, the inn is strictly twentieth century.

In the elegant entry the walls are sponge-painted an apricot color, and there's a massive floral display on a Federal sideboard. The drawing room has a grand piano and sofas and chairs grouped near a gracious fireplace. The library is furnished with green leather chairs, another fireplace, and numerous books in built-in cases. Games are available here also for the enjoyment of the guests. To the rear an enclosed stone terrace has an abundance of plants, iron tables and chairs, and a fireplace at one end. This is where breakfast is served, overlooking the formal gardens and gazebo, and dinner on occasion as well.

The guest rooms all have fireplaces and are furnished with antiques. Room 5 has a window seat overlooking the croquet lawn, a sofa in pink damask, and a pencil-post bed. The quaint rooms in the Old Livery Buildings overlook the lake. They have bead-board walls and cabbage rose fabric covering sofas and chairs in the sitting areas, which also have fireplaces. Beds are located on raised platforms; baths have old-fashioned tubs with bead-board surrounds, tiled showers, and built-in benches. On this visit we stayed in Blue Ridge, a funky room in the main house, with an entrance through a private sunporch that leads through the bathroom. As with all the rooms it's loaded with charm, but you must do some gymnastics to crawl into the deep soaking tub, and the commode is hidden behind a pair of louvered doors. The double-sized tiled shower, however, has wonderful multiple shower-heads, and the antique bed, which sits next to the fireplace, is dressed with fine linens.

The estate was turned into an inn in 1987, but since Craig Hartman became the innkeeper in 1992, it's gained a wide following for its distinguished cuisine as well as its rooms. Craig has a notable restaurant background and he's a graduate of the Culinary Institute of America. Dinner is an event. We dressed in our finest and gathered in the drawing room for wine. Craig soon came in and described each of the items on tonight's menu. As we listened to the description of the luscious courses we were about to sample, we ate pheasant liver mousse on toast points. We were then escorted to our tables in the dining rooms.

We dined on the enclosed stone-floored terrace, which has paned windows, a shingled wall, and a stone fireplace. At our table an appetizer of thinly sliced smoked salmon with long threads of portobello mushrooms and little potato cakes waited. Our soup, a fabulous marriage of buttered squash and apple bisque, followed. A salad of organic greens with blue cheese and walnuts, lightly drizzled with a pungent dressing, was next, trailed by a tiny intermezzo of warm dried fruits macerated in cognac. Our entree was a thick fillet of mahi mahi in a tarragon-truffle butter sauce with Yukon gold potatoes, shoestring carrots, and *haricot verts*. The perfect finale to this perfect meal consisted of a white chocolate mousse with fresh berries and three sauces. It was served with a beautiful mint flower that perfumed the entire dish. Naturally, there's a fine wine list.

Were Thomas Jefferson still alive, I have no doubt this would be his favorite place to dine.

HOW TO GET THERE: From I-64 east of Charlottesville, take exit 25 onto Route 250 south. Go 2 miles and turn right onto Route 729. Travel for ¼ mile and turn left at the discreet sign into the inn's driveway.

## Creative Moments

Craig Hartman loves a challenge, so one time when he was asked to create a memorable meal for a man who wanted to ask his girlfriend to marry him, Craig did the following. When it was time for dessert, Craig had prepared an elaborate cake with a chocolate filigree rose standing in the center. The sparkling engagement ring was hanging from the rose. It was presented to the couple at the table and amidst a very tender moment, the lady tearfully said "yes."

# Silver Thatch Inn
## Charlottesville, Virginia 22911-7422

**INNKEEPERS:** Jim and Terri Petrovits

**ADDRESS/TELEPHONE:** 3001 Hollymead Drive; (804) 978–4686; fax (804) 973–6156

**ROOMS:** 7; all with private bath and air-conditioning; 4 with fireplace. Children over the age of 8 welcome. No smoking inn.

**RATES:** $135 to $170, double occupancy; includes continental breakfast. Two-night minimum weekends April to June and September to November.

**OPEN:** All year.

**FACILITIES AND ACTIVITIES:** Dinner Tuesday to Saturday (entrees $16 to $25); tavern. Swimming pool (shared with neighborhood). Nearby: Monticello, Ash Lawn-Highland, University of Virginia, Blue Ridge Parkway, vineyards, antiquing.

'll never forget my first visit to the Silver Thatch Inn. A freshly baked sheet of chocolate chip cookies had just emerged from the oven, and the lovely aroma was as welcoming as a visit to grandmother's house. But the inn held no resemblance to *my* grandmother's house.

The original part of the inn was built by German mercenaries, who were captured in the Battle of Saratoga (New York) during the Revolutionary War and marched to Virginia. This section, now called the Hessian Room, is built of logs and mortar. In 1812 the center clapboard section was built, and the buildings housed a boys' school. Later the house and its surrounding 300 acres were used as a tobacco or melon farm until, in 1984, it became an inn. Jim and Terri Petrovits purchased it in 1998.

The guest rooms are charming; each is named for a president. Three are in the main building and four are in an adjacent cottage. In the main building Jefferson has a four-poster canopy bed, a carved armoire, and a fireplace; Madison has a pencil-post canopy bed, a fireplace, and a lovely view across the courtyard. Washington is the grandest of the cottage accommodations, with a magnificent matching bedroom suite that includes a burled mahogany armoire, a marble-topped dresser, and an intricately carved mahogany headboard.

Dinner is served in three rooms; two of them have fireplaces, and the third is the sunroom, where breakfast is also served. One night we started with sautéed sweetbreads served with caramelized onions, apples, and pecans and topped with a Riesling sauce. One of our entrees consisted of a grilled breast of duck with a roasted garlic–saffron sauce and pearl couscous; the other of us had grilled Atlantic salmon with a mango–red pepper sauce, rice pilaf, and pickled daikon. For dessert the triple-layered chocolate mousse, served in a stemmed glass, won raves.

The Silver Thatch Inn is in an unusual setting. This authentic country inn, parts of which date to 1780, is encircled by modern homes on spacious lots. Nevertheless they all blend harmoniously into a secluded little neighborhood, where the community swimming pool and tennis court are shared by inn guests.

HOW TO GET THERE: From Washington, D.C., take I–66 west to exit 43 (Gainsville). Follow Route 29 south for about 85 miles. Continue on Route 29 for 1 mile past the Charlottesville Airport (the inn is 7 miles north of Charlottesville). At a traffic light turn left onto Hollymead Drive (Route 1520). The inn is ²⁄₁₀ mile up the hill on the right.

# 200 South Street Inn
## Charlottesville, Virginia 22902

**INNKEEPERS:** Brendan and Jenny Clancy

**ADDRESS/TELEPHONE:** 200 South Street; (804) 979-0200 or (800) 964-7008; fax (804) 979-4403

**E-MAIL:** clancyb@efw.com

**WEB SITE:** www.southstreetinn.com

**ROOMS:** 20, including 2 suites; all with private bath, air-conditioning, telephone with dataport, television, and radio; 8 with fireplace, 6 with whirlpool tub. Wheelchair accessible. Children welcome. Restricted smoking.

**RATES:** $105 to $195, double occupancy; includes continental breakfast. Two-night minimum weekends April, May, and September to November.

**OPEN:** All year.

**FACILITIES AND ACTIVITIES:** Patio, wraparound veranda, access to full-service health club. Nearby: located in downtown Charlottesville near Charlottesville's spectacular Ice Park, with indoor ice skating and skating lessons. Restaurants, art galleries, and boutiques are within a block. Virginia has more than sixty wineries, many of them near Charlottesville. Tours are encouraged.

**BUSINESS TRAVEL:** In-town location, convenient to downtown businesses. Telephone with dataport and television in all rooms; desk in 10 rooms; fax and concierge service available.

*T*he buttercup-yellow houses with white trim—one in brick and the other in clapboard—sit beside each other behind fancy wrought-iron fences on a quiet back street in Charlottesville, close to the new mall with its shops, restaurants, and wonderful Ice Park. The huge verandas, furnished with sparkling white wicker, offer refreshing places to relax before venturing out in the morning or before going out to dinner. If you want a downtown location, this can't be beat.

Jenny and Brendan Clancy have owned the inn since 1991, and they have renovated and decorated in a sophisticated blend of modern comfort and old-world elegance. There are stunning antiques. There's a charming, book-case-filled library, for example, painted a deep tomato red, with a walnut gateleg table as a centerpiece. On one recent visit wine and cheese were waiting in this urbane retreat for all takers. Breakfast can be eaten here or on the back veranda, which has more white wicker and overlooks the garden. A gallery on the first floor has walls lined with paintings of exotic animals. Upstairs there's a hideaway study where guests can watch television.

The guest rooms feature English and Belgian antiques. Several rooms have canopy beds, gas fireplaces, and fabulously carved armoires. There are polished wide-plank floors topped by kilims. The baths are beautifully finished with tile floors and brass fixtures, and six have whirlpool tubs.

If you are a light sleeper, you should know that a secondary line of the railroad runs behind the inn, although trains generally do not run at night.

**HOW TO GET THERE:** From Washington, D.C., take I-66 to U.S. 29 south. Take Route 250 bypass east to the third traffic light. Turn right onto McIntire Road. At the second traffic light, turn left onto South Street. Travel ⅔ block and turn into the driveway on the right between two gateposts. Park in the inn's parking lot and come in the red door in back.

# Eldon—The Inn at Chatham
## Chatham, Virginia 24531

**INNKEEPERS:** Joy and Bob Lemm

**ADDRESS/TELEPHONE:** 1037 Chalk Level Road (SR 685);
(804) 432–0935; restaurant (804) 432–0934

**E-MAIL:** eldoninn@gamewood.net

**WEB SITE:** www.inngetaways.com

**ROOMS:** 4, including 2 suites; 2 with private bath; all with air-conditioning, 3 with telephone, television, radio, porch, and decorative fireplace. Children over the age of 12 welcome. No smoking inn.

**RATES:** $70 to $85, double occupancy; includes full breakfast.

**OPEN:** All year.

**FACILITIES AND ACTIVITIES:** Restaurant serving dinner Wednesday to Saturday (entrees $11 to $20) and Sunday Brunch (prix fixe $9.95); wine parlor. On thirteen and one-half acres with formal English gardens, orchard, herb and vegetable gardens, swimming pool, fishpond with fountain, croquet, bocci. Nearby: Chatham Hall, a private girls' school;

Hargrave Military Academy; Danville (last capital of the Confederacy); wineries, antiquing, fishing, golfing.

**BUSINESS TRAVEL:** Meeting room, telephone, and television in most rooms.

*C*hatham is located in a little-traveled region of Virginia known as Southside—an area of lovely rolling fields of tobacco and textile plants almost on the North Carolina border. As one brochure said of Pittsylvania County, "Its bread and butter is farming." Nevertheless Chatham is a pretty little town with a handsome Greek Revival courthouse with an ornate gold-leafed ceiling, a brick courtyard with a fountain, and a lovely park.

Eldon—The Inn at Chatham is a distinguished white, thirteen-room mansion with a broad front veranda supported by fluted columns. The brick walkway in front skirts a fish pond and fountain. The house was built by Chatham attorney James Whittle in 1835 as the centerpiece of his 500-acre tobacco plantation. Its most prominent owner was Claude A. Swanson, a man who served as Virginia's governor from 1906 to 1910 and also held positions as congressman, senator, and Secretary of the Navy. When Joy and Bob Lemm purchased the estate in 1991, however, although it ended their five-year search for the "perfect" inn, it took them a full year to upgrade the heating, wiring, plumbing, and structure to the point where it could be used.

Today the inn features a fine-dining room where the Lemm's son, Joel Wesley, a graduate of the Culinary Institute of America, and his wife and pastry chef, Peggy, preside. Dinner is served in three elegant dining rooms (beautiful fluted columns lead the way to the library dining room) or on the terrace. Perhaps you'll sample Maryland crab cakes with sundried tomato tartar sauce followed by grilled quail stuffed with fruit dressing and accompanied by roasted apple puree. Desserts can be selected from the pastry cart and may include chocolate truffle cake with raspberry sauce, tiramisu, or coconut-apricot layer cake.

The guest rooms, which are located upstairs in the inn, are furnished with fine antiques. The James Whittle Guest Room has a wonderful Georgian full-tester bed and an antique armoire; the Whitehead Guest Suite, which has two connected rooms that share a large bath, has mahogany twin beds in one room and a sleigh bed in the other. It's decorated with red French toile wallpaper. My favorite room, however, is the Governor Swanson Room, which has a fabulous four-poster, carved-cherry tobacco bed and an antique dresser. It's decorated in blue and white, and Joy has painted blue stencils on the white walls.

Breakfast is Joy's specialty. In addition to fresh fruit, juice, and muffins, she may prepare eggs Benedict, a spinach frittata, or sour-cream Belgium waffles.

**HOW TO GET THERE:** From Lynchburg take Route 29 south for 48 miles to Chatham. From Chatham follow State Road 685 (Chalk Level Road) east ¹/₁₀ mile to the inn.

## Ode to Eldon

Visitors to Eldon—The Inn at Chatham have been so moved by the historic buildings and their surroundings that several have composed poems in its behalf. The following is one of them.

*Broad-roofed and welcoming it stands,*

*Like a kind host, with out-stretched hands,*

*To greet all those who enter in,*

*Comrade or stranger, friend or kin.*

*Sometimes within it, and around,*

*The happy children's voices sound.*

*Sometimes o'er those who lie asleep,*

*It seems a midnight watch to keep.*

*It offers balm for bitter grief,*

*For troubled minds a sweet relief.*

*And if as some, half jesting, say*

*Within these rooms and hallways stray*

*Sad visitants from days long past,*

*May they too here find peace at last.*

# The Oaks Victorian Inn
## Christiansburg, Virginia 24073

**INNKEEPERS:** Margaret and Tom Ray

**ADDRESS/TELEPHONE:** 311 East Main Street; (540) 381–1500 or (800) 336–OAKS; fax (540) 381–3036

**WEB SITE:** www.bbhost.com/theoaksinn

**ROOMS:** 7; all with private bath, air-conditioning, private line telephones with dataport, television, desk, radio, minirefrigerator, and robes; 5 with fireplace, 3 with VCR, 2 with whirlpool tub. Children over the age of 12 welcome. No smoking inn.

**RATES:** $115 to $160, double occupancy; $85 single occupancy Sunday to Thursday; all include full breakfast. Additional person $15. Two-night minimum in October and special-event weekends.

**OPEN:** All year, except first two weeks in January.

**FACILITIES AND ACTIVITIES:** Parlor, patio, hot tub, bicycles available. Nearby: state-of-the-art fitness center, bicycle trails, 26 miles to Blue Ridge Parkway; Transportation Museum in Roanoke, antiquing, outlet shopping, Long Way Home Outdoor Drama; hiking, Mill Mountain Theatre, Virginia Tech University, Radford University.

**BUSINESS TRAVEL:** Desk, private line telephone with dataport, television, and minirefrigerator in all rooms. Corporate rates; valet service.

*T*here had been a terrific snow storm several days earlier, and mounds of freshly plowed snow lined the streets of Christiansburg. Twilight had turned the evening into shades of black and white. And there, straight ahead at the fork in the road, stood a magical and welcoming scene. The Oaks Victorian Inn was brilliantly lighted from top to bottom, its lights twinkling in the reflection of the pristine white snow. This was my first sight of The Oaks—an unforgettable one.

Presided over by seven majestic white oak trees (one is 400 years old), the grand Victorian is a medley of porches and turrets and gables and bays. Tom and Margaret bought the house in 1989, and today it's hard to imagine the crumbling edifice they purchased, since the restoration is so perfect in every way. The house is now listed on the National Register of Historic Places.

From the grand wraparound porch, with its Kennedy rockers mingled with white wicker, you can admire the lovely gardens, and in the back there's a brick terrace with wrought-iron tables and chairs, a fish pond with a fountain, and a gazebo containing a hot tub.

The common rooms include a rust-colored study with an elegant antique walnut buffet and a fireplace. Family photos grace the mantel. A parlor is entered beneath fanciful Victorian fretwork. There are turret windows, another fireplace, and an oil painting of a beautiful young woman. There are wonderful examples of stained glass in the house, especially in the stair landing.

The guest rooms are equally impressive. Bonnie Victoria, on the second floor, is a favorite. It has a  bow-top bed with a fishnet canopy and a gas fireplace and two baths—one for him and one for her. It's decorated in rich hues of burgundy, green, and cream. Both the Julia Pierce and the Major Pierce rooms have fabulous hand-painted slate fireplace mantels. Julia Pierce has an elegant carved Victorian bed, wicker chairs, a polished cherry chest dating to 1820, and a romantic bath with a Jacuzzi for two. Major Pierce has an iron canopy bed and a diamond-patterned quilt. A stained-glass lamp and an oak chest of drawers complete the picture. I believe my favorite room, however, is the hideaway called Lady Melodie's Turret, located on the third floor. The blue-and-white motif is richly used on the half-canopy bed and the tiles of the bath. It's also carried out in a Victorian lamp with a deep blue stained-glass shade. A table and chair in the turret offer the ideal vantage for watching the sunset.

If you want to be totally pampered, I can't imagine a better place to come. The warmth and solicitousness of Tom and Margaret are incredible. I heard them ask one guest, "Can we turn on your VCR for you?" To another they said, "Your private refrigerator is already stocked with soft drinks, but since it was a special occasion, we thought we'd tuck in a bottle of our own wine." Special chocolates and a decanter of sherry await bedside in the evening.

Margaret turns breakfast into an event. It's served by candlelight in an oak-floored sunroom that has another fireplace. She uses her elegant sterling silver and antique Dresden china that once belonged to Tom's grandmother. She might feature shirred eggs in a spinach nest and whole-wheat-buttermilk pancakes topped by a praline syrup with toasted pecans and maple cream for entrees.

**HOW TO GET THERE:** From I-81 take exit 114. Turn left if approaching from the south and right if coming from the north, and you will be on Main Street. Continue for approximately 2 miles to fork at Park and Main Streets. Bear right onto Park, then left into The Oaks driveway.

# Go West, Young Man, and Grow Up with the Country

These famous words by Horace Greeley were taken literally by thousands of men and women in the early nineteenth century. The old Indian trail that is now Route 11, which hugged the valley between the Shenandoah Mountains and the Blue Ridge, was known at that time as the Wilderness Trail. It led through Christiansburg and eventually through the Cumberland Gap to the great plains.

In Christiansburg the Wilderness Trail passed along a route that is now the Main Street of the town—and directly past The Oaks Victorian Inn. Among the legendary pioneers who made this journey, Lewis and Clark were the first. They were eventually followed by Daniel Boone and Davey Crockett. Records even show that Abraham Lincoln's father came this route with his family when they migrated to their new home in Illinois.

# The Bailiwick Inn
## Fairfax, Virginia 22030

INNKEEPERS: Bob and Annette Bradley

ADDRESS/TELEPHONE: 4023 Chain Bridge Road; (703) 691–2266 or (800) 366–7666; fax (703) 934–2112

ROOMS: 14, including 1 suite; all with private bath, private line telephone, and air-conditioning; 10 with television, 4 with fireplace and VCR, 2 with whirlpool bath. Wheelchair access. No smoking inn. Children welcome.

RATES: $130 to $299, double occupancy; includes full breakfast and afternoon tea.

OPEN: All year.

FACILITIES AND ACTIVITIES: Belvoir Dining Room serving lunch Fridays (prix fixe $20 to $25); afternoon tea Thursday or Sunday (prix fixe $20); and dinner Wednesday, Thursday, and Sunday (prix fixe $45); Friday and Saturday (prix fixe $55); health club available to guests. Nearby: restaurants (within walking distance), Washington, D.C., Manassas Civil War Park, George Mason University, Mount Vernon, swimming, golf, tennis, historic sites.

BUSINESS TRAVEL: Located 17 miles from Washington, D.C. Telephone in room; desk in 11 rooms; fax and secretarial services available; corporate rates.

*A* fine historic restoration always captures my fancy, but The Baliwick Inn is far more than a physical restoration of a building. Each of the guest rooms is named for a famous Virginian, and they are decorated just as that individual decorated his or her own home. Thomas Jefferson, for example, features his favorite colors of red and gold and is modeled after his bedroom at Monticello. The pretty Antonia Ford room has a sitting room with Chippendale furnishings, a bedroom with dormer windows, and a bath with a Jacuzzi (a slight digression from the period), but this is the most-often requested room for honeymooning couples. All the rooms feature downy featherbeds and luxurious linens.

Thoughtful little touches include a glass jar of freshly baked cookies on an upstairs chest and chocolates on the pillow at night.

The common rooms are equally refined. In the two parlors Sheraton and Duncan Phyfe tables gleam, and chairs and sofas are upholstered in raspberry and ivory damasks. Fires crackle in the elegant fireplaces and museum-quality oil paintings hang on the walls.

Dinner is served Wednesdays through Sundays in the two-tiered dining room and also in the walled English courtyard with its bubbling fountain

when the weather is nice. The meal is relaxed and elegant. It will start with a glass of wine and hors d'oeuvres in the parlor. The four-course meal might begin with a tuna tartare salad dressed with a ginger curry sauce and accompanied by avocado and a confetti of red and yellow peppers or a saffron ravioli filled with shrimp, scallop, and tarragon. You might try a light bisque next, followed by a tenderloin of Black Angus beef with a sauce bordelaise or a seared fillet of salmon with a tomato buerre blanc. For dessert a warm-centered chocolate fondant cake is excellent, but I had one of the best desserts of my life here once—a small crème brûlée that had a soft chocolate center. It was outstanding!

Historic Fairfax has streets lined with Federal-style brick homes and a charming downtown of interesting shops and restaurants. The old courthouse (where George and Martha Washington's wills are on file) sits across the street. The inn is located in the gracious home that Joshua Gunnell built sometime between 1800 and 1812 with bricks he imported from England. Significant additions were made to the house over the years, but it remains true to its Federal origins. The house, listed on the National Register of Historic Places, became The Bailiwick Inn in 1989.

HOW TO GET THERE: From I–66 take exit 60 onto Route 123 east (Chain Bridge Road) toward George Mason University. It's 1½ miles to the inn, which is opposite the old courthouse. Off-street parking behind the inn.

# Richard Johnston Inn

## Fredericksburg, Virginia 22401

**INNKEEPER:** Susan T. Williams

**ADDRESS/TELEPHONE:** 711 Caroline Street; (540) 899–7606

**E-MAIL:** rjinn@aol.com

**ROOMS:** 9, including 2 suites; all with private bath and air-conditioning; 4 with television and minirefrigerator. No smoking inn. Children welcome.

**RATES:** $95 to $145, double occupancy; includes continental breakfast.

**OPEN:** All year except one week at Thanksgiving.

**FACILITIES AND ACTIVITIES:** Courtyard. Nearby: golf; historic sites include Ferry Farm, Kenmore, James Monroe Museum, Belmont, and Fredericksburg/Spotsylvania National Military Park.

When they say in Fredericksburg that "George Washington slept here," it's probably true. This is George Washington's hometown. The streets, which are lined with handsome brick buildings, look much as they did when George Washington and James Monroe walked here. You can visit Washington's boyhood home, Ferry Farm, and the home that he later bought for his mother. In addition you can tour Kenmore, the elaborate and elegant plantation house that his sister occupied, and Rising Sun Tavern, where his brother once lived.

The Richard Johnston Inn witnessed much of this history. Located in a pair of brick townhouses in the heart of town—one built in 1754 and the other in 1780—they were occupied for many years by Richard Johnston, who was the mayor of Fredericksburg in 1809 and 1810. Susan Williams has been the owner and innkeeper since 1992.

The inn has handsome main-floor rooms that are furnished with Federal-period antiques and have 12-foot ceilings. The living room has a fireplace, an Oriental rug on heart-pine floors, and a navy-and-rose color scheme. One of the most appreciated amenities of the inn is its large parking lot in back, however, because it is sometimes difficult to find parking space on the busy streets.

The guest rooms are furnished with fine antiques and period reproductions. Room 5 has a handsome, ornately carved 1830s plantation-style bed, 12-foot ceilings, and a pretty bath; but one of my favorites is Room 9, which is located in the original brick-floored kitchen and has two antique double beds. Two suites on the ground floor have their own entrances off the courtyard and contain wet bars, refrigerators, and televisions. Although every room has a private bath, several are located across the hallway from the room.

Breakfast is served at a polished cherry Duncan Phyfe table in the formal dining room. Susan puts out her fine china, silver, and linens and serves a continental breakfast of freshly baked muffins and breads, fruit, juice, and coffee.

Following breakfast guests can step right outside the inn's front door to walk in the path of history.

HOW TO GET THERE: From I–95 take exit 130A onto Route 3 east and travel 3 miles to Fredericksburg. Follow the signs to the Fredericksburg Visitor Center. The inn is across the street and has a parking lot just behind, on Sophia Street.

# Killahevlin
## Front Royal, Virginia 22630

INNKEEPERS: Susan and John Lang

ADDRESS/TELEPHONE: 1401 North Royal Avenue; (540) 636–7335 or (800) 847–6132; fax (540) 636–8694

E-MAIL: kllhvln@shentel.net

WEB SITE: www.shenwebworks.com:8001/kllhvln

ROOMS: 6, including 2 suites; all with air-conditioning, telephone, and fireplace; 5 with whirlpool tub, 2 with TV. Children over the age of 12 welcome. No smoking inn.

RATES: $120 to $200, double occupancy; includes full breakfast. Two-night minimum weekends April to November and major holidays.

OPEN: All year.

**FACILITIES AND ACTIVITIES:** On three acres with gazebos, pond, and waterfall. Nearby: Massanutten and Blue Ridge Mountains, Belle Grove Plantation, Skyline Drive, Luray Caverns, Shenandoah National Park, golfing, hiking, canoeing, tennis.

**BUSINESS TRAVEL:** Desks in all rooms; corporate rates, meeting room.

*S*ituated on the highest point of land in the area to take advantage of the spectacular views of the Blue Ridge and Massanutten Mountains, the brick Edwardian manor house was built in 1905 by William Edward Carson, who made his fortune quarrying limestone. He named the house for a favorite childhood haunt in Northern Ireland. When Susan and John Lang first saw the house in 1990, they knew it was perfect for the inn they wanted to create. They decided to capitalize on its Irish heritage, since they claim Irish ancestry themselves.

The charming Irish Pub is the first example of their creativity that guests encounter. Guests can step up to the oak bar with its brass footrail and help themselves to Irish draft beer on tap, as well as wine, soft drinks, and snacks. Or they can sit at one of the tables to play a game of backgammon or cribbage. The elegantly restored house, which has beautiful maple floors throughout the first floor, also includes a formal parlor with a lovely fireplace and a reception room, which has another fireplace.

A full breakfast is served in the formal dining room. It will include freshly squeezed juices, fresh fruit, cereals, gourmet coffee and tea, and Susan's homemade muffins and breads, as well as, perhaps, eggs Benedict or Irish-style scrambled eggs and sausage.

The guest rooms are spacious and lovely. Four rooms are located on the second floor of the main house. My two favorites are the Blue Room, which has a four-poster bed facing the fireplace, a bath with a two-person indigo-blue whirlpool tub, and a private porch offering mountain and sunset views, and the Raspberry Room, which has a marvelous, antique high four-poster bed and an antique French armoire. Antique tiles surround the fireplace and there's a columned and mirrored mantel. This bath has a restored antique pedestal sink and a raspberry-colored double whirlpool tub.

Behind the house, with even more beautiful views of the mountains, there are two suites in a brick building with a three-story tower that once was used to collect rainwater to irrigate the grounds. The Plum Cottage Suite has hand-painted period furniture in numerous shades of plum. A private porch faces south, and there's a fireplace in the living room with an antique mantel, as well as a television. The bath has a double whirlpool tub and also provides access to the room's north-facing porch. The Jade Tree Suite, on the second floor, also has two porches. From the entrance a winding staircase leads to the top of the tower, where the views are breathtaking.

The inn has been impeccably restored in every detail and is listed on the National Register of Historic Places.

HOW TO GET THERE: From I-66 take exit 6 and turn south (right) onto Route 522/340. Travel approximately 2 miles and turn left onto Fifteenth Street, which dead ends at North Royal Avenue. Turn left onto North Royal Avenue and then turn right into the first driveway. (Watch for KILLAHEVLIN on the mail box.)

# The Hummingbird Inn
Goshen, Virginia 24439

INNKEEPERS: Diana and Jeremy Robinson

ADDRESS/TELEPHONE: 30 Wood Lane (mailing address: P.O. Box 147); (540) 997-9065 or (800) 397-3214; fax (540) 997-0289

E-MAIL: hmgbird@cfw.com

WEB SITE: www.hummingbirdinn.com

ROOMS: 5; all with private bath and air-conditioning; 2 with fireplace and Jacuzzi. Children over the age of 12 welcome. Dogs permitted with prior permission. No smoking inn.

RATES: $105 to $145, double occupancy; includes full breakfast. Two-night minimum weekends May to November.

OPEN: All year.

FACILITIES AND ACTIVITIES: Four-course dinner served Saturday nights with advance reservations (prix fixe $35); on one and three-tenths acres of landscaped grounds; in-room massages arranged. Nearby: historic sights in Lexington including the Stonewall Jackson House, Museum, and Memorial Cemetery; the Robert E. Lee Chapel; Virginia Military Institute; and Washington and Lee University; baths at Warm Springs, Garth Newell Music Center, hiking, fishing, biking, horseback riding, canoeing.

RECOMMENDED COUNTRY INNS® TRAVELERS' CLUB BENEFIT: 10 percent discount, Monday to Thursday.

he earliest part of the house was built in 1780, and the den still exhibits the hand-hewn posts and beams, paneled walls, polished heart-pine floors, and stone fireplace from that era. It's a cozy, comfortable, and informal room with braided rugs on the floor and plump pillows on the sofa. The rest of the inn harks to an 1853 expansion that increased the house from 5 rooms to 18. A formal living room boasts a handsome wood carved mantel over the fireplace and an elegant antique settee and chairs.

The most distinguishing feature of the handsome white-clapboard house with black shutters is its double wraparound verandas. In front, however, the house exhibits all the characteristics of a Carpenter Gothic Victorian, with steeply peaked gable roofs, an arched window, and gingerbread trim. A picket fence neatly encloses the yard.

The guest rooms are all decorated in period antiques. Martha, for example, has a canopied pencil-post bed and a fireplace. The bath includes a double whirlpool tub. Abigail has a white-iron bed and oak furniture; Eleanor contains a beautiful bird's-eye maple bed and a claw-foot tub in the bath.

## The Thread of Life

The great textile centers that flourished in New England in the 1800s had closed by the time Franklin Delano Roosevelt became president. Many plants had moved to the southern states, however, and in 1935 the president implored his wife, Eleanor, to visit the Stillwater Fabric plants in Goshen, Craigsville, and Augusta Springs, Virginia, to see (and to report back to him about) the modern facilities—and particularly to learn about the humane treatment of the workers and the modern housing provided for them. She came and stayed at the huge old house owned by Pearl and Joe Wood. Pearl was an indomitable woman. She was the first principal of the Goshen school and the chairperson of the county Democratic committee, and she was born in this house and lived here all her life. It's this same house that Jeremy and Diana Robinson turned into an inn in 1993.

A four-course dinner is served at the inn every Saturday night when advance reservations have been made. Among the entrees, you might sample a lavender and herb roasted Cornish game hen or a fillet of salmon en croute.

HOW TO GET THERE: From I–81 take exit 191 onto I–64 west and travel 12½ miles to exit 43. Follow Route 780 north for 9½ miles to Goshen. Route 780 ends just before Goshen at the intersection with Route 39. Turn left onto Route 39 and follow this for 1 mile into Goshen. Bear left onto Alternate Route 39 and follow this around the corner and across the railroad tracks. Immediately turn left onto Wood Lane. The inn is the fourth house on the right.

# The Joshua Wilton House
## Harrisonburg, Virginia 22801

INNKEEPERS: Craig and Roberta Moore; Pat Spicer and Sean Pugh, managers

ADDRESS/TELEPHONE: 412 South Main Street; (540) 434–4464; fax (540) 432–9525

E-MAIL: jwhouse@rica.net

WEB SITE: www.rica.net/jwhouse

ROOMS: 5, all with private bath, telephone, and air-conditioning; 1 with fireplace. No smoking inn. Children over the age of 10 welcome.

RATES: $95 to $105, double occupancy; includes full breakfast.

OPEN: All year.

FACILITIES AND ACTIVITIES: Dinner Tuesday to Saturday (fixed-price menu, $40 to $55; cafe entrees $10 to $19), tavern. Nearby: Massanutten, New Market Battlefield, Shenandoah Valley, fishing, hiking.

Harrisonburg is a charming little university town—the home of James Madison University. The mellow brick buildings of the campus are merely steps away along a broad boulevard from the Joshua Wilton House, a gracious 1888 brick Victorian painted sage green with cream and brick-colored trim.

Craig and Roberta Moore have owned the house since 1988, when they turned it into an inn. The main floor rooms are devoted to its dining room, which is elegant and refined in the front rooms and more casual in back. A pretty, reclusive lounge has a bar with a green marble top and leather chairs pulled up before a fireplace, which has a maroon faux-marble mantel.

The dining rooms feature rose carpets and pink tablecloths on tables that hold little lamps with pink pleated shades. There are stained-glass windows and faux-marble fireplaces, and the walls are decorated with beautiful watercolors that change frequently, as they are the work of members of the Shenandoah Valley Watercolor Society, and they are for sale. The casual cafe rooms are accessed through the brick courtyard in back, which also has seating under umbrellas and is warmed by gas heaters when the weather turns cooler.

I had an excellent dinner here one night that started with pan-seared scallops with toasted almond pesto cream sauce followed by the Joshua Wilton salad, a pile of mixed greens topped with blue cheese, artichoke bottoms, hearts of palm, cherry tomatoes, and bacon and served with a raspberry vinaigrette. My entree con-

sisted of herb-crusted rack of lamb with a Cabernet sauce, and I had a lovely chocolate hazelnut cheesecake for dessert. The five-course meal is $40 if you want to select your own bottle of wine from the inn's wine list or $55 if you choose to have a glass of the wine they recommend with each of the courses. The menu in the cafe is a la carte.

The guest rooms, which are furnished with lovely antiques, are on the second floor. My favorite room is Number 4, located in the turret. It has a wonderful Chinese wedding bed covered with a pretty white cutwork spread. A Victorian armoire, a vanity, and a table and chairs in the turret complete the furnishings. The beautiful tile bath is spacious. Other rooms have either four-poster or antique high-headboard beds.

HOW TO GET THERE: From I–81 take exit 245 and go west on Port Republic Road to Main Street, turn right, and continue approximately 1 mile to the inn on the right.

# The Inn at Fairfield Farm
Hume, Virginia 22639

**INNKEEPER:** Irene Voglsam; Jerry Cooper, general manager

**ADDRESS/TELEPHONE:** Marriott Ranch, 5305 Marriott Lane; (540) 364–3221; fax (540) 364–2498

**ROOMS:** 8, including 1 suite and 1 cottage; all with private bath, air-conditioning, radio, and desk; 5 with fireplace, 4 with telephone and dataport and/or private porch, 2 with kitchen, 1 with whirlpool tub. Wheelchair accessible. Children welcome. No smoking in guest rooms.

**RATES:** $125 to $500, double occupancy; includes full breakfast and afternoon tea.

**OPEN:** All year.

**FACILITIES AND ACTIVITIES:** On 4,500-acre cattle ranch with gardens, pond, river for fishing, horseback riding, and hiking. Scheduled trail rides, occasional cattle drives, river and mountain rides. Jeep tours, picnic lunches, and winery and vineyard tours available. Nearby: Skyline Drive, Shenandoah National Park, numerous wineries.

**BUSINESS TRAVEL:** Desk in all rooms; meeting rooms, fax, telephone, dataport, coffeemaker, hair dryers, iron, and ironing boards available.

*T*he Marriott family manage one of the finest hotel empires in America, so it makes sense that the inn they opened in December 1997 on their vast 4,500-acre cattle ranch would draw from the lessons learned in more than forty years of owning and managing hotels.

J. Willard Marriott purchased Fairfield Farm in 1951 because it reminded him of the ranch he grew up on in Marriott, Utah. The centerpiece of the ranch is the distinguished brick manor house, built in 1814 by James Markham Marshall, brother of Chief Justice John Marshall. Although it had been vacant for thirty years, Marriott accomplished a historically accurate restoration of the house so that the rooms look today much as they did when the house was new.

From the beginning, however, the ranch has been much more than a rich man's toy. It is very much a working ranch, where meat from the vast herds of cattle are destined for the tables of Marriott restaurants. Corporate meetings take place here, also, as well as an annual management outing. The stables, which are about 1½ miles from the inn, are the site of daily scheduled trail rides. Inn guests can participate in these (there's a fee) as well as in occasional cattle drives.

The centerpiece of the inn is the manor house. The common rooms on the main floor include a dining room, a parlor—where a piano is located—and a library, as well as the foyer. A large porch set with white-iron cafe tables offers panoramic views of sunsets over the Blue Ridge Mountains. There are four guest rooms on the second floor. Each is elegantly furnished with four-poster beds and hardwood floors covered by Oriental rugs. One room has curtains and bed coverings in a red-and-black rose fabric; another used a blue-and-yellow color scheme.

The carriage house has an additional three rooms. The finest lodging, however, is The Baroness Cottage, named for Baroness Jeanne von Reininghaus Lambert of Belgium, who purchased Fairfield Farm just before World War II. She converted a small log cabin into this charming three-bedroom cottage for herself and her children. Today the eat-in kitchen, family room with a fireplace, and configuration of bedrooms and baths make it an ideal place to relax for an extended stay or for a family getaway.

The old smokehouse, where hams and wild turkeys were cured over slow hickory fires, is now a common room in which guests might gather. There's a bar with a fireplace, and the old smokey beams still impart a faint hint of hickory.

A full breakfast of fresh fruit, home-made muffins and pastries, and, perhaps, an egg entree or French toast stuffed with mascarpone and pecans is served every morning.

HOW TO GET THERE: From Washington, D.C., take I–66 west for approximately 40 miles to exit 27 (the second Marshall exit). Turn left at the stop sign, crossing over I–66. Make an immediate right onto Route 647. Go 4 miles and turn right onto Route 635; proceed 9½ miles to the main entrance of the ranch, which is on the left.

# Keswick Hall 👪 📱
## Keswick, Virginia 22947

**GENERAL MANAGER:** Stephen Beaumont; Sir Bernard Ashley, proprietor

**ADDRESS/TELEPHONE:** 701 Club Drive; (804) 979–3440 or (800) ASHLEY–1; fax (804) 977–4171

**WEB SITE:** www.keswick@keswick.com

**ROOMS:** 48, including 4 suites; all with private bath, air-conditioning, telephone, television, VCR, desk, radio, hair dryer, and robes; 17 with decorative fireplace, 11 with private balcony or terrace, 4 with whirlpool tub. Wheelchair accessible. Children welcome. Smoking permitted.

**RATES:** $250 to $645, double occupancy; includes full breakfast and afternoon tea. Packages available. Two-night minimum weekends in spring, summer, and fall.

**OPEN:** All year.

**FACILITIES AND ACTIVITIES:** Breakfast, lunch, afternoon tea, and dinner (prix fixe $58) available. Bistro restaurant, English pub. On 600 acres with Arnold Palmer–designed golf course, clay tennis courts, indoor-outdoor swimming pool, fitness center, sauna, massage therapy, gift shop, snooker table, garden, croquet lawn. Nearby: Charlottesville (5 miles), Monticello, Ashlawn, University of Virginia.

**BUSINESS TRAVEL:** Telephone and desk in room; conference and meeting facilities including audiovisual, fax, Internet access.

*I*f you have considered redecorating your house in Laura Ashley fashion, you should definitely book a night or two at Keswick Hall first. But then you should stay here even if you've never considered such a thought. For Keswick Hall is one of the grandest country house inns in America, equal in every respect to the grand country house estates of England—and for good reason.

Sir Bernard Ashley, cofounder of the Laura Ashley design and fabric firm, searched the countryside until he found this elegant 600-acre estate known as Villa Crawford. To the imposing 1912 Tuscan villa that he found in 1990 he added wings that created a 60,000-square-foot mansion, and then he

painted it corn-muffin yellow with bottle-green trim. Keswick became the triple crown in Sir Bernard's stable of elegant inns. He also owns The Inn at Perry Cabin in Maryland and Llangoed Hall in Wales.

Elegant and sophisticated, the public areas at Keswick Hall combine period antiques and Laura Ashley fabrics—all in the BA style, as his staff refer to Sir Bernard. In the tile-floored Great Hall stately columns define intimate seating areas about the fireplace. The Crawford Lounge is furnished with down-filled, yellow velvet sofas and needlepoint pillows. White predominates in the Morning Room; the red Snooker Room offers a snooker table, a fireplace, Oriental rugs, and soft leather chairs. The inn also boasts an impressive collection of museum-quality oil paintings. A 30-foot-wide terrace, which has an outside fireplace, offers sweeping views of the rolling golf course. This is a popular evening retreat—often the only sound is the croaking of frogs in the pond.

The guest rooms are lavishly decorated with sophisticated Laura Ashley fabrics. Wooden shutters filter the sun, upholstered window seats invite stargazing, and overstuffed chairs are accented with needlepoint pillows. The baths have tile floors and double pedestal sinks. Rockingham is one of my favorites. The spacious room is elegantly dressed in cowslip yellow and sage green and has an antique Chinoise theme. It has French doors that open to a balcony with views of the golf course and such amenities as heated towel bars and a jetted tub in the bath.

Guests should be sure to arrive in time for afternoon tea, as we did one day. We sampled light-as-a-feather scones with lemon curd and clotted cream, fresh fruit, delectable pastries, and tea. Had we requested the extended tea, we would have received cucumber, watercress, and tomato sandwiches as well. It's all so civilized, you see. Breakfast, lunch, and dinner are served in the dining room downstairs, which has a terrace overlooking the golf course. The relaxed and leisurely dinner is outstanding.

Light meals and snacks also are available at the members-only Keswick Club. Overnight guests may use its facilities, which include three outdoor tennis courts and a championship eighteen-hole golf course designed by Arnold Palmer. The Pavilion Clubhouse offers an indoor/outdoor pool; a fitness center; an excellent gift shop; the Bistro restaurant, which overlooks the golf course; and the British-style Pub, complete with wooden floors, leather chairs, and ale on tap. Bicycles are available for touring the estate's miles of paved roads, which lead past a series of elegant new homes being built on part of the property.

**HOW TO GET THERE:** From Washington, D.C., take I-66 west to exit 43. Follow Route 29 south for 85 miles to the Route 250 bypass eastbound. Follow this to the exit for Route 22, traveling east toward the towns of Cismont and Boyd's Tavern. After approximately 2 miles turn right onto Route 744 (Hunt Club Drive). At the next stop sign, the gates of Keswick Hall are directly ahead.

# The Suites at Prince Michel
## Leon, Virginia 22725

**MAITRE D'HOTEL:** Andrew Ferlazzo; Jean LeDucq, proprietor

**ADDRESS/TELEPHONE:** Route 29 south (mailing address: HCR 4, Box 77); (540) 547-9720 or (800) 800-WINE; fax (540) 547-3088

**WEB SITE:** www.princemichel.com

**ROOMS:** 4 suites; all with private bath, air-conditioning, telephone with dataport, fax, television, VCR, Jacuzzi, fireplace, two porches or patios, CD player, and minibar. Wheelchair accessible. Rooms suitable for two people only. Smoking on patios only.

**RATES:** $350 Thursday, $400 Friday and Saturday, double occupancy; includes continental breakfast and champagne on arrival.

**OPEN:** Thursday to Sunday mid-July through late December and mid-January through late June.

**FACILITIES AND ACTIVITIES:** Restaurant serving lunch Thursday to Sunday (prix fixe $25 to $40) and dinner Thursday to Saturday (prix fixe $70 to $80); on grounds of 155-acre winery offering tours and tastings daily 10 A.M. to 5:00 P.M.; wine museum. Limousine service available. Nearby: golfing, Shenandoah National Park and Skyline Drive, canoeing and tubing on Rapidan River, bicycling, Brandy Station and Cedar Mountain battlefields.

**BUSINESS TRAVEL:** Desk, telephone with dataport, television, VCR, and fax available in all rooms.

French businessman Jean LeDucq established Prince Michel and Rapidan River Vineyards in 1983, and it hasn't stopped growing ever since. The vineyards, which are planted with a combination of Cabernet Sauvignon, Merlot, Cabernet Franc, Riesling, and Gewürztraminer, stretch for 155 acres, and the winery now bottles some 35,000 cases annually, making it one of the largest in Virginia.

In 1992 Mr. LeDucq opened a fine-dining restaurant at the winery featuring the cuisine of Chef Alain Lecomte, who grew up and trained in France. His cooking marries the bounty of local produce, meats, fruit, and herbs with his classical French training to produce an imaginative and unique regional cuisine.

The pretty cellar dining room is refreshing in cool teal, peach, and white. Trellises are hung with antique vineyard implements, and the walls are painted with murals of the port of Bordeaux. There's a flower-bordered patio for summer luncheons. Dinner is a sumptuous and elegant repast that deserves dress-up attire, although it's not required. You might start with a hot foie gras with three different combinations of apple and Virginia cider sauce or a crab and lobster coussinet with a crayfish butter sauce. For an entree you might try the red snapper on a spinach cushion with a light saffron butter sauce or the medallions of venison with a Grand Veneur sauce.

In 1998 the operation was expanded even more by the addition of four stunning suites for overnight guests. Charming and delightful as an *auberge* or *mas* in Provence, each of the suites, with names like La Tour Eiffel and Les Champs Elysées, combines the ultimate in luxury with the casual charm of its sunny vineyard setting. The rooms are decorated with sponged, ragged, or faux-marble walls in shades of blue, green, yellow, and red and accented with bright provincial fabrics. Distressed painted headboards, tables, and chests, as well as chairs with paintings on their backs, lend comfort and appeal. Every room has a fireplace, both a front and back porch or patio, a telephone with dataport, fax, minibar, television and VCR, and a CD player. The rooms are equipped with surround-sound, and the music is even piped to one of the patios.

The baths are equally luxurious, finished in tumbled marble in colors coordinated with the room—blue, green, and white. Each has a Jacuzzi that includes a neck massage, and there's a bidet as well.

If you're planning a trip to Virginia's wine country—and such an excursion is well worthwhile—this is the perfect place to stay and to dine.

**HOW TO GET THERE:** From Washington, D.C., take I-66 west to exit 43 (Gainsville). Follow Route 29 south for 48 miles to the winery, which is 10 miles south of Culpeper.

# *Virginia Is for Lovers— Wine Lovers*

According to Marguerite Thomas, author of *Wineries of the Eastern States* (Berkshire House Publishers: Lee, MA, 1996), Virginia is the sleeper in the burgeoning wine regions in the East. She says:

"Virginia could be the most promising eastern wine-producing state. Lying between the cold weather extreme of the Northeast and the intense heat and humidity of the South . . . this region may prove to have the most grape-friendly climate. Forty-six Virginia wineries are now in operation [there are more than sixty now], a remarkable number considering that the first successful *vinifera* grape wines were made here less than twenty years ago. Remarkably supportive state legislation that encourages growers and wineries is one of the principal factors contributing to this success. Virginia has one of the most liberal farm winery laws in the nation. Unlike many other states in the East, wine can even be sold in Virginia's food stores. Another bonus is the affluent and educated population in the Washington, D.C., area, which supports the local wine industry."

She gives Prince Michel a three-bottle rating.

# Brierley Hill Country Inn
Lexington, Virginia 24450

**INNKEEPERS:** Carole Speton

**ADDRESS/TELEPHONE:** Bordon Road (mailing address: Route 2, Box 21A); (540) 464–8421 or (800) 422–4925; fax (540) 464–8925

**E-MAIL:** cspeton@cfw.com

**WEB SITE:** www.brierleyhill.com

**ROOMS:** 5, including 1 suite; all with private bath and air-conditioning; 2 with fireplace and TV; 1 with whirlpool tub, porch, and minirefrigerator. Children over the age of 14 welcome. No smoking inn.

**RATES:** $95 to $160, double occupancy; includes full breakfast and afternoon tea. Two-night minimum weekends in May and October and holiday weekends.

**OPEN:** All year.

**FACILITIES AND ACTIVITIES:** Restaurant serving dinner Saturday (prix fixe $35 including wine) by advance reservation. On eight acres with gardens. Nearby: Virginia Military Institute and the George C. Marshall Museum, Washington and Lee University, Stonewall Jackson House, Natural Bridge, Virginia Horse Center, canoeing and kayaking on the James River.

**BUSINESS TRAVEL:** Fax, copier available; corporate rates.

*C*arole and Barry Speton started their enterprise by purchasing an eight-acre parcel of land high on a sunny hilltop above historic Lexington that offered views of the Blue Ridge Mountains and the Shenandoah Valley. Then they designed their dream inn, incorporating the best features of the many inns they had stayed in over the years.

To reach the inn you climb and climb up a hill, and when you reach the top you feel as though you are on top of the world. The blue-clapboard farmhouse-style Colonial has white trim and a wraparound porch from which there are panoramic views of the Blue Ridge Mountains. It's surrounded by spacious gardens and ample parking.

Just inside the entry hall of the inn stands an 1850s tall-case clock made in Brierley Hill, England, which was the inspiration for the inn's name. In the inn's parlor the sofas and drapes are lavishly covered with a floral Laura Ashley pattern called Lewes, so the room is named the Lewes Sitting Room. A beautiful twisted-leg table, an ornate upright piano, and a child's Chinese stroller decorate the room. There's a gas fireplace and an Oriental rug covering the oak floors. In another sitting room upstairs, sofas provide places to watch television, and a corner holds a semicircular table where the inn's telephone is located.

The guest rooms, which are named for flowers in the garden, are crisp and spritely. Cowslip is a medley of yellows and includes a canopy bed, an oak armoire, and a lovely painted table. Peony is a large room with an iron canopy bed, as well as a sleigh bed. A gas fireplace with a pretty wood mantle and wicker chairs complete the decor. Primrose features a magnificent antique brass bed and pink-and-white striped walls. The baths are thoroughly modern and bright, although they are a bit spartan. All have stall showers—except the suite, that is. Rose Suite has a bath that includes a two-person whirlpool tub. It also has a beautiful pine bed with a high headboard and footboard and a sitting room with a gas fireplace. French doors lead to a huge private patio.

Carole is a great cook. She rises early in the morning to begin baking breakfast breads. She may serve her apple turnovers or her oat-bran bread. Entrees may include her wine-and-cheese baked-egg casserole or, maybe, Grand Marnier French toast. She also serves a light afternoon tea either in the dining room or on the veranda. In summer she might prepare lemonade and cookies or cake; in the winter she'll have hot tea with scones and little sandwiches.

On Saturday nights a four-course meal is served if advance reservations have been made. A sample menu might include wild mushroom soup with a homemade French baguette, followed by a green salad with pears and blue cheese and then an entree of salmon fillets with garlic-and-herb salsa that Carole serves with sweet potato-and-artichoke hash. The dessert with such a meal might be an orange napoleon with crème anglaise. The Saturday night dinner is offered for $35, including a selection of wines from the inn's list.

HOW TO GET THERE: From I–81 traveling north take exit 188B onto Route 60 west. Follow Route 60 through Lexington (it becomes Nelson Street). Turn left onto Borden Road and continue for 1 mile to Brierley Hill, which is on the left. From I–81 traveling south take exit 191 onto I–64 west. Continue on I–64 to exit 55 and then follow Route 11 south to Lexington, passing Virginia Military Institute and Washington and Lee University. At Route 60 (Nelson Street) turn right and proceed west to Borden Road. Then follow directions above.

# The Inn at Meander Plantation 🖼 📱 ♥
## Locust Dale, Virginia 22948

**INNKEEPERS:** Suzanne Thomas, Suzie Blanchard, Bob Blanchard

**ADDRESS/TELEPHONE:** James Madison Highway (Route 15) (mailing address: HCR 5 Box 460A); (540) 672–4912 or (800) 385–4936; fax (540) 672–0405

**E-MAIL:** inn@meander.net

**WEB SITE:** www.meander.net

**ROOMS:** 8, including 2 suites and 4 dependencies; all with private bath, air-conditioning, telephone with dataport, and radio; 6 with porch or patio, 5 with fireplace, 4 with television. Wheelchair accessible. Children welcome. Pets permitted in dependencies with prior permission. No smoking inn.

**RATES:** $105 to $250, double occupancy; includes full breakfast and afternoon snacks. Two-night minimum in May and October and on holidays.

**OPEN:** All year.

**FACILITIES AND ACTIVITIES:** Restaurant for inn guests Saturday by reservation (prix fixe $37.50); on eighty acres including pastures for horses (guests may bring their own), stables, horseback riding; gardens; river for fishing, tubing, and swimming; exercise room with treadmill, stationary bike, health rider. Nearby: numerous wineries, antiques shops, Civil War battlefields, Plow and Hearth catalog outlet store, Shenandoah National Park, hot-air ballooning.

**BUSINESS TRAVEL:** Telephone with dataport in room; corporate rates; access to computer, printer, fax; meeting rooms; early breakfast.

*G*eorge Washington may not have stayed here, but Thomas Jefferson did—many times. Tom's father, Peter, was a friend of Colonel Joshua Fry, who was a member of the House of Burgesses, and the patent holder of this plantation. He built the original house on the property, which was enlarged later by his son, Henry, who was a friend of Tom's. History marched past here during both the Revolutionary War and the Civil War. General Lafayette, James Madison, and George Washington visited, and Stonewall Jackson crossed the Robinson River with his troops on the property.

The gracious manor house has been lovingly restored by Suzanne, Suzie, and Bob, who purchased the estate in 1991 with the intention of turning it into an inn. Offering an abundance of enthusiasm and genuine warmth, the innkeepers are hospitable and delightful.

The formal rooms of the inn have beautiful dentil moldings, elegant antique furniture, solid paneled doors, and handsome fireplaces mantels. There's a formal reception room with a fireplace and a living room with another fireplace. Games and books are available here for guests to use.

All the guest rooms are beautifully furnished with period antiques and elegant fabrics, but be sure to ask which ones have the bath in the hallway.

My favorites are the rooms located in the dependencies. The Summer Kitchen is joined to the manor house by an arched brick colonnade. This has a living room on the main floor, a beautiful bedroom on the second floor with a fireplace, and a private bath with a claw-foot tub and a separate shower. Two other dependencies and a former groom's cottage are also charmingly and romantically furnished.

Suzie is not only an innkeeper but also a food writer and editor, which naturally means that she loves to cook. Her breakfasts are wonderful, but she also offers Saturday night dinners to inn guests. Candles twinkle against a backdrop of fine linen, elegant china, polished silver, and stemmed crystal, and a fire crackles in the fireplace in winter. A typical spring menu might consist of baby asparagus wrapped in proscuitto with lemon herb sauce, a salad of mixed greens with Parmesan-garlic dressing, a fruit sorbet, an entree of, perhaps, honey and orange glazed Cornish game hen or smoked bacon–wrapped filet mignon topped with Danish blue cheese on a bed of fresh wilted spinach. The coconut crème brûlée is a fabulous finale.

And who knows, maybe that perennial sleep-about George Washington stayed here, too. He couldn't have had a room as elegantly decorated as you will, however.

**HOW TO GET THERE:** From Washington, D.C., go west on I-66 to exit 43A (Gainsville). Take Route 29 south to the third Culpeper exit, and follow Route 15 south for 9 miles. The inn is on the right, just past Crooked Run.

# The Red Fox Inn 🖼 📱
## Middleburg, Virginia 22117

**INNKEEPER:** F. Turner Reuter, Jr.; Frank Vitale and Alberta Loos, managers

**ADDRESS/TELEPHONE:** 2 East Washington Street (mailing address: P.O. Box 385); (540) 687-6301 or (800) 223-1728; fax (540) 687-6053

**WEB SITE:** www.redfox.com

**ROOMS:** 24, including 8 suites and 1 cottage; all with private bath, air-conditioning, telephone, television, desk, and robes; 7 with fireplace, 4 with porch. Wheelchair accessible. Children welcome. Guest pets permitted with prior permission. Smoking permitted; designated nonsmoking rooms.

**RATES:** $150 to $250, double occupancy; includes continental breakfast. Cot $25.

**OPEN:** All year.

**FACILITIES AND ACTIVITIES:** Two restaurants, The Red Fox Inn and Mosby's Tavern, serving breakfast, lunch, and dinner (entrees $19 to $29); gift shop, art gallery. Nearby: Upperville Colt and Horse Show (June), Stable Tour (Memorial Day), Point to Point Races, equestrian meets, polo on Sunday (June to September), vineyard tours, biking.

**BUSINESS TRAVEL:** Desks, telephone, and television in all rooms; fax available; meeting rooms; corporate rates.

We were on our honeymoon, enjoying a leisurely drive from New York to Dallas, where we were going to live, and we stopped at The Red Fox Inn for a bite of lunch. An hour became two and then three, and eventually we spent the night. I wondered at the time how many other couples had done exactly the same through the years.

Folks started pulling up to the door in a stagecoach when the mellow stone building was first built in 1728. How grateful they must have been for some respite from the dusty road and the constant bouncing of the wagon! Chinn's Ordinary was its name at the time. Throughout its 270 years, it's continued to be the focal point of the charming village of Middleburg, and it's grown and changed with the demands of the times.

Today the complex includes twenty-four rooms in five buildings that range from the original tavern to several historic houses. Alas, the rooms at The Red Fox Inn have more similarities to a chain hotel than to a charming country inn. The rooms come in various sizes, but all have standard private baths and are furnished mostly with reproduction pieces. There are no hands-on innkeepers who look after guest's needs, and all the rooms are similar in style and decor. Nevertheless, the historical ambience of the inn makes its inclusion here possible.

Dinner might be taken in one of the inn dining rooms on the second floor. The numerous rooms all have fireplaces and paneled walls hung with

oil paintings. Travelers also might eat in the charming tavern or over at Mosby's Tavern, about a block away.

The various buildings that make up The Red Fox Inn are all within walking distance of the wonderful antiques, interior design, and gift shops that line the streets of Middleburg. The inn has its own art gallery in the Stray Fox Stable, where you can buy fine original nineteenth-century paintings or bronze statues of animals. This is the heart of Virginia's hunt country, and you're likely to see numerous references to the sport in town. There's even a riding stable right in town.

One place I never miss when I travel through town is the tiny, old-fashioned Upper Crust Bakery, a wonderful mélange of heady smells, outstanding coffees, delicious bakery goods, and sandwiches. You can put together a picnic for the road here, or you can eat in the tiny room in back.

HOW TO GET THERE: From Washington, D.C., take I–66 west to exit 57 (Winchester, near Fair Oaks Mall). Follow Route 50 west for 26 miles to Middleburg. The inn is on the right in the center of town at the traffic light. Ample parking is located behind the inn.

# Fort Lewis Lodge ▦ ▩
## Millboro, Virginia 24460

INNKEEPERS: John and Caryl Cowden

ADDRESS/TELEPHONE: HCR 3, Box 21A; (540) 925–2314;
fax (540) 925–2352

WEB SITE: www.svta.org/ftlewis/

ROOMS: 17, including 4 suites and 2 log cabins; all with private bath;
cabins with fireplace. Wheelchair accessible. Children welcome. Smoking limited to some common rooms.

RATES: $140 to $195, double occupancy; $90, single occupancy;
includes breakfast and dinner; additional person over 12, $35; children
3 to 12, $25; those under 2 are free. Two-night minimum weekends.

OPEN: April through mid-October.

FACILITIES AND ACTIVITIES: Picnic lunches prepared by reservation
($5.00 to $7.00), wine and beer service. Guest fridge, playroom; basketball court, hot tub, five bicycles, two canoes; 3,200 acres; swimming,
fishing, hiking, biking, birding, towers for wildlife viewing, spelunking.
Nearby: hot springs, golf courses, Garth Newel Chamber Music Center,
Lime Kiln Theater, Museum of American Frontier Culture.

Snuggled into the Allegheny Mountains, Fort Lewis Lodge sits amid
3,200 acres of natural forests, meadows, and farmland laced with
streams and hiking trails. In 1754 Colonel Charles Lewis built a stock-
ade here to protect his family from Indian raids. Lewis died in 1774 at the
Battle of Point Pleasant, considered by some historians to have been the first
engagement of the American Revolution. Over its long history the property
has remained remarkably unchanged. In the 1950s it was purchased by
Robert Cowden as his retirement retreat, and he raised Black Angus cattle on
the land. Today his son and daughter-in-law, John and Caryl Cowden, own
and operate the property as a country inn and cattle ranch.

The country roads on the way to Fort Lewis Lodge wind past a breathtaking view of Goshen Pass and may offer glimpses of deer feeding by a
mountain stream. Turning onto the gravel lane that leads to the inn, you'll
pass over a cattle guard and see a silo rising ahead and, down by the pond, a
perfectly restored gristmill.

Fort Lewis Lodge is anything but ordinary, and that's true of its owners
as well. By anyone's standards, John is a master craftsman; the inn is his mas-

terpiece. He meticulously restored the nineteenth-century gristmill, with its 2-foot-thick stone walls. It now serves as the dining room, where Caryl offers such hearty home-cooked dinners as a harvest roast with scalloped apples, fresh vegetables from the garden, homemade biscuits, and sinfully rich chocolate pie. Meals are served buffet-style and with complimentary wines. Guests may opt to sit at individual tables or at one of the large family-style tables. Buck's Bar, a screened porch overlooking the old millpond, is the place to get acquainted before dinner. In the evening the old piano near the woodstove gets a workout during impromptu sing-alongs.

Guest rooms are scattered among several buildings and are furnished in Shaker-style simplicity with cherry, walnut, red oak, and chestnut furniture made by a local craftsman. John himself built the two-story cedar-shake lodge, right down to the milled pine floors, as well as the adjoining silo, which is an exact replica of the original that was here; it contains three guest rooms offering panoramic views across the fields. At the very top is an observation tower, reached by a spiral staircase. Two rustic log cabins (one dating

from the 1860s and the other from the 1890s) were transported to the property in 1993 and now provide romantic retreats. They have stone fireplaces, front porches with rockers or a swing, patchwork quilts, and pioneer artifacts. The "Little House on the Prairie" ambience is conveyed in all the rooms by clothes pegs on the walls instead of closets, patchwork quilts on the beds, and simple but utilitarian bathrooms. The outdoor hot tub, on the other hand, is strictly a 1990s refinement.

HOW TO GET THERE: From I–81 north take exit 240 (Bridgewater) and follow Route 257 west to Bridgewater. At the intersection with Route 42, follow this south for 16 miles to Churchville. In Churchville turn onto Route 250 west, go 10 miles to the junction with Route 629, and turn left. Stay on Route 629 for 22 miles through Deerfield. Turn right onto Route 678 and go 4 miles to Route 625. Turn left and you will see the lodge entrance on the left in 2/10 mile.

# The Mark Addy
## Nellysford, Virginia 22958

**INNKEEPERS:** John Storck Maddox and Joanne R. Maddox

**ADDRESS/TELEPHONE:** 56 Rodes Farm Drive; (804) 361–1101 or (800) 278–2154; fax (804) 361–2425

**E-MAIL:** markaddy@symweb.com

**WEB SITE:** www.symweb.com/rockfish/mark.html

**ROOMS:** 9, including 1 suite; all with private bath and air-conditioning; 4 with private porch or deck, 3 with whirlpool tub. Wheelchair accessible. Children over the age of 12 welcome. No smoking inn.

**RATES:** $100 to $150, double occupancy; includes full breakfast. Two-night minimum weekends in February, May, June, September, and October.

**OPEN:** All year.

**FACILITIES AND ACTIVITIES:** Restaurant serving dinner to inn guests Saturday (prix fixe $40). On thirteen acres with gardens, hammock, croquet; The Storck's Nest, a fine-gift and home-furnishings shop. Nearby: Blue Ridge Parkway, Appalachian Trail, George Washington National Forest, Oak Ridge Estate, Walton's Mountain Museum, Wintergreen resort (12 miles away) where there's downhill and cross-country skiing, hiking, and golfing; wineries.

**BUSINESS TRAVEL:** Meeting rooms, fax and telephone available; on-premise catering.

**RECOMMENDED COUNTRY INNS® TRAVELERS' CLUB BENEFIT:** 10 percent discount, Sunday to Thursday.

*A*lthough a thick layer of snow covered the lawn, the sun shone brightly as I drove up the inn's driveway, offering a hint of the spring that was soon to come. Yet the sunny, butter-yellow Victorian was so welcoming I felt as though winter was already an old memory. The house sits high on a hill surrounded by voluptuous summer flower gardens, its white trim and green shutters giving it just the right sense of style. And no wonder. Style is John Storck Maddox's forte, as witnessed by the lamps he designs and the antiques he collects.

John and his mother, Joanne, purchased Dr. John C. Everett's historic 1837 home to give John a place to showcase his talents. His collections of china—including some delicate and rare pieces of Belleek—are only a few examples. Visitors to the inn are able to purchase some of the antiques that are on display at the inn, or they can visit The Storck's Nest, John's home furnishings, gift, and antiques shop, which is located on the grounds.

The inn is on a thirteen-acre parcel of land in Virginia's remote Nelson County, where it offers superb views of the Blue Ridge Mountains and Rockfish Valley from its hilltop perch. There are five porches from which to view this wonderland, and it's not unusual for those who rise early to witness a herd of deer feeding in a nearby field.

Guests enter the inn through a columned covered porch. There's a broad entry hall with peach walls and white trim. The polished wood floor is covered with an Oriental rug. The inn has a lovely Victorian parlor containing a beautiful antique buffet and a library with book-filled bookcases. A sitting room has a television and VCR. A beautiful and well-designed kitchen, available for guests to use, contains a refrigerator, microwave, and coffeemaker. Two of the main floor rooms are devoted to the dining room, where John fixes an acclaimed Saturday night dinner for his guests.

The guest rooms are stunning—each with a different theme. Tiger Lily, on the main floor, is a spacious room designed in a British Raj scheme. It has peach walls, an elephant coffee table on a green carpet, and a bath with green faux-marble walls and a whirlpool tub. Mimosa, on the second floor, contains a white iron bed on a gray carpet and a bath with a claw-foot tub and a pedestal sink. Kensington offers its occupants an English Country ambience with its deep green walls and duvet on the bed.

A full breakfast is served every morning in one of the dining rooms. In addition to John's decorating capabilities, he was previously a caterer in New York, and his meals reflect his ingenuity in combining flavors and textures. One of his unusual breakfasts might be a salmon loaf topped with eggs and dressed with a light béarnaise sauce. This would be accompanied by fried green tomatoes and cheese grits. Or perhaps he'll serve caramel-walnut stuffed French toast.

Saturday night dinners begin with a variety of hors d'oeuvres in the parlor, accompanied by a glass of wine. A typical entree might be a roast pork loin with spinach, shiitakes, and walnuts in a rosemary sauce and a sundried tomato pilaf, or perhaps he'll serve roasted salmon in a lime and dill sauce. He serves a salad following the entree and then a delicious dessert such as cream cheesecake with blackberry sauce. Wines are served at the table.

For nights when the restaurant is not open, you may want to walk down the road to the Rodes Farm Inn, where you will be served fabulous local country fare, family-style, in an old farmhouse with a broad front porch. John Lennon, Mick Jagger, and Muhammad Ali have eaten here in the past.

**HOW TO GET THERE:** From I–64 take exit 107 (Crozet) and follow Route 250 west for 5 miles. Turn left onto Route 151 and travel south for 10 miles. At the junction with Route 613, turn right and follow Route 613 west. The inn is the first driveway on the right.

# The Garden and The Sea Inn
## New Church, Virginia 23415

**INNKEEPERS:** Sara and Tom Baker

**ADDRESS/TELEPHONE:** 4188 Nelson Road (Route 710); (757) 824–0672 (fax also) or (800) 824–0672

**E-MAIL:** baker@shore.intercom.net

**WEB SITE:** www.bbhost.com/gardenandseabnb

**ROOMS:** 6; all with private bath, air-conditioning, and radio; 4 with whirlpool tub. Wheelchair accessible. Children over the age of 12 welcome on weekends; those over the age of 6 welcome weekdays. Pets permitted. No smoking inn.

**RATES:** $75 to $175, double occupancy; includes hearty continental breakfast and afternoon snacks. Two-night minimum weekends; three-night minimum holidays; four-night minimum last week in July.

**OPEN:** Mid-March to November.

**FACILITIES AND ACTIVITIES:** Dinner Wednesday to Sunday in July and August; Thursday to Sunday in June, September, October, and November; Friday to Sunday in April. Four-course fixed price, $30; also a la carte (entrees $18 to $25). Two parlors. Nearby: Chincoteague National Wildlife Refuge, Assateague National Seashore, wildlife, swimming, boating, village touring.

**RECOMMENDED COUNTRY INNS® TRAVELERS' CLUB BENEFIT:** Stay two nights get third night free, Sunday to Thursday, except July and August. July and August, 10 percent discount each night, Sunday to Thursday. No discounts Fridays and Saturdays and last week in July.

*T*his handsome Victorian inn is on a quiet side street in the sleepy village of New Church. It was built in 1802 and known then as Bloxom's Tavern. In 1901 the colonial tavern was substantially enlarged and embellished to transform it into the Victorian home we see today. That's when all the gables, stained glass, and gingerbread trim were added. In 1988 the home underwent another metamorphosis when it was converted into a country inn with dining rooms on the first floor. It acquired its name then—a recognition that the restaurant serves the freshest bounty from both the garden and the sea. An adjacent building, known as the Garden House, was added to the property in 1993 to supplement the increasingly popular overnight accommodations. Tom and Sara Baker have owned the complex since 1994.

Tom graduated from the Culinary Institute of America and prepares excellent meals with a Continental twist using fresh locally caught fish and vegetables and herbs from the kitchen garden. A sautéed breast of chicken with apricots and brandy cream sauce one night was outstanding; so was the grilled boneless lamb ribeye with currant-rosemary sauce. There's a nice wine list to accompany the meal.

There are three guest rooms in the Victorian house. This includes a gorgeous new room that was incorporated into a former private dining room in

1998. Chardonnay has a carved Victorian bed covered with an ivory duvet, an Oriental rug, and lace curtains. But the bath is the pièce de résistance. It has a skylighted cathedral ceiling, a stained-glass window, a dressing area, and both a double-sized Jacuzzi and a separate shower.

The Garden House, which contains three more rooms, has a comfortable parlor with a television and a VCR for guests to use and a small kitchen. Refreshments are set out every afternoon and often include fresh fruit, sherry, brownies, or chocolate chip cookies.

Since the season in this section of the DelMarVa Peninsula is defined, the inn closes from December through mid-March.

**HOW TO GET THERE:** Take Route 13 south from Dover, Delaware, or Route 50 south from Washington, D.C., to Salisbury, Maryland. Continue south on Route 13 for approximately 29 miles to Route 710 (1 mile past the Virginia border). Turn right onto Route 710. The inn is on the right just beyond the Virginia Welcome Center.

# The Page House Inn 📱 💟
## Norfolk, Virginia 23507

**INNKEEPERS:** Stephanie and Ezio DeBelardino

**ADDRESS/TELEPHONE:** 323 Fairfax Avenue; (757) 625–5033 or (800) 599–7659; fax (757) 623–9451

**E-MAIL:** innkeeper@pagehouseinn.com

**WEB SITES:** www.pagehouseinn.com and www.boatandbreakfast.com

**ROOMS:** 7, including 3 suites; all with private bath, air-conditioning, television, telephone with dataport, radio, coffeemaker, hair dryer, robes, iron, and ironing board; 4 with fireplace and/or CD player, 3 with whirlpool tub and/or VCR. Children over the age of 12 welcome. No smoking inn.

**RATES:** $120 to $200, double occupancy; includes full breakfast and afternoon refreshments. Two-night minimum weekends April to October.

**OPEN:** All year.

**FACILITIES AND ACTIVITIES:** Rooftop garden. Bed-and-breakfast on a boat, $200 to $300. Nearby: Chrysler Museum of Art; Virginia Opera, Symphony, and Stage Company; Naval Base Tour; Hampton Roads Naval Museum; Mariner's Museum; Harbor and Sailing Tours; Virginia Beach.

**BUSINESS TRAVEL:** Telephone with dataport, television, hair dryer, coffeemaker, iron, and ironing board in all rooms; desk in 6 rooms. Fax and copier available; meeting rooms; corporate rates.

*I* always wish I could send enthusiastic, budding innkeepers who are considering the purchase of a deteriorated old house to see Stephanie and Ezio so that they realize what an authentic restoration entails. In this case Ezio is a highly professional master craftsman who knew exactly what had to be done to stabilize, repair, and restore this house that most folks thought should be torn down. And Stephanie—well, she's absolutely indefatigable. From getting new laws passed that permitted a bed-and-breakfast in Norfolk to convincing the neighbors that this was a good idea, she never gave up, and their beautiful inn is now a lasting tribute to their hard work.

But they certainly didn't stop when the first guest arrived in 1991. In 1996, when I visited, they had just completed the conversion of the inn's formal dining room to a fabulous suite they appropriately call the Bathe Suite. It has a gold and evergreen canopy bed, a gas fireplace, and a Chippendale sofa, as well as a sunken hot tub and a large shower and steam room.

In 1997 they added Bianca Boat and Breakfast, providing overnight stays on a 43-foot Nauticat built in Finland and moored on the Elizabeth River—directly on the Intracoastal Waterway. Yes, breakfast really is served on board. How? A hot breakfast that includes fresh breads, pastries, fruit, juice, and, perhaps, an omelette wrapped around roasted peppers is delivered daily by water taxi. This is the ultimate romantic accommodation.

The inn is located in Ghent, a waterside neighborhood built between 1892 and 1912 and filled with wonderful old mansions. It's a treat to walk along Mowbray Arch with the houses on one side and a park bordering an inlet of the Elizabeth River on the other.

One chilly morning in December we took an invigorating walk along this route and returned to find hot cups of steaming coffee waiting. But that was merely a prelude to a fabulous breakfast that included a lush smoothie, a brioche bread, pound cake, and poached eggs with sausage.

HOW TO GET THERE: From I-63 east or west take exit for I-264 (toward downtown Norfolk) and follow signs (staying in left lane) to exit 9, Waterside Drive. Continue on Waterside Drive, which curves and becomes Boush Street. Turn left onto Olney Street (after Grace Street). Continue for 2 blocks and turn left onto Mowbray Arch, go 1 block to Fairfax Avenue, and turn right. Inn is on the left; park behind.

# The Ashby Inn 🫶
## Paris, Virginia 20130

**INNKEEPERS:** John and Roma Sherman; Debby Cox, manager

**ADDRESS/TELEPHONE:** 692 Federal Street; (540) 592–3900; fax (540) 592–3781

**E-MAIL:** ashbyinn@mnsinc.com

**ROOMS:** 10, including 4 suites; 8 with private bath; all with air-conditioning, 8 with telephone, 5 with fireplace and balcony, 4 with steeping tub and television. Children over the age of 10 welcome. Smoking permitted in Tap Room and Library only.

**RATES:** $130 to $220, double occupancy; includes full breakfast; $30 charge each additional guest; additional $20 to $30 surcharge for Saturday-only stay.

**OPEN:** All year.

**FACILITIES AND ACTIVITIES:** Restaurant serving dinner Wednesday to Saturday (entrees $18 to $27) and brunch Sunday (prix fixe $19); Tap Room. On four and one-half acres with perennial, herb, and vegetable gardens; horseshoe pit. Nearby: hiking Sky Meadows State Park and Appalachian Trail, Bellgrove Mansion, antiquing, vineyard tours, horse shows, trail rides, Shenandoah River sports.

*T*he tiny village of Paris (formerly known as Pun'kinville) was renamed to honor the Marquis de Lafayette, who paid the town a visit after the Revolutionary War—perhaps to stop at Ashby's Tavern, just across the street from the present Ashby Inn, with his friend George Washington.

Time has been kind to the town, which probably looks much the same as it did then. And travelers still visit primarily to partake of the fine food and spirit (both liquid and convivial) that are offered at the village inn. After a local hunt the Tap Room fills with exuberant laughter, and on Sundays a crowd in a more leisurely frame of mind arrive from the city for the buffet brunch. Dinner is my favorite time to visit, however, especially if I can merely walk upstairs or down the street to the old schoolhouse to my room.

You might sit in the lower dining room, as I have done, in one of the intimate booths, where you can watch the swirl of activity from a quiet outpost. Or you might sit in one of the more formal dining rooms. Regardless, you will probably spend a few minutes perusing the collection of books in the library, warmed by the fire in the fireplace if it's winter, before you go to dinner. And you will certainly spend time admiring the wonderful, vibrant oil paintings on the walls. Should one particularly suit your fancy, you can take it home; they are all for sale.

Maybe your meal will begin with the unique Ashby Caesar Salad that includes freshly grated Parmesan cheese and polenta croutons. I had a wonderful roasted Chilean sea bass one night with couscous, olives, and roasted red peppers. For dessert the chocolate torte with coconut ice cream and chocolate sauce was terrific.

The guest rooms are perfection. All are furnished in lovely period antiques, but they are not the pretentious sort. Instead they are the kind that make you feel comfortable and relaxed. Roma collects and repairs priceless antique quilts, and you will see one or several of these in most guest rooms. There are balloon shades in pretty floral patterns on the windows.

In the main inn the New England room, a medley of greens, has a beautiful star-patterned quilt on the hand-painted bed; the Victorian Room has a cannonball bed and a bath with a red iris pattern on the walls. The Fan Room, which has its own private entrance, has a beautiful Palladian window and its own balcony.

The nicest rooms, however, are in the converted schoolhouse just down the road. I love Lafayette. It has a fabulous porch that looks out over the fields below and to the Appalachian Mountains beyond. In the misty early morning light, you will see deer, Canada geese, and wild turkeys. The room has a cathedral ceiling, a fireplace, a canopied four-poster bed, and a window wall. A window seat stretches beneath the window, and it's overseen by wall sconces perfectly placed for reading a good book found on the shelves. I couldn't resist rereading several stories in *Great Short Stories of the Twentieth Century,* which included "The Man Who Would Be King" by Rudyard Kipling.

John and Roma are an engaging couple who had high-powered careers in Washington, D.C., before creating their sanctuary from the city. During the dinner hour especially, the inn is filled with their friends and longtime customers, who obviously appreciate their consummate professionalism.

HOW TO GET THERE: From Washington, D.C., take I–66 west to exit 23 (Delaplane/Paris). Follow Route 17 north for 7½ miles. Turn left onto Route 701, the little road that runs through the center of Paris. The inn is straight ahead.

# The Smithfield Inn
## Smithfield, Virginia 23430

INNKEEPER: Mrs. Janice Scott

ADDRESS/TELEPHONE: 112 Main Street; (757) 357–1752; fax (757) 365–4425

ROOMS: 5 suites; all with private bath, air-conditioning, telephone, television, desk, and minirefrigerator; 2 with fireplace, 1 with private porch. Children welcome. No smoking inn.

RATES: $125, double occupancy; includes full breakfast.

OPEN: All year.

FACILITIES AND ACTIVITIES: Restaurant serving lunch Tuesday to Sunday and dinner Wednesday to Saturday (entrees $16 to $23); garden with gazebo. Nearby: Williamsburg, Jamestown, Norfolk, Virginia Beach, numerous plantations to visit, bicycling, golfing, fishing.

RECOMMENDED COUNTRY INNS® TRAVELERS' CLUB BENEFIT: 10 percent discount, Monday to Thursday.

When you think of Smithfield you think of ham, right? And when you think of ham you think of Smithfield. The huge processing plant does dominate the area just north of town, but the village also has a nice collection of handsome houses, shops, restaurants, and inns.

Smithfield's chronicle began long before little porkys started giving their all. In 1607 the first English settlers landed at Jamestown, just up the James River from Smithfield, and changed the course of history. The little inn with its broad front porch that sits on Main Street was built in 1752 and has served as an inn since 1759. Once on the main stage route from Norfolk to Richmond, it has witnessed much of America's history. In 1922 it was purchased by the Sykes family, who operated Sykes Inn here for more than forty years. In 1996 it was purchased and renovated by Smithfield Foods. Mrs. Sykes was Joe Luter III's grandmother, and he is now CEO of Smithfield Foods, thus bringing the inn full circle.

Although the exterior of the inn is Colonial in appearance (it has a yellow-clapboard and brick facade with white trim and green awnings), the first floor is decidedly Victorian. There are exquisite Victorian antiques in the entry hall and parlor, and the dining rooms have heavy gold velvet drapes and gold wallpaper. The adjoining William Rand Tavern, a more casual dining room and lounge, is equally attractive. The walls here are sponged in muted brown and gold, and there's a comfortable sitting area with a stunning sofa in Russian patchwork fabrics and drapes in gray-green moire taffeta. The interior shutters have etched glass inserts. French doors lead to a brick courtyard and a side garden with a fountain. When the tiny little lights on the brick wall of the adjacent building are illuminated at night, the garden looks like a fairyland.

We were here one year for New Year's Eve, when the inn and its dining rooms were in a festive mood. The wonderful Victorian ambience was supplemented by balloons and streamers that made the rooms radiant. But you needn't wait for a holiday to dine here. A marvelous dinner might start with clam and roasted-corn fritters in a Cajun Creole sauce or Smithfield peanut soup. One time I had Chicken Smithfield, a pan-seared boneless breast of chicken fused with Smithfield ham and served with a rosemary-mushroom demiglace; another time I had jumbo lump crab cakes. For dessert the sweet potato pecan pie is decadently rich.

The five suites, all located on the second and third floors, combine a variety of styles, but all are beautifully decorated. The Joe Luter and the George Washington have bedrooms with huge murals on the walls; the Pembroke Decatur Gwaltney is very masculine with a black-and-white Egyptian fabric on the walls. There are pine floors, Oriental rugs, beds dressed with cutwork duvets, down pillows, silky sheets, televisions, telephones, and minirefrigerators. The beautiful baths are done with tile, although several have showers only.

And, yes, George Washington did actually sleep here!

HOW TO GET THERE: From Norfolk/Virginia Beach take I–264 toward downtown Norfolk, following signs for the downtown bridge-tunnel to Portsmouth. Continue on I–264 toward Newport News/Hampton and take exit 9A onto Route 17 north toward the James River Bridge. Do not cross the bridge, but turn left instead onto Route 258 south (Brewer's Neck) and follow the signs to Smithfield. When you reach Route 10 west, turn right and follow this for 5 miles to Smithfield. Take the Route 10 business route (stay in the right lane; this becomes Church Street) to go into the town of Smithfield. Turn left onto Main Street. The inn is on the right.

# Smithfield's Gift to Gastronomy

One of my most consistently used food references is the Time-Life series called *Foods of the World,* which was published in the 1960s and 1970s. Not only are the books packed with wonderful regional recipes, they are extremely well written by knowledgeable authors who are intimately familiar with the region they are describing. *American Cooking: Southern Style* (published in 1971) was written by Eugene Walter, who was raised in Alabama, and the Editors of Time-Life Books. The following is from this book.

"To the serious traveler and eater, Virginia means two things above all: history and ham . . . Smithfield is a shrine hallowed by food lovers everywhere—home of Virginia's world-famous hams.

"Smithfield is, appropriately, just a few miles from Hog Island, where the original Jamestown settlers kept their hogs. It is a placid little town with only one hostelry, Sykes Inn, which was built in 1752. The inn has a high, wide front porch and spotless rooms furnished with old wooden beds and wardrobes. My experience of its dining room reassured me that there are, indeed, places in the South where public eating is a pleasure.

"The young man who presently runs Sykes Inn is Russell Thompson, a conscientious and ingratiating host. I questioned him point-blank:

"'What *is* a Smithfield ham?'

"'. . . The hog has to be the lean type, part razorback, and usually it has been at least partly peanut-fed,' he replied. 'And you have to know how to cook it!'

"'And how *do* you cook it?'

# Smithfield Station
## Smithfield, Virginia 23430

**INNKEEPERS:** Ron and Tina Pack; Mark Mohrbach, manager

**ADDRESS/TELEPHONE:** 415 South Church Street; (757) 357–7700 (fax same)

**ROOMS:** 20, including 2 suites; all with private bath, air-conditioning, television, telephone, coffeemaker, hair dryer, iron, and ironing board; 10 with balcony, 4 with fireplace, 1 with whirlpool tub. Wheelchair accessible. Children welcome. Smoking permitted.

**RATES:** $69 to $225, double occupancy; includes continental breakfast Monday to Friday.

**OPEN:** All year.

**FACILITIES AND ACTIVITIES:** Waterfront restaurant serving breakfast, lunch, and dinner (entrees $15 to $22); raw bar and grill; swimming pool, boardwalk, marina. Nearby: boating, sailing, fishing, golfing, Isle of Wight Museum.

**BUSINESS TRAVEL:** Telephones and televisions in rooms; meeting room with full audiovisual capabilities; fax, copier available; corporate rates.

*S*tretching along a placid area of waterfront along the Pagan River, which flows into the James River nearby, Smithfield Station was built by Ron and Tina Pack in 1986. "We found we were spending so much time in Smithfield and loved it so much that we decided to create our home here," Tina told me. They started out by building a bed-and-breakfast on the highway into town. But they soon expanded by building this waterfront inn, which includes a restaurant, outside raw bar, and marina.

The main inn reminds me of a cross between a lighthouse (it's got a tower with a crow's nest) and a Mississippi riverboat (a double row of porches encircle it). The waterside restaurant has beautiful views of the water, as do many of the guest rooms. Those on the second floor have access to the porch as well; the rooms on the top floor have dormer windows.

The rooms in the main inn are well designed and handsome. The rooms are carpeted, there is custom-crafted wood furniture, and the baths are tiled. There are no cutesy or frilly extravagances, just comfortable rooms with spectacular water views.

For the romantics among us, the lighthouse, a building completed in 1991 and located several yards down the boardwalk from the main inn, is where we want to head. What a fabulous retreat! The lighthouse is an exact replica of the St. Michael's Light in St. Michaels, Maryland, and it features two suites, one on the first floor and one on the second. The first floor suite is flooded with light from the tall windows and is surrounded by a deck. It is also used on occasion for small meetings or conferences. The upstairs suite is fabulous and utterly romantic. Light streams in from dormer windows, and the ceilings are curved up to the crow's nest on top, which can be reached from a spiral stairway in the suite. There's a gas fireplace before the luxurious bed.

The convivial restaurant specializes in local seafood, although you can get a good steak or a hamburger as well. There are salads, pasta dishes, and delicious desserts.

Come to Smithfield and you'll find it's got a lot more going for it than ham.

**HOW TO GET THERE:** From Norfolk/Virginia Beach take I–264 toward downtown Norfolk, following signs for the downtown bridge-tunnel to Portsmouth. Continue on I–264 toward Newport News/Hampton and take exit 9A onto Route 17 north toward the James River Bridge. Do not cross the bridge, but turn left instead onto Route 258 south (Brewer's Neck) and follow the signs to Smithfield. When you reach Route 10 west turn right and follow this for 5 miles to Smithfield. Take the Route 10 business route (stay in the right lane, this becomes Church Street) and follow this for 2 miles. Cross the small bridge. The inn is directly on the water on the right, just across the bridge.

# The Manor at Taylor's Store
## Smith Mountain Lake, Virginia 24184

**INNKEEPERS:** Mary Lynn and Lee Tucker

**ADDRESS/TELEPHONE:** Route 122 (mailing address: Route 1, Box 533, Wirtz); (540) 721–3951 or (800) 248–6267; fax (540) 721–5243

**E-MAIL:** taylors@symweb.com

**WEB SITE:** www.symweb.com/taylors

**ROOMS:** 10, including 6 suites and 1 cottage; all with air-conditioning; 8 with private bath, 3 with whirlpool bath, 5 with fireplace, 6 with porch or patio. Wheelchair accessible. Children welcome in cottage. No smoking inn.

**RATES:** $85 to $185, double occupancy; includes full breakfast. Corporate rates available.

**OPEN:** All year.

**FACILITIES AND ACTIVITIES:** Game room, exercise room, hot tub, guest kitchen; on 120 acres, Colonial garden, walking paths, with six ponds for swimming, fishing, and canoeing; volleyball, badminton, croquet. Nearby: restaurants and Smith Mountain Lake (5 miles), antiquing, country roads, state park, plane rides, hot-air balloon rides, golf, Blue Ridge Parkway.

Taylor's Store was a significant landmark to the early pioneers who brought their goods to Skelton Taylor's establishment as early as 1799. It was on an early westward route known as the Old Warwich Road, and they undoubtedly stocked up at his store before heading into the wilderness. The building later became an ordinary, and, later still, it was turned into the general post office for the area. Mary Lynn and Lee Tucker converted the property into a country inn in 1983.

The original manor house was built in 1820 and was the centerpiece of a large tobacco plantation. It is still located on 120 acres that are laced with six ponds and a multitude of hiking trails. Swimming docks offer opportunities for swimming or sunbathing, there are canoes to use, and fishing poles for the fisherpersons. Brick pathways lead through the gardens and to a gazebo; there's another gazebo next to a pond, which is a wonderful place for a private picnic. A hot tub is located on a lattice-enclosed porch, where you can relax in private under the stars and with your favorite music softly piped in. Brick walls encircle the white-clapboard house, which has black shutters.

The manor house is the epitome of graciousness. A formal parlor is decorated with fine antiques, including a fabulous tall-case clock designed by Stanford White, a Victorian sofa and chairs, and European oil paintings. A sunroom is appreciated by both plants and people. A great room has a huge brick fireplace, a large-screen television (there's an extensive video library), and a billiards table. A

guest kitchen provides a place for guests to store picnic supplies and, perhaps, a bottle of their favorite wine. There's also an exercise room with a step machine, bicycle, and rowing machine for those who want to stay in shape while they're on the road.

The guest rooms are located in the main building and also in the West Lodge, a hand-hewn log cabin set away in the woods. Another private cottage, which has three bedrooms, two baths, a kitchen, and a den with a fireplace, is ideal for families. It has decks and lovely views of a pond and the surrounding forests.

The rooms in the manor house have antique furnishings and sophisticated decor ranging from one with an English castle theme (with a canopy bed, two antique throne chairs, prints of English castles, and a bath with a sunken tub for two) to a toy room that features an antique rocking horse, a canopy bed, and antique quilts on the walls. French doors lead to a balcony. The English Garden suite is located on the garden level. It has an antique brass bed and a private porch filled with antique wicker.

The three suites in the West Lodge share a great room with a huge stone fireplace and a front porch with rockers. Two of the rooms have their own fireplace and whirlpool tub.

Breakfast is eaten in a sunroom on wrought-iron tables with glass tops. The menu will include freshly baked breads, homemade granola, fresh fruit and juice, and, perhaps, apple puff (pancakes) with Canadian bacon.

**HOW TO GET THERE:** From I–81 in Roanoke take exit 143 onto I–581/220 south, which will take you through Roanoke. Continue on Route 220 south through Boone's Mill to the Route 122/40 exit, and then go north on Route 122 toward the Booker T. Washington National Monument and Smith Mountain Lake. Pass through Burnt Chimney and continue for exactly 1⁶/₁₀ miles to the inn, which is on the right.

# Jordan Hollow Farm Inn
Stanley, Virginia 22851

**INNKEEPERS:** Gail Kyle and Betsy Anderson

**ADDRESS/TELEPHONE:** 326 Hawksbill Park Road (Route 626); (540) 778–2285 or (888) 418–7000; fax (540) 778–1759

**E-MAIL:** JHF@jordanhollow.com

**WEB SITE:** www.jordanhollow.com

**ROOMS:** 20; all with private bath, telephone, air-conditioning, and porch; 8 with television, 4 with fireplace and whirlpool bath. No smoking inn. Children welcome.

**RATES:** $110 to $154, double occupancy; $83 to $127, single occupancy; both include full breakfast; additional person $25; children 16 and under stay in parents room free.

**OPEN:** All year.

**FACILITIES AND ACTIVITIES:** Farmhouse Restaurant serving breakfast and dinner (entrees $15 to $25); pub; on 150 acres with hiking and cross-country trails, mountain biking, horseback riding ($20 per hour), horse boarding for guests' horses. Nearby: swimming pool, fishing, golf, tennis, canoeing, museums, antiques shops, Luray Caverns.

**BUSINESS TRAVEL:** Telephone in all rooms; fax available; conference center with all facilities.

**RECOMMENDED COUNTRY INNS® TRAVELERS' CLUB BENEFIT:** Stay two nights, get third night free, Monday to Thursday, subject to availability.

The complex that makes up Jordan Hollow Farm Inn is composed of numerous buildings. Guests will check in at an office recently created in a restored carriage house. This is also where the Great Room, a gathering room with a fireplace, a television, and books, is located. The Farmhouse Restaurant is nearby in a log cabin dating from 1785. The hand-hewn beams are still visible and there's a fireplace. Sixteen guest rooms are located in Arbor View Lodge, a building fronted by a wisteria-covered porch populated by a herd of Kennedy rockers and offering panoramic views of the Blue Ridge or Massanutten Mountains. Four more rooms in Mare Meadow have fireplaces and whirlpool tubs.

The property has been a working horse farm for two centuries, and it continues to be a horse farm today. Gail Kyle and Betsy Anderson have owned it since 1996, and they encourage guests to bring their own horses, but you can also ride one of the inn's horses. The accomplished staff members lead guests on trail rides. Depending on your skills, you can take a gentle beginner ride or join the advanced treks into the mountains.

All this activity will undoubtedly make you hungry, but not to worry. The evening often begins in the Watering Trough, a rustic bar that's been carved out of a former stable. Convivial conversation centers on the pool table and other games.

Dinner is not a dress-up affair at Jordan Hollow Farm. The dining room is located in the original log cabin, which has heart-pine floors and chestnut posts and beams, conveying the rustic simplicity of its origins. The food, just like the furnishings, will be homey and hearty. The menu  includes fresh trout, chicken, and pasta dishes. There are house-baked breads, fresh-from-the-garden salads and vegetables, and desserts such as pear crisp and chocolate mousse cake. A complete wine and beer selection is available.

Arbor View Lodge has cozy, homespun rooms decorated in a lively and fresh manner with old tables and chests, farm and horse paraphernalia, quilts, and twiggy headboards. Each room includes a small bookshelf that is selectively filled. The baths are straightforward and modest, and the sinks are in the room.

Mare Meadow Lodge, on the other hand, appeals to those who want a bit more luxury. The rooms have hand-hewn pine furniture, fireplaces, and whirlpool tubs.

There are numerous activities to occupy you if you don't care to horseback ride one day. A canoeing outfitter, for example, will make arrangements for a day on the Shenandoah River, or the inn has 5 miles of hiking and mountain biking trails. The property abounds with cats, goats, horses, and sheep, as well as three dogs, who will charm even the most confirmed city slickers.

**HOW TO GET THERE:** From I–66 take exit 13 (Front Royal and Linden) onto Route 55 traveling to Front Royal. At the third traffic light in Front Royal turn left onto Highway 340 south business. You will reach Luray in about 24 miles. Continue on Highway 340 beyond the traffic light in Luray for 6 more miles. Continue past the Exxon station on the left for $^1/_{10}$ mile and turn left onto Route 624. At the next stop sign turn left onto Route 689 and cross the bridge. In $^1/_2$ mile turn right onto Route 626. The inn's entrance is on the right in $^1/_4$ mile.

# Osceola Mill Country Inn
Steeles Tavern, Virginia 24476

**INNKEEPERS:** Brian Domino and Mercer Balliro

**ADDRESS/TELEPHONE:** Route 56 (mailing address: General Delivery); (540) 377–MILL (fax also)

**ROOMS:** 13, including 1 suite and 1 cottage; all with private bath; 8 with air-conditioning; cottage with fireplace, television with VCR, CD player, and whirlpool tub. Wheelchair accessible. Children welcome. No smoking inn.

**RATES:** $89 to $169, double occupancy; includes full breakfast. Two-night minimum in October.

**OPEN:** All year.

**FACILITIES AND ACTIVITIES:** Marl Creek Tavern Friday and Saturday serving dinner (entrees $10 to $19); on eleven acres with pool, bicycling. Nearby: Blue Ridge Parkway, Appalachian Trail, the National Bike Trail, wineries, antiques shops.

The huge, gray weathered mill with its enormous overshot wheel is a rustic reminder of the days when Cyrus McCormick, who was raised on his father's farm here, invented the McCormick reaper, thus industrializing the farms of America. Before his reaper was used in 1830, it took twenty hours to harvest an acre of wheat; afterward this was reduced to less than one hour. The mill is on property that was once part of the McCormick farm, and it is the largest of seven mills that ground wheat into flour on Marl Creek. It operated from 1849 through 1969, but today the quaint rooms serve as the dining rooms for the inn.

The Marl Creek Tavern, as the dining room is called, has chestnut timbers, and you can see the old millstone. There's a large porch where you can watch the creek rushing by. You might sample a chicken breast stuffed with ham and smoked Gouda in a basil-cream sauce and served with angel hair pasta or a grilled bourbon and maple–basted tenderloin of beef.

There are four guest rooms upstairs in the mill. They have exposed timbers, quilts on the beds, and views of the Blue Ridge Mountains and of Marl Creek. They all have private baths, although two have only a shower. The rest of the guest rooms are located across the street in The Mangus House, a neat and trim gray weathered farmhouse dating to 1873 that once belonged to the successful miller. It has been meticulously restored and includes a parlor, music room, game room, and porches, all of which are available for guests to use.

The rooms here are furnished with Victorian-era antiques. Some have brass beds, others have beds with oak or walnut headboards, and several are four-poster beds. There are quilts here also. The ultimate retreat, however, and one that is often preferred by honeymooners, is the Mill Store, a separate cottage. It has vaulted ceilings, a huge stone fireplace, and a whirlpool tub.

Brian and Mercer have owned the inn since 1993, and they serve a fabulous full breakfast. You will start with fresh fruit and homemade granola accompanied by home-baked muffins, scones, bread, and pastries. For an entree you might receive banana- or pear-stuffed French toast with warm maple syrup or, perhaps, a four-cheese quiche with herbs.

HOW TO GET THERE: From I–81 take exit 205 (Raphine) and turn right if traveling north and turn left if traveling south. Continue on this road for 1³/₁₀ miles to Route 11. Turn left and then take the next right onto Route 56. Follow this for ⁷/₁₀ mile to the inn, which is on the right.

# Steeles Tavern Manor Country Inn

## Steeles Tavern, Virginia 24476

**INNKEEPERS:** Bill and Eileen Hoernlein

**ADDRESS/TELEPHONE:** Route 11 (mailing address: P.O. Box 39);
(540) 377–9261 or (800) 743–8666; fax (540) 377–5937

**E-MAIL:** hoernlei@cfw.com

**WEB SITE:** www.steelestavern.com

**ROOMS:** 5, including 2 suites; all with private bath, air-conditioning,
television, VCR, video library, whirlpool tub, robes, iron, and ironing
board; 4 with fireplace. Not suitable for children. No smoking inn.

**RATES:** $130 to $160, double occupancy; includes full breakfast, afternoon tea, and evening sherry. Packages available. Two-night minimum
weekends.

**OPEN:** All year, except several weeks in winter.

**FACILITIES AND ACTIVITIES:** Restaurant serving dinner for house
guests with prior reservations (prix fixe $55 to $80 per couple, including
a bottle of Virginia wine), on fifty-five acres with hiking trails, fishing
pond, stream. Nearby: Blue Ridge Parkway, skiing and golfing at Wintergreen Resort, Wade's Mill, Buffalo Springs, Herb Farm, wineries,
antiquing.

**RECOMMENDED COUNTRY INNS® TRAVELERS' CLUB BENEFIT:** 10 percent discount, Monday to Thursday.

The handsome gray-stucco building with its imposing double-
height white columns and black shutters is actually as warm and
inviting as its host and hostess. Eileen and Bill Hoernlein, who
purchased the building in 1995, have created an intimate and romantic adult
retreat in the heart of the Blue Ridge Mountains. The inn was built in 1916,
and the Hoernleins had to add modern plumbing, heating, air-conditioning,
and even new windows to create just the right atmosphere they were seeking.

When David Steele moved to this area in 1781, he and his young wife
provided housing to travelers on this well-traveled post road. Soon the stage
came along and the tavern became a place to change horses and eat, and the
area grew to include a general store, several flour mills, a cooper shop, a
blacksmith shop, and a schoolhouse. In 1834 David's son John encouraged
his friend Cyrus McCormick to give the first demonstration of his newfan-
gled reaper in the field of oats in front of the tavern.

There are several lovely common rooms. The living room has a fireplace with a painted wooden mantel and interesting family heirlooms. There's a mantel clock that had belonged to Eileen's great-grandmother, a walnut table with a marble top, and brass candlesticks from Bill's family. Recessed shelves hold volumes of books and videos.

The dining room, which is romantically Victorian, is decorated in dark colors. Breakfast is served to inn guests here at individual tables, or it can be delivered to your room for a romantic breakfast in bed. Eileen is a great cook. She or Bill deliver coffee to your door early in the morning. Breakfast, which is generally served in the dining room between 8:30 and 9:30, will include a freshly baked breakfast bread, fresh fruit, and, perhaps, scrambled eggs with gingerbread pancakes and sausage. It will be served by candlelight and on fine china, crystal, and silver.

The guest rooms, which are named for flowers, are charming cocoons of elegance. A basket of wine and snacks will be waiting for your arrival, and each of the rooms, as well as the common rooms of the inn, contain antique clothing—perhaps several parasols or beaded bags—that had belonged to Bill's aunt. Hyacinth has a king-size sleigh bed; Buttercup has an antique oak high-headboard and footboard bed. There are lace curtains on the windows and pretty floral fabrics on the beds. The baths all have large, two-person whirlpool tubs.

Eileen loves to cook, and her dinners are as special as her breakfasts. If you make reservations in advance, you can have dinner at the inn. The Hoernleins are very knowledgeable about Virginia wines, and they have a nice selection that they offer their dinner guests along with the meal. The five-course menu will include freshly baked bread, a soup course, a salad course, perhaps an entree of Rock Cornish game hen, and a dessert. The wine is complimentary with the meal.

The inn is on fifty-five acres that include hiking trails, a stream, and a fishing pond with relaxing lounge chairs beside it.

HOW TO GET THERE: From I–81 take exit 205 and follow signs for Steeles Tavern, following Route 606 east for 1½ miles to Route 11. Turn right onto Route 11 and then make a quick left into the inn's driveway.

# Sugar Tree Inn 🦢
## Steeles Tavern, Virginia 24476

**INNKEEPERS:** Sarah and Hal Davis

**ADDRESS/TELEPHONE:** Highway 56; (540) 377–2197 or
(800) 377–2197; fax (540) 377–6776

**WEB SITE:** www.sugartreeinn.com

**ROOMS:** 11, including 2 suites; all with private bath, fireplace, and coffeemaker; 8 with private porch, 7 with air-conditioning, 4 with VCR,
3 with whirlpool tub. Wheelchair accessible. Not appropriate for children. Smoking permitted in 1 room only.

**RATES:** $100 to $150, double occupancy; includes full breakfast. Two-
night minimum weekends in May, early June, October, and all holidays.

**OPEN:** April 1 to November.

**FACILITIES AND ACTIVITIES:** Restaurant serving gourmet dinners by
reservation (entrees $16 to $21); live music some nights; on twenty-eight
acres with hiking trails, a creek, a front porch with 40-mile sunset view;
wildflower, herb, and vegetable gardens. Nearby: Blue Ridge Parkway,
Appalachian Trail, hiking, biking, and walking trails less than a mile
away; wineries, golfing.

*I*t may look as old as the hills whence these logs came, but the main
inn and one guest house were actually built in the mid 1980s using
logs that had been salvaged from 125+-year-old log cabins,
churches, and stores. There are chinked log walls using authentic dovetail
construction and native stone fireplaces in every room.

Although the interior of the inn has an Early American feeling, it is done
with utmost sophistication. And no wonder, for Sarah and Hal Davis are
excellent interior designers. They've owned the inn since 1994, and the work
they've done is incredible. Inside the main lodge there are wood plank ceilings, massive hand-hewn beams, and log walls in the Great Room. A stone
fireplace rises two stories to a skylight, which separates the Great Room from
the Sign of the Swine tavern—a relaxed, brick-floored spot in which to have
a glass of wine or beer. There's a library filled with books, games, and videos
upstairs in a loft.

The guest rooms are located in the main lodge, Caithness Cabin, and Chellowe House. All the rooms are decorated with spritely quilts and have stone fireplaces, log walls, and beamed ceilings. Sugar Tree Country, in the main lodge, has a whirlpool tub in the room. It offers both a mountain and fireplace view when bathing. Antique circus posters decorated the walls of the P. T. Barnum room in Chellowe House and Jefferson Davis has a fabulously carved antique walnut Victorian bed.

During the week a hot or cold basket dinner is prepared for inn guests, which they can eat wherever they like. Dinner is served to inn guests as well as the public on weekends with soft classical music playing in the background, and sometimes there will be entertainment such as a blue grass band. The menu features haute country gourmet dishes that use local ingredients. A spring menu, for example, might start with a garden pizza or cock-a-leekie soup, followed by a salad of carrots with a honey-ginger glaze. The entree might be pork loin with mustard cream sauce accompanied by tarragon buttered beets, red and green peppers au gratin, and Aunt Gertie's corn pudding. For dessert there

may be a key lime pie or a "corn likker" pecan pie. The dining room is a glass enclosed room with another stone fireplace. Iron chandeliers and candlelight give a soft glow to the beamed ceiling and log walls.

You can sit on the front porch here and listen to the array of birdsongs or watch a woodpecker search for bugs. Repose quietly as a raccoon ambles by, and at dawn and dusk see the deer feed in the nearby meadows. On clear nights the sunsets are spectacular, and you will have a 40-mile view from this perch at the 2,800-foot level.

Sugar Tree Inn has won more awards than it's possible to mention. And this special inn deserves every one of them.

**HOW TO GET THERE:** From I–81 take exit 205 onto Route 606 and follow that for 1½ miles to Steeles Tavern. Turn left onto Route 11 and then take an immediate right onto Route 56. Follow this through Vesuvius and go left across the railroad tracks before climbing 2⁸/₁₀ miles up the twisting mountain road to Sugar Tree Inn, which is on the right.

# The Inn at Vaucluse Spring
## Stephens City, Virginia 22655

**INNKEEPERS:** Karen and Mike Caplanis; Neil and Barry Myers

**ADDRESS/TELEPHONE:** 140 Vaucluse Spring Lane; (540) 869–0200 or (800) 869–0525; fax (540) 869–9544

**E-MAIL:** mail@vauclusespring.com

**WEB SITE:** www.vauclusespring.com

**ROOMS:** 12, including 2 suites and 2 cottages; all with private bath, air-conditioning, fireplace (some suites have two fireplaces), and radio; telephone and dataport available for all rooms; 11 with whirlpool tub, 4 with porch or patio. Wheelchair accessible. Children over the age of 10 welcome. No smoking inn.

**RATES:** $145 to $250, double occupancy; includes full breakfast. Two-night minimum from mid-April through mid-June and from mid-September through mid-November, as well as holidays, if stay includes Saturday night.

**OPEN:** All year except Thanksgiving and Christmas.

**FACILITIES AND ACTIVITIES:** Four-course dinner Saturday night to house guests only (prix fixe $35 plus 15 percent gratuity); on 103 acres with swimming pool, spring, millpond, stream, gardens with perennial border, two herb gardens, and one hundred acres of pasture for small herd of Holstein cattle. Nearby: golfing, winery tours, hiking, antiquing, canoeing, visits to Route 11 potato chip plant, historic house tours at Belle Grove and Glen Burnie, Wayside Theatre.

**BUSINESS TRAVEL:** Telephone with dataport available for all rooms; desk in 7 rooms. Meeting space, fax, copier, word processor available.

**RECOMMENDED COUNTRY INNS® TRAVELERS' CLUB BENEFIT:** 10 percent discount, Monday to Thursday, subject to availability.

What a perfect little country inn! It has a secluded country setting, friendly innkeepers who have thought of everything to make a stay flawless, beautifully restored historic buildings, and exceptional decor. Oh, yes, also lovely romantic dinners on Saturday nights exclusively for their guests. I would like to move into the Mill House Studio for six months to write a novel. But instead I must content myself to stay here on occasion.

Karen and Mike, along with Neil and Barry, purchased their 103-acre enterprise in 1995. It had formerly been the studio and home of John Chumley, a well-known local artist. The picturesque tumble of buildings housed his studio, which overlooked a spring pond, an art gallery with a porch across the front, and a charming "home place" where he and his wife lived. A grand Federal brick manor house stood high on the hill, desperately in need of restoration.

The farm originally belonged to Gabriel Jones, known throughout the area as the "valley lawyer." In about 1785 Gabriel's son Strother built the magnificent manor house. Hard times brought on by the Civil War descended on the family, however, and they lost "Vaucluse." The manor house was abandoned for some fifty years, and only the brick chimney was left of Mr. Jones's original law office.

Those hard-luck days are well behind the estate now. The manor house has been fully restored, and this is where the reception area is now located. Massive triple-hung, 10-foot-high Jeffersonian windows and dramatic cherry

and walnut doors rise almost to the 11-foot ceilings. The deep claret–red living room has an 1830s Greek Revival fireplace mantel, plus a chintz sofa and piles of books on the coffee table.

The inn's two dining rooms are located here also, where breakfast is served every morning and dinner is served to inn guests on Saturday nights. The menus are inventive, colorful, and yet uncomplicated. Dinner guests might start with a twin pepper soup (red and yellow pepper soups poured into the same bowl and topped with a disc of Boursin cheese), followed by a salad of baby greens dressed with a maple Balsamic vinaigrette. For an entree there might be a salmon fillet crusted with smoked salmon and topped with warm horseradish sauce. This could be served with southern creamed rice and broccoli sautéed with caramelized shallots. A dessert might be cinnamon apples in phyllo shells topped with ginger ice cream and caramel sauce.

For nights when they are not serving dinner at the inn, you might go to One Block West in Winchester, as I did one night. I had a delicious meal of grilled shrimp, followed by a salad of marinated Bermuda onions with a

# The Buttons on Gabriel's Coat

Gabriel Jones and his progency lived on the estate known as Vaucluse for some hundred years, and many of his descendants continue to live nearby today. Gabriel was King's Attorney for Frederick County and served several terms in Colonial Virginia's House of Burgesses. He was the first "legal gentleman" to cross the Blue Ridge Mountains, and he was known up and down the Shenandoah Valley as the "valley lawyer."

A story is still told of a card game Jones played in 1750 with several notable gentlemen that included James Wood, the founder of the town of Winchester. The game was played at Wood's estate, Glen Burnie. Gabriel was dressed in the style of the time with a pigtailed wig and a fine coat with silver buttons. The hour grew late and the mistress of the house sent her young house servant to see how the game was progressing. The breathless youngster returned to report that the game must be almost over because, "They're down to the last button of Master Gabe's coat."

To this day, when things are scarce, descendants of Gabriel Jones talk about being down to "the last button on old Gabe's coat."

tomato marmalade and pesto sauce. A dish of grilled chicken came with garlicky mashed potatoes and spinach. For dessert I had a fabulous bread pudding with Jack Daniels sauce.

My favorite guest rooms are not in the manor house, where they are undeniably beautiful, but in the Chumley Home Place, where a common room called the Keeping Room has log walls, beamed ceilings, and a huge stone fireplace. There's a pretty stone-floored terrace room with wicker furniture and a wall of windows that look out to the perennial garden. The guest rooms here are quirky and wonderful, with low ceilings and lots of little nooks and crannies. My ultimate favorite accommodation, however, is the Mill House Studio. It has a living room on the main floor with a fireplace, and a terrace and it sits on the banks of the millpond. Upstairs there's a bedroom with a brass bed, Chumley prints on the wall, and a view of the water.

You can hear the sound of the water rushing over a waterfall beside the studio and on into the stream.

**HOW TO GET THERE:** From I–66 westbound take exit 1B onto I–81 north. Go 1 mile and take exit 302 onto Route 627 toward Middletown. At the end of Route 627 turn right onto Route 11. Go 2 miles and turn left onto Route 638 (Vaucluse Road). Go ¾ mile and turn left at the sign for the inn.

# Prospect Hill 🎞️ 📱 💝
Trevilians, Virginia 23093

**INNKEEPERS:** Michael and Laura Sheehan

**ADDRESS/TELEPHONE:** 2887 Poindexter Road; (540) 967–2574 or (800) 277–0844; fax (540) 967–0102

**E-MAIL:** michael@prospecthill

**WEB SITE:** www.prospecthill.com

**ROOMS:** 13, including 3 suites and 6 cottages; all with private bath, air-conditioning, fireplace, radio, and robes; 10 with desk, minirefrigerator, and coffeemaker; 9 with private porch or patio; 8 with whirlpool tub. Children welcome. Smoking permitted except in dining rooms.

**RATES:** $280 to $365, double occupancy; includes full breakfast, afternoon tea, bowl of fruit and a split of Virginia wine in room, and dinner. 10 percent discount Monday to Thursday. Two-night minimum if stay includes Saturday night.

**OPEN:** All year except Christmas Eve and Christmas Day.

**FACILITIES AND ACTIVITIES:** Dinner served nightly (prix fixe Sunday to Friday $48; Saturday and holidays $50); Board Room downstairs where wine and beer are served. On fifty acres with swimming pool, croquet, hammocks, extensive cutting gardens, trails. Nearby: carriage rides, fishing, golfing, horseback riding, tennis, winery tours, hot-air ballooning, Monticello, Ash Lawn-Highland, antiques shops.

**BUSINESS TRAVEL:** Desk, coffeemaker, and minirefrigerator in most rooms; fax and copier available; meeting room.

*M*ichael Sheehan greets you with a firm handshake and ushers you into this former plantation house, which dates back to 1732. This is reputedly the oldest continuously operating plantation in America; it traces its roots to the 1600s. As families grew and plantation activities increased, dependency buildings were added to the grounds: a smokehouse, carriage house, and summer kitchen, to name a few. These structures have been turned into charming guest rooms, all connected to the main house by a stone pathway.

One of my favorites is the Boy's Cabin, a log cabin that dates back to 1699. It has log walls, a brick fireplace, and a simple bed that is covered with a quilt; nevertheless, the bath is large and absolutely modern. Another favorite is the Overseer's Cottage, which has a four-poster bed, a fireplace, and a step-down sitting room with a private deck. Each of the cottages is impeccably furnished in a style that is appropriate to its original use, but with all the comforts we love today. There are five rooms in the plantation house as well; these are the most elegant.

Bill and Mireille Sheehan created the inn in 1977. Eventually they eased out of hands-on innkeeping, and their son Michael stepped into the innkeepers' shoes. When I asked if he and his wife, Laura, are training their daughter and son to eventually assume the responsibility, he replied they wear T-shirts that read: "Innkeeper in training."

Behind the inn stretches a lawn shaded with massive old leafy trees. A hammock is suspended between the trees. A pool and cabana entice sunlovers on warm days. Large white wicker chairs cuddle the afternoon reader on the small porch in back, while the Board Room downstairs, with its soft  leather chairs and fireplace, serves the purpose in cool weather. There's also a formal living room with a stereo to listen to classical music.

Dinner at Prospect Hill is an experience that should not be missed. For many years Mireille was the chef, preparing meals inspired by the foods of Provence, where she grew up. Today Michael prepares classically inspired French cuisine spiced up with a bit of Provence, as his mother used to, but with his own twist. He uses herbs from his kitchen garden and garnishes each dish with flowers, making them as pretty as they are delicious.

The dining rooms (there are three separate rooms) are charmingly decorated, as if they were plucked directly from the French countryside. There are wide-plank polished floors, fireplaces in two of the rooms, and French antiques and fabrics used throughout.

Dinner begins with a wine reception. The five-course menu changes every night, but typically it will include a creative appetizer, then a soup, followed by a salad. The entree may be a pan-seared tenderloin of veal forestière. For dessert perhaps Michael will have prepared a blackberry-and-Drambuie cheese torte served with a blackberry coulis. All this is accompanied by wines from the extensive selection. It's a wonderfully romantic way to spend an evening.

Prospect Hill is one of my favorite inns—an enchanting getaway in the country, where exceptional food, gracious innkeepers, charming rooms, and a relaxed style blend to create a perfect stay.

**HOW TO GET THERE:** From I-64 take exit 136 onto Route 15 south and go to Zion Crossroads. At the intersection with Route 250, turn left (east) and go 1 mile to Route 613. Turn left onto Route 613 and travel 3 miles. Prospect Hill is on the left.

---

# 1763 Inn 🎎 🖼
## Upperville, Virginia 20184

**INNKEEPER:** Uta Kirchner

**ADDRESS/TELEPHONE:** 10087 John Mosby Highway (Route 50); (540) 592-3848; fax (540) 592-3208

**WEB SITE:** www.1763INN.com

**ROOMS:** 18, including 1 cottage and 4 log cabins; all with private bath, air-conditioning, telephone, television, private porch or patio, minirefrigerator, coffeemaker, and hair dryer; 15 with fireplace, 14 with whirlpool tub. Children welcome in some rooms. Smoking permitted.

**RATES:** $100 to $205, double occupancy; includes full breakfast; additional person $40. One box firewood provided; additional is extra. Two-night minimum if Saturday stay included. Corporate rates.

**OPEN:** All year.

**FACILITIES AND ACTIVITIES:** Lunch Saturday and Sunday, dinner Wednesday to Sunday and holidays ($14 to $22). Tavern, fifty acres in

Virginia horse country, pond, swimming pool, tennis, trails through private woods. Nearby: wineries, horseback riding, polo matches and steeplechase races, hiking, fishing, canoeing, bicycling, antiques shops in Middleburg.

**BUSINESS TRAVEL:** Telephone, television, minirefrigerator, and coffeemaker in all rooms; desks in some rooms. Meeting rooms; fax, copier available.

When you walk up the pathway to the stone and half-timber main building of this popular inn and restaurant, you'll be greeted by a smiling wooden sculpture made by a local lumberjack. When a gala event is going on, he can spit fire from his mouth. The sculpture symbolizes the variety of interests that have been combined to create this unique inn. Don and Uta Kirchner purchased the property, which incidentally once belonged to George Washington, in 1983, and they've added something new every year.

The main building, with portions that date to 1763, contains the restaurant; this is the centerpiece of the inn. There's a romantic and intimate timbered lounge upstairs, which has a stone fireplace, and an outside deck overlooking the pond, which often has swans frisking about.

The dining tables are distributed among several small and intimate rooms. The most romantic, in my opinion, is the French Room, which has several booths as well as tables. French plates decorate the walls. It's a secluded and seductive room. The George Washington Room has a stone fireplace that dates to 1763 and oil paintings that literally cover the walls.

The German Room has another fireplace, and the walls hold photographs of Uta's family, who are German.

The restaurant specializes in German cuisine, so you might include a schnitzel or rouladen in your evening meal or, perhaps, have the Rheinischer sauerbraten, a wonderful roast that's been marinated for several days, slow-roasted, and then finished with a gingersnap gravy. Desserts include apple strudel and Hot Love, a potion of vanilla ice cream and hot raspberry sauce.

The guest rooms were thoroughly updated in 1996, and they are lovely. Some are located in the main building; others are in a duplex cottage and in a converted barn. There are also individual accommodations in the carriage house and in four log cabins that Don purchased in West Virginia. He dismantled them, shipped them here, and reassembled them in private spots in the woods. They offer the ultimate in romantic retreats. All the log cabins have stone woodburning fireplaces, quilt-covered beds with fishnet canopies, double whirlpool tubs, and separate showers.

One of my favorite rooms is the Mosby Suite, which is located in the main building. It has a four-poster bed, a huge stone fireplace, and a whirlpool tub that separates the bedroom from the bath. There's a lovely deck with a view of the pond.

The inn is located on fifty acres in the Virginia hunt country. There's a pool and a tennis court on the property, as well as the pond and hiking trails.

**HOW TO GET THERE:** From I–66 take exit 23 (Paris/Delaplane) onto Route 17 north. Travel 9 miles to the stop sign at Route 50. Turn right and go 1½ miles to the inn, which is on the right.

---

# The Inn at Gristmill Square
## Warm Springs, Virginia 24484

**INNKEEPERS:** The McWilliams Family; Bruce McWilliams, manager

**ADDRESS/TELEPHONE:** Main Street (mailing address: P.O. Box 359); (540) 839–2231; fax (540) 839–5770

**E-MAIL:** grist@va.tds.net

**WEB SITE:** www.vainns.com/grist.htm

**ROOMS:** 17, including 1 suite; all with private bath, air-conditioning, television, telephone with dataport, and minirefrigerator; 8 with fireplace, 6 with porch or balcony, 1 with whirlpool tub. Limited wheelchair accessibility. Children welcome. Smoking permitted in guest rooms.

**RATES:** $80 to $140, double occupancy; includes continental breakfast; $155 to $210, per couple; includes breakfast and dinner.

**OPEN:** All year.

**FACILITIES AND ACTIVITIES:** Waterwheel Restaurant closed Mondays during winter. Full breakfast available, dinner (entrees $17 to $22), Sunday brunch, pub. Swimming pool, three tennis courts, sauna ($5.00 fee). Nearby: natural hot springs; carriage rides, horseback rides, golfing, fishing, hunting, Garth Newel Music Center, skiing at the Homestead.

**BUSINESS TRAVEL:** Telephone with dataport, television, minirefrigerator in all rooms; desk in 5 rooms; corporate rates; conference room.

Nestled in a quiet village around a brook is the enticing and romantic Inn at Gristmill Square. It's a combination of five buildings that surround a stone-paved square. The flavor is that of a nineteenth-century mill village, with rooms located in a former miller's house, blacksmith shop, hardware store, and town residence.

The inn's romantic Waterwheel Restaurant, located in an old stone Purina mill, has a foundation that dates back to 1771. Although the mill subsequently burned, it was rebuilt in 1900 and continued to operate until 1970. The Simon Kenton pub, the world's tiniest bar, is named for a boy who once worked here after fleeing his home because he thought he had killed a rival suitor. Before dining you can descend to the wine cellar to select your own wine.

The atmosphere in the restaurant is utterly charming. There are beamed ceilings, rough-sawn pine walls that have been painted white, and a view of the huge old grain hopper. Downstairs in the pebble-floored wine cellar, you can see the old gears. Fresh daisies graced the tables when I last ate there, and tall green tapers cast a flickering light across the rooms.

The fare includes fresh grilled trout served with herb butter, fresh pan-fried trout dipped in crushed black walnuts and cornmeal and sautéed until

crisp, or grilled ribeye steak. Desserts include bread pudding with whiskey sauce and deep-dish apple pie. It's an unpretentious meal in a delightful setting.

The guest rooms are located in four buildings near the mill, and each room is distinctively decorated. Esther McWilliams and her husband single-handedly restored and built this inn, respecting the quality of the construction and adding interesting materials wherever they found them. Their son, Bruce, is the manager now.

One of the buildings is the old village hardware store. It's located just across the brick courtyard from the old mill. It has one round room with a fireplace, called the Silo Room, and another called the Board Room because it has walls made of rescued barnwood. Rag rugs cover bare floors and the bath includes a claw-foot tub. The Dinwiddie Room has a stone fireplace made by Hessian soldiers and rescued from one of George Washington's early forts. Other rooms are located in the Blacksmith Shop, which is where the office is also located, and in two houses across the street—the Miller House and the Steel House. All the rooms have modern baths.

The grounds include the old mill stream, a swimming pool, three tennis courts, and a sauna.

HOW TO GET THERE: From I–64 take exit 16 (Covington) and travel north on Route 220 for 25 miles through Hot Springs to Warm Springs. In the village turn left (west) onto Route 619 and then turn right onto Main Street. The inn is on the right in less than a block.

# The Black Horse Inn
## Warrenton, Virginia 20187

INNKEEPER: Lynn A. Pirozzoli

ADDRESS/TELEPHONE: 8393 Meetze Road; (540) 349–4020; fax (540) 349–4242

E-MAIL: blackhrs@citizen.infi.net

WEB SITE: www.blackhorseinn.com

ROOMS: 9, including 2 suites; all with private bath and air-conditioning; 4 with fireplace and whirlpool tub. Wheelchair accessible. Children over the age of 12 welcome. No smoking inn. Inquire about policy on pets.

RATES: $125 to $295, double occupancy; includes full breakfast and afternoon "hunt country" tea. Generally two-night minimum weekends April to June and September to November.

OPEN: All year except Christmas Day.

FACILITIES AND ACTIVITIES: On twenty acres with riding stables, jogging trail, formal gardens with gazebo, area with stationary bicycles, exercise videos, mountain bicycles. Nearby: steeplechase racing, wineries, horseback riding, golfing, boating, hiking in Shenandoah Mountains, Appalachian Trail, biking and cross-country skiing across street on Rails-to-Trails path.

Although this gracious 1850s white-clapboard mansion has been welcoming travelers since 1986, when Lynn Pirozzoli purchased it in 1993, she undertook a top-to-bottom renovation. Calling it The Black Horse Inn, she opened it again in 1995. The inn recalls the Black Horse Cavalry, a prestigious mounted unit that was conceived by Warrenton lawyers in 1838. It led a successful battle against Union forces in the first battle of Manasses.

The original part of the gracious country manor was built in 1850, but significant renovation and expansion took place in 1910. It served as a hospital during the Civil War. Guests enter the inn through the double-height columned veranda.

Located in the heart of Virginia's hunt country, the inn has it own hunter stables (guests are encouraged to bring their own equine companions), and the activities associated with fox hunts and point-to-point races swirl around the inn during the season. Lynn, who is an accomplished rider herself, will prepare picnic lunches and tailgate baskets so that even her guests with their feet on the ground can participate. When races are not under way, the mead-

ows surrounding the house are filled with tranquilly grazing horses and will frequently yield sights of white-tail deer, wild turkeys, and cautious red foxes.

Lynn has appropriately chosen a hunt theme for the decor of her inn. The first thing you'll notice is the grand circular stairway that winds to the second floor. There's a living room with comfortable overstuffed chairs and sofas. There are statues, lamps, and objects d'art in a horse or dog motif. There's also a cherry-paneled library filled with shelves of books and with another fireplace. A porch offers views of the gardens and gazebo.

The guest rooms are romantic, intimate, and alluring and filled with beautiful antiques. One of my favorites is Hunters Haven, a spacious, masculine room that has the feel of a very elegant hunting lodge. There's a rock fireplace, an antique Chippendale canopy bed, and a beautiful chest. The deep green spread on the bed reflects the greens in the hound-dog wallpaper border. A fabulous tile bath has wainscoted walls, a whirlpool tub, and a separate glass shower. Lynn reports that more than forty-five proposals of marriage have been accepted in this room. She asserts, "Perhaps the room brings out the 'hunter' in men. To the best of my knowledge our hunters have never been refused."

Reynard's Retreat has a wonderful ambience as well. It includes a twisted-post canopy bed, an oak bookcase, an oak rolltop desk, and a fireplace with a marble mantel. The bath has a whirlpool tub and a pedestal sink. The most romantic room, however, and one frequently reserved for honeymooners, is Great Expectations. It has a bed with a carved headboard covered in a frothy white spread, a fireplace, an antique cubbyhole desk, and a sofa in an ivory damask. It also has its own private sunporch. In the bath there's a whirlpool tub for two and a separate shower.

A full breakfast is served in the formal dining room. Lynn is noted for her great meals. A typical menu will include gourmet coffee, fresh juice, and

# There's Still Gold in Them Hills

Have you ever dreamed of striking it rich—of winning a multi-million dollar lottery or of finding your own gold mine?

Well, Lynn Pirozzoli, owner and innkeeper of The Black Horse Inn in Warrenton, Virginia, did just that. She had worked in corporate America for eighteen years as Vice President of Environmental and Government Affairs for several major companies. But her most lucrative job, ironically, was the one that allowed her to transition into a new life of owning and operating The Black Horse Inn.

Lynn struck gold—literally—in the Mojave desert in an area that had been discovered by the Forty-niners during the mid-1800s California Gold Rush. When the mines petered out they were abandoned. With new technology, however, the area was reclaimed, and Lynn was there to help. Gold that earlier miners could not extract was removed, launching Lynn on a new career. She invested the proceeds in the restoration and renovation of The Black Horse Inn. And she hasn't looked back since!

muffins hot from the oven. There will be fresh or baked fruit, depending on the season. Her creative entrees might include Little Washington French Toast (a recipe she received from The Inn at Little Washington), stuffed with brown sugar, pecans, and mascarpone cheese or, perhaps, Beggars Purse, a poached egg served on a bed of spinach, enclosed in phyllo, and tied to look like a purse. It's served with hollandaise sauce and one of Lynn's special sausages.

Everything about this inn is perfection, and in our opinion that will be the sum of your stay here—perfection.

HOW TO GET THERE: From I-66 take exit 43A (Warrenton) and travel south on Route 29 for approximately 13 miles to the second exit for Warrenton, which is Route 643 (Meetze Road). Turn left and go 1⁶⁄₁₀ miles; the inn is on the left.

# Bleu Rock Inn 🖼
## Washington, Virginia 22747

INNKEEPERS: Bernard and Jean Campagne; Richard Mahan, manager

ADDRESS/TELEPHONE: 12567 Lee Highway; (540) 987-3190 or (800) 537-3652; fax (540) 987-3193

E-MAIL: therock@monumental.com

WEB SITE: www.insiders.com

ROOMS: 5, all with private bath; air-conditioning, desk, and hair dryer; 4 with balcony. Wheelchair accessible. Children welcome. Pets permitted with prior permission. Smoking in lounge or outside only.

RATES: $109 to $195, double occupancy; includes full breakfast and French brandy in room; extra person over 8 years old $35.

OPEN: All year; closed Mondays.

FACILITIES AND ACTIVITIES: Restaurant serving dinner Wednesday to Sunday (entrees $18 to $22) and Sunday brunch ($7.00 to $17.00). On eighty acres with vineyards, orchards, gardens, and pond stocked with trout for fishing. Nearby: Skyline Drive, Shenandoah National Park, Appalachian Trail, antiquing, golf, horseback riding, hiking, and wineries.

The white-stucco farmhouse with its blue roof had been the center-piece of a horse stud farm for many years, and the red stables are still located beside the circular driveway. But in 1990 when Bernard and Jean Campagne, who hark from the Basque region of France and also own LaBergerie Restaurant in Alexandria, purchased the farm, they converted the farmhouse into a charming and very popular restaurant plus five guest rooms. The inn sits high on a hill overlooking its eighty acres of vineyards and orchards and with the Blue Ridge Mountains in the distance. Pastoral and peaceful, there's even a pond on the property that's stocked with bass, catfish, and bluegill for fishing.

As one can imagine, the bounty of the farm figures prominently in the cuisine served at the restaurant. The vineyards are planted in Cabernet Sauvignon, Chardonnay, and Seyval vines, and the inn bottles its own wines. Nectarine, apricot, peach, and apple trees produce fruit for picking and for cooking. The cuisine is imaginative and grounded in classical French methods. The Alsatian choucroute garnie is marvelous, but a typical meal might begin with a Caesar salad with

spicy crabmeat fritters followed by medallions of local free-range veal tenderloin served with risotto. Desserts are heavenly and include a toasted pecan cake with praline cream and warm caramel sauce and a walnut-prune Armagnac cherry roulade with an English custard sauce.

There are three delightful dining rooms to choose from: One has beautiful flowers painted on the walls, another has floral oil paintings, and all include charming stone fireplaces. A broad slate patio offers additional dining in the summer and has panoramic views of the pond, vineyards, and mountains. A lounge has another stone fireplace as well as a piano, games, and books for guests to enjoy.

The restaurant is clearly the focal point here, as the guest rooms are quite plain and ordinary compared with the dining rooms. Four of the rooms have balconies, but the beds have motel-like headboards attached to the wall, and the baths are standard with few amenities.

**HOW TO GET THERE:** From Washington, D.C., take I-66 west to exit 43A (Gainsville). Follow Route 29 south for 12 miles into Warrenton. In Warrenton take Route 211 west and travel for 24 miles, passing both entrances to Washington, Virginia. The inn is on Route 211, on the right.

# Shhhh! Don't Wake the Cardinal

The farmland surrounding Bleu Rock Inn in Washington, Virginia, is populated with a variety of beautiful birds year-round. The cardinals are especially numerous, and guests frequently enjoy watching them feed near the terrace.

Although a poll has never been taken, there is perhaps one cardinal who is sometimes met with less than enthusiasm. Someone must have told her that her job at the inn is to act as an alarm clock; every day, precisely at 7:15 A.M., she begins her daily wake-up calls. She flies around the inn going from the window of one guest room to the next, pecking on each window and balcony door until she has worked her way around the entire inn.

Her daily job done for her humans, she flies away to join her bird buddies—thus allowing those who preferred to snooze a bit later to drift back to sleep.

# The Inn at Little Washington
Washington, Virginia 22747

**INNKEEPERS:** Patrick O'Connell and Reinhardt Lynch; D. Scott Little, general manager

**ADDRESS/TELEPHONE:** Middle and Main Streets (mailing address: P.O. Box 300); (540) 675–3800; fax (540) 675–3100

**ROOMS:** 14, including 4 suites; all with private bath, air-conditioning, telephone, and robes; 9 with balconies or patios, 4 with Jacuzzis, 1 with a fireplace. Wheelchair accessible. Children welcome. Pets permitted, but they must stay in a separate building; guests bring their own cage. Smoking permitted except in dining rooms.

**RATES:** $275 to $575, double occupancy, Sunday to Thursday; $385 to $685, all Fridays and every day in October as well as selected holiday weekends; $440 to $730, all Saturdays and Valentine's Day; all include continental breakfast and afternoon tea.

**OPEN:** All year except Tuesdays and Christmas Day.

**FACILITIES AND ACTIVITIES:** Dinner Wednesday, Thursday, and Sunday, $88 per person; four-course, full-choice menu; Friday evening, $98; Saturday evening, $118 per person, seven-course, full-choice menu; beverages additional). Nearby: vineyard tours, antiquing, horse events, The Theatre at Washington Virginia, Skyline Drive, Shenandoah National Park.

he Inn at Little Washington is the mecca and nirvana for gourmets and oenophiles around the world. At least once in every food-lover's lifetime, a pilgrimage should be made to this hallowed spot. It has won every possible award, including five stars, five diamonds, and Restaurant of the Year from the James Beard Foundation, and *Zagats* readers made it the number-one restaurant in America for food, decor, and service. It is a member of the prestigious *Relais & Chateaux* organization. Expensive? Yes. Worth it? Yes! Yes! Yes! Every penny.

The restaurant and inn are located in the town the inn built. It has literally grown up with the restaurant. When Patrick O'Connell and Reinhardt Lynch opened their inn in 1978 in a little building that formerly housed a garage and then a general store, the town was a wide spot on a little country road that had been passed by. Not so today. There are now antiques shops, galleries, a theatre, and a multitude of bed-and-breakfast establishments.

If the decor and furnishings at The Inn at Little Washington seem a bit dramatic, it's no accident. They were designed by Joyce Conway-Evans, a London theatrical designer, whose charming sketches for each of the guest rooms are framed in the upstairs hallway. Unusual touches include walls papered with wallpaper and borders created by hand-cut paper flowers; the entryway ceiling is covered with a spectacular collage. Fabrics—used lavishly in window treatments, draping canopy beds, tenting the dining room, or creating a canopy for a sofa in a guest room—are exotic and lush. The baths are a medley of brass and marble. Lavish bouquets of fresh flowers sit by the bed, on the desk, and in the baths, and a bowl of fruit awaits guests' arrival. Museum-quality antiques and custom-made furniture are found throughout. Patrick and Reinhardt are inveterate collectors (how do they find time?), and some of their whimsical or elegant pieces in each of the rooms add to their charm.

As beautiful as the rooms are (and two new rooms were added in 1998), the dining room is the raison d'être for coming. Its decor is equally elegant, but it's the wonderful cuisine that we've come for. Patrick is the chef, and he

completed a stunning new kitchen in 1998 that is absolutely fabulous. It has one wall of windows that look out onto the gardens and another wall finished in blue-and-white tiles. Two chef tables right in the kitchen can be reserved for those who like to watch the behind-the-scene action.

A tiny sampling of the vast selections on the menu include an appetizer of a seared slab of goose foie gras served with pears poached in Sauternes and pickled cranberries; there's an intermezzo of lemon-rosemary sorbet with vermouth. One entree features a sandwich of veal and veal sweetbreads with oyster mushrooms, country ham, and onion-plum confiture. Desserts, of course, are fabulous—such as the warm Valrhona chocolate cake with molten center, with a side of roasted-banana ice cream. The menu changes every day, however, so you might have entirely different choices to make. Naturally there's an exceptional wine selection—some 13,000 bottles in the cellar, when I last asked.

If you can think about breakfast the next morning, you could have it brought to the room. It will include a basket of just-baked breads, juice, and a bowl of fresh fruit (we had perfect little raspberries one time) topped with crème fraîche, and coffee or tea.

**HOW TO GET THERE:** From Washington, D.C., take I–66 west 22 miles to Exit 43A (Gainsville). Follow Route 29 south for 12 miles to Warrenton and turn right onto Route 211 west. Go 23 miles, turn right at sign for Washington Business district. Go ½ mile to stop sign; the inn is on the right.

# The Iris Inn
## Waynesboro, Virginia 22980

**INNKEEPERS:** Iris and Wayne Karl

**ADDRESS/TELEPHONE:** 191 Chinquapin Drive; (540) 943–1991; fax (540) 942–2093

**E-MAIL:** irisinn@cfw.com

**WEB SITE:** www.irisinn.com

**ROOMS:** 9, including 2 suites; all with private bath, air-conditioning, telephone with dataport, television, radio, minirefrigerator, hair dryer, and robes; 8 with balconies, desks, and CD players; 3 with whirlpool tub; 2 with fireplace. Wheelchair accessible. Children over the age of 10 welcome. No smoking inn.

**RATES:** $80 to $140, double occupancy; includes full breakfast. Packages available. Two-night minimum weekends.

**OPEN:** All year.

**FACILITIES AND ACTIVITIES:** On twenty-one acres. Hot tub, observation tower, gardens, massage by reservation ($25 for 45 minutes). BYOB (Virginia beverage law permits wine consumption in your private room). Nearby: P. Buckley Moss Museum, Virginia Metalcrafters, Waynesboro Factory Outlet Mall, Fishburne Military School, Skyline Drive, and Blue Ridge Parkway. Vineyard tours, Wintergreen Resort for downhill skiing, golf, and horseback riding.

**BUSINESS TRAVEL:** Telephone with dataport, television, and minirefrigerator in all rooms; desk in 8 rooms. Early breakfast; fax and copier available; corporate rates.

*I*ris and Wayne Karl looked throughout the countryside for their ideal inn, and when they couldn't find it, they decided to build their dream inn on this hilltop aerie. The inn fits neatly among tall native trees and has a cedar-and-brick exterior with a double-decked porch from which to enjoy the views of the Shenandoah Valley and the wonderful forest smells, sounds, and sights. A steep driveway lined with brilliant irises leads up to the inn and gives the inn its name—that and the fact that it's the name of the owner as well.

The inn is as different from the precious and fussy antique-filled inns as a luxury resort is from a motel. We entered a great room that is the focal point of the inn. Light floods the room from windows that reach to the 20-foot-high cathedral ceilings; there's a fieldstone fireplace whose chimney also reaches the ceiling. All along one wall wildlife artist Joan Henley has painted a charming woodland scene of graceful deer, curious raccoons, bash-

ful bunnies, and a multitude of squirrels, chipmunks, herons, bluebirds, and robins amidst a tangle of greenery and on a carpet of flowers. Her work is featured throughout the inn. In a loft above the great room, guests can sit to read, watch the birds at the various feeders, or just gaze at the panorama of the Shenandoah Valley before them.

Each of the guest rooms is unique and themed to birds, animals, or flowers, and the tiled baths have hand-painted tiles that coordinate with the theme. The Bird Room has a pine pineapple-post bed and a lovely armoire. The room offers a terrific view. The Wildflower Room includes a pretty lingerie chest and a bath with a double whirlpool tub. Guests can climb to the top of the observation tower for an even better view. A hot tub on the deck offers a relaxing end to the day.

A new building was constructed in 1997 to house two luxury suites. Deep Woods has a stone fireplace, a cathedral ceiling, and a huge deck overlooking the woods. Joan painted foxes on a wooden box that hides the television. There's a four-poster canopy bed and a loft with a single bed as well. A private treadmill in the room and a kitchen are especially welcome to traveling businesspeople. (There are several major corporations nearby.) The Garden Suite has similar amenities, but several whimsical touches give it a special character. There's a chest on which Joan painted a cute little squirrel who is obviously looking for his acorns, which she painted inside the drawer. *Pot Man,* a large sculpture made of red clay flower pots, sits on a ledge of the loft overlooking the room.

Iris fixes a full breakfast for her guests, and it's not at all unusual for everyone to sit at the table and talk for hours. I remember one time when I arrived about noon and the conversation was so lively that no one could tear themselves away. Her entrees range from waffles and pancakes to an egg strata dish.

HOW TO GET THERE: From I–64 take exit 96 (Waynesboro-Lyndhurst) and turn south onto Route 624 toward Lyndhurst. Almost immediately turn left onto Chinquapin Drive. The iris-lined driveway up to the inn is on the left in approximately ³/₁₀ mile.

# L'Auberge Provençale
White Post, Virginia 22663

INNKEEPERS: Alain and Celeste Borel; Clay Morris and Albert Leach, managers

ADDRESS/TELEPHONE: Route 340 (mailing address: P.O. Box 119); (540) 837–1375 or (800) 638–1702; fax (540) 837–2004

E-MAIL: cborel@shentel.net

WEB SITE: www.laubergeprovencale.com

ROOMS: 14, including 4 suites; all with private bath and air-conditioning; 2 with steam shower. Children over the age of 10 welcome. Smoking in sitting room only.

RATES: $145 to $295, double occupancy; includes full breakfast. Additional person $25.

OPEN: All year except two weeks in January.

FACILITIES AND ACTIVITIES: Restaurant serving five-course dinner Wednesday to Sunday (prix fixe $55); on nine acres with gardens and *petangue* field (French game similar to bocci); other property, La Campagnette, on eighteen acres with a swimming pool and hot tub (open to all guests). Nearby: White Post Restorations, winery tours, restored mill, antiques shops, Blandy Farm, Skyline Drive, point-to-point races, horse shows, horseback riding, Apple Blossom Festival.

**BUSINESS TRAVEL:** Desk and telephone jack in three rooms; fax and secretarial services available; conference facility.

**RECOMMENDED COUNTRY INNS® TRAVELERS' CLUB BENEFIT:** 10 percent discount, Monday to Thursday.

*Y*ou will feel as though you are in a French country auberge in the heart of Provence the minute you walk into L'Auberge Provençale. Celeste Borel has filled the inn with spritely Provençale fabrics and country-French antiques. *Mais oui!* Alain was raised in Avignon, the heart of Provence. In fact, the immersion in a French ambience is so complete it's hard to imagine that this rural inn is actually in a village with a solid American past. It was named White Post when a young surveyor in the early eighteenth century set up white markers to plot the land. His name was George Washington.

The handsome stone manor house, which was built as a private home in 1753, sits on nine acres. A barn and other outbuildings give it the appearance of a rural French farm. There are three spacious rooms in the oldest part of the building, but the rest of the rooms are contained in two wings: one that

was added in 1983 and the other in 1993. They also have a French-country decor with pine canopy beds with turned posts, sleigh beds, and an antique cannonball bed. Seven of the rooms have fireplaces.

In 1998 the Borels purchased and renovated La Campagnette, a lovely eighteen-acre property about 3 miles from the inn that has a distinguished 1890s manor house, as well as a swimming pool and a hot tub. They have renovated this property into two fabulous suites and a beautiful room. The pool and hot tub here may be used by all guests.

Alain began acquiring his considerable culinary talent in his grandfather's restaurant kitchen when he was merely thirteen years old. Today the prix-fixe menu includes such French delicacies as an appetizer of *les escargots à la crème de Roquefort* (escargots with Roquefort cream and wild rice), a first course of *la salade composée au confit de caneton* (warm duck confit salad with field greens, apples, pinenuts, and sherry vinaigrette), *l'entr'acte* (an intermission) of a warm pear with cloves, an entree of *le red snapper de golfe à l'aubergine* (grilled red snapper with a rosemary-eggplant pancake and marjoram caper oil), and a dessert of poached peach in a nutty caramel sauce served with nutmeg cream.

Every year Alain and Celeste make improvements. It's always exciting to see what they will do next.

**HOW TO GET THERE:** From Washington, D.C., take I–66 west to exit 23 (Delaplane/Paris). Follow Route 17 north for 9 miles to Route 50. Turn left onto Route 50 and go to the first traffic light. Turn left onto Route 340 and proceed south for 1 mile to the inn, which is on the left.

# The Cedars Bed & Breakfast
## Williamsburg, Virginia 23185

**INNKEEPERS:** Carol Malecha and Jim and Bróna Malecha

**ADDRESS/TELEPHONE:** 616 Jamestown Road; (757) 229–3591 or (800) 296–3591; fax (757) 229–0756

**E-MAIL:** cedars@w.domaker.com

**WEB SITE:** www.ontheline.com/cedars

**ROOMS:** 9, including 2 suites and 1 cottage; all with private bath and air-conditioning; 2 with fireplace. Children welcome. No smoking inn.

**RATES:** $95 to $180, double occupancy; includes full breakfast. Two-night minimum most weekends and some holiday and special-event weekends.

**OPEN:** All year.

**FACILITIES AND ACTIVITIES:** Nearby: golf and beaches, Colonial Williamsburg, Jamestown, Yorktown, James River Plantations, Busch Gardens.

Carol, Jim, and Bróna Malecha purchased this gracious brick Georgian house in 1993. Although it had been a guest house since the 1930s, it needed considerable updating to turn it into a fine 1990s inn—and that's exactly what they did.

I entered a lovely foyer with a stairway leading to the second and third floors. To the left the elegant sitting room has a fireplace and attractively upholstered sofas and chairs. The bright room beyond seemed to beckon, however. The tavern porch is the heart of this inn. The light and sunny room has a tile floor, windows on three sides, and an abundance of plants. There are games to play, stacks of books, and a huntboard set with tea and soft drinks for arriving guests as well as stay-overs in the afternoon. Breakfast is served here in the morning amidst an abundance of flowers and candles in hurricane lamps.

The guest rooms are attractively decorated with antiques and reproductions. The George Washington Suite on the main floor has a reproduction four-poster canopy bed, an antique armoire, and a beautiful antique writing desk. The rest of the rooms in the main house are on the second and third floors. At the top of the stairs, a decanter of sherry and a bowl of macadamia nuts are set out for guests' enjoyment. The Christopher Wren room, on the third floor, is the inn's largest. It has a canopy bed with plum bed coverings,

a plaid sofa, a fabulous antique desk, and a window seat under the dormer window.

Additional rooms are located in the brick carriage house. The Lord Botetourt Room, on the top floor, has a cozy feeling with a slanted ceiling, a gas fireplace, and a pine wardrobe. The bath is modern and attractive.

The breakfast served at The Cedars is one of the most inventive I've run across. Carol is a marvelous cook, and she's adapted several old Colonial recipes to today's standards. In addition to fresh fruit, juice, and freshly baked breads, she may include her oatmeal-pudding entree—a dish made with oatmeal, eggs, milk, cottage cheese, nutmeg, and cinnamon. Brandied raisins and maple syrup are served on the side.

The inn is in a terrific location. It's directly across the street from the College of William and Mary and within walking distance of Colonial Williamsburg and Merchant Square.

HOW TO GET THERE: From I-64 take exit 242A (Busch Gardens) onto Route 199. Follow Route 199 for 4 miles. Turn right onto Route 5 east (Jamestown Road). Go 1²/₁₀ miles to The Cedars, which is on the right.

# Colonial Houses
# Historic Lodging 🖼️ 📱
## Williamsburg, Virginia 23187

INNKEEPER: Gillian Murphy; Steve Erickson, manager

ADDRESS/TELEPHONE: 302 East Francis Street (mailing address: P.O. Box 1776); (757) 229–1000 or (800) HISTORY; fax (757) 565–8797

E-MAIL: cwres@cwf.org

WEB SITE: www.history.org

ROOMS: 77 accommodations in 27 buildings, including 15 suites; all with private bath, air-conditioning, telephone with dataport, television, radio, hair dryer, porch or patio, iron, and ironing board; 24 with fireplace. Children welcome. Smoking permitted; designated nonsmoking rooms.

RATES: $90 to $515, double occupancy. Two-night minimum some weekends and holidays.

OPEN: All year.

FACILITIES AND ACTIVITIES: Numerous restaurants serving breakfast, lunch, afternoon tea, and dinner (entrees $20 to $30), bar in taverns and in inn; extensive gift shop and Craft House, where you can buy Williamsburg reproductions. All facilities of the Williamsburg Inn available, including golf course, swimming pools, tennis courts, fitness center, lawn bowling, croquet lawns, parlors, recitals, Christmas ceremonies.

BUSINESS TRAVEL: Telephone with dataport, television, iron and ironing board in all rooms; desk in most rooms; fax, copier, cellular telephones available; business center with secretarial services, computers; audiovisual equipment; conference center.

From 1699 to 1780 Williamsburg was the political, social, and cultural center of Virginia. But in 1780 the capital was moved to Richmond. In 1926, however, John D. Rockefeller came for a visit and appreciated the wealth of Colonial buildings still intact. He spearheaded the restoration of some eighty-eight original structures and the reconstruction of fifty others, and today the streets of Williamsburg look and feel much as they did in Colonial days. Here twentieth-century visitors can experience eighteenth-century history. Time has stopped and it's 1770 again.

Colonial character interpreters, dressed in Colonial attire, have assumed the identity of actual Williamsburg citizens. You may see a shepherd and his flock going down the street or listen to the Reverend Samuel Henley discuss his students and their education. Perhaps Duncan Steward will tell you about his store as he waits for a shipment or Mr. Kidd, the upholsterer, will show you his fabrics.

In my opinion there's no better way to experience this unique history lesson than to stay in the heart of the restoration, in one of the seventy-seven rooms and suites in twenty-seven of the restored houses and taverns. They are furnished with Colonial Williamsburg reproduction furnishings—some more elegant than others—to reflect the style of the house.

You might stay in a room in the Market Square Tavern, for example, where Thomas Jefferson and Patrick Henry once stayed or in one of the individual houses. One year we visited during the Christmas holidays and stayed in a charming little two-level cottage with its own private garden. There was

a fireplace in the living room and a four-poster bed up the narrow stairs in the bedroom. We were able to walk out our front door to admire the multitude of wreaths decorating each doorway and to watch the evening illumination of Duke of Gloucester Street. Huge torches of twigs were lighted by a runner, just as they must have been in Colonial days. Every evening a different historic mansion was also illuminated and a guide recited its history.

Another advantage to staying in the Colonial houses is that you can walk down the street to one of the Colonial taverns for dinner. On this trip we dined at Christiana Campbell's Tavern, a handsome building with a porch across the front and numerous dining rooms. There are pine floors, paneled walls, and candles lighting the tables. The waiters (our waiter, Russell, had worked for Colonial Williamsburg for thirty-four years) are dressed in Colonial attire, and there are strolling violinists and minstrels. Don't miss the wonderful spoon bread and the sweet potato–pecan muffins.

Colonial Williamsburg is a wonderful place for children and adults alike. You can visit numerous times and learn something new with every visit. All the facilities of the Williamsburg Inn are available to guests staying in the Colonial houses as well. There are swimming pools, a golf course, tennis courts, an extensive fitness center, croquet lawns, and numerous restaurants.

**HOW TO GET THERE:** From I–64 take exit 238. Go ½ mile and turn right onto Route 132 south and follow the signs for the Williamsburg business district and William and Mary College. Route 132 becomes Henry Street. After crossing the railroad tracks, go to the second traffic light. Turn left onto Francis Street. In approximately ¼ mile you will reach the Orell Kitchen, where registration for the Colonial Houses takes place. It is on the right.

# Trillium House 📷 📱
## Wintergreen, Virginia 22958

**INNKEEPERS:** Ed and Betty Dinwiddie

**ADDRESS/TELEPHONE:** Wintergreen Drive (mailing address: P.O. Box 280, Nellysford, VA 22958); (804) 325–9126; for reservations (800) 325–9126 (9:00 A.M. to 8:00 P.M.); fax (804) 325–1099

**WEB SITE:** www.trilliumhouse.com

**ROOMS:** 12, including 2 suites; all with private bath, air-conditioning, telephone, and desk; 1 with a patio; television available. Wheelchair accessible. Well-behaved children with responsible parents welcome. No smoking inn. Pets sometimes permitted with prior permission.

**RATES:** $105 to $160, double occupancy; includes full breakfast. Additional person $35; crib $10. Two-night minimum if stay includes Saturday; three-night minimum holiday weekends.

**OPEN:** All year.

**FACILITIES AND ACTIVITIES:** Dinner by reservation Friday and Saturday ($24 to $32), full beverage license. Activities at 11,000-acre Wintergreen Resort (additional charge), including skiing, nature trails, indoor swimming pool, outdoor pool, fitness center, whirlpool spa, golf, tennis, horseback riding, picnicking, sixteen-acre lake for boating and fishing, mountains and valleys. Nearby: restaurants, Monticello, Ash Lawn-Highland, Woodrow Wilson Birthplace, antiquing, universities, factory outlets.

**BUSINESS TRAVEL:** Desk and telephone in all rooms; television, fax and copier available.

rillium House is located in the 11,000-acre Wintergreen Resort, a mountaintop oasis of downhill ski slopes, 27 miles of hiking trails, cross-country skiing, golf courses, swimming pools, and almost every other imaginable form of outdoor activity. Located in the Blue Ridge Mountains, the views from up here are breathtaking. Just across the road from Trillium House, the Wintergarden has a full-service fitness center that includes both an indoor and an outdoor pool.

The dove-gray cedar exterior of the inn blends quietly into a grove of trees, almost becoming a part of the natural environment, just as a mountain lodge should. Ed and Betty Dinwiddie had the inn built to their specifications in 1983. In spring, when the little trillium flowers (for which the inn is named) are in bloom, the forest floor is carpeted in pink and white.

Guests enter a cathedral-ceilinged great room with a welcoming stone fireplace flanked by comfortable sofas and chairs. Oriental rugs sit on pegged-oak floors. On the other side of the fireplace, another fireplace warms the television room, where a large-screen television becomes the focal point when a sporting event is in progress or when a classic movie is being

played on the VCR. There's a little closet bar here from which guests can be served mixed drinks, wine, and beer. In a loft above the television room, a library contains more than 6,000 volumes. There are snug leather chairs on Oriental rugs for reading or gazing out the Palladian window at the forest.

The guest rooms are immaculate and comfortable. There are Shaker-style beds and Formica counters in the modern baths.

On Friday and Saturday nights delicious dinners using imaginative recipes are served in a dining room decorated with Betty's Majolica collection. A winter meal included a salad of mixed greens with a roasted-garlic vinaigrette and topped with Parmesan cheese, followed by an entree of glazed duck breasts with pear chutney and served with cornbread timbales and spiced crackling green beans. For dessert there were chocolate pancakes with banana cream.

Trillium House is located just 1 mile from the Blue Ridge Parkway and is an ideal place to stay if you are hiking the Appalachian Trail or simply want to enjoy nature in all its glory.

**HOW TO GET THERE:** From the north or east follow I–64 to exit 107 (Crozet) and then take Route 250 west to Route 151. From the west take I–64 to exit 99 (past Waynesboro) and then follow Route 250 east to Route 151. Follow Route 151 south for 14 miles; turn right onto Route 664 and follow this for 4½ miles to the entrance to Wintergreen Resort. From the entry gates follow Wintergreen Drive for 3 miles up the mountain, passing the Mountain Inn on the way. As you reach the top and level off, Trillium House is on the left just past Trillium Place.

# The Inn at Narrow Passage
## Woodstock, Virginia 22664

**INNKEEPERS:** Ed and Ellen Markel, Jr.

**ADDRESS/TELEPHONE:** Route 11 south at Route 672 (Chapman Landing Road) (mailing address: P.O. Box 608); (540) 459–8000 or (800) 459–8002; fax (540) 459–8001

**E-MAIL:** innkeeper@innatnarrowpassage.com

**WEB SITE:** www.innatnarrowpassage.com

**ROOMS:** 12; all with private bath and air-conditioning; 7 with fireplace, 10 with porch; shared telephones. Children welcome. Wheelchair accessible. No smoking inn.

**RATES:** $95 to $145, double occupancy; includes full breakfast. Two-night minimum weekends in spring, fall, and on holidays.

**OPEN:** All year except Christmas.

**FACILITIES AND ACTIVITIES:** On five acres; Shenandoah River canoeing and fishing. Nearby: restaurants (within 3 miles), Orkney Springs, New Market Battlefield, Belle Grove Plantation, Shenandoah Caverns, Shenandoah Valley Music Festival, skiing at Bryce Mountain, horseback riding, hiking, bicycling, antiquing.

**BUSINESS TRAVEL:** Desk in 6 rooms; conference room.

The heart of The Inn at Narrow Passage is the charming living room, which has wide-plank pine floors, chinked log walls, and a massive limestone fireplace. One can imagine the stories this room has to tell. It was built as a little log cabin beside the Great Wagon Road in 1740. Those stopping at the cabin had probably just come along the trail as it passed through a limestone ridge so narrow that there was room for only one wagon at a time—a spot where travelers were often subjected to Indian attack. From here they would journey along the Great Wagon Road to the Cumberland Gap in the southwest corner of Virginia, where they would traverse the mountains on their way to the western frontier.

The inn sits on a five-acre knoll above the Shenandoah River and has a porch lined with rockers that stretches across the back, affording lovely views

of the river and Massanutten Mountain just beyond.

Since innkeepers Ed and Ellen Markel purchased the inn in 1983, they have made numerous improvements. One of them is the addition of a wing that added another living room. In building it they created the same Early American atmosphere as the original cabin by using old pine flooring and paneling so cleverly that it's hard to distinguish it from its authentically old neighbor.

The guest rooms are furnished with Early American reproduction furniture, combined with interesting Colonial decor. All the beds are hand-crafted of pine, and each is different. Some have curved headboards, and others have canopy beds dressed with fishnet. Seven of the rooms have brick fireplaces, and ten of them have access to the porch.

Ellen fixes a full breakfast for her guests every morning. In addition to fresh fruit, juice, and a breakfast bread such as a cherry-almond coffee cake, there will be an entree of, perhaps, French toast with sausage and apples. It's hearty fare—just what folks who have come to canoe, hike, or bicycle need.

**HOW TO GET THERE:** From I–81 take exit 283 (Woodstock) to Route 11 south. The inn is 2 miles south on Route 11, on the left side of the road at Chapman Landing Road.

# Morrison-Clark

## Washington, D.C. 20001

**GENERAL MANAGER:** Josette Shelton; R.B. Associates, proprietor

**ADDRESS/TELEPHONE:** Massachusetts Avenue and Eleventh Street, NW; (202) 898–1200 or (800) 332–7898; fax (202) 289–8576

**ROOMS:** 54, including 13 suites; all with private bath, air-conditioning, telephone with dataport, refrigerator, and cable television; 3 with fireplace. Wheelchair accessible. Children welcome. Smoking permitted; designated nonsmoking rooms.

**RATES:** $165 to $250, double occupancy; includes continental breakfast; children under 16 stay free. Weekend rates, especially during summer. Covered valet parking, $15 per day.

**OPEN:** All year.

**FACILITIES AND ACTIVITIES:** Dinner served nightly ($18 to $22), lunch Monday to Friday ($11 to $20), and Sunday brunch ($20). Fitness center. Nearby: Metro stop (4 blocks), Smithsonian Museum, Kennedy Center, White House.

**BUSINESS TRAVEL:** Five-minute Metro ride to downtown. Telephone with dataport in room; desk in 36 rooms; fax and copier available; meeting room; corporate rates.

**RECOMMENDED COUNTRY INNS® TRAVELERS' CLUB BENEFIT:** $99 on Friday and Saturday, $145 Sunday through Thursday, double occupancy, subject to availability.

*T*he Morrison-Clark has a long and distinguished history. It was originally two separate townhouses: one built for David Morrison and the other for Reuben Clark. At some previous time one of the houses took on an Oriental look by sprouting a Chinese Chippendale porch and a Shanghai roof. The houses were eventually joined into one.

In 1923 the complex became the Soldiers, Sailors, Marines, and Airmen's Club, and for sixty years it functioned as an inexpensive hostel for servicemen traveling to Washington, D.C. During its peak in 1943, some 45,000 servicemen, many fresh from the front, slept here. Traditionally the club was under the wing of the First Lady, who held teas and benefits to raise operating funds. Mamie Eisenhower and Jacqueline Kennedy, in particular, expended considerable effort on its behalf.

In 1987 the building was turned into an inn, the restoration earning it a place in the National Register of Historic Places. A new wing and courtyard were added at this time. It has been under the current ownership since 1993.

The common rooms continue to display the original, elaborately carved marble mantelpieces, crystal chandeliers, and mirrors that reach almost to the 13-foot ceilings. The nicest guest rooms are located in the original Victorian houses, where several of the rooms have elegant antiques. Room 313, a rather small room where we stayed one night, has a wonderful balcony with an elaborate wrought-iron railing, a burled-walnut Victorian headboard, and an armoire that hides the television. There are wide moldings, thick doors, and a marble bathroom. The rooms in the wing are decorated either in French-country decor or with a Neoclassical theme.

The dining room on the main floor is elegant and refined. Its distinctive features include two fireplaces and a round banquette in the center of the room topped with a floral display that's so huge it almost touches the ceiling. Unfortunately the food on our last visit received a less-than-enthusiastic response.

**HOW TO GET THERE:** From I-95 south take exit 22-B, Baltimore–Washington Parkway, to Washington, D.C. Follow signs and exit New York Avenue in 5 miles. Continue 4 $^7/_{10}$ miles on New York Avenue to Fourth Street, N.W. Cross Fourth Street (you're now on L Street) and continue to Eleventh Street. Inn is on right on corner. Short-term parking in front for unloading. Or take Metro to Metro Center and exit L Street. Inn is 4-block walk.

# Select List of Other Inns in Virginia

## Summerfield Inn

101 West Valley Street
Abingdon, VA 24210
(540) 628–5905 or (800) 668–5905

*7 rooms; all with private bath; in lovely inn on quiet street in town.*


## White Birches

268 Whites Mill Road
Abingdon, VA 24210
(540) 676–2140 or (800) BIRCHES

*3 rooms; all with private bath; in B&B with lovely decor and lush gardens.*


## Little River Inn

Route 50
Aldie, VA 22001
(703) 327–6742

*10 rooms in various buildings; some with private bath; in village setting.*


## Dulwich Manor Inn

550 Richmond Highway (Route 5)
Amherst, VA 24521
(804) 946–7207

*6 rooms; 4 with private bath and 3 with fireplace.*

## Henry Clay Inn

114 North Railroad Avenue
Ashland, VA 23005
(804) 798–3100 or (800) 798–3100

*15 rooms; all with private bath; in inn and restaurant rebuilt in 1991 after a fire.*

## Edgewood Plantation

4800 John Tyler Memorial Highway (Route 5)
Charles City, VA 23030
(804) 829–6908 or (800) 296–3343

*7 rooms; all with private bath; in Victorian house filled with Victorian furnishings.*

## North Bend Plantation B&B

12200 Weyanoke Road
Charles City, VA 23030
(804) 829–5176 or (800) 841–1479

*4 rooms; all with private bath; in 1819 plantation house on working farm.*

## Piney Grove at Southall's Plantation

16920 Southall Plantation Lane
Charles City, VA 23030
(804) 829–2480

*5 rooms; all with private bath; in country setting. Authentic restoration of log house.*

## The Watson House Bed & Breakfast and The Inn at Poplar Corner

4240 and 4248 Main Street
Chincoteague, VA 23336
(757) 336–6115 or (800) 336–6787

*12 rooms; all with private bath; in two Victorian houses on Virginia's Eastern Shore.*

## Chester House Inn

43 Chester Street
Front Royal, VA 22630
(540) 635–3937 or (800) 621–0441

*6 rooms; 4 with private bath; in turn-of-the-century home.*

## The Willows B&B

5344 Roanes Wharf Road
Gloucester, VA 23061
(804) 693–4066

*4 rooms; all with private bath; in rural country setting.*

## Kings Victorian Inn

Route 220
Hot Springs, VA 24445
(540) 839–3134

*6 rooms; 4 with private bath; in elegantly restored Victorian.*

## The Hope and Glory Inn

634 King Carter Drive
Irvington, VA 22480
(804) 438–6053 or (800) 497–8228

*11 rooms; all with private bath; in delightfully decorated old schoolhouse and adjacent cottages.*

## The Norris House Inn

108 Loudoun Street, SW
Leesburg, VA 20175
(703) 777–1806 or (800) 644–1806

*6 rooms; all with shared bath; in 1760 brick Federal house in village setting.*

## Woodruff House

330 Mechanic Street
Luray, VA 22835
(540) 743–1494

*6 rooms; all with private bath; in 1882 Victorian with fireplaces and whirlpool tubs.*

# Federal Crest Inn Bed & Breakfast

1101 Federal Street
Lynchburg, VA 24504
(804) 845–6155 or (800) 818–6155

*5 rooms; all with private bath; in 8,000-square-foot mansion in Federal Hill Historic District.*

# Lynchburg Mansion Inn

405 Madison Street
Lynchburg, VA 24504
(804) 528–5400 or (800) 352–1199

*5 rooms; all with private bath; in elegant 9,000-square-foot mansion with beautiful antiques.*

# Hidden Inn

249 Caroline Street
Orange, VA 22960
(540) 672–3625 or (800) 841 1253

*10 rooms; all with private bath; on six acres with gardens.*

# Willow Pond Farm Country House

137 Pisgah Road
Raphine, VA 24472
(540) 348 1310 or (800) WIL POND

*4 rooms; all with private bath; in 1800s house on 174 acres with pool, fireplaces.*

# The Morris House

Lower Main Street
Reedville, VA 22539
(804) 453–7016

*5 rooms; all with private bath; in ornate Victorian in quaint fishing village in Virginia's Tidewater.*

## The Emmanuel Hutzler House

2036 Monument Avenue
Richmond, VA 23220
(804) 353-6900

*4 rooms; all with private bath; in lovely townhouse in historic district of Richmond.*


## Chester B&B

243 James River Road
Scottsville, VA 24590
(804) 286-3960

*5 rooms; all with private bath; in 1847 Greek Revival mansion.*


## The Sampson Eagon Inn

238 East Beverley Street
Staunton, VA 24401
(540) 886-8200 or (800) 597-9722

*5 rooms; all with private bath; in elegantly restored 1840s Greek Revival mansion; lovely antiques.*


## Thornrose House at Gypsy Hill

530 Thornrose Avenue
Staunton, VA 24401
(540) 885-7026

*5 rooms; all with private bath; across from 500-acre park.*


## The Middleton Inn

176 Main Street
Washington, VA 22747
(540) 675-2020 or (800) 816-8157

*5 rooms; all with private bath; in lovely brick Federal manor house on six-acre horse farm.*

## Sycamore Hill House and Gardens

110 Menefee Mountain Lane
Washington, VA 22747
(540) 675–3046

*3 rooms; all with private bath; in hilltop bed-and-breakfast and artist's home with panoramic views.*


## Liberty Rose Bed & Breakfast Inn

1022 Jamestown Road
Williamsburg, VA 23185
(757) 253–1260 or (800) 545–1825

*4 rooms; all with private bath; in utterly romantic bed-and-breakfast outside town.*


## River'd Inn

1972 Artz Road
Woodstock, VA 22664
(540) 459–5369 or (800) 637–4561

*8 rooms; all with private bath; inn on 25 acres in Shenandoah Valley.*

# West Virginia

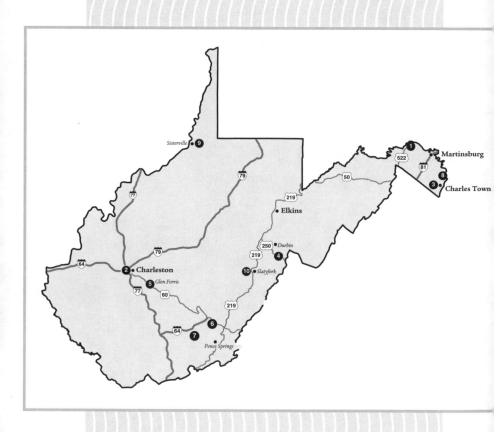

Sisterville • ⑨

79

77

50

522 ① Martinsburg
81
③ ⑧
Charles Town

219

• Elkins

250 • Durbin
219
④

79

64

② • Charleston

⑤ Glen Ferris

77
60

⑩ • Slatyfork

219

64 ⑥
⑦
Pence Springs

# West Virginia

*Numbers on map refer to towns numbered below.*

1.  Berkeley Springs, The Glens Country Estate* ............... 436
2.  Charleston, The Brass Pineapple .......................... 438
3.  Charles Town,
    The Cottonwood Inn .................................... 440
    Hillbrook Inn* ......................................... 441
4.  Durbin, Cheat Mountain Club ........................... 443
5.  Glen Ferris, The Glen Ferris Inn ........................ 445
6.  Lewisburg, General Lewis Inn ........................... 447
7.  Pence Springs, Pence Springs Hotel ..................... 448
8.  Shepherdstown,
    Bavarian Inn & Lodge* ................................ 450
    Thomas Shepherd Inn ................................. 452
9.  Sistersville, The Wells Inn .............................. 453
10. Slatyfork, Elk River Inn ................................ 455

*A Top Pick Inn

# The Glens Country Estate 🖤
## Berkeley Springs, West Virginia 25411

**INNKEEPER:** C. G. Everhart

**ADDRESS/TELEPHONE:** New Hope Road (mailing address: P.O. Box 160); (304) 258–4536

**WEB SITE:** www.wvglens.com

**ROOMS:** 8; all with private bath, air-conditioning, telephone, private deck, television, and VCR; 3 with Jacuzzi. Not appropriate for children. Wheelchair accessible. No smoking inn.

**RATES:** Rates, which include full breakfast, dinner, and all taxes, are discussed when reservation made. Two-night minimum weekends.

**OPEN:** All year except closed Monday and Tuesday nights.

**FACILITIES AND ACTIVITIES:** Dinner served Wednesday to Sunday to inn guests (included in room rate); swimming pool, two outdoor hot tubs, video library, private massages arranged; limousine pickup arranged.

*W*e needed time together—just the two of us—far from the pressures of our stress-filled jobs. Romance was definitely on our minds. We couldn't have chosen more wisely.

The Glens Country Estate is unique among country inns. It was conceived and built as a romantic adult retreat. Located on twenty serene acres that include two mountain streams and a duck pond and surrounded by several hundred acres of woods and meadows, it is peaceful, quiet, and lovely. There are seven acres of manicured lawns, bordered in places by flower beds.

We reveled in the calm. Shortly after our arrival we heard a soft knock on the door, and there was the masseuse we had inquired about. An hour later we were thoroughly relaxed and utter tranquility had set in.

The manor house, which is the centerpiece of the inn, was built in 1910 with plans purchased from the Sears and Roebuck catalog. After Chase Everhart bought the property in 1991, however, he completely transformed the cute farmhouse into an elegant manor. We entered a hallway with a 30-foot cathedral ceiling. Two oak staircases lead to the upper floors. There's a charming sitting room in burgundy and rose. A Victorian sofa is inviting, and wingback chairs sit before a large fireplace. An oak table for backgammon or cards awaits takers, and a 700-volume video library offers selections to please any taste.

The guest rooms are furnished with beautiful antique-reproduction oak beds with high carved headboards and carved dressers. Pretty floral fabrics cover down comforters and feather pillows, and the all-natural cotton sheets are freshly pressed. Most rooms have examples of the owner's fine collection of lithographs. Every room has a television and VCR as well as a private deck, and all the private baths have tile floors; three have Jacuzzis. There are luxurious robes in every room.

We were anticipating dinner and we were not disappointed. We dressed for the occasion because we were in the mood, but a jacket and tie are not required. The handsome dining room, with old-world moldings and door trim, is a medley of oak, and the oak tables are covered with crisp white tablecloths.

Dinner is served on Lenox china with Gorham silverware and crystal stemware.

All breads, desserts, soups, stocks—literally everything—are made on the premises, and there are raised beds of herbs and vegetables from which the chef can choose her ingredients. The five-course meal will start with, perhaps, an herbed potato soup, which is followed by The Glens' garden salad. A light sorbet (perhaps a summer lime) will follow. We chose an entree of baked Atlantic salmon wrapped in phyllo and served with a creamy dill sauce, which was accompanied by jumbo shrimp and tri-bell confetti, as well as an order of pan-seared broiled lamb with mint jelly and herbed potatoes. For dessert one of us devoured a rich Southern pecan pie with homemade vanilla ice cream; the other had a chocolate-walnut bourbon pie with homemade cinnamon ice cream.

Following dinner we headed out beyond the pool to one of the hot tubs. We sat under the stars sipping a cool drink and were ever so relaxed as we talked and planned together.

We rose the next morning to see deer, wild turkey, and birds from our deck in the early-morning mist. We had brought our bicycles, and we spent a leisurely morning riding along the C & O Canal Trail. After our return we lazed away the afternoon near the swimming pool. Tomorrow we would play golf.

Both breakfast and dinner are included in the room rate, and the breakfasts are as lavish as dinner. For guests who make arrangements in advance, Mr. Everhart will have a limousine pick them up and bring them to the inn. The limo is equipped with two televisions and a VCR so that guests can watch a movie both coming and going.

HOW TO GET THERE: Directions given when reservation made.

# The Brass Pineapple
## Charleston, West Virginia 25311

INNKEEPER: Sue Pepper; Bobbie Morris, manager

ADDRESS/TELEPHONE: 1611 Virginia Street East; (304) 344–0748 (fax same) or (800) CALLWVA

E-MAIL: pineapp104@aol.com

WEB SITE: www.wvweb.com/brasspineapple

ROOMS: 6, including 1 suite; all with private bath, air-conditioning, telephone with dataport, television, VCR, desk, and robes; 1 with minirefrigerator and CD player. Children over the age of 8 welcome. No smoking inn.

RATES: $69 to $109, double occupancy; includes full breakfast and afternoon tea. Additional person $25.

OPEN: All year except major holidays.

FACILITIES AND ACTIVITIES: Bicycles, video library. Nearby: State Capitol, West Virginia Cultural Center, Sunrise: restored mansion, planetarium, and children's museum, cruise aboard West Virginia Belle, dog racing, antiques shopping, and seasonal events—Sternwheel Regatta.

BUSINESS TRAVEL: Telephone with dataport and voicemail, TV, VCR, and desk in room; fax available; guest laundry, valet services, courtesy airport and train pickup service. Corporate apartments available complete with kitchens. Conference facilities at Benedict Haid House, 10 miles away.

*S*ue Pepper contends that she and her husband should have been born one hundred years earlier. They love antiques, old houses, and restoration. We're glad they were born just when they were, however. Otherwise the fine restoration of The Brass Pineapple might not have taken place.

When Sue and her husband found the 1910 buff-colored brick Craftsman-style house, which has a tile roof, it had been used as an apartment house for many years. (The inn is part of a National Historic District that contains the largest concentration of buildings with tile and slate roofs in the country). The gracious stair railings and spindles were gone (they had been replaced by solid walls), and the stained-glass windows in the stairway were barely visible. They found the original stair pieces in the basement, however, and cleaned the stained-glass window. They polished the pine floors and covered them with Oriental rugs, and they filled the rooms with lovely antiques.

My favorite guest room is the English Gentleman's, which has lovely antique walnut Victorian bedroom furniture that includes a carved, high-headboard bed, an armoire, a marble topped dresser, and even an antique desk. There's walnut wainscoting on the walls, and the decor is done mostly in rich browns and greens, making this a refined and elegantly masculine room. Every room is well equipped for today's business traveler, as it has a telephone with a computer hookup and voice mail, a desk with plenty of good lighting, and a television and VCR.

Sue or her staff prepare a hearty breakfast. It might include scalloped apples and Southern biscuit muffins to start, followed by scrambled eggs, cottage fries with green peppers, sausage, and pumpkin bread. Or she might fix stuffed orange French toast with warm maple syrup and bacon and a fruit salad of grapefruit, pineapple tidbits, and orange sections accompanied by blueberry muffins.

The inn is located in the historic district of Charleston within walking distance of the State Capitol building. Do not miss a walk through this area. Should you prefer to stay in an apartment with a kitchen, Sue can make those arrangements as well. She also owns three fully furnished apartments several blocks away. You might also inquire about the Pepper's farm, the Benedict Haid Farm, where additional rooms are located and where weddings and special events often take place.

**HOW TO GET THERE:** From I-64 take exit 99 (Capitol exit), turn south onto Greenbrier Street, and continue to second light. Turn right onto Kanawha Boulevard, right onto Elizabeth Street, and take another right onto Virginia Street. Look for waving brass pineapple flag and American flag on the right; park behind inn.

# The Cottonwood Inn
## Charles Town, West Virginia 25414

**INNKEEPERS:** Joe and Barbara Sobol

**ADDRESS/TELEPHONE:** Mill Lane (mailing address: Route 2, Box 61S); (304) 725–3371 or (800) 868–1188; fax (304) 728–4763

**E-MAIL:** travels@mydestination.com

**WEB SITE:** www.mydestination.com/cottonwood

**ROOMS:** 7; all with private bath, air-conditioning, and desks; 6 with television. Children over the age of 12 welcome. No smoking inn.

**RATES:** $75 to $115, double occupancy; $65 to $105, single occupancy; both include full breakfast; all rooms $75 Sunday to Thursday; two-night minimum holiday weekends.

**OPEN:** All year.

**FACILITIES AND ACTIVITIES:** On six acres with a stream and walking trails; picnic pavilion. Nearby: Charles Town Races, Old Opera House (live theatrical performances), Harpers Ferry National Historic Park.

*J*oe and Barbara Sobol are folks with many talents. In addition to running this lovely inn, they have their own travel video company. They produce video tours of European destinations, especially concentrating on driving tours outside major cities. All their editing, splicing, and production work is done right here in their studio at the inn, and they often invite their guests into the studio to see how it's all done.

The inn, which the Sobols purchased in 1995, offers the ultimate quiet and secluded getaway. Located on six acres in the country, it's reached by driving down country roads and then crossing a bridge across Bullskin Run, a stream that rushes along the periphery of the property. The 1840s farmhouse inn has a broad porch across the front where guests can sit to listen to the birds or count the stars.

Barbara has decorated the common rooms with lovely examples of antique and contemporary quilts as well as clocks and antique furniture. The kitchen, where breakfast is served, has a huge stone cooking fireplace, plank walls, wide pine floors, a woodstove, and a beamed ceiling. A pretty little bar stands in the corner. The comfortable living room has a brick fireplace and a piano as well as a plethora of books in shelves.

The guest rooms are charming. Room 2 has a fireplace, plank walls, natural pine floors, and a sleigh bed; Room 3 has a brick wall, a four-poster maple bed on blue carpeting, and a claw-foot tub in the bath. Room 5 includes beamed ceilings, a king-size bed with a matelassé spread, and a wicker daybed.

There are excellent restaurants within an easy drive of the inn, and there are plenty of walking trails right on the property for activity during the day. You may want to bring a good book along, though, or select one from the inn library and relax in the utter peace and quiet of this hideaway.

HOW TO GET THERE: From I–81 take exit 12 (Charles Town/Martinsburg) onto Route 51 and travel east toward Charles Town. At the junction with Route 9, take Route 9 east toward Leesburg. About 1 mile after crossing Route 340, turn south onto Kabletown Road. Go 3²/₁₀ miles to Mill Lane and turn right. The inn's driveway is ²/₁₀ mile straight ahead.

# Hillbrook Inn
## Charles Town, West Virginia 25414

INNKEEPER: Gretchen Carroll

ADDRESS/TELEPHONE: Route 13 (mailing address: Route 2, Box 152); (304) 725–4223 or (800) 304–4223; fax (304) 725–4455

ROOMS: 6; all with private bath, telephone, and air conditioning; 2 with fireplace, 1 with whirlpool tub. Not appropriate for children unless they can occupy their own room. Smoking permitted.

**RATES:** $140 to $300, double occupancy; includes full breakfast (seven-course dinner included first night of stay at $70 per person extra, including wines); procrastinator's special rate of $129 per room if booked after noon on day of stay; midwinter midweek special, $99.

**OPEN:** All year.

**FACILITIES AND ACTIVITIES:** On seventeen acres with pond and stream. Dinner (by reservation) for guests not spending the night ($70). Nearby: Charles Town Races, Old Opera House, antiquing, tour Shepherdstown or Harpers Ferry, bicycling, and hiking on C & O Canal Towpath.

**BUSINESS TRAVEL:** Telephone in all rooms; desk in two rooms; fax and copier available; meeting room.

*H*ave you ever entered a room to find the fringe on the antique Oriental rug covering the polished oak floors perfectly combed? That's the kind of place Hillbrook Inn is. This urbane, refined, and sophisticated retreat is absolute perfection.

The half-timbered wood-and-stucco Tudor house was built in seven sections. It meanders down its limestone ridge in fifteen different levels. Constructed in the 1920s the original section incorporates the log-and-chink walls of an old log cabin. The house is encircled by leaded and stained-glass windows, stone pathways and terraces, and seventeen acres of gorgeous landscaped grounds that include an English rock garden, two streams, and a pond. One stream is crossed by a 12-foot-wide Bridge of Sighs, a bridge with a Chinese Chippendale design that includes ornate lion's heads. There's a 4-foot-high chess set beside the pond.

The rooms in the inn are exquisitely designed, combining the unique architecture of the inn with Gretchen's eclectic decor that includes objects d'art that she's collected in her worldwide travels. The living room, which has 20-foot ceilings, includes deep terra-cotta walls with exposed white posts and timbers and a woodburning fireplace. There are rich silks on the sofas and chairs. Antique tables and chests display ebony statues, pottery, vases, and figurines. On the lowest level, where the garage used to be, there's now a tavern with natural oak floors placed on the diagonal, boxed beams, and English-style mullioned windows. French doors lead to a stone terrace, and tapestries decorate the walls.

The guest rooms are as distinctive as the common rooms. The Bamford Suite has a private porch and luxurious big chairs before a fireplace. There's a four-poster bed and another sitting area with Victorian furniture. The Point, a cozy retreat that is adored by everyone who stays here, is entered along a narrow tunnel-like hallway that opens to reveal an antique cannon-ball bed. All the rooms have private baths.

A seven-course dinner is served to inn guests and the general public in the evening. It's a leisurely, relaxed, and very romantic event—each course is served with appropriate wines—with soft classical or Broadway music playing in the background. Couples are seated at individual, candlelit tables, and the food is served on lovely china (much of it is by Lynn Chase) with beautiful silver and crystal. The courses include an appetizer (one night it was smoked trout in puff pastry with a cold dill sauce), a soup (a curried almond, for example), a light pasta (perhaps a farfalle in basil cream sauce), an entree (quail with pilaf one night), a salad, a cheese-and-fruit plate, and dessert (Chocolate Decadence with strawberry coulis) with coffee.

Most of the area surrounding Charles Town and the inn was owned by George Washington, who gave it to his brother, Charles, for whom the town is named. His country estate was located nearby, and some of the original log cabins are still on the property.

**HOW TO GET THERE:** From I–270 take I–70 west to Route 340 west. Past Harpers Ferry take Route 51 west to Charles Town. Continue on Route 51 west to Route 13 (Summit Point Road), which bears off to the left at the west end of town. Go 4⁸⁄₁₀ miles on Route 13 to the inn, which is on your left (past elementary school on right). Watch for stone pillars.

# Cheat Mountain Club
Durbin, West Virginia 26264

**INNKEEPER:** Cynthia Loebig

**ADDRESS/TELEPHONE:** Route 250 (mailing address: P.O. Box 28); (304) 456–4627 or (800) CALL–WVA; fax (304) 456–3192

**E-MAIL:** cheatmc@neumedia.net

**WEB SITE:** www.wvweb.com/cheatmountain

**ROOMS:** 10, including 1 suite plus third-floor dormitories; 1 with private bath, all with robes, 8 with sinks in room; separate bath facilities for men and women. Children welcome; cribs available. No smoking inn.

**RATES:** $80 to $150, per person per night; includes breakfast, lunch, and dinner; children 6 to 12 one-half adult rate; those under 5, $25. Three-night minimum holidays.

**OPEN:** All year.

**FACILITIES AND ACTIVITIES:** Dining room serving three meals a day; 180 acres; located on Shavers Fork River. Service bar. Cheat Mountain Outfitting and Guide Service, short walk from lodge, has mountain bikes, cross-country skis, canoes, and fishing equipment for rent. Fun-yaks, badminton, softball, croquet, soccer, swimming, kayaking, rafting, horseshoes, volleyball, snowshoes, fitness center including a Nordic Track and step and rowing machines available at lodge. Nearby: Cass Scenic Railroad, National Radio Astronomy Observatory, downhill skiing.

**RECOMMENDED COUNTRY INNS® TRAVELERS' CLUB BENEFIT:** Stay two nights, get third free, Monday to Thursday.

This remote hunting lodge was built in 1887 as an executive retreat. Over the years such industrialists as Thomas Edison, Henry Ford, and Harvey Firestone have sampled its peaceful and secluded setting. It sits at the 3,800-foot level of Cheat Mountain surrounded by West Virginia's highest peaks—its 180 acres are contiguous with the 900,000-acre Monongahela National Forest. Five miles of hiking, mountain biking, and

cross-country ski trails lace the inn's property, and the tumbling Shavers Fork River is noted for its exceptional trout fishing. Folks come here to take fly-fishing classes and to hunt deer, bear, grouse, and turkey, as well as to simply escape the pressures of the work world.

The lodge is rustic but well kept, with a spruce-log and pine interior. The Great Room has a massive stone fireplace, where a fire is often burning even in summer, as the nights do get cool at this level. There's an excellent stereo system and a variety of books and games to entertain guests when it's too foggy to hike, hunt, or fish.

The guest rooms, which have pine walls and maple furnishings, are on the second floor—only the Spruce Suite has its own bath—the rest have a sink in the room, but they share modern and clean men's and women's rooms that are complete with showers, tubs, and commodes. A third-floor dormitory is a great place to put kids, who will love the camp-style informality.

Meals are served in the dining room, which has another stone fireplace, or on the terrace. The meals include buckwheat pancakes and sausage for breakfast, hearty soups and stews, and outdoor barbecues in the summer for dinner.

One of the best parts of the day at Cheat Mountain is in the evening after dinner, when folks gather around the stone firepit down by the river to swap fish tales and to share the day's experiences.

**HOW TO GET THERE:** From I–81 take exit 222 (Staunton) onto Route 250 west. Follow Route 250 west for 66 miles to Durbin. Continue on Route 250 past Durbin for 9½ miles to the inn's sign, which is on the left. Turn left onto the inn's gravel road and travel 1½ miles to the lodge.

# The Glen Ferris Inn
## Glen Ferris, West Virginia 25090

**INNKEEPER:** Natalie Phillips; David and Rebecca Hill, managers

**ADDRESS/TELEPHONE:** Route 60 (mailing address: P.O. Box 128); (304) 632–1111; fax (304) 632–0113

**WEB SITE:** www.emoney.net/glenferris

**ROOMS:** 17, including 2 suites; all with private bath, air-conditioning, telephone, television, desk, and radio; 2 with minirefrigerator, coffeemaker, VCR, robes, and CD player. Wheelchair accessible. Children welcome. Smoking permitted; designated nonsmoking rooms.

**RATES:** $60 to $130, double occupancy.

**OPEN:** All year.

**FACILITIES AND ACTIVITIES:** Restaurant serving breakfast, lunch, and dinner (entrees $10 to $16); overlooking scenic Kanawha Falls, lovely landscaped gardens. Nearby: whitewater rafting, golfing, Hawks Nest State Park, Tamarack: The Best of Virginia (West Virginia Craft Center in Beckley).

As you drive along the twisting and winding road that's now called Route 60 as it meanders beside the Kanawha River, it's easy to imagine the stagecoaches that followed this same route in the early nineteenth century. Aaron Stockton, a local sawmill operator and coal entrepreneur, built his ordinary in 1839 to offer food and lodging to travelers along the James River and Kanawha Turnpike, and it's continued to fill this need through its 180+ years.

The setting, on the tumultuous, cascading Kanawha Falls, is spectacular to say the least. A local family, Dan and Rebecca Hill, purchased the historic old hotel in 1996, and they have built a new dining room with a huge window-wall and a deck that projects out over the river, giving diners a spectacular view of the falls.

This is not the first addition that the inn has experienced, however. It was in 1910 that the third floor was added, as well as the distinctive ionic columns across the front and the stone wall that surrounds the inn. In 1929 the brick wing was added to provide housing for workers on the huge ferroalloy plant—the largest in the world—built nearby by Union Carbide.

The guest rooms of the inn offer a variety of styles. Room 206 has pine furniture and a view of the waterfall. Quilts cover the beds. Suite 201 has a lovely bedroom, two baths, and a living room with a Formica-topped wet bar. Some of the rooms have tiny baths, but all rooms have private baths.

The inn is open for breakfast, lunch, and dinner, although no meals are included in the room price. Dinner entrees include old-fashioned dishes such as pork chops, ground sirloin steak, ham steak, and lots of New York, T-bone, rib-eye, and filet mignon steak selections. Cobblers and bread pudding are featured for dessert. Several recent reports indicate that improvements are needed in the kitchen.

A beautiful, formal flower garden with a gazebo adjoins the inn. The innkeepers plan to open a bookstore specializing in Civil War and West Virginia books across the street from the inn, where they also hope to open a casual cafe.

HOW TO GET THERE: From I–77 in Charleston take I–64 west for 2 to 3 miles and then exit onto Route 60 west. Follow this for 35 miles to Glen Ferris. The inn is on Route 60 on the right.

# General Lewis Inn
## Lewisburg, West Virginia 24901

**INNKEEPER:** Nan Morgan

**ADDRESS/TELEPHONE:** 301 East Washington Street; (304) 645–2600 or (800) 628–4454; fax (304) 645–2601

**ROOMS:** 25, including 2 suites; all with private bath, air-conditioning, television, and telephone. Wheelchair accessible. Pets allowed. Children welcome. No smoking inn.

**RATES:** $75 to $110, double occupancy. Additional guests and pets, $10; children under 3 free. Request winter packages. August State Fair week higher.

**OPEN:** All year.

**FACILITIES AND ACTIVITIES:** Breakfast, lunch, dinner (entrees $10 to $17) wine, beer, and cocktails. Nearby: walk through historic Lewisburg, golf at Greenbrier Hotel and Greenbrier Valley Country Club, fishing, Lost World Cavern, Organ Cave, Greenbrier River Trail, West Virginia State Fair, Greenbrier Valley Theater, Carnegie Hall, North House Museum.

When you enter The General Lewis Inn, which dates to 1834, you feel as if you've stepped back in time, and that's exactly the reason we like it so much. The handsome front desk dates to 1760 and was used by Thomas Jefferson and Patrick Henry. To the right there's a parlor with a fireplace and numerous antique tables and chairs. Fascinating old paintings and photographs line the walls. You'll want to spend considerable time in a back hallway known as Memory Hall. The walls are absolutely covered with interesting old pioneer artifacts: guns, tools, candle molds, shoes, lanterns, kitchen equipment, and much, much more. In front a broad veranda stretches the length of the building, offering comfortable old wooden rocking chairs.

The inn has been owned by the Hock family since 1928. Nan Morgan, the third generation to operate the inn, is friendly and charming. It's this hands-on continuity and personal attention that have made the General Lewis such a consistent winner.

The guest rooms all have private baths (although several are quite small), and they are decorated with antiques. Many of the beds are original rope beds. Room 208 has a curly-maple bed and a terrific antique dresser, Room 206 has a spool bed, and Room 212 has a canopy bed and an old sewing machine.

The dining room, with its hand-hewn beamed ceiling and fireplace, serves old-fashioned comfort food. The setting is congenial and pleasant, and the food is well prepared. You might have Southern fried chicken, roast duck a l'orange, or sautéed mountain trout. For dessert there are homemade pies and cobblers.

The General Lewis Inn, as well as the town itself, is part of a National Historic District. On the front lawn of the inn you'll see an old stagecoach. There are numerous craft shops, antiques shops, art galleries, book shops, and restaurants in town. Carnegie Hall is the site of musical and theatrical productions, and North House Museum traces the history of Lewisburg.

**HOW TO GET THERE:** From I–64 take exit 169 onto Route 219 south. Travel 1 mile to Lewisburg. In town turn east (left) onto Route 60 and go 3 blocks to the inn.

# Pence Springs Hotel 🖼 💲
## Pence Springs, West Virginia 24962

**INNKEEPERS:** Ashby Berkley and Rosalee Berkley Miller

**ADDRESS/TELEPHONE:** Route 3 (mailing address: P.O. Box 90); (304) 445–2606 or (800) 826–1829; fax (304) 445–2204

**E-MAIL:** omc01508@mail.wvnet.edu

**WEB SITE:** www.wvweb.com/www/pence_springs_hotel

**ROOMS:** 15, including 7 suites; all with private baths and air-conditioning; telephones and televisions available. The Lodge has 8 more rooms that share 3½ baths. Wheelchair accessible. Children welcome. Smoking permitted.

**RATES:** $69.50 to $99.50, double occupancy; $59.50 to $89.50, single occupancy; both include full breakfast.

**OPEN:** April to December.

**FACILITIES AND ACTIVITIES:** Riverside Inn restaurant serving dinner (entrees $12 to $25); Sun Porch Cafe, Cider Press Lounge. On 400 acres, with fishing, horseback riding, hiking, bicycling, croquet, volleyball. Nearby: Sunday flea market (seasonal), Organ Cave, hiking, whitewater rafting, biking, villages for touring.

*E*arly in the twentieth century, Pence Springs was the most popular destination in West Virginia—fourteen trains a day delivered passengers here. It was known for the restorative power of its mineral springs, and its water was bottled and shipped all over the world. The Grand Hotel, an elaborate brick Georgian-style mansion, was built in 1918 and quickly became the premier place to stay—even though it was also the state's most expensive. During Prohibition hiding places for guests' liquor promoted a convivial, party-like atmosphere. Following the stock market crash of 1929, however, the hotel closed its doors—and that was the end of an era.

During the Depression Eleanor Roosevelt established a girls' school in the former hotel, but in 1947 it was converted to the West Virginia State Prison for Women; it remained a prison until 1983.

But then Ashby Berkley returned to town. Ashby's mother had been a prison officer in Pence Springs, and he grew up here. After graduating from school he went to the Culinary Institute of America and then on to Europe, where he enhanced his culinary education.

When he returned to Pence Springs, he opened a restaurant in a log cabin down by the banks of the Greenbrier River. Once that was up and running, he began the arduous task of restoring the massive old Grand Hotel, which he rechristened the Pence Springs Hotel. He chose to restore the rooms to their 1920s appearance, which means that they are plain and unadorned and furnished with 1920s-style pieces that include motel-style headboards bolted to the wall. Even Ashby Berkley calls them tacky. We can forgive him his

tasteless rooms, however, because each does have its own bath, and the common rooms are truly the focal point.

The lobby has a fireplace, as does the music room/parlor, and there are wonderful verandas for whiling away an afternoon. Several years ago, after a disastrous flood, Ashby moved The Riverside Inn restaurant to the Pence Springs Hotel. The Cider Press lounge has another fireplace, and you can still see the hidden little rooms where patrons used to stash their liquor. The inn is located on 400 acres, and there are ample opportunities for fishing, hiking, bicycling, horseback riding and whitewater rafting.

**HOW TO GET THERE:** From I–64 take exit 161 (Alta). Take Route 12 south to Alderson, where Route 12 becomes Route 3. Continue approximately 7 miles on Route 3 to the inn. You'll see the FLEA MARKET sign, then the inn.

# Bavarian Inn & Lodge 👪 📱
## Shepherdstown, West Virginia 25443

**INNKEEPERS:** Erwin and Carol Asam

**ADDRESS/TELEPHONE:** Route 480 (mailing address: Route 1, Box 30); (304) 876–2551; fax (304) 876–9355

**WEB SITE:** www.wvweb.com/www/bavarian_inn

**ROOMS:** 72, including 2 suites; all with private bath, air- conditioning, telephone, and television; 70 with private balcony or deck, 41 with fireplace, 37 with whirlpool tub, 32 with dataport. Wheelchair accessible. Children welcome. Smoking permitted; designated nonsmoking rooms.

**RATES:** $95 to $175, double occupancy. Additional person, $10. Two-night minimum holidays and special events. Sunday to Thursday winter packages and seasonal golf packages.

**OPEN:** All year.

**FACILITIES AND ACTIVITIES:** Breakfast, lunch, dinner (entrees $14 to $25). Rathskeller with entertainment on weekends. Outdoor pool, tennis court, golf course, exercise room. Nearby: C & O Canal Towpath, Harpers Ferry, Antietam Battlefield, Charles Town opera, and races.

BUSINESS TRAVEL: Telephone and desk all rooms; fax connection 32 rooms; fax and copier available; conference room.

*A*re you prepared for a unique experience? Welcome to Bavaria in West Virginia. Surprised? Don't tell owner Erwin Asam that. He was absolutely convinced from the beginning that his scheme would work.

Asam was raised in Munich, the heart of Bavaria, where he went to hotel school and then continued his education in Paris, Italy, and Switzerland. Coming to the United States to fulfill an apprenticeship, he eventually opened his own restaurant in Washington, D.C., in 1964. The restaurant was a fabulous success. But then he married Carol, they had two children, and he decided they needed to move to the country. And it wasn't so much that he found this restaurant and the fabulous stone mansion, as it found him. A former employer called and asked if he wouldn't purchase it, so he did.

Well, to make a long story short, he opened a Bavarian restaurant in rooms that have deer-horn chandeliers and stone fireplaces. You'll find such German dishes as sauerbraten, *jaegerschnitzel,* and *geschmorte rindsroulade* on the menu. Desserts include homemade apple strudel and Black Forest cake.

With the success of the restaurant assured, the couple added several elegant suites upstairs in the mansion, then they added three chalets on the bluff overlooking the Potomac River and, eventually, a new wing as well. The rooms are impeccably maintained, and most have gas fireplaces, canopy beds, and balconies with spectacular views.

The inn is located on eleven acres, and it has its own swimming pool and tennis court. There are bicycles to rent for those who want to take a ride on the C & O Canal Towpath that meanders along the Potomac. Whitewater rafting, canoeing, and golfing are nearby.

HOW TO GET THERE: From I–70 take exit 49 (Braddock Heights/Middletown) and turn left onto Alternate 40. Follow this to Boonsboro. Turn left in Boonsboro onto Maryland Route 34 and follow this through Sharpsburg to Shepherdstown. Cross the Potomac River Bridge into West Virginia. You will now be on WV Route 480. The inn is on the right overlooking the river.

# Thomas Shepherd Inn
## Shepherdstown, West Virginia 25443

INNKEEPER: Margaret Perry

ADDRESS/TELEPHONE: 300 West German Street (mailing address: P.O. Box 1162); (304) 876–3715 or (888) 889–8952; fax (304) 876–3313

E-MAIL: mrg@intrepid.net

WEB SITE: www.intrepid.net/thomasshepherd

ROOMS: 7; all with private bath and air-conditioning; telephone available on request. No smoking inn. Well-behaved children over the age of 8 welcome.

RATES: $85 to $135, double occupancy; includes full breakfast. Corporate midweek rates. Senior and AARP rates. Two-night minimum on weekends if Saturday stay included, April to Thanksgiving.

OPEN: All year.

FACILITIES AND ACTIVITIES: Picnic lunch; dinner served on request midweek ($20 to $30); BYOB. Library with television and VCR. Nearby: restaurants, C & O Canal, antiquing, canoeing, hiking, Harpers Ferry, Antietam Battlefield, Charles Town Races, outlet shopping.

BUSINESS TRAVEL: Telephone, fax, and desk available; corporate rates; meeting room.

The handsome creamy brick building with its green shutters was built as the parsonage for the town's Lutheran church in 1868. It joined other distinguished buildings along the streets of this town, which is the oldest in West Virginia. Founded by German settlers in 1727, the entire town is now on the National Register of Historic Places.

Margaret Perry, an effervescent woman, purchased her inn in 1989. Guests relax in a living room with wide-plank pine floors covered with Oriental rugs, green-checked sofas, and cranberry-colored wing chairs in which they can warm their toes before a fireplace. There's also a library on the second floor, with a wide selection of books and a television, VCR, and video library. Just off the library, a treetop porch with a lattice wall has white rockers and an abundance of plants.

The guest rooms are simple and functional, and several have private baths in the hallway. The nicest rooms are Number 1, which includes a beau-

tiful Victorian half-tester bed, a sitting area with a decorative fireplace, and a nice bath; and Number 2, which has a sleigh bed and a new bath.

Margaret loves to cook, and her breakfasts reflect her interest. She may fix strawberry pancakes with maple-flavored sausage and Vermont maple syrup, for example, and she will undoubtedly decorate the plates with colorful edible flowers and herbs. Guests sit in a dining room at antique tables, where they can also admire the corner cupboard and its array of gifts available for purchase.

**HOW TO GET THERE:** From I-70 take exit 49 (Braddock Heights/Middletown) and turn left onto Alternate 40. Follow this to Boonsboro. Turn left in Boonsboro onto Maryland Route 34 and follow this through Sharpsburg to Shepherdstown. Cross the Potomac River Bridge into West Virginia. You will now be on WV Route 480. Follow this into Shepherdstown. The inn is at the intersection of Route 480, 45, and 230 in the center of town, on the corner of West German and Duke Streets.

# The Wells Inn
## Sistersville, West Virginia 26175

**INNKEEPER:** Walker Boyd; Nel Smith, manager

**ADDRESS/TELEPHONE:** 316 Charles Street; (304) 652-1312 or (800) 648-3984; fax (304) 652-1354

**ROOMS:** 36, including 6 suites; all with private bath, telephone, and television; 25 with VCR, 18 with air-conditioning and desk, 12 with dataport. Children welcome. Pets permitted with prior permission. Smoking permitted; designated nonsmoking rooms.

**RATES:** $69, double occupancy; $59, single occupancy.

**OPEN:** All year.

**FACILITIES AND ACTIVITIES:** Black and Gold Room serving breakfast and lunch, main dining room serving dinner (entrees $10 to $21), on-premises bakery, The Wooden Derrick pub; heated swimming pool, hot tub, exercise room with extensive equipment. Nearby: fishing, golfing, hiking, historic town of Sistersville with Townhouse Gallery, The General Store (arts and crafts outlet), the Ohio River and Sistersville Ferry, Gaslight Theater.

**BUSINESS TRAVEL:** Desk, television, VCR, telephone with dataport in all rooms; fax and copier available; room service, twenty-four-hour front desk service, meeting rooms, audiovisual equipment; same-day valet and laundry.

*W*alker Boyd worked for Union Carbide for thirty-seven years, but when he left the company, he certainly didn't choose a quiet retired life of playing golf or lying on the beach. Instead he and his wife, Jody, flew headlong into the restoration of the old Hotel Wells, which they purchased at auction in 1994.

The hotel and the town have an interesting history. In the late nineteenth century, oil was discovered near Sistersville. Suddenly the quiet town was booming with fortune seekers and bounty hunters. Numerous boarding houses provided overnight lodging. Bankers, financial supporters, and astute businessmen also came to town. Charles Wells built the elegant Hotel Wells, which opened in 1895, for their pleasure.

But a century later the once-grand hotel was on such hard times that it was feared it would never open again, and it was sold at auction. Now, more than a million dollars later, the inn includes the Black and Gold Room and a restored main dining room with a gold metal ceiling, a bakery, The Wooden Derrick pub, and thirty-six guest rooms. It is listed on the National Register of Historic Places.

The guest rooms (which I have not seen) are purported to be small and simply furnished with a smattering of antiques, but all do have private baths, and they are all equipped with air-conditioning, telephones with dataports, televisions, and VCRs.

Sistersville, a Victorian-era boomtown on the banks of the Ohio River, has retained its brick sidewalks, streets, and alleys, as well as a downtown with brick buildings and Victorian houses. An ornate Victorian-era theater was restored in 1998, so you can walk across the street from the inn to see live entertainment and first-run movies in a thoroughly Victorian theater. There is an interesting arts and craft store, an art gallery, and a summertime ferry offering excursions on the Ohio River.

**HOW TO GET THERE:** From I–77 in Parkersburg take exit 179 onto Route 2 north and travel 32 miles to Sistersville. The inn is on Route 2 on the corner of Charles Street in the center of town.

# Elk River Inn
## Slatyfork, West Virginia 26291

**INNKEEPERS:** Gil and Mary Willis

**ADDRESS/TELEPHONE:** Route 219 (mailing address: HC 69, Box 7); (304) 572–3771; fax (304) 572–3741

**E-MAIL:** elk@neumedia.com

**WEB SITE:** www.ertc.com

**ROOMS:** 13, including 3 cabins; 8 with private bath; all with radio. Two cabins have telephones, coffeemakers, and tape players. Children welcome. No smoking inn.

**RATES:** $50 to $85, double occupancy; includes full breakfast. Children under 9 free. Additional person, $5. Request package and midweek rates. Two-night minimum weekends.

**OPEN:** All year.

**FACILITIES AND ACTIVITIES:** Dinner (entrees $11 to $16; $4 for children). Hot tub on 150 acres; fly-fishing for trout, 25-kilometer cross-country trail, 2 kilometers with night lighting; ski shop, bike shop, mountain bike rental, cross-country ski rental, hiking trails. Adjacent to Monongahela National Forest, skiing at Snowshoe and Silver Creek (5 miles away).

Rugged outdoor individuals head for the Elk River Inn, in the heart of the Monongahela National Forest, where they can partake of healthy outdoor activities four seasons of the year. There's hiking on 5 kilometers of groomed trails, mountain bike tours for riders at all levels, trout fishing in the inn's fabulous trout streams, and 25 kilometers of cross-country ski trails (2 kilometers are lighted for night skiing). The inn also has mountain bicycle and cross-country ski rentals, and Gil Willis leads treks throughout the forest.

The fact that people can return to a cozy, warm inn and enjoy a hearty meal at the end of a strenuous day is a tremendous plus. You may have a drink on the large deck, and you will enjoy a relaxing dinner while you gaze at the Elk River and listen to the crackle of the logs in the stone fireplace.

The dinner menu is an eclectic one, ranging from fresh-baked Elk River trout topped with lemon pepper to chicken, steak, or vegetable fajitas. Desserts feature apple-cranberry crumb pie and bread pudding with a caramel glaze. Mary is the chef.

Five guest rooms are located in an eighty-five-year-old farmhouse that was originally the centerpiece of a sheep farm. Although all the rooms here share a bath, you can wake in the morning to watch deer feed in the adjacent meadow, or you can read in a little sitting room. The inn, a separate building built in 1988 on the site of the original barn, contains a sitting area that

includes a television. The nicest rooms are located here, as they all have private baths, although none would be considered elegant or cosmopolitan. They have simple furnishings and utilitarian baths.

Mary prepares a full and hearty breakfast—designed to sustain folks headed out for an active day in the outdoors. There will be pancakes or French toast, omelettes accompanied by country-fried potatoes and grits, and homemade granola, fruit, and juice.

**HOW TO GET THERE:** From I–64 take exit 169 onto Route 219 north in Lewisburg. Go 40 miles to Marlinton. From Marlinton, continue north on Route 219 for 15⁹⁄₁₀ miles. The inn is on the left at sign: ELK RIVER LODGE. Cross one-lane bridge over Elk River.

# Select List of Other Inns
# in West Virginia

## Edgewood Manor B&B

Route 11
Bunker Hill, WV 25413
(304) 229-9353 or (888) 453-2960

*6 rooms; all with private bath; in gracious brick manor house on fifty-two acres.*

## North Fork Mountain Inn

Smoke Hole Road
Cabins, WV 26855
(304) 257-1108 or (800) CALL-WVA

*6 rooms; all with private bath; in log-style lodge built in 1995.*

## The Carriage Inn

417 East Washington Street
Charles Town, WV 25414
(304) 728-8003 or (800) 367-9830

*5 rooms; all with private bath; in 1836 mansion on one acre in village setting.*

## Tunnel Mountain B&B

Route 33
Elkins, WV 26241
(304) 636-1684

*3 rooms; all with private bath; in a stone and wood lodge on five acres in the country.*

## The Warfield House Bed and Breakfast

318 Buffalo Street
Elkins, WV 26241
(304) 636-1457 or (888) 636-4555

*5 rooms; 3 with private bath; in 1901 Victorian beauty in village across from park and college.*

## Harpers Ferry Guest House

800 Washington Street
Harpers Ferry, WV 25425
(304) 535-6955

*3 rooms; all with private bath; in village across from Appalachian Trail Conference headquarters.*

## The Farmhouse on Tomahawk Run

1 Tomahawk Run Place
Hedgesville, WV 25427
(304) 754-7350

*5 rooms; all with private bath; on 280 acres in lovely farmhouse restored in 1994.*

## Hutton House B&B

Routes 250 and 219
Huttonsville, WV 26273
(304) 355-6701

*6 rooms; all with private bath; in elaborate 1898 Queen Anne Victorian.*

## McMechan House B&B

109 North Main Street
Moorefield, WV 26836
(304) 538-7841 or (800) 298-2466

*7 rooms; 5 with private bath; in 1853 Greek Revival mansion.*

## Avery-Savage House

420-13th Street
Parkersburg, WV 26101
(304) 422-9820 or (800) 315-7121

*3 rooms; all with private bath; in Queen Anne Victorian.*

## Elmhurst Manor B&B

1606 Pleasant Avenue
Wellsburg, WV 26070
(304) 737–2876 or (800) 584–8718

*3 rooms; all with private bath; in historic Greek Revival mansion with view of
Ohio River.*

## The Eckhart House

810 Main Street
Wheeling, WV 26003
(304) 232–5439

*5 rooms; with private and shared baths; in Victorian Old Town section.*

## The James Wylie House

208 East Main Street
White Sulphur Springs, WV 24986
(304) 536–9444

*6 rooms; all with private bath; in brick Georgian Colonial-style house built
in 1819.*

# Indexes

## Alphabetical Index to Inns

Acorn Inn (NY) . . . . . . . . . . . . . . . . . . . . . 109
Adelphi Hotel (NY) . . . . . . . . . . . . . . . . . 207
Albergo Allegria Bed & Breakfast (NY) . 235
American Hotel (NY). . . . . . . . . . . . . . . . . 204
Antietam Overlook Farm (MD). . . . . . . . 37
Antrim 1844 Country Inn (MD) . . . . . . . 57
Armitage Inn (DE) . . . . . . . . . . . . . . . . . . 8
Asa Ransom House (NY) . . . . . . . . . . . . . 123
Ashby 1663 Bed and Breakfast MD) . . . . 29
Ashby Inn, The (VA) . . . . . . . . . . . . . . . . 380
Atlantic Hotel (MD) . . . . . . . . . . . . . . . . 15
Aubergine (NY) . . . . . . . . . . . . . . . . . . . . 157
B&B Inn of the Princess and European
    Bakery (PA) . . . . . . . . . . . . . . . . . . . . . 318
Bailiwick Inn, The (VA) . . . . . . . . . . . . . 350
Barley Sheaf Farm (PA) . . . . . . . . . . . . . . 285
Batcheller Mansion Inn (NY) . . . . . . . . . 209
Bavarian Inn & Lodge (WV) . . . . . . . . . . 450
Beaverkill Valley Inn (NY) . . . . . . . . . . . 172
Bed and Breakfast on the Park (NY) . . . 178
Beekman Arms (NY) . . . . . . . . . . . . . . . . 198
Belhurst Castle & White Springs Manor
    (NY) . . . . . . . . . . . . . . . . . . . . . . . . . . . 151
Belvedere Mansion (NY) . . . . . . . . . . . . . 200
Bernards Inn, The (NJ) . . . . . . . . . . . . . . 67
Bird & Bottle Inn, The (NY) . . . . . . . . . 149
Black Horse Inn, The (VA) . . . . . . . . . . . 406
Bleu Rock Inn (VA) . . . . . . . . . . . . . . . . . 409
Brampton Bed & Breakfast (MD) . . . . . . 25
Brass Pineapple, The (WV) . . . . . . . . . . . 438
Brewster Inn, The (NY) . . . . . . . . . . . . . . 113
Bridgehampton Inn (NY) . . . . . . . . . . . . 108
Bridgeton House on the Delaware (PA) 320
Brierley Hill Country Inn (VA) . . . . . . . . 366
Buttermilk Falls Bed & Breakfast (NY) . 159
Carmel Cove Inn (MD) . . . . . . . . . . . . . . 43
Carnegie House (PA) . . . . . . . . . . . . . . . . 315
Cashelmara Inn (NJ) . . . . . . . . . . . . . . . . 66
Cashtown Inn (PA) . . . . . . . . . . . . . . . . . 257
Castle at Tarrytown, The (NY) . . . . . . . . 229
Catoctin Inn, The (MD) . . . . . . . . . . . . . 19
Cedars Bed & Breakfast, The (VA) . . . . . 418
Celie's Waterfront Bed & Breakfast (MD) 12
Cheat Mountain Club (WV) . . . . . . . . . . 443
Chequit Inn (NY) . . . . . . . . . . . . . . . . . . 213
Chestnut Hill on the Delaware (NJ) . . . . 86

Clifton: The Country Inn (VA) . . . . . . . . 338
Colonial Houses Historic Lodging (VA) 420
Combsberry (MD) . . . . . . . . . . . . . . . . . . 47
Cooper Inn, The (NY) . . . . . . . . . . . . . . . 126
Cottonwood Inn, The (WV) . . . . . . . . . . 440
Crescent Lodge and Country Inn (PA) . 266
Cromwell Manor Inn (NY) . . . . . . . . . . . 128
Doctors Inn at Kings Grant, The (NJ) . . . 79
Eagles Mere Inn (PA) . . . . . . . . . . . . . . . . 269
East Hampton Point Cottages (NY) . . . 136
Eldon—The Inn at Chatham (VA) . . . . . 344
Elk River Inn (WV) . . . . . . . . . . . . . . . . . 455
Elk Lake Lodge (NY) . . . . . . . . . . . . . . . . 185
Elliott House Victorian Inn (MD) . . . . . . 34
EverMay On-the-Delaware (PA) . . . . . . . 276
Fairville Inn (PA) . . . . . . . . . . . . . . . . . . . 293
Fort Lewis Lodge (VA) . . . . . . . . . . . . . . 372
428 Mt. Vernon—A B&B Inn (NY) . . . . . 202
Fox & Hound Bed & Breakfast of New
    Hope, The (PA) . . . . . . . . . . . . . . . . . 301
French Manor, The (PA) . . . . . . . . . . . . . 313
Friends Lake Inn, The (NY) . . . . . . . . . . 121
Garden and The Sea Inn, The (VA) . . . . 376
Gaslight Inn, The (PA) . . . . . . . . . . . . . . . 281
General Lewis Inn (WV) . . . . . . . . . . . . . 447
Genesee Country Inn (NY) . . . . . . . . . . . 174
Geneva on the Lake Resort (NY) . . . . . . 153
Glasbern (PA) . . . . . . . . . . . . . . . . . . . . . . 279
Glen Ferris Inn, The (WV) . . . . . . . . . . . 445
Glendorn, A Lodge in the Country (PA) 254
Glens Country Estate, The (WV) . . . . . . 436
Golden Pheasant Inn (PA) . . . . . . . . . . . . 277
Gramercy Mansion B&B (MD) . . . . . . . . 56
Great Oak Manor (MD) . . . . . . . . . . . . . . 26
Greenville Arms 1889 Inn (NY) . . . . . . . 155
Hanshaw House Bed & Breakfast (NY) . 161
Hedges Inn, The (NY) . . . . . . . . . . . . . . . 138
Highwinds Inn (NY) . . . . . . . . . . . . . . . . 187
Hillbrook Inn (WV) . . . . . . . . . . . . . . . . . 441
Historic Smithton Inn (PA) . . . . . . . . . . . 272
Hobbit Hollow Farm (NY) . . . . . . . . . . . 218
Holly Hedge Estate Bed & Breakfast
    (PA) . . . . . . . . . . . . . . . . . . . . . . . . . . . 303
Horned Dorset Inn, The (NY) . . . . . . . . . 171
Hummingbird Inn, The (VA) . . . . . . . . . 355
Huntting Inn, The (NY) . . . . . . . . . . . . . . 139

Inn at the Canal (MD) . . . . . . . . . . . . . . . 21
Inn at Fairfield Farm, The (VA) . . . . . . . 359
Inn at the Falls (NY) . . . . . . . . . . . . . . . . 195
Inn at Georgian Place, The (PA) . . . . . . . 311
Inn at Gristmill Square, The (VA) . . . . . 404
Inn at Irving Place, The (NY) . . . . . . . . . 179
Inn at Jim Thorpe, The (PA) . . . . . . . . . . 287
Inn at Lambertville Station, The (NJ) . . . 83
Inn at Little Washington, The (VA) . . . . 412
Inn at Meander Plantation, The (VA) . . 368
Inn at Millrace Pond, The (NJ) . . . . . . . . 80
Inn at Montchanin Village, The (DE) . . . . 5
Inn at Narrow Passage, The (VA) . . . . . . 424
Inn at Olde New Berlin, The (PA) . . . . . 299
Inn at Osprey Point, The (MD) . . . . . . . . 49
Inn at Perry Cabin, The (MD) . . . . . . . . . . 51
Inn at Phillips Mill, The (PA) . . . . . . . . . 305
Inn at Quogue, The (NY) . . . . . . . . . . . . . 196
Inn at Turkey Hill, The (PA) . . . . . . . . . . 252
Inn at Twin Linden, The (PA) . . . . . . . . . 261
Inn at Vaucluse Spring, The (VA) . . . . . . 397
Inn New York City (NY) . . . . . . . . . . . . . 181
Inns at Doneckers, The (PA) . . . . . . . . . . 274
Iris Inn, The (VA) . . . . . . . . . . . . . . . . . . . 414
J. Harper Poor Cottage (NY) . . . . . . . . . . 141
Jordan Hollow Farm Inn (VA) . . . . . . . . 389
Joshua Wilton House, The (VA) . . . . . . . 357
Keswick Hall (VA) . . . . . . . . . . . . . . . . . . . 361
Killahevlin (VA) . . . . . . . . . . . . . . . . . . . . 353
King's Cottage, The (PA) . . . . . . . . . . . . . 289
L'Auberge Provençale (VA) . . . . . . . . . . . 416
La Maison—A B&B and Gallery (NJ) . . . . 88
Lafayette Inn, The (PA) . . . . . . . . . . . . . . 271
Lake Placid Lodge (NY) . . . . . . . . . . . . . . 168
Lake Pointe Inn (MD) . . . . . . . . . . . . . . . . 39
Lakehouse Inn...On Golden Pond (NY) 224
Lambertville House (NJ) . . . . . . . . . . . . . . 84
Lamplight Inn Bed and Breakfast,
     The (NY) . . . . . . . . . . . . . . . . . . . . . . . 166
Le Chambord (NY) . . . . . . . . . . . . . . . . . . 158
Le Refuge (NY) . . . . . . . . . . . . . . . . . . . . . 183
Lighthouse Club Hotel...at Fager's Island,
     The (MD) . . . . . . . . . . . . . . . . . . . . . . . 45
Lincklaen House (NY) . . . . . . . . . . . . . . . 115
Lindenmere Estate B&B, The (NY) . . . . 116
Magoffin Inn, The (PA) . . . . . . . . . . . . . . 295
Maidstone Arms, The (NY) . . . . . . . . . . . 143
Mainstay Inn, The (NJ) . . . . . . . . . . . . . . . 69
Manor House Inn (NJ) . . . . . . . . . . . . . . . 71
Manor at Taylor's Store, The (VA) . . . . . 387
Mansion Inn, The (PA) . . . . . . . . . . . . . . 307
Maple Inn, The (NY) . . . . . . . . . . . . . . . . 119
Mark Addy, The (VA) . . . . . . . . . . . . . . . . 376

Mercersburg Inn, The (PA) . . . . . . . . . . . 296
Merry Sherwood Plantation (MD) . . . . . . 17
Morgan-Samuels B&B Inn (NY) . . . . . . . 111
Morrison House (VA) . . . . . . . . . . . . . . . . 336
Morrison-Clark (DC) . . . . . . . . . . . . . . . . 426
Mr. Mole Bed & Breakfast (MD) . . . . . . . 14
New Devon Inn (DE) . . . . . . . . . . . . . . . . . . 4
Normandy Inn (NJ) . . . . . . . . . . . . . . . . . . 90
Oaks Victorian Inn, The (VA) . . . . . . . . 347
Old Drovers Inn (NY) . . . . . . . . . . . . . . . 130
Old Chatham Sheepherding Company
     Inn (NY) . . . . . . . . . . . . . . . . . . . . . . . 189
Olde Country Inn (NY) . . . . . . . . . . . . . . 215
Oliver Loud's Inn (NY) . . . . . . . . . . . . . . 193
Osceola Mill Country Inn (VA) . . . . . . . 391
Pace One Country Inn (PA) . . . . . . . . . . . 317
Page House Inn, The (VA) . . . . . . . . . . . . 378
Pence Springs Hotel (WV) . . . . . . . . . . . 448
Plumbush Inn (NY) . . . . . . . . . . . . . . . . . 125
Point, The (NY) . . . . . . . . . . . . . . . . . . . . 205
Priory—A City Inn, The (PA) . . . . . . . . . 309
Prospect Hill (VA) . . . . . . . . . . . . . . . . . . 400
Queen Victoria, The (NJ) . . . . . . . . . . . . . 73
Ragged Edge Inn, The (PA) . . . . . . . . . . . 259
Ram's Head Inn, The (NY) . . . . . . . . . . . 216
Red Fox Inn, The (VA) . . . . . . . . . . . . . . . 370
Reynolds Mansion, The (PA) . . . . . . . . . 248
Richard Johnston Inn (VA) . . . . . . . . . . . 352
River House Inn (MD) . . . . . . . . . . . . . . . . 54
Rose Inn (NY) . . . . . . . . . . . . . . . . . . . . . . 163
Roycroft Inn, The (NY) . . . . . . . . . . . . . . 133
Sayre Mansion Inn, The (PA) . . . . . . . . . 251
Sea Crest by the Sea (NJ) . . . . . . . . . . . . . 91
Settlers Inn, The (PA) . . . . . . . . . . . . . . . 283
1708 House, The (NY) . . . . . . . . . . . . . . . 221
1763 Inn (VA) . . . . . . . . . . . . . . . . . . . . . . 402
1770 House (NY) . . . . . . . . . . . . . . . . . . . 145
Sherwood Inn (NY) . . . . . . . . . . . . . . . . . 220
Ship Watch Inn (MD) . . . . . . . . . . . . . . . . 22
Sign of the Sorrel Horse (PA) . . . . . . . . . 268
Silver Thatch Inn (VA) . . . . . . . . . . . . . . 341
Smithfield Station (VA) . . . . . . . . . . . . . . 385
Smithfield Inn, The (VA) . . . . . . . . . . . . . 382
Southern Mansion, The (NJ) . . . . . . . . . . 75
Steeles Tavern Manor Country Inn (VA) 393
Stockton Inn, The (NJ) . . . . . . . . . . . . . . . 94
Stone Manor (MD) . . . . . . . . . . . . . . . . . . . 41
Sugar Tree Inn (VA) . . . . . . . . . . . . . . . . . 395
Suites at Prince Michel, The (VA) . . . . . 363
Swiss Woods Bed & Breakfast (PA) . . . . 290
Tara—A Country Inn (PA) . . . . . . . . . . . . 264
Taughannock Farms Inn (NY) . . . . . . . . 231
Thomas Shepherd Inn (WV) . . . . . . . . . . 452

Three Village Inn (NY) .............. 227
Trillium House (VA) ................. 422
Troutbeck (NY) ..................... 105
Turning Point Inn, The (MD) ......... 31
200 South Street Inn (VA) ........... 343
Tyler-Spite Inn (MD) ................ 33
Union Gables Bed & Breakfast (NY) ... 211
Vagabond Inn, The (NY) ............. 176
Vandiver Inn (MD) .................. 36

Virginia Hotel, The (NJ) ............. 77
Wells Inn, The (WV) ................ 453
Whistling Swan Inn, The (NJ) ......... 93
White Inn, The (NY) ................ 146
Whitewing Farm Bed & Breakfast (PA) . 322
William Seward Inn, The (NY) ........ 233
William Page Inn (MD) .............. 11
Woolverton Inn, The (NJ) ............ 96

# The Most Romantic Inns

### Delaware
VInn at Montchanin Village, The ........ 5

### Maryland
Antietam Overlook Farm .............. 37
Antrim 1844 Country Inn ............. 57
Ashby 1663 Bed and Breakfast ........ 29
Combsberry ......................... 47
Great Oak Manor ................... 26
Lake Pointe Inn ..................... 39
Lighthouse Club Hotel...at Fager's Island,
   The ............................. 45
Merry Sherwood Plantation ........... 17
Mr. Mole Bed & Breakfast ............ 14
Stone Manor ....................... 41
Turning Point Inn, The .............. 31
Tyler-Spite Inn ..................... 33

### New Jersey
Chestnut Hill on the Delaware ........ 86
La Maison—A B&B and Gallery ........ 88
Lambertville House .................. 84
Mainstay Inn, The .................. 69
Southern Mansion, The .............. 75
Woolverton Inn, The ................ 96

### New York
1708 House, The .................... 221
Batcheller Mansion Inn .............. 209
Bed and Breakfast on the Park ........ 178
Belvedere Mansion .................. 200
Bird & Bottle Inn, The .............. 149
Castle at Tarrytown, The ............ 229
Cromwell Manor Inn ................ 128
Geneva on the Lake Resort ........... 153
Hobbit Hollow Farm ................ 218
Inn New York City .................. 181
Inn at Irving Place, The ............. 179
J. Harper Poor Cottage .............. 141

Lake Placid Lodge .................. 168
Lakehouse Inn...On Golden Pond...... 224
Lindenmere Estate B&B, The ......... 116
Old Drovers Inn .................... 130
Old Chatham Sheepherding Company
   Inn ............................ 189
Oliver Loud's Inn .................. 193
Point, The ......................... 205
Rose Inn .......................... 163
Vagabond Inn, The ................. 176

### Pennsylvania
Glasbern .......................... 279
Glendorn, A Lodge in the Country .... 254
Golden Pheasant Inn ................ 277
Holly Hedge Estate Bed &
   Breakfast ....................... 303
Inn at Twin Linden, The ............ 261
Inn at Phillips Mill, The ............ 305
Mansion Inn, The .................. 307
Ragged Edge Inn, The .............. 259
Reynolds Mansion, The ............. 248
Tara—A Country Inn ............... 264
Whitewing Farm Bed & Breakfast ..... 322

### Virginia
Ashby Inn, The .................... 380
Bailiwick Inn, The ................. 350
Black Horse Inn, The ............... 406
Clifton: The Country Inn ............ 338
Inn at Vaucluse Spring, The ......... 397
Inn at Meander Plantation, The ....... 368
Inn at Little Washington, The ........ 412
Killahevlin ........................ 353
Oaks Victorian Inn, The ............ 347
Page House Inn, The ............... 378
Prospect Hill ...................... 400
Smithfield Station ................. 385
Steeles Tavern Manor Country Inn .... 393

Sugar Tree Inn . . . . . . . . . . . . . . . . . . . . . . 395
Suites at Prince Michel, The . . . . . . . . . . 363

**West Virginia**
Glens Country Estate, The . . . . . . . . . . 436
Hillbrook Inn . . . . . . . . . . . . . . . . . . . . . 441

# Best Buys in the Mid-Atlantic States

*Delaware*
New Devon Inn . . . . . . . . . . . . . . . . . . . . . 4

*Maryland*
Atlantic Hotel . . . . . . . . . . . . . . . . . . . . 15
Gramercy Mansion B&B . . . . . . . . . . . . . 56
Inn at the Canal . . . . . . . . . . . . . . . . . . . 21
Lighthouse Club Hotel...at Fager's Island,
    The . . . . . . . . . . . . . . . . . . . . . . . . . . . . 45
Turning Point Inn, The . . . . . . . . . . . . . 31
Vandiver Inn . . . . . . . . . . . . . . . . . . . . . 36

*New Jersey*
Cashelmara Inn . . . . . . . . . . . . . . . . . . . . 66
Manor House Inn . . . . . . . . . . . . . . . . . . 71
Queen Victoria, The . . . . . . . . . . . . . . . 73
Virginia Hotel, The . . . . . . . . . . . . . . . . 77

*New York*
Albergo Allegria Bed & Breakfast . . . . . 235
Aubergine . . . . . . . . . . . . . . . . . . . . . . . 157
Belvedere Mansion . . . . . . . . . . . . . . . . 200
Chequit Inn . . . . . . . . . . . . . . . . . . . . . 213
Cooper Inn, The . . . . . . . . . . . . . . . . . . 126
Genesee Country Inn . . . . . . . . . . . . . . 174
Hanshaw House Bed & Breakfast . . . . . 161
Highwinds Inn . . . . . . . . . . . . . . . . . . . 187
Le Refuge . . . . . . . . . . . . . . . . . . . . . . . 183
Maple Inn, The . . . . . . . . . . . . . . . . . . . 119
Olde Country Inn . . . . . . . . . . . . . . . . . 215
Ram's Head Inn, The . . . . . . . . . . . . . . 216
Sherwood Inn . . . . . . . . . . . . . . . . . . . . 220
White Inn, The . . . . . . . . . . . . . . . . . . . 146
William Seward Inn, The . . . . . . . . . . . . 233

*Pennsylvania*
B&B Inn of the Princess and European
    Bakery . . . . . . . . . . . . . . . . . . . . . . . . 318

Fox & Hound Bed & Breakfast of New
    Hope, The . . . . . . . . . . . . . . . . . . . . . 301
Golden Pheasant Inn . . . . . . . . . . . . . . . 277
Historic Smithton Inn . . . . . . . . . . . . . . 272
Inn at Olde New Berlin, The . . . . . . . . . 299
Inn at Phillips Mill, The . . . . . . . . . . . . 305
Inn at Jim Thorpe, The . . . . . . . . . . . . . 287
Inns at Doneckers, The . . . . . . . . . . . . . 274
Pace One Country Inn . . . . . . . . . . . . . . 317
Priory—A City Inn, The . . . . . . . . . . . . 309
Ragged Edge Inn, The . . . . . . . . . . . . . . 259
Sign of the Sorrel Horse . . . . . . . . . . . . 268

*Virginia*
Eldon—The Inn at Chatham . . . . . . . . . 344
Fort Lewis Lodge . . . . . . . . . . . . . . . . . . 372
Garden and The Sea Inn, The . . . . . . . . 376
Inn at Gristmill Square, The . . . . . . . . . 404
Iris Inn, The . . . . . . . . . . . . . . . . . . . . . 414
Manor at Taylor's Store, The . . . . . . . . . 387
Osceola Mill Country Inn . . . . . . . . . . . 391
Smithfield Station . . . . . . . . . . . . . . . . . 385

*West Virginia*
Brass Pineapple, The . . . . . . . . . . . . . . . 438
Cheat Mountain Club . . . . . . . . . . . . . . 443
Cottonwood Inn, The . . . . . . . . . . . . . . 440
Elk River Inn . . . . . . . . . . . . . . . . . . . . 455
General Lewis Inn . . . . . . . . . . . . . . . . . 447
Glen Ferris Inn, The . . . . . . . . . . . . . . . 445
Pence Springs Hotel . . . . . . . . . . . . . . . 448
Thomas Shepherd Inn . . . . . . . . . . . . . . 452
Wells Inn, The . . . . . . . . . . . . . . . . . . . . 453

# Inns Especially Suited to Family Travel

## Delaware
Inn at Montchanin Village, The ......... 5

## Maryland
Atlantic Hotel ...................... 15
Brampton Bed & Breakfast ............ 25
Catoctin Inn, The ................... 19
Gramercy Mansion B&B ............ 56
Inn at Perry Cabin, The ............. 51
Inn at Osprey Point, The ............ 49
Merry Sherwood Plantation .......... 17
River House Inn .................... 54
Ship Watch Inn ..................... 22
Turning Point Inn, The ............. 31
Vandiver Inn ...................... 36

## New Jersey
Bernards Inn, The .................. 67
Cashelmara Inn ..................... 66
Doctors Inn at Kings Grant, The ....... 79
Inn at Millrace Pond, The ............ 80
Inn at Lambertville Station, The ...... 83
Mainstay Inn, The .................. 69
Normandy Inn ..................... 90
Queen Victorian, The ............... 73
Stockton Inn, The .................. 94
Virginia Hotel, The ................. 77

## New York
Adelphi Hotel ..................... 207
Albergo Allegria Be & Breakfast ....... 235
American Hotel .................... 204
Asa Ransom House .................. 123
Aubergine ......................... 157
Beaverkill Valley Inn ................ 172
Bed and Breakfast on the Park ....... 178
Beekman Arms ..................... 198
Belvedere Mansion .................. 200
Brewster Inn, The .................. 113
Bridgehampton Inn ................. 108
Buttermilk Falls Bed & Breakfast ..... 159
Castle at Tarrytown, The ............ 229
Chequit Inn ....................... 213
Cooper Inn, The ................... 126
Cromwell Manor Inn ................ 128
East Hampton Point Cottages ........ 136
Elk Lake Lodge .................... 185
Geneva on the Lake Resort .......... 153
Hanshaw House Bed & Breakfast ..... 161
Hedges Inn, The ................... 138

Highwinds Inn .................... 187
Huntting Inn, The ................. 139
Inn at the Falls ................... 195
Inn at Quogue, The ............... 196
J. Harper Poor Cottage ............. 141
Lake Placid Lodge ................. 168
Lakehouse Inn...On Golden Pond ..... 224
Le Refuge ........................ 183
Le Chambord ..................... 158
Lincklaen House ................... 115
Maidstone Arms, The .............. 143
Morgan-Samuels B&B Inn .......... 111
Old Chatham Sheepherding
    Company Inn ................... 189
Ram's Head Inn, The .............. 216
Roycroft Inn, The ................. 133
Sherwood Inn .................... 220
Taughannock Farms Inn ............ 231
Three Village Inn ................. 227
Union Gables Bed & Breakfast ....... 211
White Inn, The ................... 146
William Seward Inn, The ........... 233

## Pennsylvania
B&B Inn of the Princess and European
    Bakery ......................... 318
Barley Sheaf Farm ................. 285
Bridgeton House on the Delaware ..... 320
Cashtown Inn .................... 257
Eagles Mere Inn ................... 269
French Manor, The ................ 313
Glasbern ......................... 279
Golden Pheasant Inn ............... 277
Historic Smithton Inn .............. 272
Holly Hedge Estate Bed & Breakfast ... 303
Inn at Turkey Hill, The ............ 252
Inn at Jim Thorpe, The ............ 287
Inn at Twin Linden, The ........... 261
Inn at Phillips Mill, The ........... 305
Inn at Olde New Berlin, The ........ 299
Inns at Doneckers, The ............ 274
King's Cottage, The ............... 289
Lafayette Inn, The ................ 271
Magoffin Inn, The ................ 295
Mercersburg Inn, The .............. 296
Pace One Country Inn ............. 317
Priory—A Country Inn, The ........ 309
Ragged Edge Inn, The ............. 259
Sayre Mansion Inn, The ............ 251
Settlers Inn, The .................. 283

Swiss Woods Bed & Breakfast ........ 290
Whitewing Farm Bed & Breakfast ..... 322

### Virginia
Bailiwick Inn, The ................... 350
Bleu Rock Inn ...................... 409
Cedars Bed & Breakfast, The ......... 418
Clifton: The Country Inn ............ 338
Colonial Houses Historic Lodging .... 420
Fort Lewis Lodge .................... 372
Inn at Gristmill Square, The ......... 404
Inn at Narrow Passage, The .......... 424
Inn at Little Washington, The ........ 412
Inn at Meander Plantation, The ....... 368
Inn at Fairfield Farm, The ........... 359
Jordan Hollow Farm Inn ............. 389
Keswick Hall ....................... 361
Manor at Taylor's Store, The ......... 387
Morrison House ..................... 336
Osceola Mill Country Inn ........... 391
Prospect Hill ....................... 400

Red Fox Inn, The ................... 370
Richard Johnston Inn .............. 352
1763 Inn .......................... 402
Silver Thatch Inn .................. 341
Smithfield Inn, The ................ 382
Smithfield Station ................. 385
Trillium House ..................... 422
200 South Street Inn ............... 343

### Washington, D.C.
Morrison-Clark .................... 426

### West Virginia
Bavarian Inn & Lodge ............. 450
Brass Pineapple, The .............. 438
Cheat Mountain Club ............. 443
Elk River Inn ..................... 455
General Lewis Inn ................. 447
Glen Ferris Inn, The .............. 445
Pence Springs Hotel .............. 448
Wells Inn, The .................... 453

# Inns Especially Suited to Business Travelers

### Delaware
Armitage Inn........................ 8
Inn at Montchanin Village, The ......... 5

### Maryland
Antrim 1844 Country Inn ............. 57
Catoctin Inn, The ................... 19
Celie's Waterfront Bed and Breakfast ... 12
Inn at the Canal .................... 21
Inn at Perry Cabin, The ............. 51
Inn at Osprey Point, The ............ 49
Lake Pointe Inn ..................... 39
Lighthouse Club Hotel...at Fager's Island,
  The .............................. 45
Mr. Mole Bed & Breakfast ........... 14
Ship Watch Inn ..................... 22

### New Jersey
Bernards Inn, The ................... 67
Doctors Inn at Kings Grant, The ...... 79
Inn at Lambertville Station, The ...... 83
Inn at Millrace Pond, The ........... 80
Lambertville House .................. 84
Southern Mansion, The .............. 75
Stockton Inn, The ................... 94
Virginia Hotel, The ................. 77
Whistling Swan Inn, The ............. 93

### New York
Adelphi Hotel ..................... 207
Albergo Allegria Bed & Breakfast ..... 235
Asa Ransom House ................. 123
Beaverkill Valley Inn ............... 172
Beekman Arms ..................... 198
Belhurst Castle & White Springs
  Manor ........................... 151
Castle at Tarrytown, The ........... 229
Chequit Inn ....................... 213
Cooper Inn, The ................... 126
428 Mt. Vernon—A B&B Inn ......... 202
Geneva on the Lake Resort ......... 153
Huntting Inn, The ................. 139
Inn at Irving Place, The ............ 179
Inn New York City ................. 181
Inn at the Falls ................... 195
J. Harper Poor Cottage ............. 141
Lake Placid Lodge ................. 168
Lamplight Inn Bed & Breakfast, The .. 166
Le Chambord ..................... 158
Lincklaen House ................... 115
Maidstone Arms, The .............. 143
Old Chatham Sheepherding Company
  Inn ............................. 189
Oliver Loud's Inn ................. 193
Rose Inn .......................... 163

Roycroft Inn, The . . . . . . . . . . . . . . . . . . 133
1708 House, The . . . . . . . . . . . . . . . . . . . 221
Three Village Inn . . . . . . . . . . . . . . . . . . 227
Troutbeck . . . . . . . . . . . . . . . . . . . . . . . . 105
Union Gables Bed & Breakfast . . . . . . . 211
White Inn, The . . . . . . . . . . . . . . . . . . . 146

### Pennsylvania
B&B Inn of the Princess and European
   Baker . . . . . . . . . . . . . . . . . . . . . . . . . . 318
Barley Sheaf Farm . . . . . . . . . . . . . . . . 285
Bridgeton House on the Delaware . . . . . 320
Carnegie House . . . . . . . . . . . . . . . . . . . 315
Crescent Lodge and Country Inn . . . . . . 266
Fairville Inn . . . . . . . . . . . . . . . . . . . . . . 293
Gaslight Inn, The . . . . . . . . . . . . . . . . . 281
Glasbern . . . . . . . . . . . . . . . . . . . . . . . . 279
Glendorn, A Lodge in the Country . . . . 254
Holly Hedge Estate Bed & Breakfast . . . 303
Inn at Olde New Berlin, The . . . . . . . . . 299
Inn at Turkey Hill, The . . . . . . . . . . . . . 252
Lafayette Inn, The . . . . . . . . . . . . . . . . . 271
Mansion Inn, The . . . . . . . . . . . . . . . . . 307
Mercersburg Inn, The . . . . . . . . . . . . . . 296
Priory—A City Inn, The . . . . . . . . . . . . . 309
Ragged Edge Inn, The . . . . . . . . . . . . . . 259
Sayre Mansion Inn, The . . . . . . . . . . . . . 251
Settlers Inn, The . . . . . . . . . . . . . . . . . . 283
Tara—A Country Inn . . . . . . . . . . . . . . . 264

### Virginia
Bailiwick Inn, The . . . . . . . . . . . . . . . . . 350
Black Horse Inn, The . . . . . . . . . . . . . . . 406
Colonial Houses Historic Lodging . . . . 420
Inn at Gristmill Square, The . . . . . . . . . 404
Inn at Fairfield Farm, The . . . . . . . . . . . 359
Inn at Vaucluse Spring, The . . . . . . . . . . 397
Inn at Meander Plantation, The . . . . . . 368
Iris Inn, The . . . . . . . . . . . . . . . . . . . . . 414
Jordan Hollow Farm Inn . . . . . . . . . . . . 389
Keswick Hall . . . . . . . . . . . . . . . . . . . . . 361
Killahevlin . . . . . . . . . . . . . . . . . . . . . . 353
Morrison House . . . . . . . . . . . . . . . . . . . 336
Oaks Victorian Inn, The . . . . . . . . . . . . 347
Page House Inn, The . . . . . . . . . . . . . . . 378
Prospect Hill . . . . . . . . . . . . . . . . . . . . . 400
Red Fox Inn, The . . . . . . . . . . . . . . . . . 370
1763 Inn . . . . . . . . . . . . . . . . . . . . . . . . 402
Smithfield Station . . . . . . . . . . . . . . . . . 385
Suites at Prince Michel, The . . . . . . . . . 363
Trillium House . . . . . . . . . . . . . . . . . . . 422
200 South Street Inn . . . . . . . . . . . . . . . 343

### Washington, D.C.
Morrison-Clark . . . . . . . . . . . . . . . . . . . 426

### West Virginia
Bavarian Inn & Lodge . . . . . . . . . . . . . . 450
Brass Pineapple, The . . . . . . . . . . . . . . . 438
Cottonwood Inn, The . . . . . . . . . . . . . . 440
Wells Inn, The . . . . . . . . . . . . . . . . . . . . 453

# Inns with Wheelchair Accessibility

### Delaware
Inn at Montchanin Village, The . . . . . . . 5
New Devon Inn . . . . . . . . . . . . . . . . . . . 4

### Maryland
Antrim 1844 Country Inn . . . . . . . . . . . 57
Atlantic Hotel . . . . . . . . . . . . . . . . . . . . 15
Brampton Bed & Breakfast . . . . . . . . . . 25
Catoctin Inn, The . . . . . . . . . . . . . . . . . 19
Celie's Waterfront Bed and Breakfast . . . 12
Elliott House Victorian Inn . . . . . . . . . . 34
Inn at Perry Cabin, The . . . . . . . . . . . . . 51
River House Inn . . . . . . . . . . . . . . . . . . 54
Ship Watch Inn . . . . . . . . . . . . . . . . . . . 22
Stone Manor . . . . . . . . . . . . . . . . . . . . . 41
Turning Point Inn, The . . . . . . . . . . . . . 31
Tyler-Spite Inn . . . . . . . . . . . . . . . . . . . 33
Vandiver Inn . . . . . . . . . . . . . . . . . . . . . 36

### New Jersey
Chestnut Hill on the Delaware . . . . . . . . 86
Doctors Inn at Kings Grant, The . . . . . . 79
Inn at Millrace Pond, The . . . . . . . . . . . 80
Inn at Lambertville Station, The . . . . . . 83
La Maison—A B&B and Gallery . . . . . . . 88
Lambertville House . . . . . . . . . . . . . . . . 84
Mainstay Inn, The . . . . . . . . . . . . . . . . . 69
Queen Victoria, The . . . . . . . . . . . . . . . 73
Woolverton Inn, The . . . . . . . . . . . . . . . 96

### New York
Albergo Allegria Bed & Breakfast . . . . . . 235
Asa Ransom House . . . . . . . . . . . . . . . . . 123
Beaverkill Valley Inn . . . . . . . . . . . . . . . 172
Beekman Arms . . . . . . . . . . . . . . . . . . . 198
Belhurst Castle & White Springs Manor 151
Bird & Bottle Inn, The . . . . . . . . . . . . . 149

Brewster Inn, The ................... 113
Buttermilk Falls Bed & Breakfast ..... 159
Castle at Tarrytown, The ............ 229
Chequit Inn ....................... 213
Cromwell Manor Inn ............... 128
428 Mt. Vernon—A B&B Inn ......... 202
Geneva on the Lake Resort .......... 153
Greenville Arms 1889 Inn ........... 155
Inn at Quogue, The ............... 196
Inn at the Falls .................... 195
Lake Placid Lodge ................. 168
Lamplight Inn Bed and Breakfast, The . 166
Le Chambord ...................... 158
Lincklaen House .................. 115
Lindenmere Estate B&B, The ........ 116
Maple Inn, The .................... 119
Oliver Loud's Inn ................. 193
Roycroft Inn, The ................. 133
Taughannock Farms Inn ............ 231
White Inn, The ................... 146
William Seward Inn, The ........... 233

*Pennsylvania*
B&B Inn of the Princess and European
    Bakery ........................ 318
Barley Sheaf Farm ................. 285
Carnegie House ................... 315
Eagles Mere Inn ................... 269
French Manor, The ................ 313
Gaslight Inn, The ................. 281
Glasbern ......................... 279
Historic Smithton Inn ............. 272
Holly Hedge Estate Bed & Breakfast ... 303
Inn at Jim Thorpe, The ............ 287
Inn at Olde New Berlin, The ........ 299
Inns at Doneckers, The ............ 274
King's Cottage, The ............... 289
Priory—A City Inn, The ............ 309

Sayre Mansion Inn, The ............ 251
Tara—A Country Inn ............... 264
Whitewing Farm Bed & Breakfast ..... 322

*Virginia*
Bailiwick Inn, The ................. 350
Black Horse Inn, The .............. 406
Bleu Rock Inn ..................... 409
Clifton: The Country Inn ........... 338
Fort Lewis Lodge .................. 372
Garden and The Sea Inn, The ....... 376
Inn at Vaucluse Spring, The ........ 397
Inn at Little Washington, The ....... 412
Inn at Narrow Passage, The ........ 424
Inn at Fairfield Farm, The ......... 359
Inn at Meander Plantation, The ...... 368
Iris Inn, The ...................... 414
Keswick Hall ..................... 361
Manor at Taylor's Store, The ....... 387
Mark Addy, The .................. 376
Morrison House ................... 336
Osceola Mill Country Inn .......... 391
Red Fox Inn, The ................. 370
Smithfield Station ................. 385
Sugar Tree Inn .................... 395
Suites at Prince Michel, The ........ 363
Trillium House .................... 422
200 South Street Inn .............. 343

*Washington, D.C.*
Morrison-Clark .................... 426

*West Virginia*
Bavarian Inn & Lodge ............. 450
General Lewis Inn ................. 447
Glen Ferris Inn, The .............. 445
Glens Country Estate, The ......... 436
Pence Springs Hotel .............. 448

# Inns That Accept Pets
## (with prior permission)

*Maryland*
Inn at Perry Cabin, The ............. 51
River House Inn ................... 54
Turning Point Inn, The ............ 31

*New Jersey*
La Maison—A B&B and Gallery ........ 88

*New York*
Acorn Inn ......................... 109
Adelphi Hotel ..................... 207
Aubergine ........................ 155
Beekman Arms .................... 198
Belvedere Mansion ................. 200
East Hampton Point Cottages ........ 136

Geneva on the Lake Resort . . . . . . . . . . 153
Horned Dorset Inn, The . . . . . . . . . . . . 171
Inn at Quogue, The . . . . . . . . . . . . . . . 196
Lake Placid Lodge . . . . . . . . . . . . . . . . . 168
Lincklaen House . . . . . . . . . . . . . . . . . . 115
Old Drovers Inn . . . . . . . . . . . . . . . . . . 130
Point, The . . . . . . . . . . . . . . . . . . . . . . . 205
Union Gables Bed & Breakfast . . . . . . . 211

*Pennsylvania*
B&B Inn of the Princess and European
    Bakery . . . . . . . . . . . . . . . . . . . . . . . 318
Fox & Hound Bed & Breakfast of New
    Hope, The . . . . . . . . . . . . . . . . . . . . . 301
Golden Pheasant Inn . . . . . . . . . . . . . . 277
Historic Smithton Inn . . . . . . . . . . . . . 272

Inn at Georgian Place, The . . . . . . . . . . 311
Inn at Turkey Hill, The . . . . . . . . . . . . . 252

*Virginia*
Black Horse Inn, The . . . . . . . . . . . . . . 406
Bleu Rock Inn . . . . . . . . . . . . . . . . . . . . 409
Garden and The Sea Inn, The . . . . . . . . 376
Hummingbird Inn, The . . . . . . . . . . . . . 355
Inn at Meander Plantation, The . . . . . . . 368
Inn at Little Washington, The . . . . . . . . 412
Red Fox Inn, The . . . . . . . . . . . . . . . . . 370
Trillium House . . . . . . . . . . . . . . . . . . . 422

*West Virginia*
General Lewis Inn . . . . . . . . . . . . . . . . . 447
Wells Inn, The . . . . . . . . . . . . . . . . . . . . 453

# Inns Offering Travelers' Club Benefits

*Maryland*
VBrampton Bed & Breakfast . . . . . . . . . . . 25
Catoctin Inn, The . . . . . . . . . . . . . . . . . . 19
Lighthouse Club Hotel...at Fager's Island,
    The . . . . . . . . . . . . . . . . . . . . . . . . . . . 45
Merry Sherwood Plantation . . . . . . . . . . . 17
River House Inn . . . . . . . . . . . . . . . . . . . 54

*New Jersey*
Doctors Inn at Kings Grant, The . . . . . . . 79
Lambertville House . . . . . . . . . . . . . . . . . 84
Mainstay Inn, The . . . . . . . . . . . . . . . . . . 69
Manor House Inn . . . . . . . . . . . . . . . . . . 71
Normandy Inn . . . . . . . . . . . . . . . . . . . . 90
Queen Victoria, The . . . . . . . . . . . . . . . . 73
Woolverton Inn, The . . . . . . . . . . . . . . . 96

*New York*
Aubergine . . . . . . . . . . . . . . . . . . . . . . . 157
Bird & Bottle Inn, The . . . . . . . . . . . . . . 149
Genesee Country Inn . . . . . . . . . . . . . . . 174
Greenville Arms 1889 Inn . . . . . . . . . . . 155
Lakehouse Inn...On Golden Pond . . . . . 224
Lincklaen House . . . . . . . . . . . . . . . . . . 115
Maple Inn, The . . . . . . . . . . . . . . . . . . . 119
Morgan-Samuels B&B Inn . . . . . . . . . . 111
Rose Inn . . . . . . . . . . . . . . . . . . . . . . . . 163
White Inn, The . . . . . . . . . . . . . . . . . . . 146

*Pennsylvania*
B&B Inn of the Princess and European
    Bakery . . . . . . . . . . . . . . . . . . . . . . . 318
Barley Sheaf Farm . . . . . . . . . . . . . . . . . 285
Cashtown Inn . . . . . . . . . . . . . . . . . . . . 257
Gaslight Inn, The . . . . . . . . . . . . . . . . . 281
Golden Pheasant Inn . . . . . . . . . . . . . . 277
Holly Hedge Estate Bed & Breakfast . . . 303
Inn at Olde New Berlin, The . . . . . . . . . 299
Inn at Jim Thorpe, The . . . . . . . . . . . . . 287
King's Cottage, The . . . . . . . . . . . . . . . . 289
Mercersburg Inn, The . . . . . . . . . . . . . . 296
Ragged Edge Inn, The . . . . . . . . . . . . . . 259
Reynolds Mansion, The . . . . . . . . . . . . . 248
Sign of the Sorrel Horse . . . . . . . . . . . . 268

*Virginia*
Garden and The Sea Inn, The . . . . . . . . 376
Hummingbird Inn, The . . . . . . . . . . . . . 355
Inn at Vaucluse Spring, The . . . . . . . . . 397
Jordan Hollow Farm Inn . . . . . . . . . . . 389
Steeles Tavern Manor Country Inn . . . . 393

*Washington, D.C.*
Morrison-Clark . . . . . . . . . . . . . . . . . . . 426

*West Virginia*
Cheat Mountain Club . . . . . . . . . . . . . . 443